ACRONYMS

ACK	acknowledgment flag; TCP header
ANSI	American National Standards Institute
API	application program interface
ARP	Address Resolution Protocol
ARPANET	Advanced Research Projects Agency network
ASCII	American Standard Code for Information Interchange
BPF	BSD Packet Filter
BSD	Berkeley Software Distribution
CC	connection count; T/TCP
CERT	Computer Emergency Response Team
CR	carriage return
DF	don't fragment flag; IP header
DNS	Domain Name System
EOL	end of option list
FAQ	frequently asked question
FIN	finish flag; TCP header
FTP	File Transfer Protocol
GIF	graphics interchange format
HTML	Hypertext Markup Language
HTTP	Hypertext Transfer Protocol
ICMP	Internet Control Message Protocol
IEEE	Institute of Electrical and Electronics Engineers
INN	InterNet News
INND	InterNet News Daemon
IP	Internet Protocol
IPC	interprocess communication
IRTP	Internet Reliable Transaction Protocol
ISN	initial sequence number
ISO	International Organization for Standardization
ISS	initial send sequence number
LAN	local area network
LF	linefeed
MIME	multipurpose Internet mail extensions
MSL	maximum segment lifetime
MSS.	maximum segment size
MTU	maximum transmission unit

ACRONYMS

NCSA	National Center for Supercomputing Applications
NFS	Network File System
NNRP	Network News Reading Protocol
NNTP	Network News Transfer Protocol
NOAO	National Optical Astronomy Observatories
NOP	no operation
OSF	Open Software Foundation
OSI	open systems interconnection
PAWS	protection against wrapped sequence numbers
PCB	protocol control block
POSIX	Portable Operating System Interface
PPP	Point-to-Point Protocol
PSH	push flag; TCP header
RDP	Reliable Datagram Protocol
RFC	Request for Comment
RPC	remote procedure call
RST	reset flag; TCP header
RTO	retransmission time out
RTT	round-trip time
SLIP	Serial Line Internet Protocol
SMTP	Simple Mail Transfer Protocol
SPT	server processing time
SVR4	System V Release 4
SYN	synchronize sequence numbers flag; TCP header
TAO	TCP accelerated open
TCP	Transmission Control Protocol
TTL	time-to-live
Telnet	remote terminal protocol
UDP	User Datagram Protocol
URG	urgent pointer flag; TCP header
URI	uniform resource identifier
URL	uniform resource locator
URN	uniform resource name
VMTP	Versatile Message Transaction Protocol
WAN	wide area network
WWW	World Wide Web

Praise for *TCP/IP Illustrated, Volume 3: TCP for Transactions, HTTP, NNTP, and the UNIX® Domain Protocols*

"An absolutely wonderful example of how to apply scientific thinking and analysis to a technological problem...it is the highest caliber of technical writing and thinking."

— Marcus J. Ranum, Firewall Architect

"A worthy successor that continues the series' standards of excellence for both clarity and accuracy. The coverage of T/TCP and HTTP is particularly timely, given the explosion of the World Wide Web."

— Vern Paxson, Network Research Group,
Lawrence Berkeley National Laboratory

"The coverage of the HTTP protocol will be invaluable to anyone who needs to understand the detailed behavior of web servers."

— Jeffrey Mogul, Digital Equipment Corporation

"Volume 3 *is a natural addition to the series. It covers the network aspects of Web services and transaction TCP in depth."*

— Pete Haverlock, Program Manager, IBM

"In this latest volume of TCP/IP Illustrated, *Rich Stevens maintains the high standards he set up in the previous volumes: clear presentation and technical accuracy to the finest detail."*

— Andras Olah, University of Twente

"This volume maintains the superb quality of the earlier ones in the series, extending the in-depth examination of networking implementation in new directions. The entire series is a must for anybody who is seriously interested in how the Internet works today."

— Ian Lance Taylor, Author of GNU/Taylor UUCP

TCP/IP Illustrated, Volume 3

Addison-Wesley Professional Computing Series

Brian W. Kernighan, Consulting Editor

Ken Arnold/John Peyton, *A C User's Guide to ANSI C*
Tom Cargill, *C++ Programming Style*
William R. Cheswick/Steven M. Bellovin, *Firewalls and Internet Security: Repelling the Wily Hacker*
David A. Curry, *UNIX® System Security: A Guide for Users and System Administrators*
Erich Gamma/Richard Helm/Ralph Johnson/John Vlissides, *Design Patterns: Elements of Reusable Object-Oriented Software*
David R. Hanson, *C Interfaces and Implementations*
John Lakos, *Large-Scale C++ Software Design*
Scott Meyers, *Effective C++: 50 Specific Ways to Improve Your Programs and Designs*
Scott Meyers, *More Effective C++: 35 New Ways to Improve Your Programs and Designs*
Robert B. Murray, *C++ Strategies and Tactics*
David R. Musser/Atul Saini, *STL Tutorial and Reference Guide: C++ Programming with the Standard Template Library*
John K. Ousterhout, *Tcl and the Tk Toolkit*
Craig Partridge, *Gigabit Networking*
J. Stephen Pendergrast Jr., *Desktop KornShell Graphical Programming*
Radia Perlman, *Interconnections: Bridges and Routers*
David M. Piscitello/A. Lyman Chapin, *Open Systems Networking: TCP/IP and OSI*
Stephen A. Rago, *UNIX® System V Network Programming*
Curt Schimmel, *UNIX® Systems for Modern Architectures: Symmetric Multiprocessing and Caching for Kernel Programmers*
W. Richard Stevens, *Advanced Programming in the UNIX® Environment*
W. Richard Stevens, *TCP/IP Illustrated, Volume 1: The Protocols*
W. Richard Stevens, *TCP/IP Illustrated, Volume 3: TCP for Transactions, HTTP, NNTP, and the UNIX® Domain Protocols*
Gary R. Wright/W. Richard Stevens, *TCP/IP Illustrated, Volume 2: The Implementation*

TCP/IP Illustrated, Volume 3

TCP for Transactions, HTTP, NNTP, and the UNIX Domain Protocols

W. Richard Stevens

Pearson Education Asia

ISBN 81-7808-340-X

First ISE Reprint, 1999
Second Indian Reprint, 2000
Third Indian Reprint, 2001

Published by Addison Wesley Longman (Singapore) Pte. Ltd., Indian Branch, 482 F.I.E. Patparganj, Delhi 110 092, India

Printed in India by Ram Printograph Pvt. Ltd.

To my many mentors over the past years, from whom I have learned so much, especially Jim Brault, Dave Hanson, Bob Hunt, and Brian Kernighan.

Contents

Preface

Introduction and Organization of the Book

This book is a logical continuation of the *TCP/IP Illustrated* series: [Stevens 1994], which we refer to as *Volume 1*, and [Wright and Stevens 1995], which we refer to as *Volume 2*. This book is divided into three parts, each covering a different topic:

1. TCP for transactions, commonly called T/TCP. This is an extension to TCP designed to make client–server transactions faster, more efficient, and reliable. This is done by omitting TCP's three-way handshake at the beginning of a connection and shortening the TIME_WAIT state at the end of a connection. We'll see that T/TCP can match UDP's performance for a client–server transaction and that T/TCP provides reliability and adaptability, both major improvements over UDP.

   A transaction is defined to be a client request to a server, followed by the server's reply. (The term *transaction* does not mean a database transaction, with locking, two-phase commit, and backout.)

2. TCP/IP applications, specifically HTTP (the Hypertext Transfer Protocol, the foundation of the World Wide Web) and NNTP (the Network News Transfer Protocol, the basis for the Usenet news system).
3. The Unix domain protocols. These protocols are provided by all Unix TCP/IP implementations and on many non-Unix implementations. They provide a form of interprocess communication (IPC) and use the same sockets interface used with TCP/IP. When the client and server are on the same host, the Unix domain protocols are often twice as fast as TCP/IP.

Part 1, the presentation of T/TCP, is in two pieces. Chapters 1–4 describe the protocol and provide numerous examples of how it works. This material is a major expansion of the brief presentation of T/TCP in Section 24.7 of Volume 1. The second piece, Chapters 5–12, describes the actual implementation of T/TCP within the 4.4BSD-Lite networking code (i.e., the code presented in Volume 2). Since the first T/TCP implementation was not released until September 1994, about one year after Volume 1 was published and right as Volume 2 was being completed, the detailed presentation of T/TCP, with examples and all the implementation details, had to wait for another volume in the series.

Part 2, the HTTP and NNTP applications, are a continuation of the TCP/IP applications presented in Chapters 25–30 of Volume 1. In the two years since Volume 1 was published, the popularity of HTTP has grown enormously, as the Internet has exploded, and the use of NNTP has been growing about 75% per year for more than 10 years. HTTP is also a wonderful candidate for T/TCP, given its typical use of TCP: short connections with small amounts of data transferred, where the total time is often dominated by the connection setup and teardown. The heavy use of HTTP (and therefore TCP) on a busy Web server by thousands of different and varied clients also provides a unique opportunity to examine the actual packets at the server (Chapter 14) and look at many features of TCP/IP that were presented in Volumes 1 and 2.

The Unix domain protocols in Part 3 were originally considered for Volume 2 but omitted when its size reached 1200 pages. While it may seem odd to cover protocols other than TCP/IP in a series titled *TCP/IP Illustrated*, the Unix domain protocols were implemented almost 15 years ago in 4.2BSD alongside the first implementation of BSD TCP/IP. They are used heavily today in any Berkeley-derived kernel, but their use is typically "under the covers," and most users are unaware of their presence. Besides being the foundation for Unix pipes on a Berkeley-derived kernel, another heavy user is the X Window System, when the client and server are on the same host (i.e., on typical workstations). Unix domain sockets are also used to pass descriptors between processes, a powerful technique for interprocess communication. Since the sockets API (application program interface) used with the Unix domain protocols is nearly identical to the sockets API used with TCP/IP, the Unix domain protocols provide an easy way to enhance the performance of local applications with minimal code changes.

Each of the three parts can be read by itself.

Readers

As with the previous two volumes in the series, this volume is intended for anyone wishing to understand how the TCP/IP protocols operate: programmers writing network applications, system administrators responsible for maintaining computer systems and networks utilizing TCP/IP, and users who deal with TCP/IP applications on a daily basis.

Parts 1 and 2 assume a basic understanding of how the TCP/IP protocols work. Readers unfamiliar with TCP/IP should consult the first volume in this series, [Stevens 1994], for a thorough description of the TCP/IP protocol suite. The first half of Part 1

(Chapters 1–4, the concepts behind T/TCP along with examples) can be read independent of Volume 2, but the remainder of Part 1 (Chapters 5–12, the implementation of T/TCP) assumes familiarity with the 4.4BSD-Lite networking code, as provided with Volume 2.

Many forward and backward references are provided throughout the text, to both topics within this text, and to relevant sections of Volumes 1 and 2 for readers interested in more details. A thorough index is provided, and a list of all the acronyms used throughout the text, along with the compound term for the acronym, appears on the inside front covers. The inside back covers contain an alphabetical cross-reference of all the structures, functions, and macros described in the book and the starting page number of the description. This cross-reference also refers to definitions in Volume 2, when that object is referenced from the code in this volume.

Source Code Copyright

All the source code in this book that is taken from the 4.4BSD-Lite release contains the following copyright notice:

```
 *
 * Copyright (c) 1982, 1986, 1988, 1990, 1993, 1994
 *      The Regents of the University of California.  All rights reserved.
 *
 * Redistribution and use in source and binary forms, with or without
 * modification, are permitted provided that the following conditions
 * are met:
 * 1. Redistributions of source code must retain the above copyright
 *    notice, this list of conditions and the following disclaimer.
 * 2. Redistributions in binary form must reproduce the above copyright
 *    notice, this list of conditions and the following disclaimer in the
 *    documentation and/or other materials provided with the distribution.
 * 3. All advertising materials mentioning features or use of this software
 *    must display the following acknowledgement:
 *      This product includes software developed by the University of
 *      California, Berkeley and its contributors.
 * 4. Neither the name of the University nor the names of its contributors
 *    may be used to endorse or promote products derived from this software
 *    without specific prior written permission.
 *
 * THIS SOFTWARE IS PROVIDED BY THE REGENTS AND CONTRIBUTORS ``AS IS'' AND
 * ANY EXPRESS OR IMPLIED WARRANTIES, INCLUDING, BUT NOT LIMITED TO, THE
 * IMPLIED WARRANTIES OF MERCHANTABILITY AND FITNESS FOR A PARTICULAR PURPOSE
 * ARE DISCLAIMED.  IN NO EVENT SHALL THE REGENTS OR CONTRIBUTORS BE LIABLE
 * FOR ANY DIRECT, INDIRECT, INCIDENTAL, SPECIAL, EXEMPLARY, OR CONSEQUENTIAL
 * DAMAGES (INCLUDING, BUT NOT LIMITED TO, PROCUREMENT OF SUBSTITUTE GOODS
 * OR SERVICES; LOSS OF USE, DATA, OR PROFITS; OR BUSINESS INTERRUPTION)
 * HOWEVER CAUSED AND ON ANY THEORY OF LIABILITY, WHETHER IN CONTRACT, STRICT
 * LIABILITY, OR TORT (INCLUDING NEGLIGENCE OR OTHERWISE) ARISING IN ANY WAY
 * OUT OF THE USE OF THIS SOFTWARE, EVEN IF ADVISED OF THE POSSIBILITY OF
 * SUCH DAMAGE.
 */
```

The routing table code in Chapter 6 contains the following copyright notice:

```
/*
 * Copyright 1994, 1995 Massachusetts Institute of Technology
 *
 * Permission to use, copy, modify, and distribute this software and
 * its documentation for any purpose and without fee is hereby
 * granted, provided that both the above copyright notice and this
 * permission notice appear in all copies, that both the above
 * copyright notice and this permission notice appear in all
 * supporting documentation, and that the name of M.I.T. not be used
 * in advertising or publicity pertaining to distribution of the
 * software without specific, written prior permission.  M.I.T. makes
 * no representations about the suitability of this software for any
 * purpose.  It is provided "as is" without express or implied
 * warranty.
 *
 * THIS SOFTWARE IS PROVIDED BY M.I.T. ``AS IS''.  M.I.T. DISCLAIMS
 * ALL EXPRESS OR IMPLIED WARRANTIES WITH REGARD TO THIS SOFTWARE,
 * INCLUDING, BUT NOT LIMITED TO, THE IMPLIED WARRANTIES OF
 * MERCHANTABILITY AND FITNESS FOR A PARTICULAR PURPOSE. IN NO EVENT
 * SHALL M.I.T. BE LIABLE FOR ANY DIRECT, INDIRECT, INCIDENTAL,
 * SPECIAL, EXEMPLARY, OR CONSEQUENTIAL DAMAGES (INCLUDING, BUT NOT
 * LIMITED TO, PROCUREMENT OF SUBSTITUTE GOODS OR SERVICES; LOSS OF
 * USE, DATA, OR PROFITS; OR BUSINESS INTERRUPTION) HOWEVER CAUSED AND
 * ON ANY THEORY OF LIABILITY, WHETHER IN CONTRACT, STRICT LIABILITY,
 * OR TORT (INCLUDING NEGLIGENCE OR OTHERWISE) ARISING IN ANY WAY OUT
 * OF THE USE OF THIS SOFTWARE, EVEN IF ADVISED OF THE POSSIBILITY OF
 * SUCH DAMAGE.
 */
```

Typographical Conventions

When we display interactive input and output we'll show our typed input in a **bold font**, and the computer output `like this`. *Comments are added in italics.*

```
sun % telnet www.aw.com 80          connect to the HTTP server
Trying 192.207.117.2...             this line and next output by Telnet client
Connected to aw.com.
```

We always include the name of the system as part of the shell prompt (sun in this example) to show on which host the command was run. The names of programs referred to in the text are normally capitalized (e.g., Telnet and Tcpdump) to avoid excessive font changes.

> Throughout the text we'll use indented, parenthetical notes such as this to describe historical points or implementation details.

Acknowledgments

First and foremost I thank my family, Sally, Bill, Ellen, and David, who have endured another book along with all my traveling during the past year. This time, however, it really is a "small" book.

I thank the technical reviewers who read the manuscript and provided important feedback on a tight timetable: Sami Boulos, Alan Cox, Tony DeSimone, Pete Haverlock, Chris Heigham, Mukesh Kacker, Brian Kernighan, Art Mellor, Jeff Mogul, Marianne Mueller, Andras Olah, Craig Partridge, Vern Paxson, Keith Sklower, Ian Lance Taylor, and Gary Wright. A special thanks to the consulting editor, Brian Kernighan, for his rapid, thorough, and helpful reviews throughout the course of the book, and for his continued encouragement and support.

Special thanks are also due Vern Paxson and Andras Olah for their incredibly detailed reviews of the entire manuscript, finding many errors and providing valuable technical suggestions. My thanks also to Vern Paxson for making available his software for analyzing Tcpdump traces, and to Andras Olah for his help with T/TCP over the past year. My thanks also to Bob Braden, the designer of T/TCP, who provided the reference source code implementation on which Part 1 of this book is based.

Others helped in significant ways. Gary Wright and Jim Hogue provided the system on which the data for Chapter 14 was collected. Doug Schmidt provided a copy of the public domain TTCP program that uses Unix domain sockets, for the timing measurements in Chapter 16. Craig Partridge provided a copy of the RDP source code to examine. Mike Karels answered lots of questions.

My thanks once again to the National Optical Astronomy Observatories (NOAO), Sidney Wolff, Richard Wolff, and Steve Grandi, for providing access to their networks and hosts.

Finally, my thanks to all the staff at Addison-Wesley, who have helped over the past years, especially my editor John Wait.

As usual, camera-ready copy of the book was produced by the author, a Troff diehard, using the Groff package written by James Clark. I welcome electronic mail from any readers with comments, suggestions, or bug fixes.

Tucson, Arizona
November 1995

W. Richard Stevens
rstevens@noao.edu
http://www.noao.edu/~rstevens

Part 1

TCP for Transactions

1

T/TCP Introduction

1.1 Introduction

This chapter introduces the concepts of a client–server transaction. We start with a UDP client–server application, the simplest possible. We then write the client and server using TCP and examine the resulting TCP/IP packets that are exchanged between the two hosts. Next we use T/TCP, showing the reduction in packets and the minimal source code changes required on both ends to take advantage of T/TCP.

We then introduce the test network used to run the examples in the text, and look at a simple timing comparison between the UDP, TCP, and T/TCP client–server applications. We look at some typical Internet applications that use TCP and see what would change if the two end systems supported T/TCP. This is followed by a brief history of transaction processing protocols within the Internet protocol suite, and a description of existing T/TCP implementations.

Throughout this text and throughout the T/TCP literature, the term *transaction* means a request sent by a client to a server along with the server's reply. A common Internet example is a client request to a Domain Name System (DNS) server, asking for the IP address corresponding to a domain name, followed by the server's response. We do *not* use the term to imply the semantics often associated with database transactions: locking, two-phase commit, backout, and so on.

1.2 UDP Client–Server

We begin with a simple UDP client–server example, showing the client source code in Figure 1.1. The client sends a request to the server, the server processes the request and sends back a reply.

udpcli.c

```
 1 #include    "cliserv.h"

 2 int
 3 main(int argc, char *argv[])
 4 {                                   /* simple UDP client */
 5     struct sockaddr_in serv;
 6     char    request[REQUEST], reply[REPLY];
 7     int     sockfd, n;

 8     if (argc != 2)
 9         err_quit("usage: udpcli <IP address of server>");

10     if ((sockfd = socket(PF_INET, SOCK_DGRAM, 0)) < 0)
11         err_sys("socket error");

12     memset(&serv, 0, sizeof(serv));
13     serv.sin_family = AF_INET;
14     serv.sin_addr.s_addr = inet_addr(argv[1]);
15     serv.sin_port = htons(UDP_SERV_PORT);

16     /* form request[] ... */

17     if (sendto(sockfd, request, REQUEST, 0,
18                (SA) &serv, sizeof(serv)) != REQUEST)
19         err_sys("sendto error");

20     if ((n = recvfrom(sockfd, reply, REPLY, 0,
21                       (SA) NULL, (int *) NULL)) < 0)
22         err_sys("recvfrom error");

23     /* process "n" bytes of reply[] ... */

24     exit(0);
25 }
```

udpcli.c

Figure 1.1 Simple UDP client.

> This is the format used for all the source code in the text. Each nonblank line is numbered. The text describing portions of the code begins with the starting and ending line numbers in the left margin, as shown below. Sometimes the paragraph is preceded by a short descriptive heading, providing a summary statement of the code being described. The horizontal rules at the beginning and end of the code fragment specify the source code filename. Often these source filenames refer to files in the 4.4BSD-Lite distribution, which we describe in Section 1.9.

We discuss the relevant features of this program but do not describe the socket functions in great detail, assuming the reader has a basic understanding of these functions. Additional details on these functions can be found in Chapter 6 of [Stevens 1990]. We show the `cliserv.h` header in Figure 1.2.

Create a UDP socket

10–11 The `socket` function creates a UDP socket, returning a nonnegative descriptor to the process. The error-handling function `err_sys` is shown in Appendix B.2 of [Stevens 1992]. It accepts any number of arguments, formats them using `vsprintf`, prints the Unix error message corresponding to the `errno` value from the system call, and then terminates the process.

Fill in server's address

12–15 An Internet socket address structure is first zeroed out using `memset` and then filled with the IP address and port number of the server. For simplicity we require the user to enter the IP address as a dotted-decimal number on the command line when the program is run (`argv[1]`). We `#define` the server's port number (`UDP_SERV_PORT`) in the `cliserv.h` header, which is included at the beginning of all the programs in this chapter. This is done for simplicity and to avoid complicating the code with calls to `gethostbyname` and `getservbyname`.

Form request and send it to server

16–19 The client forms a request (which we show only as a comment) and sends it to the server using `sendto`. This causes a single UDP datagram to be sent to the server. Once again, for simplicity, we assume a fixed-sized request (`REQUEST`) and a fixed-sized reply (`REPLY`). A real application would allocate room for its maximum-sized request and reply, but the actual request and reply would vary and would normally be smaller.

Read and process reply from server

20–23 The call to `recvfrom` blocks the process (i.e., puts it to sleep) until a datagram arrives for the client. The client then processes the reply (which we show as a comment) and terminates.

> This program will hang forever if either the request or reply is lost, since there is no timeout on the `recvfrom`. Indeed, this lack of robustness from real-world errors of this type is one of the fundamental problems with UDP client–servers. We discuss this in more detail at the end of this section.
>
> In the `cliserv.h` header we `#define SA` to be `struct sockaddr *`, that is, a pointer to a generic socket address structure. Every time one of the socket functions requires a pointer to a socket address structure, that pointer must be cast to a pointer to a generic socket address structure. This is because the socket functions predate the ANSI C standard, so the `void *` pointer type was not available in the early 1980s when these functions were developed. The problem is that "`struct sockaddr *`" is 17 characters and often causes the source code line to extend past the right edge of the screen (or page in the case of a book), so we shorten it to `SA`. This abbreviation is borrowed from the BSD kernel sources.

Figure 1.2 shows the `cliserv.h` header that is included in all the programs in this chapter.

cliserv.h

```
/* Common includes and defines for UDP, TCP, and T/TCP
 * clients and servers */

#include    <sys/types.h>
#include    <sys/socket.h>
#include    <netinet/in.h>
#include    <arpa/inet.h>
#include    <stdio.h>
#include    <stdlib.h>
#include    <string.h>
#include    <unistd.h>
```

```
#define REQUEST 400                 /* max size of request, in bytes */
#define REPLY   400                 /* max size of reply, in bytes */

#define UDP_SERV_PORT   7777        /* UDP server's well-known port */
#define TCP_SERV_PORT   8888        /* TCP server's well-known port */
#define TTCP_SERV_PORT  9999        /* T/TCP server's well-known port */

    /* Following shortens all the type casts of pointer arguments */
#define SA  struct sockaddr *

void    err_quit(const char *,...);
void    err_sys(const char *,...);
int     read_stream(int, char *, int);
```

cliserv.h

Figure 1.2 `cliserv.h` header that is included by the programs in this chapter.

Figure 1.3 shows the corresponding UDP server.

udpserv.c

```
#include    "cliserv.h"

int
main()
{                                   /* simple UDP server */
    struct sockaddr_in serv, cli;
    char    request[REQUEST], reply[REPLY];
    int     sockfd, n, clilen;

    if ((sockfd = socket(PF_INET, SOCK_DGRAM, 0)) < 0)
        err_sys("socket error");

    memset(&serv, 0, sizeof(serv));
    serv.sin_family = AF_INET;
    serv.sin_addr.s_addr = htonl(INADDR_ANY);
    serv.sin_port = htons(UDP_SERV_PORT);

    if (bind(sockfd, (SA) &serv, sizeof(serv)) < 0)
        err_sys("bind error");

    for (;;) {
        clilen = sizeof(cli);
        if ((n = recvfrom(sockfd, request, REQUEST, 0,
                          (SA) &cli, &clilen)) < 0)
            err_sys("recvfrom error");

        /* process "n" bytes of request[] and create reply[] ... */

        if (sendto(sockfd, reply, REPLY, 0,
                   (SA) &cli, sizeof(cli)) != REPLY)
            err_sys("sendto error");
    }
}
```

udpserv.c

Figure 1.3 UDP server corresponding to UDP client in Figure 1.1.

Create UDP socket and `bind` local address

8–15 The call to `socket` creates a UDP socket, and an Internet socket address structure is filled in with the server's local address. The local IP address is set to the wildcard (`INADDR_ANY`), which means the server will accept a datagram arriving on any local interface (in case the server's host is multihomed, that is, has more than one network interface). The port number is set to the server's well-known port (`UDP_SERV_PORT`) which we said earlier is defined in the `cliserv.h` header. This local IP address and well-known port are bound to the socket by `bind`.

Process client requests

16–25 The server then enters an infinite loop, waiting for a client request to arrive (`recvfrom`), processing that request (which we show only as a comment), and sending back a reply (`sendto`).

This is the simplest form of UDP client–server application. A common real-world example is the Domain Name System (DNS). A DNS client (called a *resolver*) is normally part of a client application (say, a Telnet client, an FTP client, or a WWW browser). The resolver sends a single UDP datagram to a DNS server requesting the IP address associated with a domain name. The reply is normally a single UDP datagram from the server.

If we watch the packets that are exchanged when our client sends the server a request, we have the time line shown in Figure 1.4. Time increases down the page. The server is started first, shown on the right side of the diagram, and the client is started sometime later.

We distinguish between the function call performed by the client and server, and the action performed by the corresponding kernel. We use two closely spaced arrows, as in the two calls to `socket`, to show that the kernel performs the requested action and returns immediately. In the call to `sendto`, although the kernel returns immediately to the calling process, a UDP datagram is sent. For simplicity we assume that the sizes of the resulting IP datagrams generated by the client's request and the server's reply are both less than the network's MTU (maximum transmission unit), avoiding fragmentation of the IP datagram.

In this figure we also show that the two calls to `recvfrom` put the process to sleep until a datagram arrives. We denote the kernei routines as `sleep` and `wakeup`.

Finally, we show the times associated with the transaction. On the left side of Figure 1.4 we show the transaction time as measured by the client: the time to send a request to the server and receive a reply. The values that comprise this transaction time are shown on the right side of the figure: RTT + SPT, where *RTT* is the network round-trip time, and *SPT* is the server processing time for the request. The transaction time for the UDP client–server, RTT + SPT, is the minimum possible.

> We implicitly assume that the path from the client to the server accounts for ½ RTT and the return path accounts for the other ½ RTT. This is not always the case. In a study of about 600 Internet paths, [Paxson 1995b] found that 30% exhibited a major asymmetry, meaning that the routes in the two directions visited different cities.

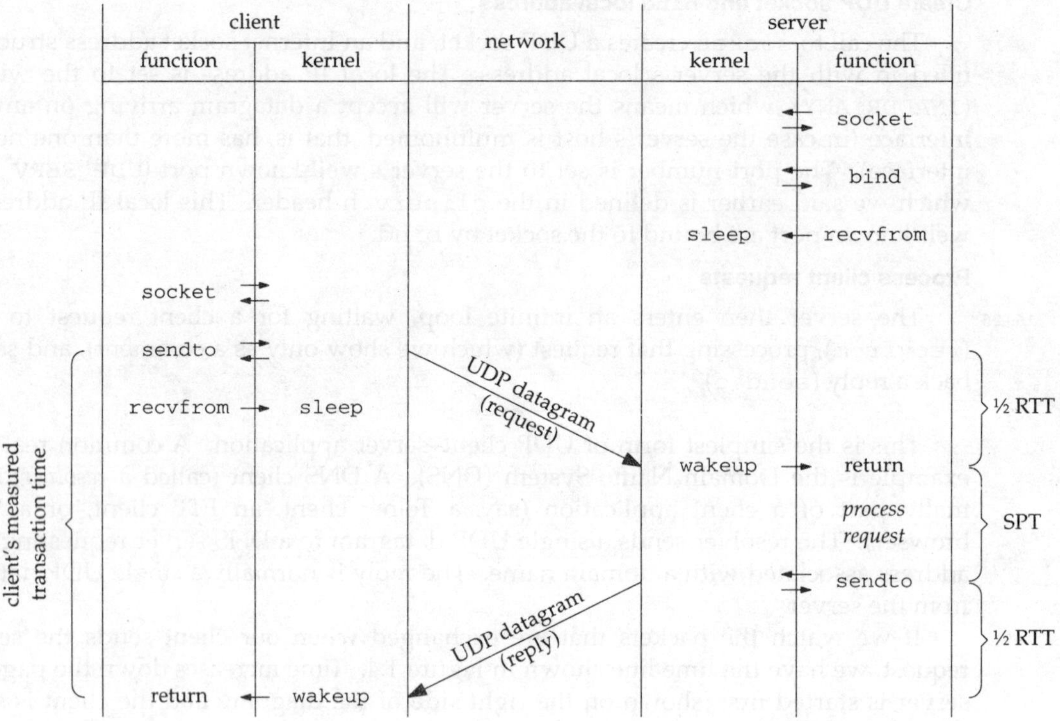

Figure 1.4 Time line of UDP client–server transaction.

Although our UDP client–server looks simple (each program contains only about 30 lines of networking code), the programs are not robust enough for real-world applications. Since UDP is an unreliable protocol, datagrams can be lost, reordered, or duplicated, and a real application needs to handle these problems. This normally involves placing a timeout on the client's call to `recvfrom`, to detect lost datagrams, and retransmitting the request. If a timeout is going to be used, the client must measure the RTT and update it dynamically, since RTTs on an internet can vary widely and change dramatically over time. But if the reply was lost, instead of the request, the server will process the same request a second time, which can lead to problems for some types of services. One way to handle this is for the server to save the reply for each client's latest request, and retransmit that reply instead of processing the request another time. Finally, the client typically sends an identifier with each request, and the server echoes this identifier, allowing the client to match responses with requests. Section 8.4 of [Stevens 1990] details the source code required to handle some of these problems with a UDP client–server, but this adds about 500 lines of code to each program.

While many UDP applications add reliability by performing all of these additional steps (timeouts, RTT measurements, request identifiers, etc.), these steps are continually being reinvented as new UDP applications are developed. [Partridge 1990b] notes that

"To develop a 'reliable UDP' you'll need state information (sequence number, retransmission counts, round-trip time estimator), in principle you'll need just about all the information currently in the TCP connection block. So building a 'reliable UDP' is essentially as difficult as doing a TCP."

Some applications don't implement all of the required steps: for example, they place a timeout on the receive, but do not measure and update the RTT dynamically, which can lead to problems when the application moves from one environment (a LAN) to another (a WAN). A better solution is to use TCP instead of UDP, taking advantage of all the reliability provided by TCP. But this solution increases the client's measured transaction time from RTT + SPT to 2×RTT + SPT, as shown in the next section, and greatly increases the number of network packets exchanged between the two systems. There is a solution to these new problems, using T/TCP instead of TCP, and we examine it in Section 1.4.

1.3 TCP Client–Server

Our next example of a client–server transaction application uses TCP. Figure 1.5 shows the client program.

Create TCP socket and `connect` to server

10–17 A TCP socket is created by `socket` and then an Internet socket address structure is filled in with the IP address and port number of the server. The call to `connect` causes TCP's three-way handshake to occur, establishing a connection between the client and server. Chapter 18 of Volume 1 provides additional details on the packet exchanges when TCP connections are established and terminated.

Send request and half-close the connection

19–22 The client's request is sent to the server by `write`. The client then closes one-half of the connection, the direction of data flow from the client to the server, by calling `shutdown` with a second argument of 1. This tells the server that the client is done sending data: it passes an end-of-file notification from the client to the server. A TCP segment containing the FIN flag is sent to the server. The client can still read from the connection—only one direction of data flow is closed. This is called TCP's *half-close*. Section 18.5 of Volume 1 provides additional details.

Read reply

23–24 The reply is read by our function `read_stream`, shown in Figure 1.6. Since TCP is a byte-stream protocol, without any form of record markers, the reply from the server's TCP can be returned in one or more TCP segments. This can be returned to the client process in one or more `reads`. Furthermore we know that when the server has sent the complete reply, the server process closes the connection, causing its TCP to send a FIN segment to the client, which is returned to the client process by `read` returning an end-of-file (a return value of 0). To handle these details, the function `read_stream` calls `read` as many times as necessary, until either the input buffer is full, or an end-of-file is returned by `read`. The return value of the function is the number of bytes read.

tcpcli.c

```
#include    "cliserv.h"

int
main(int argc, char *argv[])
{                                   /* simple TCP client */
    struct sockaddr_in serv;
    char    request[REQUEST], reply[REPLY];
    int     sockfd, n;

    if (argc != 2)
        err_quit("usage: tcpcli <IP address of server>");

    if ((sockfd = socket(PF_INET, SOCK_STREAM, 0)) < 0)
        err_sys("socket error");

    memset(&serv, 0, sizeof(serv));
    serv.sin_family = AF_INET;
    serv.sin_addr.s_addr = inet_addr(argv[1]);
    serv.sin_port = htons(TCP_SERV_PORT);

    if (connect(sockfd, (SA) &serv, sizeof(serv)) < 0)
        err_sys("connect error");

    /* form request[] ... */

    if (write(sockfd, request, REQUEST) != REQUEST)
        err_sys("write error");
    if (shutdown(sockfd, 1) < 0)
        err_sys("shutdown error");

    if ((n = read_stream(sockfd, reply, REPLY)) < 0)
        err_sys("read error");

    /* process "n" bytes of reply[] ... */

    exit(0);
}
```

tcpcli.c

Figure 1.5 TCP transaction client.

readstream.c

```
#include    "cliserv.h"

int
read_stream(int fd, char *ptr, int maxbytes)
{
    int     nleft, nread;

    nleft = maxbytes;
    while (nleft > 0) {
        if ((nread = read(fd, ptr, nleft)) < 0)
            return (nread);     /* error, return < 0 */
        else if (nread == 0)
            break;              /* EOF, return #bytes read */
        nleft -= nread;
        ptr += nread;
    }
    return (maxbytes - nleft);  /* return >= 0 */
}
```

readstream.c

Figure 1.6 `read_stream` function.

There are other ways to delineate *records* when a stream protocol such as TCP is used. Many Internet applications (FTP, SMTP, HTTP, NNTP) terminate each record with a carriage return and linefeed. Others (DNS, RPC) precede each record with a fixed-size record length. In our example we use TCP's end-of-file flag (the FIN) since we send only one request from the client to the server, and one reply back. FTP also uses this technique with its data connection, to tell the other end when the end-of-file is encountered.

Figure 1.7 shows the TCP server.

tcpserv.c

```
 1 #include    "cliserv.h"

 2 int
 3 main()
 4 {                                  /* simple TCP server */
 5     struct sockaddr_in serv, cli;
 6     char    request[REQUEST], reply[REPLY];
 7     int     listenfd, sockfd, n, clilen;

 8     if ((listenfd = socket(PF_INET, SOCK_STREAM, 0)) < 0)
 9         err_sys("socket error");

10     memset(&serv, 0, sizeof(serv));
11     serv.sin_family = AF_INET;
12     serv.sin_addr.s_addr = htonl(INADDR_ANY);
13     serv.sin_port = htons(TCP_SERV_PORT);

14     if (bind(listenfd, (SA) &serv, sizeof(serv)) < 0)
15         err_sys("bind error");

16     if (listen(listenfd, SOMAXCONN) < 0)
17         err_sys("listen error");

18     for (;;) {
19         clilen = sizeof(cli);
20         if ((sockfd = accept(listenfd, (SA) &cli, &clilen)) < 0)
21             err_sys("accept error");

22         if ((n = read_stream(sockfd, request, REQUEST)) < 0)
23             err_sys("read error");

24         /* process "n" bytes of request[] and create reply[] ... */

25         if (write(sockfd, reply, REPLY) != REPLY)
26             err_sys("write error");

27         close(sockfd);
28     }
29 }
```

tcpserv.c

Figure 1.7 TCP transaction server.

Create listening TCP socket

8–17 A TCP socket is created and the server's well-known port is bound to the socket. As with the UDP server, the TCP server binds the wildcard as its local IP address. The call to `listen` makes the socket a listening socket on which incoming connections will be accepted, and the second argument of SOMAXCONN specifies the maximum number of pending connections the kernel will queue for the socket.

> SOMAXCONN is defined in the <sys/socket.h> header. Historically its value has been 5, although some newer systems define it to be 10. But busy servers (e.g., systems providing a World Wide Web server) have found a need for even higher values, say 256 or 1024. We talk about this more in Section 14.5.

accept a connection and process request

18–28 The server blocks in the call to `accept` until a connection is established by the client's `connect`. The new socket descriptor returned by `accept`, `sockfd`, refers to the connection to the client. The client's request is read by `read_stream` (Figure 1.6) and the reply is returned by `write`.

> This server is an *iterative* server: it processes each client's request completely before looping around to `accept` the next client connection. A *concurrent* server is one that handles multiple clients concurrently (i.e., at the same time). A common technique for implementing concurrent servers on Unix hosts is for the server to `fork` a child process after `accept` returns, letting the child handle the client's request, allowing the parent to `accept` another client connection immediately. Another technique is for the server to create a thread (called a lightweight process) to handle each request. We show the iterative server to avoid complicating the example with process control functions that don't affect the networking aspects of the example. (Chapter 8 of [Stevens 1992] discusses the `fork` function. Chapter 4 of [Stevens 1990] discusses iterative versus concurrent servers.)
>
> A third option is a *pre-forked* server. Here the server calls `fork` a fixed number of times when it starts and each child calls `accept` on the same listening descriptor. This approach saves a call to `fork` for each client request, which can be a big savings on a busy server. Some HTTP servers use this technique.

Figure 1.8 shows the time line for the TCP client–server transaction. The first thing we notice, compared to the UDP time line in Figure 1.4, is the increased number of network packets: nine for the TCP transaction, compared to two for the UDP transaction. With TCP the client's measured transaction time is *at least* 2×RTT + SPT. Normally the middle three segments from the client to the server—the ACK of the server's SYN, the request, and the client's FIN—are spaced closely together, as are the later two segments from the server to the client—the reply and the server's FIN. This makes the transaction time closer to 2×RTT + SPT than it might appear from Figure 1.8.

The additional RTT in this example is from the establishment of the TCP connection: the first two segments that we show in Figure 1.8. If TCP could combine the establishment of the connection with the client's data and the client's FIN (the first four segments from the client in the figure), and then combine the server's reply with the server's FIN, we would be back to a transaction time of RTT + SPT, the same as we had with UDP. Indeed, this is basically the technique used by T/TCP.

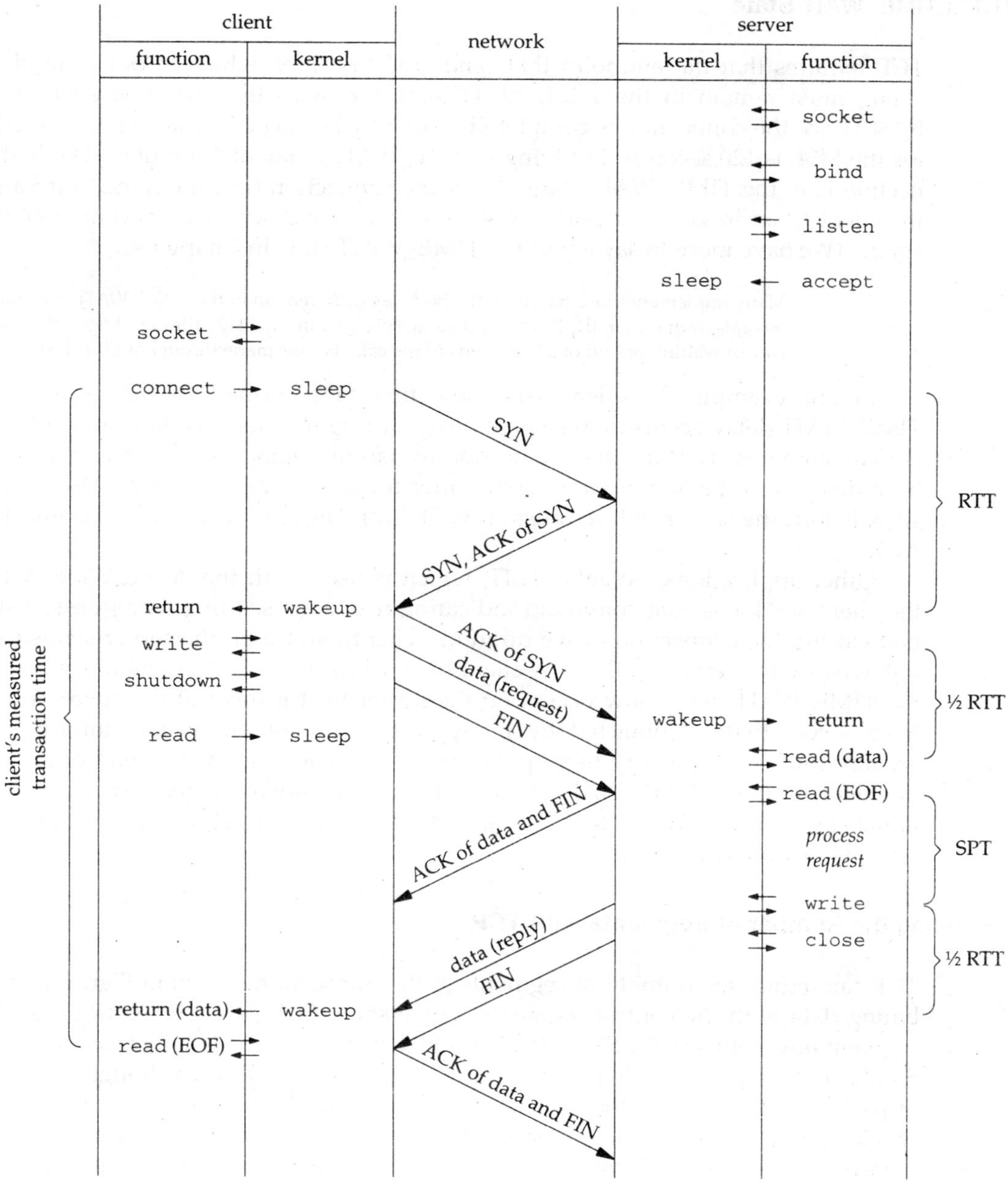

Figure 1.8 Time line of TCP client–server transaction.

TCP's TIME_WAIT State

TCP requires that the endpoint that sends the first FIN, which in our example is the client, must remain in the TIME_WAIT state for twice the *maximum segment lifetime* (MSL) once the connection is completely closed by both ends. The recommended value for the MSL is 120 seconds, implying a TIME_WAIT delay of 4 minutes. While the connection is in the TIME_WAIT state, that same connection (i.e., the same four values for the client IP address, client port, server IP address, and server port) cannot be opened again. (We have more to say about the TIME_WAIT state in Chapter 4.)

> Many implementations based on the Berkeley code remain in the TIME_WAIT state for only 60 seconds, rather than the 240-second value specified in RFC 1122 [Braden 1989]. We assume the correct waiting period of 240 seconds in the calculations made throughout this text.

In our example the client sends the first FIN, termed the *active close*, so the TIME_WAIT delay occurs on the client host. During this delay certain state information is maintained by TCP for this connection to handle segments correctly that may have been delayed in the network and arrive after the connection is closed. Also, if the final ACK is lost, the server will retransmit its FIN, causing the client to retransmit the final ACK.

Other applications, notably HTTP, which is used with the World Wide Web, have the client send a special command indicating it is done sending its request (instead of half-closing the connection as we do in our client), and then the server sends its reply, followed by the server's FIN. The client then sends its FIN. The difference here is that the TIME_WAIT delay now occurs on the server host instead of the client host. On a busy server that is contacted by many clients, the required state information can account for lots of memory tied up on the server. Therefore, which end of the connection ends up in the TIME_WAIT state needs to be considered when designing a transactional client–server. We'll also see that T/TCP shortens the TIME_WAIT state from 240 seconds to around 12 seconds.

Reducing the Number of Segments with TCP

TCP can reduce the number of segments in the transaction shown in Figure 1.8 by combining data with the control segments, as we show in Figure 1.9. Notice that the first segment now contains the SYN, data, and FIN, not just the SYN as we saw in Figure 1.8. Similarly the server's reply is combined with the server's FIN. Although this sequence of packets is legal under the rules of TCP, the author is not aware of a method for an application to cause TCP to generate this sequence of segments using the sockets API (hence the question mark that generates the first segment from the client, and the question mark that generates the final segment from the server) and knows of no implementations that actually generate this sequence of segments.

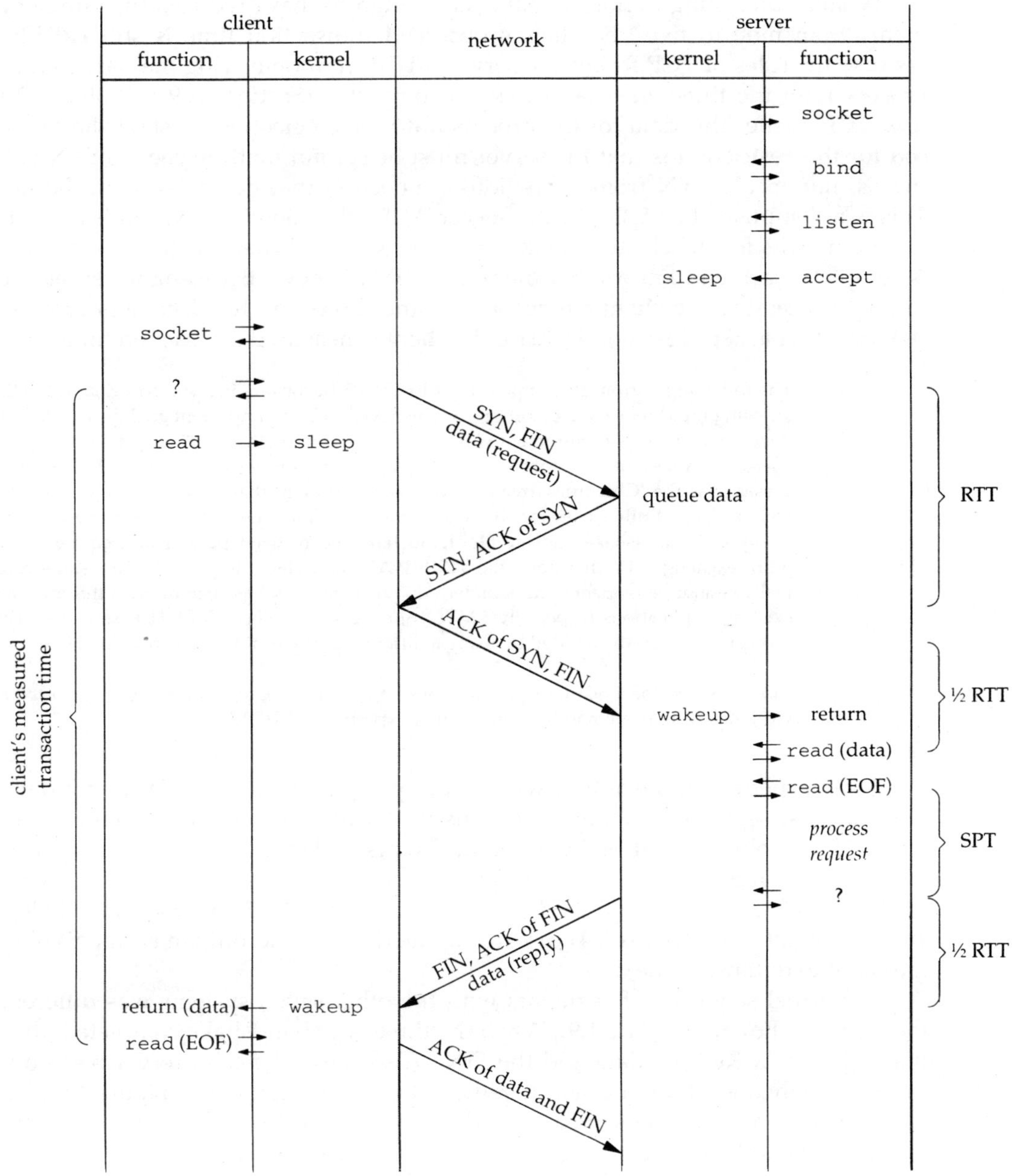

Figure 1.9 Time line of minimal TCP transaction.

What is interesting to note is that even though we have reduced the number of segments from nine to five, the client's observed transaction time is still 2×RTT + SPT because the rules of TCP forbid the server's TCP from delivering the data to the server process until the three-way handshake is complete. (Section 27.9 of Volume 2 shows how TCP queues this data for the process until the connection is established.) The reason for this restriction is that the server must be certain that the client's SYN is "new," that is, not an old SYN from a previous connection that got delayed in the network. This is accomplished as follows: the server ACKs the client's SYN, sends its own SYN, and then waits for the client to ACK the server's SYN. When the three-way handshake is complete, each end knows that the other's SYN is new. Because the server is unable to start processing the client's request until the three-way handshake is complete, the reduction in packets does not decrease the client's measured transaction time.

The following is from the Appendix of RFC 1185 [Jacobson, Braden, and Zhang 1990]: "Note: allowing rapid reuse of connections was believed to be an important goal during the early TCP development. This requirement was driven by the hope that TCP would serve as a basis for user-level transaction protocols as well as connection-oriented protocols. The paradigm discussed was the 'Christmas Tree' or 'Kamikaze' segment that contained SYN and FIN bits as well as data. Enthusiasm for this was somewhat dampened when it was observed that the 3-way SYN handshake and the FIN handshake mean that 5 packets are required for a minimum exchange. Furthermore, the TIME-WAIT state delay implies that the same connection really cannot be reopened immediately. No further work has been done in this area, although existing applications (especially SMTP) often generate very short TCP sessions. The reuse problem is generally avoided by using a different port pair for each connection."

RFC 1379 [Braden 1992b] notes that "These 'Kamikaze' segments were not supported as a service; they were used mainly to crash other experimental TCPs!"

As an experiment, the author wrote a test program that sent a SYN with data and a FIN, the first segment in Figure 1.9. This was sent to the standard echo server (Section 1.12 of Volume 1) of eight different flavors of Unix and the resulting exchange watched with Tcpdump. Seven of the eight handled the segment correctly (4.4BSD, AIX 3.2.2, BSD/OS 2.0, HP-UX 9.01, IRIX System V.3, SunOS 4.1.3, and System V Release 4.0) with the eighth one (Solaris 2.4) discarding the data that accompanied the SYN, forcing the client to retransmit the data.

The actual sequence of segments with the other seven systems was different from the scenario shown in Figure 1.9. When the three-way handshake completed, the server immediately ACKed the data and the FIN. Also, since the echo server had no way to cause its reply and FIN to be sent together (the fourth segment in Figure 1.9), two segments were sent from the server instead: the reply, immediately followed by the FIN. Therefore the total number of segments was seven, not the five shown in Figure 1.9. We talk more about compatibility with non-T/TCP implementations in Section 3.7 and show some Tcpdump output.

Many Berkeley-derived systems cannot handle a received segment for a server that contains a SYN, a FIN, no data, and no ACK. The bug results in the newly created socket remaining in the CLOSE_WAIT state until the host is rebooted. This is a valid T/TCP segment: the client is establishing the connection, sending 0 bytes of data, and closing the connection.

1.4 T/TCP Client–Server

Our T/TCP client–server source code is slightly different from the TCP code in the previous section, to take advantage of T/TCP. Figure 1.10 shows the T/TCP client.

ttcpcli.c

```
 1 #include    "cliserv.h"

 2 int
 3 main(int argc, char *argv[])
 4 {                                   /* T/TCP client */
 5     struct sockaddr_in serv;
 6     char    request[REQUEST], reply[REPLY];
 7     int     sockfd, n;

 8     if (argc != 2)
 9         err_quit("usage: ttcpcli <IP address of server>");

10     if ((sockfd = socket(PF_INET, SOCK_STREAM, 0)) < 0)
11         err_sys("socket error");

12     memset(&serv, 0, sizeof(serv));
13     serv.sin_family = AF_INET;
14     serv.sin_addr.s_addr = inet_addr(argv[1]);
15     serv.sin_port = htons(TCP_SERV_PORT);

16     /* form request[] ... */

17     if (sendto(sockfd, request, REQUEST, MSG_EOF,
18                (SA) &serv, sizeof(serv)) != REQUEST)
19         err_sys("sendto error");

20     if ((n = read_stream(sockfd, reply, REPLY)) < 0)
21         err_sys("read error");

22     /* process "n" bytes of reply[] ... */

23     exit(0);
24 }
```

ttcpcli.c

Figure 1.10 T/TCP transaction client.

Create TCP socket

10–15 The call to `socket` is the same as for a TCP client, and an Internet socket address structure is filled in with the IP address and port of the server.

Send request to server

17–19 A T/TCP client does not call `connect`. Instead, the standard `sendto` function is called, which sends the request to the server *and* establishes the connection with the server. Additionally we specify a new flag as the fourth argument to `sendto`, `MSG_EOF`, which tells the kernel we're done sending data. This is similar to the call to `shutdown` in Figure 1.5, causing a FIN to be sent from the client to the server. This `MSG_EOF` flag is new with T/TCP implementations. Do not confuse it with the existing `MSG_EOR` flag, which is used with record-based protocols (such as the OSI transport layer) to specify end-of-record. The result of this call, as we'll see in Figure 1.12, is a single segment containing the client's SYN flag, the client's request, and the client's FIN flag. This single call to `sendto` combines the functionality of `connect`, `write`, and `shutdown`.

Read server's reply

20–21 The server's reply is read with the same call to `read_stream` as we discussed with the TCP client.

Figure 1.11 shows the T/TCP server.

ttcpserv.c

```
#include    "cliserv.h"

int
main()
{                                       /* T/TCP server */
    struct sockaddr_in serv, cli;
    char    request[REQUEST], reply[REPLY];
    int     listenfd, sockfd, n, clilen;

    if ((listenfd = socket(PF_INET, SOCK_STREAM, 0)) < 0)
        err_sys("socket error");

    memset(&serv, 0, sizeof(serv));
    serv.sin_family = AF_INET;
    serv.sin_addr.s_addr = htonl(INADDR_ANY);
    serv.sin_port = htons(TCP_SERV_PORT);

    if (bind(listenfd, (SA) &serv, sizeof(serv)) < 0)
        err_sys("bind error");

    if (listen(listenfd, SOMAXCONN) < 0)
        err_sys("listen error");

    for (;;) {
        clilen = sizeof(cli);
        if ((sockfd = accept(listenfd, (SA) &cli, &clilen)) < 0)
            err_sys("accept error");

        if ((n = read_stream(sockfd, request, REQUEST)) < 0)
            err_sys("read error");

        /* process "n" bytes of request[] and create reply[] ... */

        if (send(sockfd, reply, REPLY, MSG_EOF) != REPLY)
            err_sys("send error");

        close(sockfd);
    }
}
```

ttcpserv.c

Figure 1.11 T/TCP transaction server.

This program is nearly the same as the TCP server in Figure 1.7: the calls to `socket`, `bind`, `listen`, `accept`, and `read_stream` are identical. The only change is that the

T/TCP server sends its reply with `send` instead of `write`. This allows the `MSG_EOF` flag to be specified, which combines the server's reply with the server's FIN.

Figure 1.12 shows the time line of the T/TCP client–server transaction.

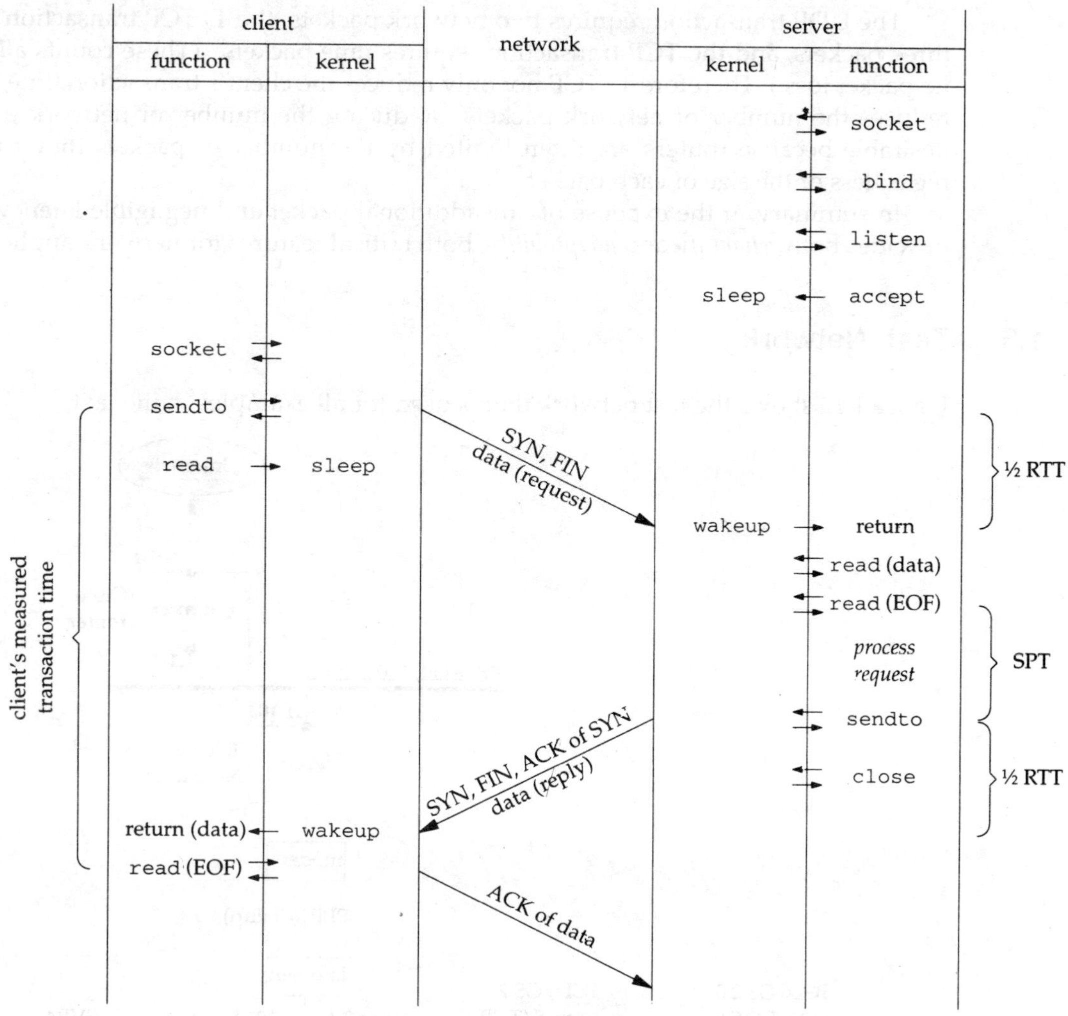

Figure 1.12 Time line of T/TCP client–server transaction.

The T/TCP client observes almost the same transaction time as the UDP client (Figure 1.4): RTT + SPT. We might expect the T/TCP time to be slightly greater than the UDP time, because more is being done by the TCP protocol than the UDP protocol, and because two `reads` are required on both ends to read the data and the end-of-file (compared to a single `recvfrom` by both ends in the UDP case). But this additional processing time on both hosts should be much less than a single network RTT. (We provide some measurements that compare our UDP, TCP, and T/TCP client–servers in Section 1.6.) We therefore conclude that the T/TCP transaction is less than the TCP transaction by about one network RTT. The savings of one RTT achieved by T/TCP is from *TAO*, TCP accelerated open, which bypasses the three-way handshake. In the next two chapters we describe how this is done and in Section 4.5 we describe why this is OK.

The UDP transaction requires two network packets, the T/TCP transaction requires three packets, and the TCP transaction requires nine packets. (These counts all assume no packet loss.) Therefore T/TCP not only reduces the client's transaction time, but also reduces the number of network packets. Reducing the number of network packets is desirable because routers are often limited by the number of packets they can route, regardless of the size of each packet.

In summary, at the expense of one additional packet and negligible latency, T/TCP provides both *reliability* and *adaptability*, both critical features for network applications.

1.5 Test Network

Figure 1.13 shows the test network that is used for all examples in the text.

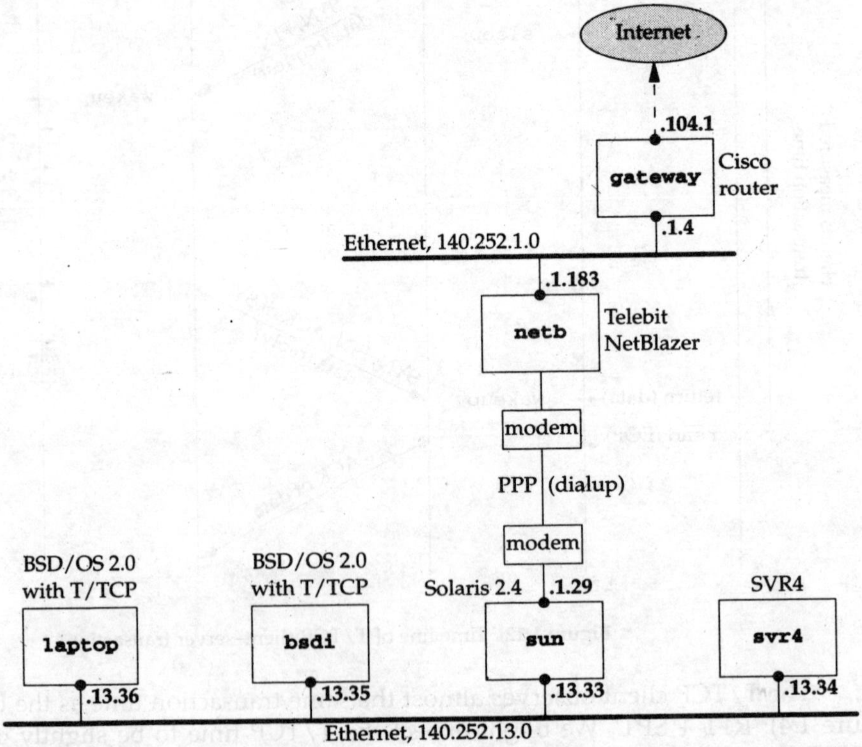

Figure 1.13 Test network used for all examples in the text. All IP addresses begin with 140.252.

Most of the examples are run on the two systems `laptop` and `bsdi`, both of which support T/TCP. All the IP addresses in this figure belong to the class B network 140.252.0.0.

All the hostnames belong to the tuc.noao.edu domain. noao stands for "National Optical Astronomy Observatories" and tuc stands for Tucson. The notation at the top of each box is the operating system running on that system.

1.6 Timing Example

We can measure the time for each of our three client–servers and compare the results. We modify our client programs as follows:

- In our UDP client we fetch the current clock time immediately before the call to sendto in Figure 1.1, and fetch it again immediately after the return from recvfrom. The difference in the two values is the transaction time measured by the client.
- For our TCP client in Figure 1.5 we fetch the clock times immediately before the call to connect and immediately after read_stream returns.
- The T/TCP client in Figure 1.10 fetches the clock times before the call to sendto and after read_stream returns.

Figure 1.14 shows the result for 14 different sizes of the request and reply. The client is the host bsdi in Figure 1.13 and the server is the host laptop. Appendix A provides additional details on these types of measurements and the factors affecting them.

The T/TCP times are always a few milliseconds greater than the corresponding UDP time. (Since the time difference is a software issue, the difference will decrease over the years as computers get faster.) The T/TCP protocol stack is doing more processing than UDP (Figure A.8) and we also noted that the T/TCP client and server both do two reads instead of a single recvfrom.

The TCP times are always about 20 ms greater than the corresponding T/TCP time. This is partly because of the three-way handshake when the connection is established. The length of the two SYN segments is 44 bytes (a 20-byte IP header, the standard 20-byte TCP header, and a 4-byte TCP MSS option). This corresponds to 16 bytes of Ping user data and in Figure A.3 we see the RTT is around 10 ms. The additional 10 ms difference is probably taken up by the additional protocol processing for the additional six TCP segments.

We can therefore state that the T/TCP transaction time will be close to, but larger than, the UDP time. The T/TCP time will be less than the TCP time by at least the RTT of a 44-byte segment.

The relative benefit (in terms of the client's measured transaction time) in using T/TCP instead of TCP depends on the relationship between the RTT and the SPT. For example, on a LAN with an RTT of 3 ms (Figure A.2) and a server with an average processing time of 500 ms, the TCP time will be around 506 ms (2×RTT + SPT) and the T/TCP time around 503 ms. But on a WAN with an RTT of 200 ms (Section 14.4) and an average SPT of 100 ms, the values are around 500 ms for TCP and 300 ms for T/TCP. Also we've shown how T/TCP requires fewer network packets (three versus nine in

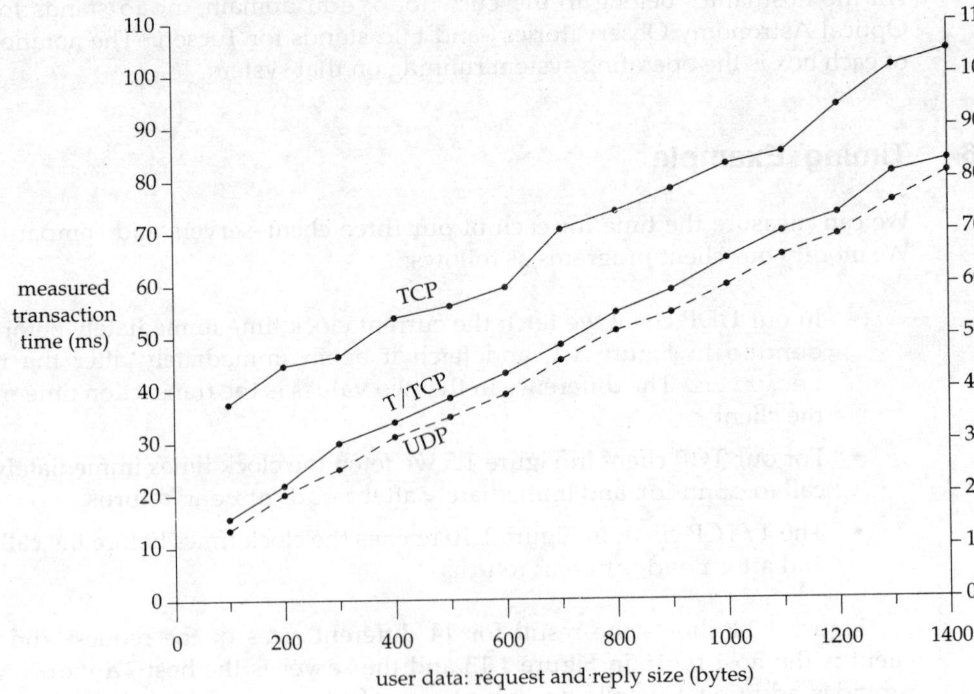

Figure 1.14 Timing for our UDP, T/TCP, and TCP client–servers.

Figures 1.8 and 1.12) so there is always a reduction in network packets using T/TCP, regardless of the actual reduction in the client's measured transaction time. Reducing the number of network packets can reduce the probability of packet loss and, in the big picture of the Internet, contributes to global network stability.

In Section A.3 we describe the difference between latency and bandwidth. The RTT depends on both, but as networks get faster, the latency becomes more important. Furthermore the latency is one variable we have little control over, since it depends on the speed of light and the distance the signals must travel between the client and server. Therefore, as networks get faster, saving an RTT becomes highly desirable, and the relative benefits of T/TCP increase significantly.

> The publicly available network performance benchmark now supports T/TCP transactions: `http://www.cup.hp.com/netperf/NetperfPage.html`.

1.7 Applications

The first benefit from T/TCP, which affects any application that uses TCP, is the potential for shortening the TIME_WAIT state. This reduces the number of control blocks that the implementation must process on a regular basis. Section 4.4 describes this protocol feature in detail. For now we just note that this benefit is available to any application that deals with short (typically less than 2-minute) TCP connections if both hosts support T/TCP.

Perhaps the greatest benefit of T/TCP is avoiding the three-way handshake, and any applications that exchange small amounts of data will benefit from the reduced latency provided by T/TCP. We'll give a few examples. (Appendix B talks about the coding changes required to avoid the three-way handshake with T/TCP.)

World Wide Web: Hypertext Transfer Protocol

The WWW and its underlying HTTP protocol (which we describe in Chapter 13) would benefit greatly from T/TCP. [Mogul 1995b] notes that: "The main contributor to Web latency, however, is network communication. . . . If we cannot increase the speed of light, we should at least minimize the number of round trips required for an interaction. The Hypertext Transfer Protocol (HTTP), as it is currently used in the Web, incurs many more round trips than necessary."

For example, in a random sample of 200,000 HTTP retrievals, [Mogul 1995b] found that the median length of the reply was 1770 bytes. (The median is often used, instead of the mean, since a few large files can skew the mean.) Mogul cites another sample of almost 1.5 million retrievals in which the median reply was 958 bytes. The client request is often smaller: between 100 and 300 bytes.

The typical HTTP client–server transaction looks similar to Figure 1.8. The client does the active open, sends a small request to the server, the server sends back a reply, and the server closes the connection. This is a perfect candidate for T/TCP, which would save the round trip of the three-way handshake by combining the client's SYN with the client's request. This also saves network packets, which now that Web traffic volume is so huge, could be significant.

FTP Data Connection

Another candidate is the FTP data connection. In one analysis of Internet traffic, [Paxson 1994b] found that the average FTP data connection transferred around 3000 bytes. Page 429 of Volume 1 shows an example FTP data connection, and it is similar to Figure 1.12 although the data flow is unidirectional. The eight segments in this figure would be reduced to three with T/TCP.

Domain Name System (DNS)

DNS client queries are sent to a DNS server using UDP. The server responds using UDP but if the reply exceeds 512 bytes, only the first 512 bytes are returned along with a "truncated" flag indicating that more information is available. The client then resends the query using TCP and the server returns the entire reply using TCP.

This technique is used because there is no guarantee that a given host can reassem ble an IP datagram exceeding 576 bytes. (Indeed, many UDP applications limit themselves to 512 bytes of user data to stay below this 576-byte limit.) Since TCP is a byte-stream protocol, the size of the reply is not a problem. The sending TCP divides the application's reply into whatever size pieces are appropriate, up to the maximum segment size (MSS) announced by the peer when the connection was established. The receiving TCP takes these segments and passes the data to the receiving application in whatever size reads the application issues.

A DNS client and server could use T/TCP, obtaining the speed of a UDP request–reply with all the added benefits of TCP.

Remote Procedure Calls (RPC)

Any paper describing a transport protocol intended for transactions always mentions RPC as a candidate for the protocol. RPC involves the client sending a request to the server consisting of the procedure to execute on the server along with the arguments from the client. The server's reply contains the return values from the procedure. Section 29.2 of [Stevens 1994] discusses Sun RPC.

RPC packages normally go to great lengths to add reliability to the RPC protocol so it can run over an unreliable protocol such as UDP, to avoid the three-way handshake of TCP. RPC would benefit from T/TCP, giving it the reliability of TCP without the cost of the three-way handshake.

Other candidates for T/TCP are all the applications that are built on RPC, such as the Network File System (NFS).

1.8 History

One of the early RFCs dealing with transaction processing is RFC 938 [Miller 1985]. It specifies IRTP, the Internet Reliable Transaction Protocol, which provides reliable, sequenced delivery of packets of data. The RFC defines a transaction as a small, self-contained message. IRTP defines a sustained underlying connection between any two hosts (i.e., IP addresses) that is resynchronized when either of the two hosts reboots. IRTP sits on top of IP and defines its own 8-byte protocol header.

RFC 955 [Braden 1985] does not specify a protocol per se, but rather provides some design criteria for a transaction protocol. It notes that the two predominant transport protocols, UDP and TCP, are far apart with regard to the services they provide, and that a transaction protocol falls into the gap between UDP and TCP. The RFC defines a transaction as a simple exchange of messages: a request to the server followed by a reply to the client. It notes that transactions share the following characteristics: asymmetrical model (one end is the client, the other is the server), simplex data transfer (data is never sent in both directions at the same time), short duration (perhaps tens of seconds, but never hours), low delay, few data packets, and message orientation (not a byte stream).

An example examined by the RFC is the DNS. It notes that the TCP/UDP choice for a name server presents an ugly dilemma. The solution should provide reliable delivery of data, no explicit connection setup or teardown, fragmentation and reassembly of messages (so that the application doesn't have to know about magic numbers like

576), and minimal idle state on both ends. TCP provides all these features, except TCP requires the connection setup and teardown.

Another related protocol is RDP, the Reliable Data Protocol, defined in RFC 908 [Velten, Hinden, and Sax 1984] with an update in RFC 1151 [Partridge and Hinden 1990]. Implementation experience is found in [Partridge 1987]. [Partridge 1990a] makes the following comments on RDP: "When people ask for a reliable datagram protocol (and before Jon Postel jumps on me, yes Jon, I know it is an oxymoron) what they typically mean is a transaction protocol—a protocol that allows them to exchange data units reliably with multiple remote systems. A sort of reliable version of UDP. RDP should be viewed as a record-oriented TCP. RDP uses connections and transmits a reliable stream of delineated data. It is not a transaction protocol." (RDP is not a transaction protocol because it uses a three-way handshake just like TCP.)

RDP uses the normal sockets API, and provides a stream socket interface (`SOCK_STREAM`) similar to TCP. Additionally, RDP provides the `SOCK_RDM` socket type (reliably delivered message) and the `SOCK_SEQPACKET` socket type (sequenced packet).

VMTP, the Versatile Message Transaction Protocol, is specified in RFC 1045 [Cheriton 1988]. It was explicitly designed to support transactions, as exemplified by remote procedure calls. Like IRTP and RDP, VMTP is a transport layer that sits on top of IP. VMTP, however, explicitly supports multicast communication, something not provided by T/TCP or the other protocols we've mentioned in this section. ([Floyd et al. 1995] make the argument that provision for reliable multicast communications belongs in the application layer, not the transport layer.)

VMTP provides a different API to the application, which is described in RFC 1045. The socket type is `SOCK_TRANSACT`.

Although many of the ideas in T/TCP appeared in RFC 955, the first specification did not appear until RFC 1379 [Braden 1992b]. This RFC defined the concepts of T/TCP and was followed by RFC 1644 [Braden 1994], which provides additional details and discusses some implementation issues.

It is interesting to compare the number of lines of C code required to implement the various transport layers, shown in Figure 1.15.

Protocol	#lines of code
UDP (Volume 2)	800
RDP	2,700
TCP (Volume 2)	4,500
TCP with T/TCP mods	5,700
VMTP	21,000

Figure 1.15 Number of lines of code required to implement various transport layers.

The additional code required to support T/TCP (about 1200 lines) is one and a half times the size of UDP. The multicast support added to 4.4BSD required about 2000 lines of code (ignoring the device driver changes and support for multicast routing).

VMTP is available from `ftp://gregorio.stanford.edu/vmtp-ip`. RDP is not generally available.

1.9 Implementations

The first implementation of T/TCP was done by Bob Braden and Liming Wei at the University of Southern California Information Sciences Institute. This work was supported in part by the National Science Foundation under Grant Number NCR-8922231. This implementation was done for SunOS 4.1.3 (a Berkeley-derived kernel) and was made available via anonymous FTP in September 1994. The source code patches for SunOS 4.1.3 can be obtained from `ftp://ftp.isi.edu/pub/braden/TTCP.tar.Z`, but you need the source code for the SunOS kernel to apply these patches.

The USC ISI implementation was modified by Andras Olah at the University of Twente (Netherlands) and put into the FreeBSD 2.0 release in March 1995. The networking code in FreeBSD 2.0 is based on the 4.4BSD-Lite release (which is described in Volume 2). We show the chronology of the various BSD releases in Figure 1.16. All of the work related to the routing table (which we discuss in Chapter 6) was done by Garrett Wollman of the Massachusetts Institute of Technology. Information on obtaining the FreeBSD implementation is available from `http://www.freebsd.org`.

The author ported the FreeBSD implementation into the BSD/OS 2.0 kernel (which is also based on the 4.4BSD-Lite networking code). This is the code running in the hosts `bsdi` and `laptop` (Figure 1.13), which are used throughout the text. These modifications to BSD/OS to support T/TCP are available through the author's home page: `http://www.noao.edu/~rstevens`.

Figure 1.16 shows a chronology of the various BSD releases, indicating the important TCP/IP features. The releases shown on the left side are publicly available source code releases containing all of the networking code: the protocols themselves, the kernel routines for the networking interface, and many of the applications and utilities (such as Telnet and FTP).

The official name of the software used as the foundation for the T/TCP implementation described in this text is *4.4BSD-Lite*, but we'll refer to it simply as *Net/3*. Also realize that the publicly available Net/3 release does not include the T/TCP modifications covered in this text. When we use the term Net/3 we refer to the publicly available release that does not include T/TCP.

4.4BSD-Lite2 is the 1995 update to 4.4BSD-Lite. From a networking perspective the changes from Lite to Lite2 are bug fixes and minor enhancements (such as the timing out of persist probes, which we discuss in Section 14.9). We show three systems that are based on the Lite code: BSD/OS, FreeBSD, and NetBSD. As of this writing all are based on the Lite code, but all three should move to the Lite2 code base with the next major release. A CD-ROM containing the Lite2 release is available from Walnut Creek CDROM, `http://www.cdrom.com`.

Throughout the text we'll use the term *Berkeley-derived implementation* to refer to vendor implementations such as SunOS, SVR4 (System V Release 4), and AIX, whose TCP/IP code was originally developed from the Berkeley sources. These implementations have much in common, often including the same bugs!

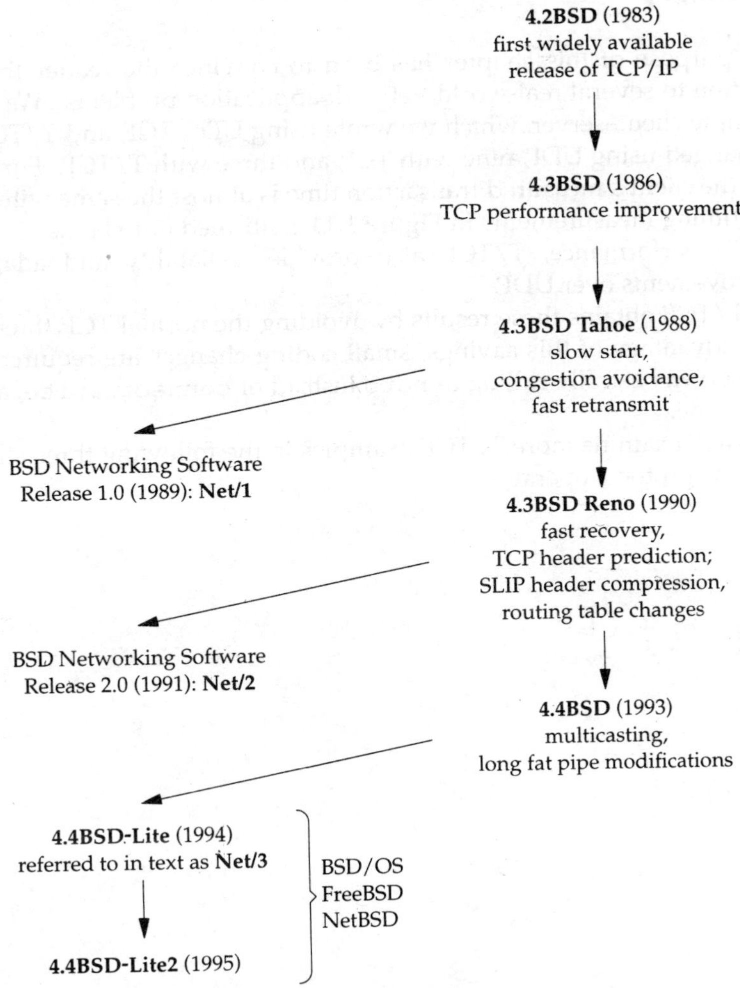

Figure 1.16 Various BSD releases with important TCP/IP features.

1.10 Summary

The purpose of this chapter has been to convince the reader that T/TCP provides a solution to several real-world network application problems. We started by comparing a simple client–server, which we wrote using UDP, TCP, and T/TCP. Two packets were exchanged using UDP, nine with TCP, and three with T/TCP. Furthermore, we showed that the client's measured transaction time is almost the same with T/TCP as with UDP. The timing measurements in Figure 1.14 confirmed our claims. In addition to matching UDP's performance, T/TCP also provides reliability and adaptability, both major improvements over UDP.

T/TCP obtains these results by avoiding the normal TCP three-way handshake. To take advantage of this savings, small coding changes are required in the T/TCP client and server, basically calling `sendto` instead of `connect`, `write`, and `shutdown` on the client side.

We'll examine more T/TCP examples in the following three chapters, as we explore how the protocol operates.

2

T/TCP Protocol

2.1 Introduction

We divide our discussion of the T/TCP protocol into two chapters (Chapters 2 and 4) so we can look at some T/TCP examples (Chapter 3) before delving into the protocol. This chapter is an introduction to the protocol techniques and the required implementation variables. The next chapter looks at some T/TCP examples, and Chapter 4 completes our look at the T/TCP protocol.

When TCP is used for client–server transactions as shown in Chapter 1, two problems arise:

1. The three-way handshake adds an extra RTT to the client's measured transaction time. We saw this in Figure 1.8.

2. Since the client does the active close (that is, the client sends the first FIN), the client's end of the connection remains in the TIME_WAIT state for 240 seconds after the client receives the server's FIN.

   The combination of the TIME_WAIT state and the 16-bit TCP port numbers limits the maximum transaction rate between any two hosts. For example, if the same client host continually performs transactions with the same server host, it must either wait 240 seconds between each transaction or it must use a different port for each successive transaction. But only 64,512 ports (65535 minus the 1023 well-known ports) are available every 240 seconds, limiting the rate to 268 transactions per second. On a LAN with an RTT around 1–3 ms, it is possible to exceed this rate.

   Also, even if the application stays below this rate, say, 50,000 transactions every 240 seconds, while the connection is in the TIME_WAIT state on the client, a control block is required to maintain the state of the connection. In the BSD implementation presented in Volume 2, an Internet protocol control block (requiring 84 bytes), a TCP control block (140 bytes), and an IP/TCP header template (40 bytes) are required. This requires 13,200,000 bytes of kernel memory, which is a lot, even as computer memory sizes increase.

T/TCP solves these two problems by bypassing the three-way handshake and shortening the TIME_WAIT state from 240 seconds to approximately 12 seconds. We'll examine both of these features in detail in Chapter 4.

The essence of T/TCP is called *TAO*, TCP accelerated open, which bypasses the three-way handshake. T/TCP assigns a unique identifier, called a *connection count* (CC), to each connection that a host establishes. Each T/TCP host remembers the most recent connection count used with each peer for some period of time. When a server receives a SYN from a T/TCP client and the SYN contains a connection count that is greater than the most recent connection count received from this peer, this guarantees that the SYN is new and allows the receiving TCP to accept the SYN without the three-way handshake. This is called the *TAO test*, and when this test fails, TCP reverts back to the three-way handshake to verify that the received SYN is new.

2.2 New TCP Options for T/TCP

Three new TCP options are used with T/TCP. Figure 2.1 shows all currently used TCP options. The first three are from the original TCP specification, RFC 793 [Postel 1981b]. The window scale and timestamp are defined in RFC 1323 [Jacobson, Braden, and Borman 1992]. The last three—CC, CCnew, and CCecho—are new with T/TCP and are defined in RFC 1644 [Braden 1994]. The rules for these last three options are as follows:

1. The CC option can be sent in an initial SYN segment: the active open performed by the client. It can also be sent in other segments but only if the other end sent a CC or a CCnew option with its SYN.
2. The CCnew option can only appear in an initial SYN segment. A client TCP sends this option instead of a CC option when the client needs to perform the normal three-way handshake.
3. The CCecho option can only appear in the second segment of a three-way handshake: the segment containing a SYN and an ACK (normally sent by the server). It echoes the client's CC or CCnew value and informs the client that the server understands T/TCP.

We'll say more about these options in this and following chapters as we look at T/TCP examples.

Notice that the three new options for T/TCP all occupy 6 bytes. To keep the options on a 4-byte boundary, which can help performance on some architectures, these three options are normally preceded by two 1-byte no-operations (NOPs).

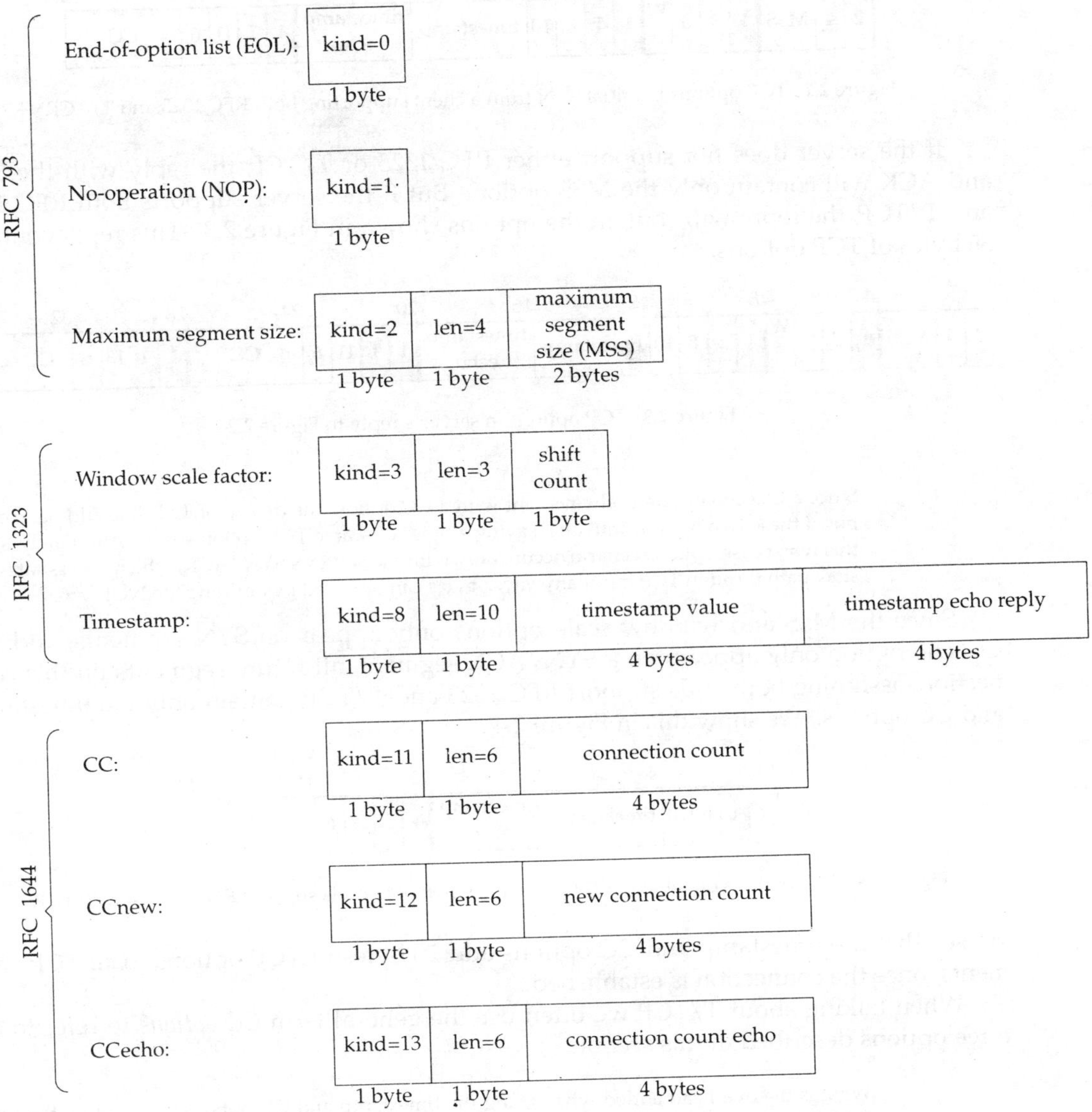

Figure 2.1 TCP options.

Figure 2.2 shows the TCP options in an initial SYN segment from a client to a server, when the client supports both RFC 1323 and T/TCP. We explicitly show the *kind* and *len* for each option, and show the NOPs as shaded boxes with a *kind* of 1. The second option is designated as "WS" for the window scale option. The numbers at the top are the byte offsets from the start of the options. This example requires 28 bytes of TCP options, which have a maximum size of 40 bytes. Notice that the padding with NOPs places all four of the 4-byte values on a 4-byte boundary.

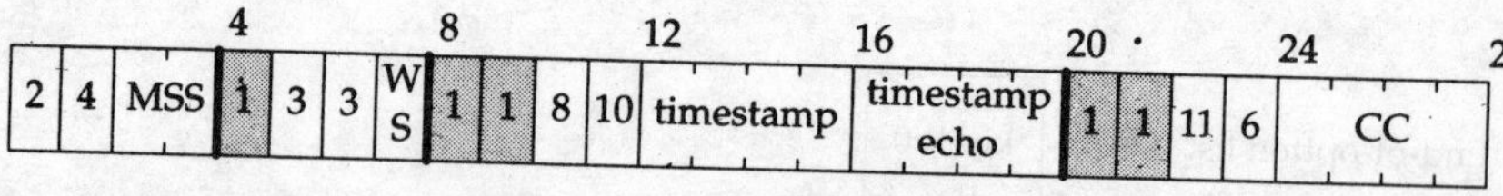

Figure 2.2 TCP options in initial SYN from a client supporting both RFC 1323 and T/TCP.

If the server does not support either RFC 1323 or T/TCP, the reply with the SYN and ACK will contain only the MSS option. But if the server supports both RFC 1323 and T/TCP, the reply will contain the options shown in Figure 2.3. This reply contains 36 bytes of TCP options.

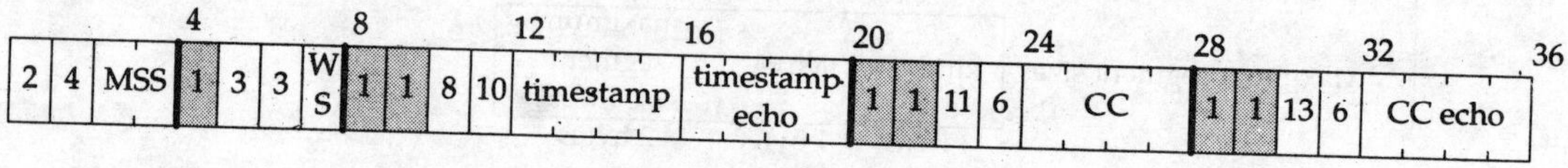

Figure 2.3 TCP options in server's reply to Figure 2.2.

> Since a CCecho option is always sent with a CC option, the design of T/TCP could have combined these two options into one, saving 4 bytes of scarce TCP option space. Alternately, since this worst case option scenario occurs only with the server's SYN/ACK, which necessitates the slow path through TCP input anyway, 7 bytes can be saved by omitting the NOP bytes.

Since the MSS and window scale options only appear on SYN segments, and the CCecho option only appears on a SYN/ACK segment, all future segments on this connection, assuming both ends support RFC 1323 and T/TCP, contain only the timestamp and CC options. We show this in Figure 2.4.

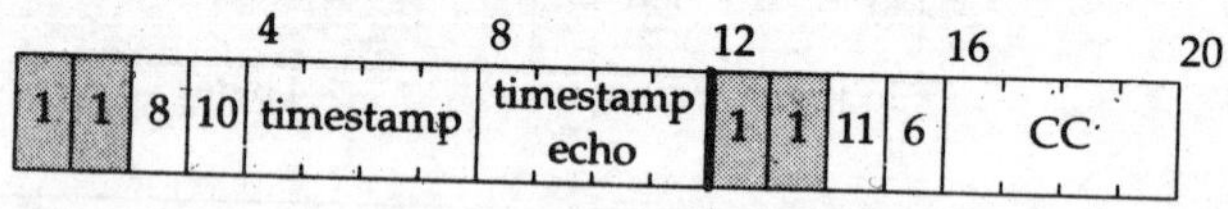

Figure 2.4 TCP options on all non-SYN segments when both ends support RFC 1323 and T/TCP.

We see that the timestamp and CC options add 20 bytes of TCP options to *all* TCP segments, once the connection is established.

When talking about T/TCP we often use the general term *CC options* to refer to all three options described in this section.

> What is the overhead added when using the timestamp and CC options? Assuming the typical 512-byte MSS between hosts on different networks, to transfer a one-million-byte file takes 1954 segments with no options and 2033 segments if both the timestamp and CC options are used, for an increase of about 4%. For hosts using an MSS of 1460 the increase in the number of segments is only 1.5%.

2.3 T/TCP Implementation Variables

T/TCP requires some new information to be maintained by the kernel. This section describes the information and later sections show how it is used.

1. `tcp_ccgen`. This is a 32-bit global integer variable containing the next CC value to use. This variable is incremented by 1 for every TCP connection established by the host, actively or passively, regardless of whether the connection uses T/TCP or not. This variable never assumes the value of 0. If, when incremented, its value becomes 0, the value is set to 1.

2. A *per-host cache* containing three new variables: `tao_cc`, `tao_ccsent`, and `tao_mssopt`. This cache is also called the *TAO cache*. We'll see that our T/TCP implementation creates a routing table entry for each host with which it communicates and stores this information in the routing table entry. (The routing table is just a convenient location for this per-host cache. A totally separate table could also be used for the per-host cache. T/TCP does not require any changes to the IP routing function.) When a new entry is created in the per-host cache, `tao_cc` and `tao_ccsent` must be initialized to 0, which means undefined.

   `tao_cc` is the last CC received from this host in a valid SYN segment without an ACK (an active open). When a T/TCP host receives a SYN with a CC option, if the option value is greater than `tao_cc`, the host knows that this is a new SYN, not an old duplicate, allowing the three-way handshake to be bypassed (the TAO test).

   `tao_ccsent` is the last CC sent to this host in a SYN without an ACK (an active open). When this value is undefined (0), it is set nonzero only when the peer demonstrates the ability to use T/TCP by sending a CCecho option.

   `tao_mssopt` is the last MSS received from this host.

3. Three new variables are added to the existing TCP control block: `cc_send`, `cc_recv`, and `t_duration`. The first is the CC value to send with every segment on this connection, the next is the CC value that we expect to receive from the other end in every segment, and `t_duration` is how long the connection is established (measured in clock ticks). When the connection is actively closed, if this tick counter indicates the connection duration was less than the MSL, the TIME_WAIT state will be truncated. We discuss this in more detail in Section 4.4.

We can represent these variables as shown in Figure 2.5. This figure assumes the implementation that we describe in later chapters.

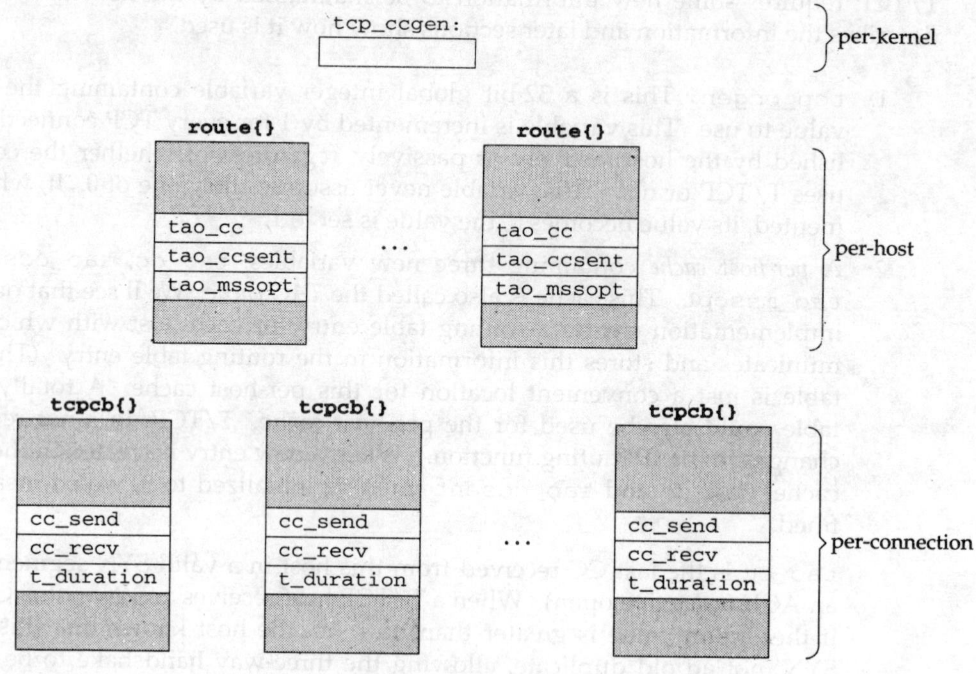

Figure 2.5 Implementation variables for T/TCP.

In this figure we use `{}` to denote a structure. We show the TCP control block as a `tcpcb` structure. Every TCP implementation must maintain a control block of some form containing all the variables for a given connection.

2.4 State Transition Diagram

The operation of TCP can be described with a state transition diagram, as shown in Figure 2.6. Most TCP state transition diagrams (such as the ones in Volumes 1 and 2) show the segment that is sent as part of each transition line. For example, the transition from CLOSED to SYN_SENT would indicate that a SYN is sent. We omit this notation from Figure 2.6, instead noting in each box the type of segment sent when in that state. For example, in the SYN_RCVD state a SYN is sent along with an acknowledgment of the received SYN. In the CLOSE_WAIT state an acknowledgment of the received FIN is sent.

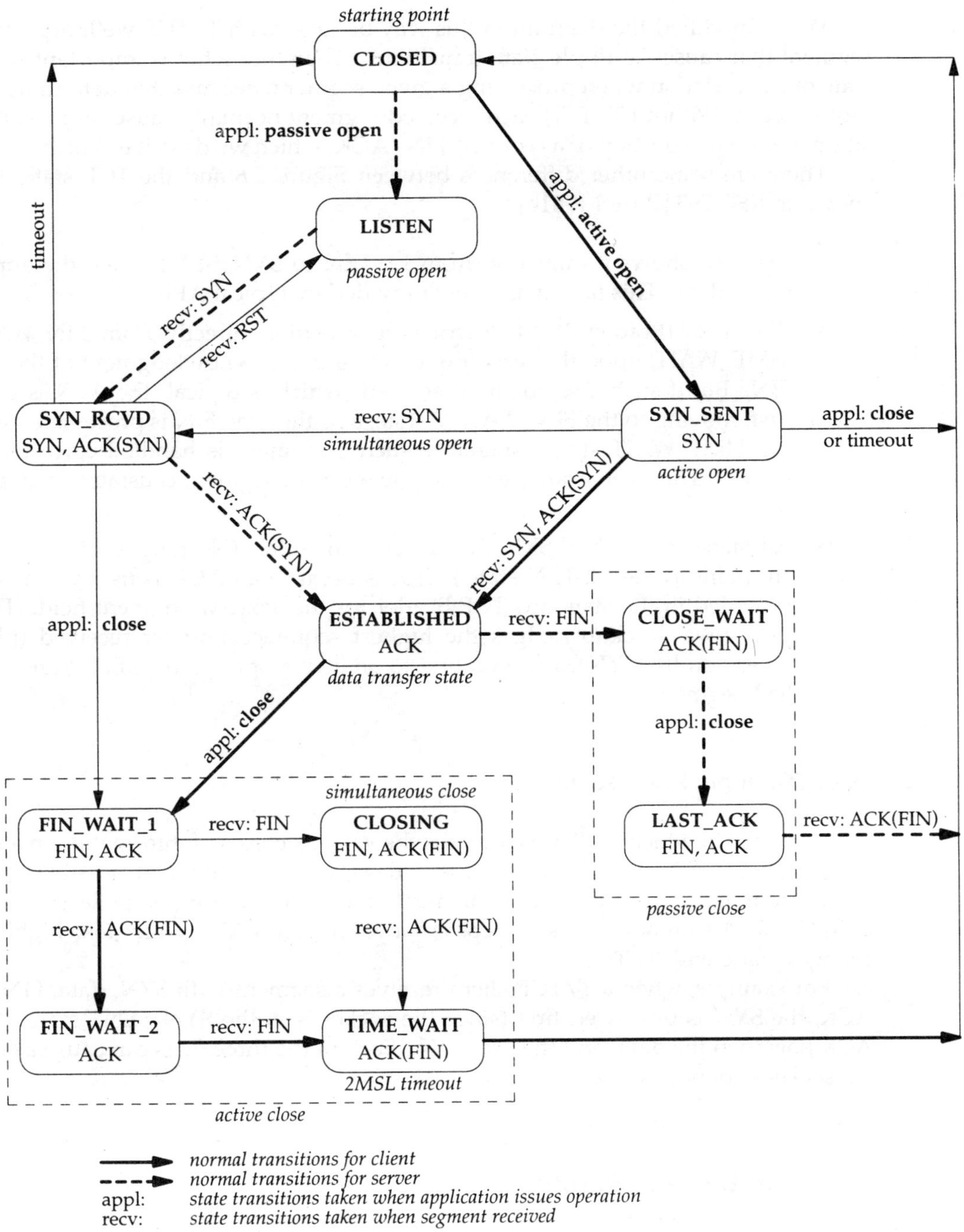

Figure 2.6 TCP state transition diagram.

We've modified the diagram in this way because with T/TCP we'll often process a segment that causes multiple state transitions. Therefore what is important is the final state of a connection when processing a given segment, because that determines what is sent in reply. Without T/TCP, each received segment normally causes at most one transition, with the exception of a received FIN/ACK, which we describe shortly.

There are some other differences between Figure 2.6 and the TCP state diagrams shown in RFC 793 [Postel 1981b].

- RFC 793 shows a transition from LISTEN to SYN_SENT when the application sends data. This facility is rarely provided by typical APIs.
- RFC 1122 [Braden 1989] describes a transition directly from FIN_WAIT_1 to TIME_WAIT, upon the receipt of a FIN and an acknowledgment of the sender's FIN. But if such a segment is received (which is typical) the ACK is processed first, moving to the FIN_WAIT_2 state, and then the FIN is processed, moving to the TIME_WAIT state. Therefore such a segment is handled correctly by Figure 2.6. This is an example of a single received segment causing two state transitions.
- All states other than SYN_SENT send an ACK. (Nothing at all is sent for an endpoint in the LISTEN state.) This is because an ACK is free: room is always provided in the standard TCP header for the acknowledgment field. Therefore TCP always acknowledges the highest sequence number received (plus one) except on the SYN corresponding to an active open (SYN_SENT) and for some RST segments.

Sequence of TCP Input Processing

The sequence in which TCP must process the various pieces of information in a received segment (SYN, FIN, ACK, URG, and RST flags, possible data, and possible options) is not random and is not up to the implementation. The ordering is spelled out explicitly in RFC 793. A summary of these steps is shown in Figure 11.1, which also highlights the changes made with T/TCP.

For example, when a T/TCP client receives a segment with SYN, data, FIN, and an ACK, the SYN is processed first (since the socket is in the SYN_SENT state), then the ACK flag, then the data, and then the FIN. Each of the three flags can cause a change in the socket's connection state.

2.5 T/TCP Extended States

T/TCP defines seven extended states, called the *starred states*: SYN_SENT*, SYN_RCVD*, ESTABLISHED*, CLOSE_WAIT*, LAST_ACK*, FIN_WAIT_1*, and CLOSING*. For example, in Figure 1.12 the client sends an initial segment containing a SYN, data, and a FIN. Sending this segment as part of an active open puts the client in the SYN_SENT* state, not the normal SYN_SENT state, since a FIN must be sent. When the server's reply is received, containing the server's SYN, data, and FIN, along with an ACK that acknowledges the client's SYN, data, and FIN, numerous state transitions take place:

- The ACK of the client's SYN moves the connection to the FIN_WAIT_1 state. The ESTABLISHED state is completely bypassed since the client has already sent its FIN.
- The ACK of the client's FIN moves the connection to the FIN_WAIT_2 state.
- The receipt of the server's FIN moves the connection to the TIME_WAIT state.

RFC 1379 details the development of a state transition diagram that includes all these starred states, but the result is much more complicated than Figure 2.6, with many overlapping lines. Fortunately there are simple relationships between the unstarred states and the corresponding starred states.

- The two states SYN_SENT* and SYN_RCVD* are identical to the corresponding unstarred states except that a FIN must be sent. That is, these two states are entered when an active endpoint is created and the application specifies `MSG_EOF` (send a FIN) before the connection is established. The normal state for the client in this scenario is SYN_SENT*. The SYN_RCVD* state is the rare occurrence of a simultaneous open, which is described in detail in Section 18.8 of Volume 1.
- The five states ESTABLISHED*, CLOSE_WAIT*, LAST_ACK*, FIN_WAIT_1*, and CLOSING* are identical to the corresponding unstarred states except that a SYN must be sent. When the connection is in one of these five states it is called *half-synchronized*. These states are entered when the endpoint is passive and receives a SYN that passes the TAO test, along with optional data and an optional FIN. (Section 4.5 describes the TAO test in detail.) The term *half-synchronized* is used because the receiver of the SYN considers the connection established (since it passes the TAO test) even though only half of the normal three-way handshake is complete.

Figure 2.7 shows these starred states, along with all the normal states. For each possible state, this table shows what type of segment is sent.

We'll see that from an implementation perspective the starred states are simple to handle. In addition to maintaining the current unstarred state, two additional flags are maintained in the per-connection TCP control block:

- `TF_SENDFIN` specifies that a FIN needs to be sent (corresponding to SYN_SENT* and SYN_RCVD*), and
- `TF_SENDSYN` specifies that a SYN needs to be sent (corresponding to the five half-synchronized starred states in Figure 2.7).

We identify the SYN and FIN flags that are turned on in the starred states by these two new flags with a bold font in Figure 2.7.

Normal state	Description	Send	Starred state	Send
CLOSED	closed	RST, ACK		
LISTEN	listening for connection (passive open)			
SYN_SENT	have sent SYN (active open)	SYN	SYN_SENT*	SYN, **FIN**
SYN_RCVD	have sent and received SYN; awaiting ACK	SYN, ACK	SYN_RCVD*	SYN, **FIN**, ACK
ESTABLISHED	established (data transfer)	ACK	ESTABLISHED*	**SYN**, ACK
CLOSE_WAIT	received FIN, waiting for application close	ACK	CLOSE_WAIT*	**SYN**, ACK
FIN_WAIT_1	have closed, sent FIN; awaiting ACK and FIN	FIN, ACK	FIN_WAIT_1*	**SYN**, FIN, ACK
CLOSING	simultaneous close; awaiting ACK	FIN, ACK	CLOSING*	**SYN**, FIN, ACK
LAST_ACK	received FIN have closed; awaiting ACK	FIN, ACK	LAST_ACK*	**SYN**, FIN, ACK
FIN_WAIT_2	have closed; awaiting FIN	ACK		
TIME_WAIT	2MSL wait state after active close	ACK		

Figure 2.7 What TCP sends based on current state (normal and starred).

2.6 Summary

The essence of T/TCP is TAO, TCP accelerated open. This allows a T/TCP server to receive a SYN from a T/TCP client and know that the SYN is new, avoiding the three-way handshake. The technique used to ensure that a received SYN is new (the TAO test) is to assign a unique identifier, the connection count, to each connection that a host establishes. Each T/TCP host remembers the most recent connection count used with each peer for some period of time, and the TAO test succeeds if a received SYN has a connection count that is greater than the most recent connection count received from this peer.

Three new options are defined by T/TCP: the CC, CCnew, and CCecho options. All contain a length field (as do the other new options defined by RFC 1323), allowing implementations that do not understand the options to skip over them. If T/TCP is used for a given connection, the CC option will appear on every segment (but sometimes the CCnew option is used instead on the client SYN).

One global kernel variable is added with T/TCP, along with three variables in a per-host cache, and three variables in the existing per-connection control block. The T/TCP implementation that we describe in this text uses the existing routing table as the per-host cache.

T/TCP adds 7 additional states to the existing 10 states in the TCP state transition diagram. But the actual implementation turns out to be simple: two new per-connection flags that indicate whether a SYN needs to be sent and whether a FIN needs to be sent are all that is needed to define the 7 new states, since the new states are extensions to existing states.

3

T/TCP Examples

3.1 Introduction

We'll now go through some T/TCP examples to see exactly how the three new TCP options are used. These examples show how T/TCP handles the following conditions:

- client reboot,
- normal T/TCP transactions,
- server receipt of an old duplicate SYN,
- server reboot,
- handling of a request or reply that exceeds the MSS, and
- backward compatibility with hosts that do not support T/TCP.

In the next chapter we consider two additional examples: SYNs that are not old duplicates but arrive out of order at the server, and client handling of duplicate SYN/ACK responses from the server.

In these examples the T/TCP client is the host `bsdi` (Figure 1.13) and the server is the host `laptop`. The programs being run are the T/TCP client from Figure 1.10 and the T/TCP server from Figure 1.11. The client sends a 300-byte request and the server responds with a 400-byte reply.

In these examples support for RFC 1323 has been turned off in the client. This prevents the client from sending window scale and timestamp options with its initial SYN. (Since the client doesn't send either option, the server won't respond with either one, so it doesn't matter whether or not RFC 1323 support is enabled on the server.) We do this to avoid complicating the examples with other factors that don't affect our discussion of T/TCP. Normally we would want to use RFC 1323 with T/TCP since the timestamp option provides additional protection against old duplicate segments being misinterpreted as part of an existing connection. That is, even with T/TCP, PAWS (protection against wrapped sequence numbers, Section 24.6 of Volume 1) is still needed on high-bandwidth connections that transfer lots of data.

3.2 Client Reboot

We start our sequence of client–server transactions immediately after the client reboots. When the client application calls `sendto`, a routing table entry is created for the server with the `tao_ccsent` value initialized to 0 (undefined). TCP therefore sends a CCnew option instead of a CC option. The receipt of the CCnew option causes the server TCP to perform the normal three-way handshake, as shown by the Tcpdump output in Figure 3.1. (Readers unfamiliar with the operation of Tcpdump and the output that it generates should refer to Appendix A of Volume 1. Also, when looking at these packet traces, don't forget that a SYN and a FIN each consumes a byte in the sequence number space.)

```
1  0.0                   bsdi.1024 > laptop.8888: SFP 36858825:36859125(300)
                                                  win 8568 <mss 1460,nop,nop,ccnew 1>
2  0.020542 (0.0205)  laptop.8888 > bsdi.1024:  S 76355292:76355292(0)
                                                  ack 36858826 win 8712
                                                  <mss 1460,nop,nop,cc 18,
                                                   nop,nop,ccecho 1>
3  0.021479 (0.0009)  bsdi.1024 > laptop.8888:  F 301:301(0)
                                                  ack 1 win 8712 <nop,nop,cc 1>
4  0.029471 (0.0080)  laptop.8888 > bsdi.1024:  .
                                                  ack 302 win 8412 <nop,nop,cc 18>
5  0.042086 (0.0126)  laptop.8888 > bsdi.1024:  FP 1:401(400)
                                                  ack 302 win 8712 <nop,nop,cc 18>
6  0.042969 (0.0009)  bsdi.1024 > laptop.8888:  .
                                                  ack 402 win 8312 <nop,nop,cc 1>
```

Figure 3.1 T/TCP client reboots and sends a transaction to server.

In line 1 we see from the CCnew option that the client's `tcp_ccgen` is 1. In line 2 the server echoes the client's CCnew value, and the server's `tcp_ccgen` is 18. The server ACKs the client's SYN but not the client's data. Since the server receives a CCnew option from the client, the server must complete a normal three-way handshake, even if it has an entry in its per-host cache for the client. The server TCP cannot pass the 300 bytes of data to the server process until the three-way handshake is complete.

Line 3 is the final segment of the three-way handshake: an acknowledgment of the server's SYN. The client resends the FIN but not the 300 bytes of data. When the server receives this segment it immediately acknowledges the data and the FIN with line 4. The ACK is sent immediately, instead of being delayed, so as to prevent the client from timing out from the data that was sent on line 1.

Line 5 is the server's reply along with the server's FIN, and both are acknowledged by the client in line 6. Notice that lines 3, 4, 5, and 6 contain a CC option. The CCnew and CCecho only appear in the first and second segments, respectively.

From this point on we will no longer show the explicit NOPs in the T/TCP segments since they are not required and they complicate our presentation. They are inserted for increased performance by forcing the 4-byte value in the option to a 4-byte boundary.

Astute readers may note that the initial sequence number (ISN) used by the client TCP, soon after the client has rebooted, does not follow the normal pattern discussed in Exercise 18.1 of Volume 1. Also, the server's initial sequence number is an even number, which normally never occurs with Berkeley-derived implementations. What's happening here is that the initial sequence number for a connection is being randomized. The increment that is added to the kernel's ISN every 500 ms is also randomized. This helps prevent sequence number attacks, as described in [Bellovin 1989]. This change was put into BSD/OS 2.0 and then 4.4BSD-Lite2 after the well-publicized Internet break-in during December 1994 [Shimomura 1995].

Time Line Diagrams

Figure 3.2 shows a time line diagram of the exchange in Figure 3.1.

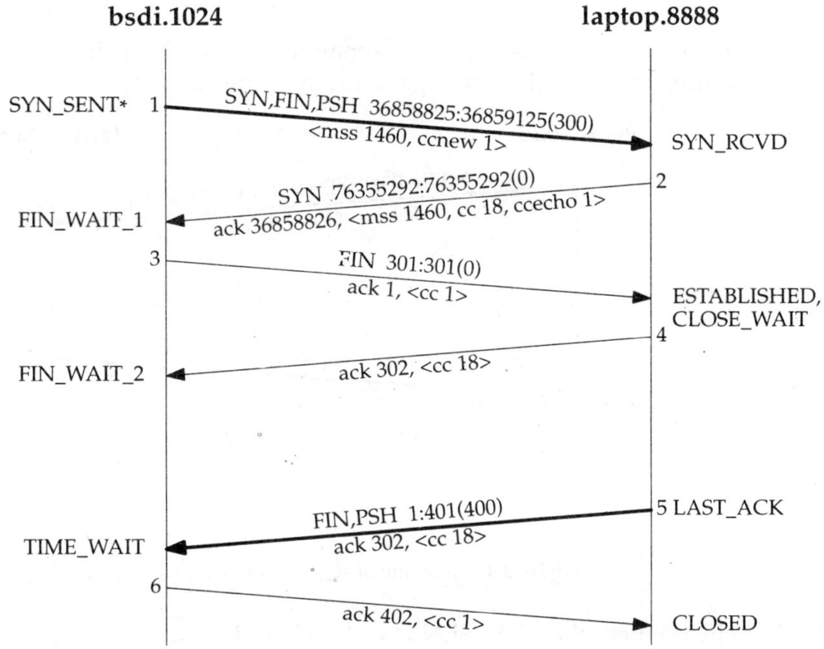

Figure 3.2 Time line of segment exchange in Figure 3.1.

We show the two segments containing data as thicker lines (segments 1 and 5). We also show the state transitions that take place with each received segment. The client starts in the SYN_SENT* state, since the client calls `sendto` specifying the `MSG_EOF` flag. Two transitions take place when segment 3 is processed by the server. First the ACK of the server's SYN moves the connection to the ESTABLISHED state, followed by the FIN moving the connection to the CLOSE_WAIT state. When the server sends its reply, specifying the `MSG_EOF` flag, the server's end moves to the LAST_ACK state. Also notice that the client resends the FIN flag with segment 3 (recall Figure 2.7).

3.3 Normal T/TCP Transaction

Next we initiate another transaction between the same client and server. This time the client finds a nonzero `tao_ccsent` value in its per-host cache for the server, so it sends a CC option with the next `tcp_ccgen` value of 2. (This is the second TCP connection established by the client since reboot.) The exchange is shown in Figure 3.3.

```
1  0.0                 bsdi.1025 > laptop.8888: SFP 40203490:40203790(300)
                                                win 8712 <mss 1460,cc 2>
2  0.026469 (0.0265)   laptop.8888 > bsdi.1025: SFP 79578838:79579238(400)
                                                ack 40203792 win 8712
                                                <mss 1460,cc 19,ccecho 2>
3  0.027573 (0.0011)   bsdi.1025 > laptop.8888: .
                                                ack 402 win 8312 <cc 2>
```

Figure 3.3 Normal T/TCP client–server transaction.

This is the normal, minimal T/TCP exchange consisting of three segments. Figure 3.4 shows the time line for this exchange, with the state transitions.

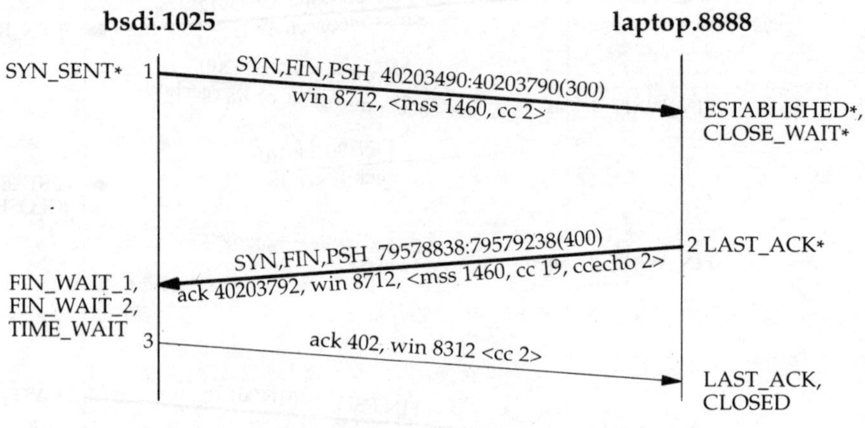

Figure 3.4 Time line of segment exchange in Figure 3.3.

The client enters the SYN_SENT* state when it sends its SYN, data, and FIN. When the server receives this segment and the TAO test succeeds, the server enters the half-synchronized ESTABLISHED* state. The data is processed and passed to the server process. Later in the processing of this segment the FIN is encountered, moving the connection to the CLOSE_WAIT* state. The server's state is still a starred state, since a SYN must still be sent. When the server sends its reply, and the process specifies the `MSG_EOF` flag, the server's end moves to the LAST_ACK* state. As indicated in Figure 2.7, the segment sent for this state contains the SYN, FIN, and ACK flags.

When the client receives segment 2, the ACK of its SYN moves the connection to the FIN_WAIT_1 state. Later in the processing of this segment the ACK of the client's FIN is processed, moving to the FIN_WAIT_2 state. The server's reply is passed to the client process. Still later in the processing of this segment the server's FIN is processed, moving to the TIME_WAIT state. The client responds with an ACK in this final state.

When the server receives segment 3, the ACK of the server's SYN moves the connection to the LAST_ACK state and the ACK of the server's FIN moves the connection to the CLOSED state.

This example clearly shows how multiple state transitions can occur in the T/TCP processing of a single received segment. It also shows how a process can receive data in a state other than the ESTABLISHED state, which occurs when the client half-closes the connection (segment 1) but then receives data while in the FIN_WAIT_1 state (segment 2).

3.4 Server Receives Old Duplicate SYN

What happens when the server receives what appears to be an old CC value from the client? We cause the client to send a SYN segment with a CC of 1, which is less than the most recent CC value that the server has received from this client (2, in Figure 3.3). This could happen, for example, if the segment with the CC of 1 were a segment from an earlier incarnation of this connection that got delayed in the network and appeared sometime later, but within MSL seconds of when it was sent.

A connection is defined by a socket pair, that is, a 4-tuple consisting of an IP address and port number on the client and an IP address and port number on the server. New instances of a connection are called *incarnations* of that connection.

We see in Figure 3.5 that when the server receives the SYN with a CC of 1 it forces a three-way handshake to occur, since it doesn't know whether this is an old duplicate or not.

```
1  0.0                    bsdi.1027 > laptop.8888: SFP 80000000:80000300(300)
                                                    win 4096 <mss 1460,cc 1>
2  0.018391 (0.0184)     laptop.8888 > bsdi.1027: S 132492350:132492350(0)
                                                    ack 80000001 win 8712
                                                    <mss 1460,cc 21,ccecho 1>
3  0.019266 (0.0009)     bsdi.1027 > laptop.8888: R 80000001:80000001(0) win 0
```

Figure 3.5 T/TCP server receives old duplicate of client SYN.

Since the three-way handshake is taking place (which we can tell because only the SYN is ACKed, not the data), the server TCP cannot pass the 300 bytes of data to the server process until the handshake is complete.

In this example segment 1 is an old duplicate (the client TCP is not currently awaiting a response to this SYN), so when the server's SYN/ACK in segment 2 arrives, the client TCP responds with an RST (segment 3). This is what should happen. The server TCP discards the 300 bytes of data when it receives the RST, and does not return from the pending `accept` that the server process is waiting for.

> Segment 1 was generated by a special test program. We are not able to have the client T/TCP generate this segment—instead we want it to appear as an old duplicate. The author tried patching the kernel's `tcp_ccgen` variable to 1, but as we'll see in Figure 12.3, when the kernel's `tcp_ccgen` is less than the last CC sent to this peer, TCP automatically sends a CCnew option, instead of a CC option

Figure 3.6 shows the next, normal, T/TCP transaction between this client and server. It is the expected three-segment exchange.

```
1  0.0                  bsdi.1026 > laptop.8888: SFP 101619844:101620144(300)
                                                 win 8712 <mss 1460,cc 3>

2  0.028214 (0.0282)    laptop.8888 > bsdi.1026: SFP 140211128:140211528(400)
                                                 ack 101620146 win 8712
                                                 <mss 1460,cc 22,ccecho 3>

3  0.029330 (0.0011)    bsdi.1026 > laptop.8888: .
                                                 ack 402 win 8312 <cc 3>
```

Figure 3.6 Normal T/TCP client–server transaction.

The server is expecting a CC value greater than 2 from this client, so the received SYN with a CC of 3 passes the TAO test.

3.5 Server Reboot

We now reboot the server and then send a transaction from the client once the server has rebooted, and once the listening server process has been restarted. Figure 3.7 shows the exchange.

```
1  0.0                  bsdi.1027 > laptop.8888: SFP 146513089:146513389(300)
                                                 win 8712 <mss 1460,cc 4>

2  0.025420 (0.0254)    arp who-has bsdi tell laptop
3  0.025872 (0.0005)    arp reply bsdi is-at 0:20:af:9c:ee:95
4  0.033731 (0.0079)    laptop.8888 > bsdi.1027: S 27338882:27338882(0)
                                                 ack 146513090 win 8712
                                                 <mss 1460,cc 1,ccecho 4>

5  0.034697 (0.0010)    bsdi.1027 > laptop.8888: F 301:301(0)
                                                 ack 1 win 8712 <cc 4>

6  0.044284 (0.0096)    laptop.8888 > bsdi.1027: .
                                                 ack 302 win 8412 <cc 1>

7  0.066749 (0.0225)    laptop.8888 > bsdi.1027: FP 1:401(400)
                                                 ack 302 win 8712 <cc 1>

8  0.067613 (0.0009)    bsdi.1027 > laptop.8888: .
                                                 ack 402 win 8312 <cc 4>
```

Figure 3.7 T/TCP packet exchange after server reboots.

Since the client does not know that the server has rebooted, it sends a normal T/TCP request with its CC of 4 (line 1). The server sends an ARP request and the client responds with an ARP reply since the client's hardware address on the server was lost when the server rebooted. The server forces a normal three-way handshake to occur (line 4), because it doesn't know the value of the last CC received from this client.

Similar to what we saw in Figure 3.1, the client completes the three-way handshake with an ACK that also contains its FIN—the 300 bytes of data are not resent. The client's data is retransmitted only when the client's retransmission timer expires, which we'll see occur in Figure 3.11. Upon receiving this third segment, the server immediately ACKs the data and the FIN. The server sends its reply (line 7), which the client acknowledges in line 8.

After the exchange in Figure 3.7 we expect to see another minimal T/TCP transaction between this client and server the next time they communicate, which is what we show in Figure 3.8.

```
1  0.0                     bsdi.1028 > laptop.8888: SFP 152213061:152213361(300)
                                                    win 8712 <mss 1460,cc 5>

2  0.034851 (0.0349)       laptop.8888 > bsdi.1028: SFP 32869470:32869870(400)
                                                    ack 152213363 win 8712
                                                    <mss 1460,cc 2,ccecho 5>

3  0.035955 (0.0011)       bsdi.1028 > laptop.8888: .
                                                    ack 402 win 8312 <cc 5>
```

Figure 3.8 Normal T/TCP client–server transaction.

3.6 Request or Reply Exceeds MSS

In all our examples so far, the client sends less than one MSS of data, and the server replies with less than one MSS of data. If the client application sends more than one MSS of data, and the client TCP knows that the peer understands T/TCP, multiple segments are sent. Since the peer's MSS is saved in the TAO cache (`tao_mssopt` in Figure 2.5) the client TCP knows the MSS of the server host but the client TCP does not know the receive window of the peer process. (Sections 18.4 and 20.4 of Volume 1 talk about the MSS and window size, respectively.) Unlike the MSS, which is normally constant for a given peer host, the window can be changed by the application if it changes the size of its socket receive buffer. Furthermore, even if the peer advertises a large window (say, 32768), if the MSS is 512, there may well be intermediate routers that cannot handle an initial burst of 64 segments from the client to the server (i.e., slow start should not be skipped). T/TCP handles these problems with the following two restrictions:

1. T/TCP assumes an initial send window of 4096 bytes. In Net/3 this is the `snd_wnd` variable, which controls how much data TCP output can send. The initial value of 4096 will be changed when the first segment is received from the peer with a window advertisement.
2. T/TCP starts a connection using slow start only if the peer is nonlocal. Slow start is when TCP sets the variable `snd_cwnd` to one segment. This local/nonlocal test is given in Figure 10.14 and is based on the kernel's

in_localaddr function. A peer is considered local if (a) it shares the same network and subnet as the local host, or (b) it shares the same network but a different subnet, but the kernel's subnetsarelocal variable is nonzero.

Net/3 starts every connection using slow start (p. 902 of Volume 2) but this prevents a transaction client from sending multiple segments to start a transaction. The compromise is to allow multiple segments, for a total of up to 4096 bytes, but only for a local peer.

Whenever TCP output is called, it sends up to the *minimum* of snd_wnd and snd_cwnd bytes of data. The former starts at the maximum value of a TCP window advertisement, which we assume to be 65535. (It is actually 65535×2^{14}, or almost 1 gigabyte, when the window scale option is being used.) For a local peer snd_wnd starts at 4096 and snd_cwnd starts at 65535. TCP output will initially send up to 4096 bytes until a window advertisement is received. If the peer's window advertisement is 32768, then TCP can continue sending until the peer's window is filled (since the minimum of 32768 and 65535 is 32768). Slow start is avoided and the amount of data sent is limited by the advertised window.

But if the peer is nonlocal, snd_wnd still starts at 4096 but now snd_cwnd starts at one segment (assume the saved MSS for this peer is 512). TCP will initially send just one segment, and when the peer's window advertisement is received, snd_cwnd will increase by one segment for each ACK. Slow start is now in control and the amount of data sent is limited by the congestion window, until the congestion window exceeds the peer's advertised window.

As an example we modified our T/TCP client and server from Chapter 1 to send a request of 3300 bytes and a reply of 3400 bytes. Figure 3.9 shows the packet exchange.

> This example shows a bug in Tcpdump's printing of relative sequence numbers for multisegment T/TCP exchanges. The acknowledgment number printed for segments 6, 8, and 10 should be 3302, not 1.

```
1  0.0                 bsdi.1057 > laptop.8888: S 3846892142:3846893590(1448)
                                                win 8712 <mss 1460,cc 7>
2  0.001556 (0.0016)   bsdi.1057 > laptop.8888: .  3846893591:3846895043(1452)
                                                win 8712 <cc 7>
3  0.002672 (0.0011)   bsdi.1057 > laptop.8888: FP 3846895043:3846895443(400)
                                                win 8712 <cc 7>

4  0.138283 (0.1356)   laptop.8888 > bsdi.1057: S 3786170031:3786170031(0)
                                                ack 3846895444 win 8712
                                                <mss 1460,cc 6,ccecho 7>
5  0.139273 (0.0010)   bsdi.1057 > laptop.8888: .
                                                ack 1 win 8712 <cc 7>
6  0.179615 (0.0403)   laptop.8888 > bsdi.1057: . 1:1453(1452)
                                                ack 1 win 8712 <cc 6>
7  0.180558 (0.0009)   bsdi.1057 > laptop.8888: .
                                                ack 1453 win 7260 <cc 7>
8  0.209621 (0.0291)   laptop.8888 > bsdi.1057: . 1453:2905(1452)
                                                ack 1 win 8712 <cc 6>
```

```
 9  0.210565 (0.0009)   bsdi.1057 > laptop.8888: .
                                                 ack 2905 win 7260 <cc 7>
10  0.223822 (0.0133)   laptop.8888 > bsdi.1057: FP 2905:3401(496)
                                                 ack 1 win 8712 <cc 6>
11  0.224719 (0.0009)   bsdi.1057 > laptop.8888: .
                                                 ack 3402 win 8216 <cc 7>
```

Figure 3.9 Client request of 3300 bytes and server reply of 3400 bytes.

Since the client knows that the server supports T/TCP it can send up to 4096 bytes immediately. Segments 1, 2, and 3 are sent in the first 2.6 ms. The first segment carries the SYN flag, 1448 bytes of data, and 12 bytes of TCP options (MSS and CC). The second segment has no flags, 1452 bytes of data, and 8 bytes of TCP options. The third segment carries the FIN and PSH flags, the remaining 400 bytes of data, and 8 bytes of TCP options. Segment 2 is unique in that none of the six TCP flags is set, not even the ACK flag. Normally the ACK flag is always on, except for a client's active open, which carries the SYN flag. (A client can never send an ACK until it receives a segment from the server.)

Segment 4 is the server's SYN and it also acknowledges everything the client sent: SYN, data, and FIN. The client immediately ACKs the server's SYN with segment 5.

Segment 6 arrives 40 ms later carrying the first segment of the server's reply. It is immediately ACKed by the client. This scenario continues with segment 8–11. The final segment from the server (10) carries the server's FIN, and the final ACK from the client acknowledges the final segment of data and the FIN.

One question is why does the client immediately ACK the first two of the three server replies, since they arrive in a short amount of time (44 ms)? The answer is in the `TCP_REASS` macro (p. 908 of Volume 2), which is invoked for each segment of data received by the client. Since the client's end of the connection enters the FIN_WAIT_2 state when segment 4 is processed, the test in `TCP_REASS` for whether the state is ESTABLISHED fails, causing an immediate ACK instead of a delayed ACK. This "feature" is not unique to T/TCP but can be seen with the Net/3 code whenever one end half-closes a TCP connection and enters the FIN_WAIT_1 or FIN_WAIT_2 state. From that point on, every segment of data from the peer is immediately ACKed. The test for the ESTABLISHED state in the `TCP_REASS` macro prevents data from being passed to the application before the three-way handshake completes. There is no need to immediately ACK in-sequence data when the connection state is greater than ESTABLISHED (i.e., this test should be changed).

TCP_NOPUSH Socket Option

When running this example another change was required to the client source code. The `TCP_NOPUSH` socket option (a new option with T/TCP) was turned on by

```
int  n;

n = 1;
if (setsockopt(sockfd, IPPROTO_TCP, TCP_NOPUSH, (char *) &n, sizeof(n)) < 0)
    err_sys("TCP_NOPUSH error");
```

This was done after the call to `socket` in Figure 1.10. The purpose of this option is to tell TCP not to send a segment for the sole reason that doing so would empty the send buffer.

To see the reason for this socket option we need to follow through the steps performed by the kernel when the process calls `sendto` to send a 3300-byte request, also specifying the `MSG_EOF` flag.

1. The kernel's `sosend` function (Section 16.7 of Volume 2) is eventually called to handle the output request. It puts the first 2048 bytes into an mbuf cluster and issues a `PRU_SEND` request to the protocol (TCP).
2. `tcp_output` is called (Figure 12.4) and since a full-sized segment can be sent, the first 1448 bytes in the cluster are sent with the SYN flag set. (There are 12 bytes of TCP options in this segment.)
3. Since 600 bytes still remain in this mbuf cluster, another loop is made through `tcp_output`. We might think that the Nagle algorithm would prevent another segment from being sent, but notice on p. 853 of Volume 2 that the `idle` variable was 1 the first time around `tcp_output`. It is not recalculated when the branch to `again` is made after the 1448-byte segment is sent. Therefore the code ends up in the fragment shown in Figure 9.3 ("sender silly window avoidance"). `idle` is true and the amount of data to send would empty the socket's send buffer, so what determines whether to send a segment or not is the current value of the `TF_NOPUSH` flag.

   Before this flag was introduced with T/TCP, this code would always send a less-than-full segment if not prevented by the Nagle algorithm and if that segment would empty the socket's send buffer. But if the application sets the `TF_NOPUSH` flag (with the new `TCP_NOPUSH` socket option) then TCP won't force out the data in the send buffer just to empty the buffer. TCP will allow the existing data to be combined with data from later write operations, in the hope of sending a larger segment.
4. If the `TF_NOPUSH` flag *is* set by the application, a segment is not sent, `tcp_output` returns, and control returns to `sosend`.

   If the `TF_NOPUSH` flag is *not* set by the application, a 600-byte segment is sent and the PSH flag is set.
5. `sosend` puts the remaining 1252 bytes into an mbuf cluster and issues a `PRU_SEND_EOF` request (Figure 5.2), which ends up calling `tcp_output` again. Before this call, however, `tcp_usrclosed` is called (Figure 12.4), moving the connection from the SYN_SENT state to the SYN_SENT* state (Figure 12.5). With the `TF_NOPUSH` flag set, there are now 1852 bytes in the socket send buffer and we see in Figure 3.9 that another full-sized segment is sent, containing 1452 bytes of data and 8 bytes of TCP options. This segment is sent because it is full sized (i.e., the Nagle algorithm has no effect). Even though the flags for the SYN_SENT* state include the FIN flag (Figure 2.7), the FIN flag is turned off (p. 855 of Volume 2) because there is still additional data in the send buffer.

6. Another loop is made through `tcp_output` for the remaining 400 bytes in the send buffer. This time around, however, the FIN flag is left on since the send buffer is being emptied. Even though the Nagle algorithm in Figure 9.3 prevents a segment from being sent, the 400-byte segment is sent because the FIN flag is set (p. 861 of Volume 2).

In this example, a 3300-byte request on an Ethernet with an MSS of 1460, setting the socket option results in three segments of sizes 1448, 1452, and 400 bytes. If the option is not set, three segments still result, of sizes 1448, 600, and 1252 bytes. But for a 3600-byte request, setting the socket option results in three segments (1448, 1452, and 700 bytes). Not setting the option, however, results in four segments (1448, 600, 1452, and 100 bytes).

In summary, when the client is sending its request with a single `sendto`, it should normally set the `TCP_NOPUSH` socket option, to cause full-sized segments to be sent if the request exceeds the MSS. This can reduce the number of segments, depending on the size of the write.

3.7 Backward Compatibility

We also need to examine what happens when a T/TCP client sends data to a host that does not support T/TCP.

Figure 3.10 shows the packet exchange when the T/TCP client on `bsdi` sends a transaction to the TCP server on `svr4` (a System V Release 4 host that does not support T/TCP).

```
1  0.0                     bsdi.1031 > svr4.8888: SFP 2672114321:2672114621(300)
                                                  win 8568 <mss 1460,ccnew 10>
2  0.006265 (0.0063)      svr4.8888 > bsdi.1031: S 879930881:879930881(0)
                                                  ack 2672114322 win 4096 <mss 1024>
3  0.007108 (0.0008)      bsdi.1031 > svr4.8888: F 301:301(0)
                                                  ack 1 win 9216
4  0.012279 (0.0052)      svr4.8888 > bsdi.1031: .
                                                  ack 302 win 3796
5  0.071683 (0.0594)      svr4.8888 > bsdi.1031: P 1:401(400)
                                                  ack 302 win 4096
6  0.072451 (0.0008)      bsdi.1031 > svr4.8888: .
                                                  ack 401 win 8816
7  0.078373 (0.0059)      svr4.8888 > bsdi.1031: F 401:401(0)
                                                  ack 302 win 4096
8  0.079642 (0.0013)      bsdi.1031 > svr4.8888: .
                                                  ack 402 win 9216
```

Figure 3.10 T/TCP client sends transaction to TCP server.

The client TCP still sends a first segment containing the SYN, FIN, and PSH flags, along with the 300 bytes of data. A CCnew option is sent since the client TCP does not have a cached value for this server. The server responds with the normal second segment of the three-way handshake (line 2), which the client ACKs in line 3. Notice that the data is not retransmitted in line 3.

When the server receives the segment in line 3 it immediately ACKs the 300 bytes of data and the FIN. (The ACK of a FIN is never delayed, as shown on p. 990 of Volume 2.) The server TCP queued the data until the three-way handshake was complete.

Line 5 is the server's response (400 bytes of data), which the client immediately ACKs in line 6. Line 7 is the server's FIN, which is then immediately ACKed by the client. Notice that the server process has no way of combining the data in line 5 with its FIN in line 7.

If we initiate another transaction from the same client to the same server, the sequence of segments is the same. The first segment from the client contains a CCnew option with a value of 11, because the client cannot send a CC option to this host, since the server did not send a CCecho option in Figure 3.10. The T/TCP client always sends a CCnew option because the per-host cache entry for the non-T/TCP server is never updated, hence `tao_ccsent` is always 0 (undefined).

The next example (Figure 3.11) is to a server host running Solaris 2.4, which although based on SVR4 (as is the server in Figure 3.10), has a completely different TCP/IP implementation.

```
1  0.0                           bsdi.1033 > sun.8888: SFP 2693814107:2693814407(300)
                                                      win 8712 <mss 1460,ccnew 12>
2  0.002808 (0.0028)             sun.8888 > bsdi.1033: S 3179040768:3179040768(0)
                                                      ack 2693814108 win 8760
                                                      <mss 1460> (DF)
3  0.003679 (0.0009)             bsdi.1033 > sun.8888: F 301:301(0)
                                                      ack 1 win 8760
4  1.287379 (1.2837)             bsdi.1033 > sun.8888: FP 1:301(300)
                                                      ack 1 win 8760
5  1.289048 (0.0017)             sun.8888 > bsdi.1033:
                                                      ack 302 win 8760 (DF)
6  1.291323 (0.0023)             sun.8888 > bsdi.1033: P 1:401(400)
                                                      ack 302 win 8760 (DF)
7  1.292101 (0.0008)             bsdi.1033 > sun.8888:
                                                      ack 401 win 8360
8  1.292367 (0.0003)             sun.8888 > bsdi.1033: F 401:401(0)
                                                      ack 302 win 8760 (DF)
9  1.293151 (0.0008)             bsdi.1033 > sun.8888:
                                                      ack 402 win 8360
```

Figure 3.11 T/TCP client sending transaction to TCP server on Solaris 2.4.

Lines 1, 2, and 3 are the same as in Figure 3.10: a SYN, FIN, PSH, and the client's 300-byte request, followed by the server's SYN/ACK, followed by the client's ACK.

This is the normal three-way handshake. Also, the client TCP sends a CCnew option, since it doesn't have a cached value for this server.

The presence of the "don't fragment" flag (DF) on each segment from the Solaris host is path MTU discovery (RFC 1191 [Mogul and Deering 1990]).

Unfortunately we now encounter a bug in the Solaris implementation. It appears the server's TCP discards the data that was sent on line 1 (the data is not acknowledged in segment 2), causing the client TCP to time out and retransmit the data on line 4. The FIN is also retransmitted. The server then ACKs the data and the FIN (line 5), and the server sends its reply on line 6. The client ACKs the reply (line 7), followed by the server's FIN (line 8) and the final client ACK (line 9).

Page 30 of RFC 793 [Postel 1981b] states: "Although these examples do not show connection synchronization using data-carrying segments, this is perfectly legitimate, so long as the receiving TCP doesn't deliver the data to the user until it is clear the data is valid (i.e., the data must be buffered at the receiver until the connection reaches the ESTABLISHED state)." Page 66 of this RFC says that when processing a received SYN in the LISTEN state "any other control or text should be queued for processing later."

One reviewer claims that calling this a "bug" is wrong since the RFCs do not *mandate* servers to accept data that accompanies a SYN. The claim is also made that the Solaris implementation is OK because it has not yet advertised a window to the client, and the server may then choose to discard the arriving data since it is outside the window. Regardless of how you choose to characterize this feature (the author still calls it a bug and Sun has assigned Bug ID 1222490 to the problem, so it should be fixed in a future release), handling scenarios such as this comes under the *Robustness Principle*, first mentioned in RFC 791 [Postel 1981a]: "Be liberal in what you accept, and conservative in what you send."

3.8 Summary

We can summarize the examples from this chapter with the following statements.

1. If the client loses state information about the server (e.g., the client reboots), the client forces a three-way handshake by sending a CCnew option with its active open.
2. When the server loses state information about the client, or if the server receives a SYN with a CC value that is less than the expected value, the server forces a three-way handshake by responding to the client's SYN with just a SYN/ACK. In this case the server TCP must wait for the three-way handshake to complete before passing any data that arrived with the client's SYN to the server process.
3. The server always echoes the client's CC or CCnew option with a CCecho option if the server wants to use T/TCP on the connection.
4. If the client and server both have state information about each other, the minimal T/TCP transaction of three segments occurs (assuming both the request and response are less than or equal to the MSS). This is the minimum number of packets and the minimum latency of RTT + SPT.

These examples also showed how multiple state transitions can occur with T/TCP, and showed the use of the new extended (starred) states.

If the client sends a segment with a SYN, data, and a FIN to a host that does not understand T/TCP, we saw that systems built from the Berkeley networking code (which includes SVR4, but not Solaris) correctly queue the data until the three-way handshake completes. It is possible, however, for other implementations to incorrectly discard the data that arrives with the SYN, causing the client to time out and retransmit the data.

4

T/TCP Protocol (Continued)

4.1 Introduction

This chapter continues our discussion of the T/TCP protocol. We start by describing how T/TCP clients should allocate a port number to their endpoint, based on whether the connection is expected to be shorter or longer than the MSL, and how this affects TCP's TIME_WAIT state. We then examine why TCP defines a TIME_WAIT state, because this is a poorly understood feature of the protocol. One of the advantages provided by T/TCP is a truncation of the TIME_WAIT state, from 240 seconds to around 12 seconds, when the connection duration is less than the MSL. We describe how this happens and why it is OK.

We complete our discussion of the T/TCP protocol by describing TAO, TCP accelerated open, which allows T/TCP client–servers to avoid the three-way handshake. This saves one round-trip time and is the biggest benefit provided by T/TCP.

4.2 Client Port Numbers and TIME_WAIT State

When writing TCP clients there is normally no concern about the client port number. Most TCP clients (Telnet, FTP, WWW, etc.) use an ephemeral port, letting the host's TCP module choose an unused port. Berkeley-derived systems normally choose an ephemeral port between 1024 and 5000 (see Figure 14.14), while Solaris chooses a port between 32768 and 65535. T/TCP clients, however, have additional choices depending on the transaction rate and duration.

Normal TCP Hosts, Normal TCP Client

Figure 4.1 depicts a TCP client (such as the one in Figure 1.5) performing three 1-second transactions to the same server, 1 second apart. The three connections start at times 0, 2, and 4, and end at times 1, 3, and 5, respectively. The *x*-axis shows time, in seconds, and the three connections are shown with thicker lines.

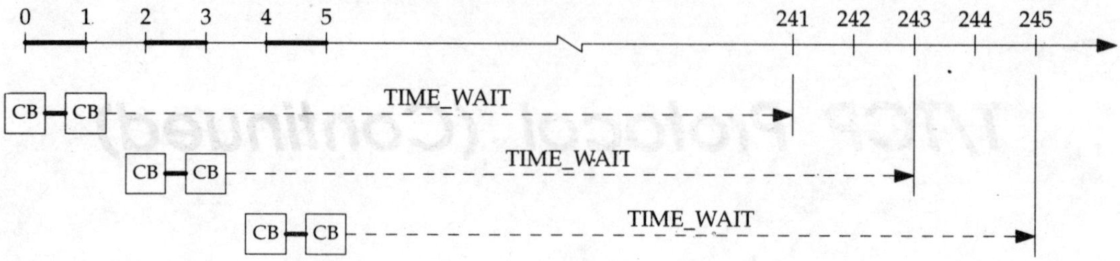

Figure 4.1 TCP client, different local port per transaction.

A different TCP connection is used for each transaction. We assume that the client does not explicitly bind a local port to the socket, instead letting its TCP module choose the ephemeral port, and we assume that the client TCP's MSL is 120 seconds. The first connection remains in the TIME_WAIT state until time 241, the second from time 3 to 243, and the third from time 5 until 245.

We use the notation CB for "control block" to indicate the combination of control blocks maintained by TCP while the connection is in use, and while it is in the TIME_WAIT state: an Internet PCB, a TCP control block, and a header template. We indicated at the beginning of Chapter 2 that the total size of these three is 264 bytes in the Net/3 implementation. In addition to the memory requirement, there is also a CPU requirement for TCP to process all the control blocks periodically (e.g., Sections 25.4 and 25.5 of Volume 2, which process all TCP control blocks every 200 and 500 ms).

> Net/3 maintains a copy of the TCP and IP headers for each connection as a "header template" (Section 26.8 of Volume 2). The template contains all the fields that do not change for a given connection. This saves time whenever a segment is sent, because the code just copies the header template into the outgoing packet being formed, instead of filling in the individual fields.

There is no way around this TIME_WAIT state with normal TCP. The client cannot use the same local port for all three connections, even with the SO_REUSEADDR socket option. (Page 740 of Volume 2 shows an example of a client attempting to do this.)

T/TCP Hosts, Different Client Ports per Transaction

Figure 4.2 shows the same sequence of three transactions although this time we assume that both hosts support T/TCP. We are using the same TCP client as in Figure 4.1. This is an important distinction: that is, the client and server *applications* need not be T/TCP aware, we only require that the client and server *hosts* support T/TCP (i.e., the CC options).

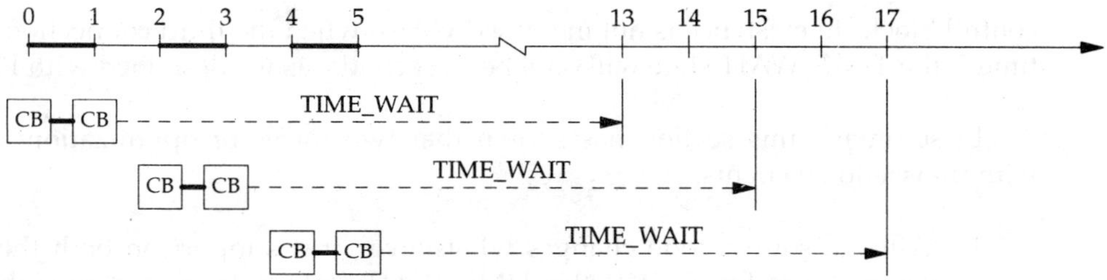

Figure 4.2 TCP client when client and server hosts both support T/TCP.

What changes in Figure 4.2, from Figure 4.1, is that the TIME_WAIT state has been truncated because both hosts support the CC options. We assume a retransmission timeout of 1.5 seconds (typical for Net/3 on a LAN, as described in [Brakmo and Peterson 1994]), and a T/TCP TIME_WAIT multiplier of 8, which reduces the TIME_WAIT state from 240 seconds to 12 seconds.

T/TCP allows the TIME_WAIT state to be truncated when both hosts support the CC options and when the connection duration is less than the MSL (120 seconds) because the CC option provides additional protection against old duplicate segments being delivered to the wrong incarnation of a given connection, as we'll show in Section 4.4.

T/TCP Hosts, Same Client Port for Each Transaction

Figure 4.3 shows the same sequence of three transactions as in Figure 4.2 but this time we assume the client reuses the same port for each transaction. To accomplish this, the client must set the `SO_REUSEADDR` socket option and then call `bind` to bind a specific local port before calling `connect` (for a normal TCP client) or `sendto` (for a T/TCP client). As in Figure 4.2, we assume both hosts support T/TCP.

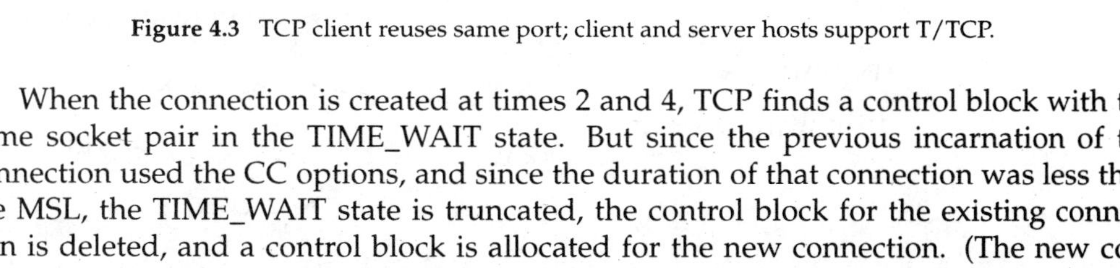

Figure 4.3 TCP client reuses same port; client and server hosts support T/TCP.

When the connection is created at times 2 and 4, TCP finds a control block with the same socket pair in the TIME_WAIT state. But since the previous incarnation of the connection used the CC options, and since the duration of that connection was less than the MSL, the TIME_WAIT state is truncated, the control block for the existing connection is deleted, and a control block is allocated for the new connection. (The new control block allocated for the new connection might be the same one that was just deleted, but that is an implementation detail. What is important is that the total number of control blocks in existence is not increased.) Also when the third connection is closed at time 5, the TIME_WAIT state will only be 12 seconds, as we described with Figure 4.2.

In summary, this section has shown that two forms of optimization are possible with transactional clients:

1. With no source code changes whatsoever, just support on both the client and server hosts for T/TCP, the TIME_WAIT state is truncated to eight times the retransmission timeout for the connection, instead of 240 seconds.
2. By changing only the client process to reuse the same port number, not only is the TIME_WAIT state truncated to eight times the retransmission timeout as in the previous item, but the TIME_WAIT state is terminated sooner if another incarnation of the same connection is created.

4.3 Purpose of the TIME_WAIT State

TCP's TIME_WAIT state is one of the most misunderstood features of the protocol. This is probably because the original specification, RFC 793, gave only a terse explanation of the feature, although later RFCs, such as RFC 1185, go into more detail. The TIME_WAIT state exists for two reasons:

1. It implements the full-duplex closing of a connection.
2. It allows old duplicate segments to expire.

Let's look in more detail at each reason.

TCP Full-Duplex Close

Figure 4.4 shows the normal exchange of segments when a connection is closed. We also show the state transitions and the measured RTT at the server.

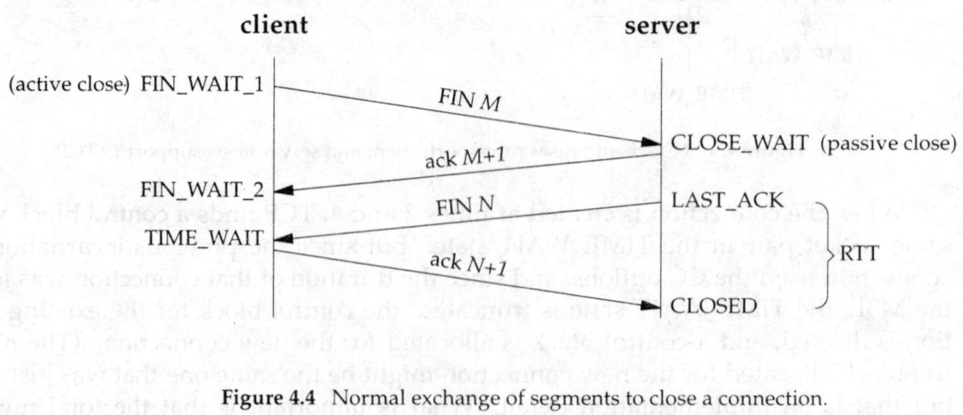

Figure 4.4 Normal exchange of segments to close a connection.

We show the left side as the client and the right side as the server, but realize that either side can do the active close. Often, however, the client does the active close.

Consider what happens if the final segment is lost: the final ACK. We show this in Figure 4.5.

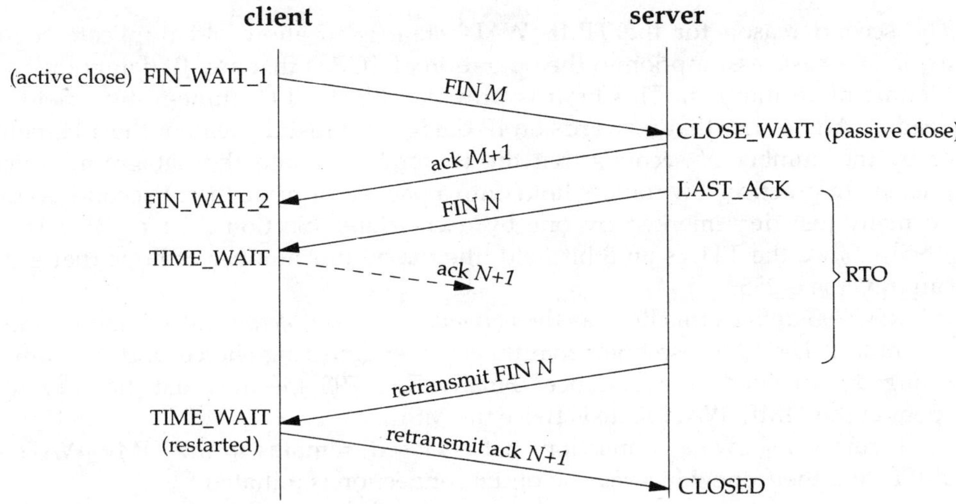

Figure 4.5 TCP close when final segment is lost.

Since the ACK is never received, the server will time out and retransmit the final FIN. We purposely show the server's RTO (the retransmission timeout) as larger than the RTT from Figure 4.4, since the RTO is the estimated RTT plus a multiple of the RTT variance. (Chapter 25 of Volume 2 provides details on the measurement of the RTT and the calculation of the RTO.) The scenario is the same if the final FIN is lost: the server still retransmits the final FIN after it times out.

This example shows why the TIME_WAIT state occurs on the end that does the active close: that end transmits the final ACK, and if that ACK is lost or if the final FIN is lost, the other end times out and retransmits the final FIN. By maintaining the state information about the connection on the end that does the active close, that end can retransmit the final ACK. If TCP didn't maintain the state information for the connection, it wouldn't be able to retransmit the final ACK, so it would have to send an RST when it received the retransmitted FIN, resulting in spurious error messages.

We also note in Figure 4.5 that if a retransmission of the FIN arrives at the host in the TIME_WAIT state, not only is the final ACK retransmitted, but the TIME_WAIT state is restarted. That is, the TIME_WAIT timer is reset to 2MSL.

The question is this: how long should the end performing the active close remain in the TIME_WAIT state to handle the scenario shown in Figure 4.5? It depends on the RTO used by the other end, which depends on the RTT for the connection. RFC 1185 notes that an RTT greater than 1 minute is highly unlikely. An RTO around 1 minute, however, is possible. This can occur during periods of congestion on a WAN, leading to multiple retransmission losses, causing TCP's exponential backoff to set the RTO to higher and higher values.

Expiration of Old Duplicate Segments

The second reason for the TIME_WAIT state is to allow old duplicate segments to expire. A basic assumption in the operation of TCP is that any IP datagram has a finite lifetime in an internet. This limit is provided by the TTL (time-to-live) field in the IP header. Any router that forwards an IP datagram must decrement the TTL field by one or by the number of seconds that the router holds onto the datagram, whichever is greater. In practice, few routers hold onto a packet for more than 1 second, so the TTL is normally just decremented by one by each router (Section 5.3.1 of RFC 1812 [Baker 1995]). Since the TTL is an 8-bit field, the maximum number of hops that a datagram can traverse is 255.

RFC 793 defines this limit as the *maximum segment lifetime* (MSL) and defines it to be 2 minutes. The RFC also notes that this is an engineering choice, and the value may be changed if dictated by experience. Finally, RFC 793 specifies that the amount of time spent in the TIME_WAIT state is twice the MSL.

Figure 4.6 shows a connection that is closed, remains in the TIME_WAIT state for 2MSL, and then a new incarnation of the connection is initiated.

Figure 4.6 A new incarnation of the connection is started 2MSL after previous incarnation.

Since a new incarnation of the connection cannot be initiated until 2MSL after the previous one, and since any old duplicates from the first incarnation will have disappeared in the first MSL of the TIME_WAIT state, we are guaranteed that old duplicates from the first connection will not appear and be misinterpreted as part of the second connection.

TIME_WAIT Assassination

RFC 793 specifies that an RST received for a connection in the TIME_WAIT state moves the connection to the CLOSED state. This is called "assassination" of the TIME_WAIT state. RFC 1337 [Braden 1992a] recommends not letting an RST prematurely terminate the TIME_WAIT state.

4.4 TIME_WAIT State Truncation

We saw in Figures 4.2 and 4.3 that T/TCP can truncate the TIME_WAIT state. With T/TCP the timeout becomes eight times the RTO (retransmission timeout) instead of twice the MSL. We also saw in Section 4.3 that there are two reasons for the TIME_WAIT state. What are the effects of TIME_WAIT truncation on each reason?

TCP Full-Duplex Close

The first reason for the TIME_WAIT state is to maintain the state information required to handle a retransmission of the final FIN. As shown in Figure 4.5, the time spent in the TIME_WAIT state really should depend on the RTO, and not on the MSL. The multiplier of eight used by T/TCP is to allow enough time for the other end to time out and retransmit the final segment. This generates the scenario shown in Figure 4.2, where each endpoint waits for the truncated TIME_WAIT period (12 seconds in that figure).

But consider what happens in Figure 4.3, when the truncation occurs earlier than eight times the RTO because a new client reuses the same socket pair. Figure 4.7 shows an example.

The final ACK is lost, but the client initiates another incarnation of the same connection before the retransmission of the server's final segment is received. When the server receives the new SYN, since the TAO test succeeds (8 is greater than 6), this implicitly acknowledges the server's outstanding segment (the second segment in the figure). That connection is closed, and a new connection is started. Since the TAO test succeeds, the data in the new SYN is passed to the server process.

It is interesting to note that since T/TCP defines the length of the TIME_WAIT state as a function of the RTO on the side performing the active close, there is an implicit assumption that the RTO values on both ends of the connection are "similar" and within certain bounds [Olah 1995]. If the side performing the active close truncates the TIME_WAIT state before the other end retransmits the final FIN, the response to the retransmitted FIN will be an RST, not the expected retransmitted ACK.

This can happen if the RTT is small, the third segment (the ACK) of the minimal three-segment T/TCP exchange is lost, and the client and server have different software clocks rates and different RTO minimums. (Section 14.7 shows some of the bizarre RTO values used by some clients.) The client can measure the small RTT while the server cannot measure an RTT at all

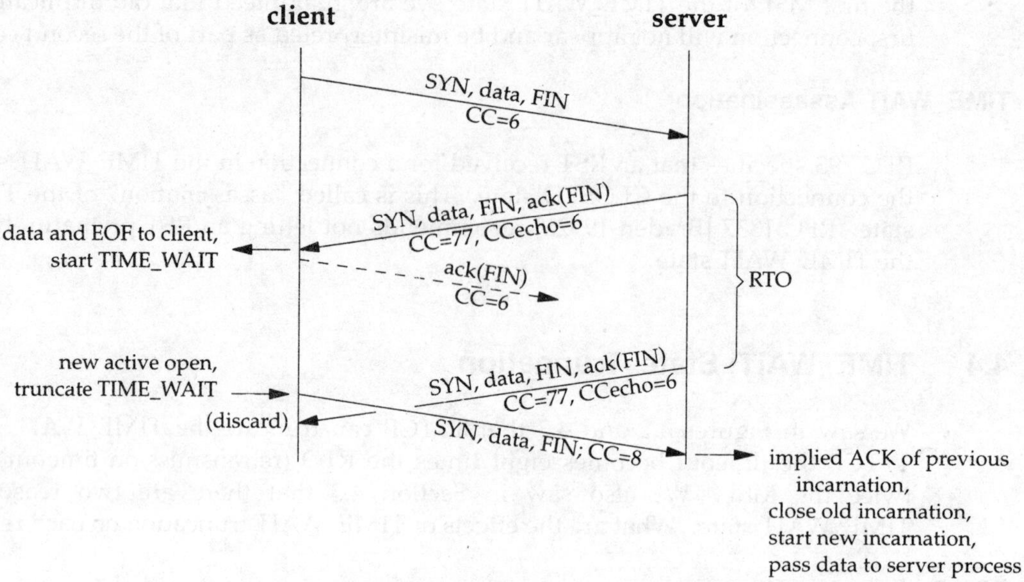

Figure 4.7 TIME_WAIT truncation when final ACK is lost.

(since the third segment is lost). For example, assume the client measures an RTT of 10 ms and has a minimum RTO of 100 ms. The client will truncate the TIME_WAIT state 800 ms after receiving the server's response. But if the server is a Berkeley-derived host, its default RTO will be 6 seconds (as seen in Figure 14.13). When the server retransmits its SYN/ACK/data/FIN after about 6 seconds, the client will respond with an RST, potentially causing a spurious error to the server application.

Expiration of Old Duplicate Segments

The TIME_WAIT state truncation is possible because the CC option provides protection against old duplicates being delivered to the wrong incarnation of a given connection, but only if the connection duration is less than the MSL. Consider Figure 4.8. We show the CC generation (`tcp_ccgen`) incrementing at the fastest rate allowable: $2^{32} - 1$ counts per 2MSL. This provides a maximum transaction rate of 4,294,967,295 divided by 240, or almost 18 million transactions per second!

Assuming the `tcp_ccgen` value starts at 1 at time 0 and increments at this maximum rate, the value will be 1 again at times 2MSL, 4MSL, and so on. Also, since the value of 0 is never used, there are only $2^{32} - 1$ values in 2MSL, not 2^{32}, therefore the value of 2,147,483,648 that we show at time MSL really occurs very shortly before time MSL.

We assume that a connection starts at time 0 using a CC of 1 and the connection duration is 100 seconds. The TIME_WAIT state starts at time 100 and goes until either time 112, or until another incarnation of the connection is initiated on the host, whichever comes first. (This assumes an RTO of 1.5 seconds, giving a TIME_WAIT duration of 12 seconds.) Since the duration of the connection (100 seconds) is less than

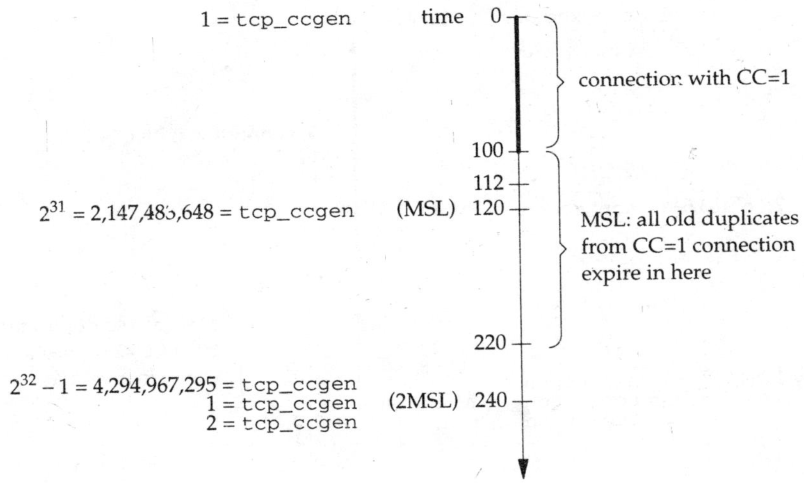

Figure 4.8 Connection with duration less than MSL: TIME_WAIT truncation is OK.

the MSL (120) we are guaranteed that any old duplicates from this connection will have disappeared by time 220. We also assume that the `tcp_ccgen` counter is being incremented at the fastest rate possible, that is, the host is establishing over 4 billion other TCP connections between times 0 and 240.

So whenever the connection duration is less than the MSL, it is safe to truncate the TIME_WAIT state because the CC values do not repeat until after any old duplicates have expired.

To see why the truncation can be performed only when the duration is less than MSL, consider Figure 4.9.

We assume again that the `tcp_ccgen` counter increments at the fastest rate possible. A connection is started at time 0 with a CC of 2, and the duration is 140 seconds. Since the duration is greater than the MSL, the TIME_WAIT state cannot be truncated, so the socket pair cannot be reused until time 380. (Technically, since we show the value of `tcp_ccgen` as 1 at time 0, the connection with a CC of 2 would occur very shortly after time 0 and would terminate very shortly after time 140. This doesn't affect our discussion.)

Between times 240 and 260 the CC value of 2 can be reused. If the TIME_WAIT state were truncated (say, somewhere between times 140 and 152), and if another incarnation of the same connection were created between times 240 and 260 using a CC of 2, since all the old duplicates may not disappear until time 260, it would be possible for old duplicates from the first incarnation to be delivered (incorrectly) to the second incarnation. It is not a problem for the CC of 2 to be reused for some other connection between times 240 and 260 (that is, for another socket pair); it just cannot be reused for a socket pair that may still have old duplicates wandering around the network.

From an application's perspective the TIME_WAIT truncation means a choice must be made by the client whether to use the same local port for a series of transactions to

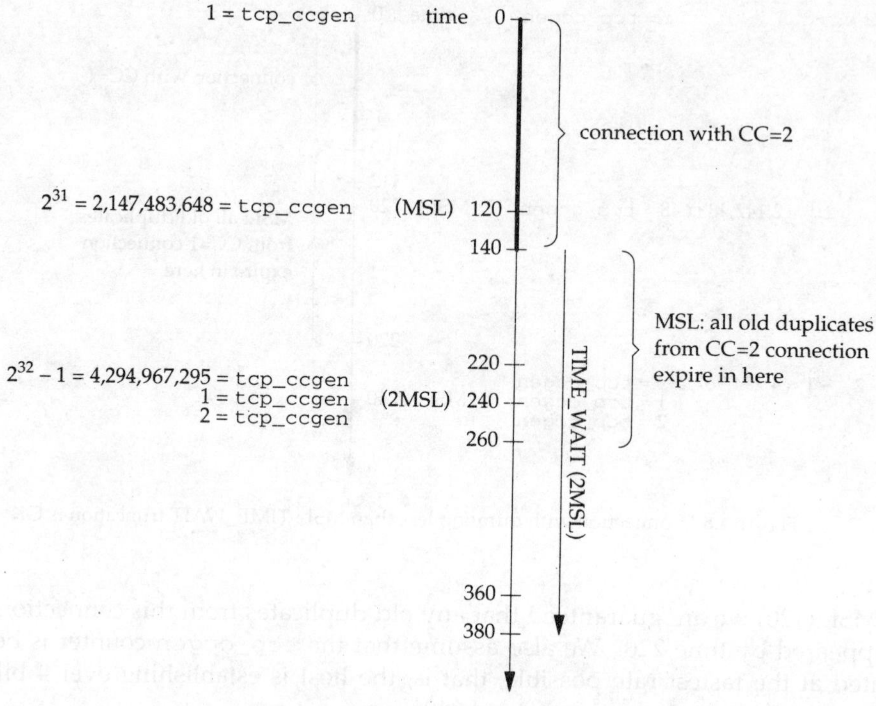

Figure 4.9 Connection with duration greater than MSL: TIME_WAIT state cannot be truncated.

the same server, or to use a different port for each transaction. If the connection duration is less than the MSL (which is typical for what we call transactions), then reusing the same local port saves TCP resources (i.e., the memory requirements of the control blocks, as shown in Figures 4.2 and 4.3). But if the client tries to use the same local port and the previous connection had a duration greater than the MSL, the error EADDRINUSE is returned when the connection is attempted (Figure 12.2).

As shown in Figure 4.2, regardless of which port strategy the application chooses, if both hosts support T/TCP and the connection duration is less than the MSL, the TIME_WAIT state is always truncated from 2MSL to 8RTO. This saves resources (i.e., memory and CPU time). This applies to any TCP connection less than MSL between two T/TCP hosts: FTP, SMTP, HTTP, and the like.

4.5 Avoiding the Three-Way Handshake with TAO

The primary benefit of T/TCP is avoidance of the three-way handshake. To understand why this is OK we need to understand the purpose of the three-way handshake. RFC 793 succinctly states: "The principal reason for the three-way handshake is to prevent old duplicate connection initiations from causing confusion. To deal with this, a special control message, reset, has been devised."

With the three-way handshake each end sends a SYN with its starting sequence number, and each end must acknowledge that SYN. This removes the potential for confusion when an old duplicate SYN is received by either end. Furthermore, normal TCP will not pass any data that arrives with a SYN to the user process until that end enters the ESTABLISHED state.

What T/TCP must provide is a way for the receiver of a SYN to be guaranteed that the SYN is not an old duplicate, without going through the three-way handshake, allowing any data that accompanies the SYN to be passed immediately to the user process. The protection against old duplicate SYNs is provided by the CC value that accompanies the SYN from the client, and the server's cached value of the most recent valid CC received from this client.

Consider the time line shown in Figure 4.10. As with Figure 4.8, we assume that the `tcp_ccgen` counter is incrementing at the fastest possible rate: $2^{32} - 1$ counts per 2MSL.

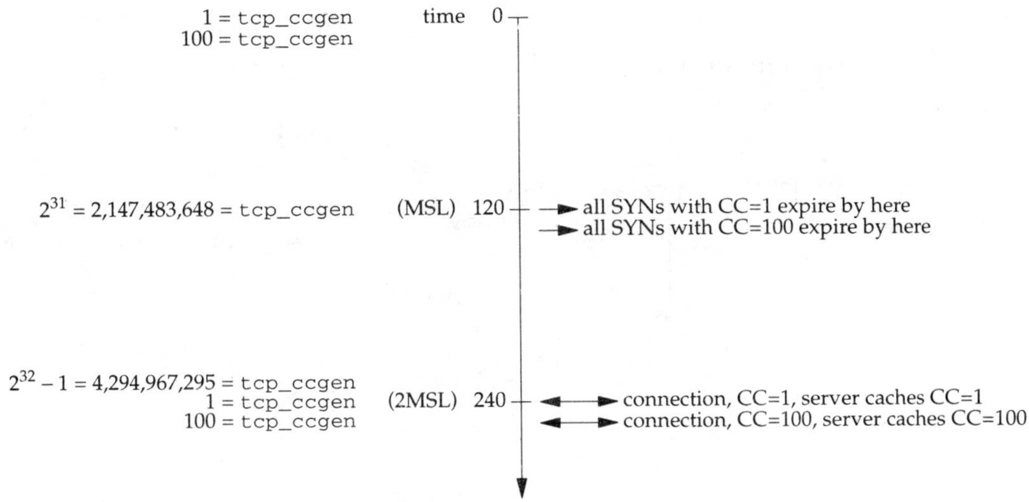

Figure 4.10 Higher CC value on SYN guarantees that SYN is not an old duplicate.

At time 0, `tcp_ccgen` is 1, and a short time later its value is 100. But because of the limited lifetime of any IP datagram, we are guaranteed that at time 120 (MSL seconds later) all SYNs with a CC of 1 have expired, and a short time after this all SYNs with a CC of 100 have expired.

A connection is then established at time 240 with a CC of 1. Assume the server's TAO test on this segment passes, so the server caches this CC value for this client. A short time after this, another connection is established to the same server host. Since the CC with the SYN (100) is greater than the cached value for this client (1), and since we're guaranteed that all SYNs with a CC of 100 expired at least MSL seconds in the past, the server is guaranteed that this SYN is not an old duplicate

Indeed, this is the TAO test from RFC 1644: "If an initial <SYN> segment (i.e., a segment containing a SYN bit but no ACK bit) from a particular client host carries a CC value larger than the corresponding cached value, the monotonic property of CC's ensures that the <SYN> segment must be new and can therefore be accepted immediately." It is the monotonic property of the CC values *and* the two assumptions that

1. all segments have a finite lifetime of MSL seconds, and
2. the `tcp_ccgen` values increment no faster than $2^{32} - 1$ counts in 2MSL seconds

that guarantee the SYN is new, and allow T/TCP to avoid the three-way handshake.

Out-of-Order SYNs

Figure 4.11 shows two T/TCP hosts and a SYN that arrives out of order. The SYN is not an old duplicate, it just arrives out of order at the server.

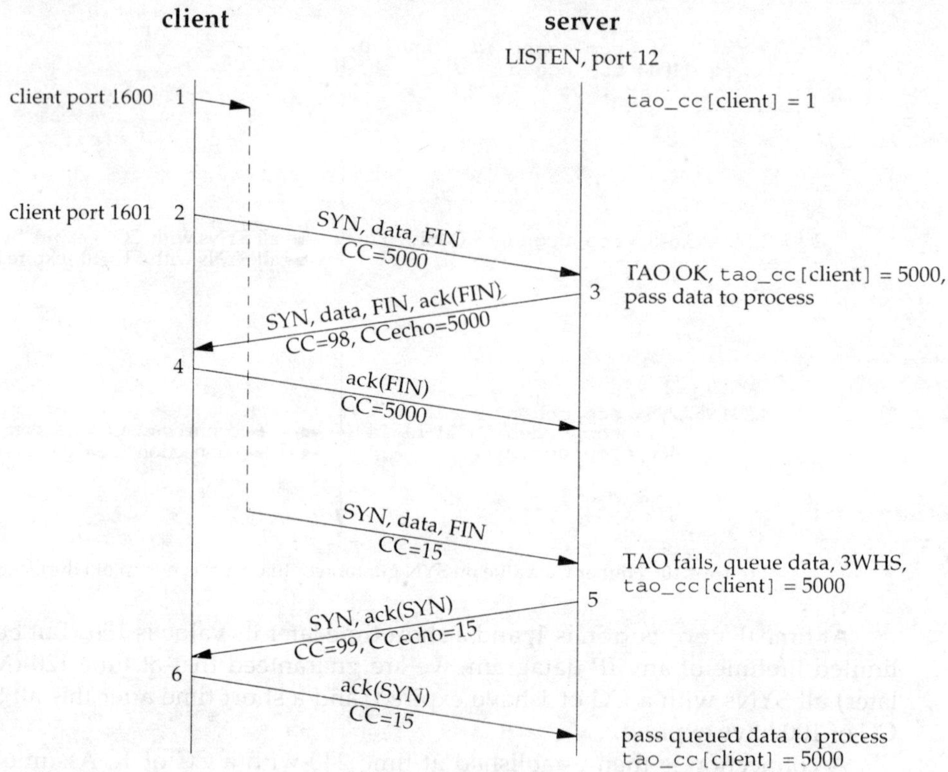

Figure 4.11 Two T/TCP hosts and a SYN that arrives out of order.

The server's cached CC for this client is 1. Segment 1 is sent from the client port 1600 with a CC of 15 but it is delayed in the network. Segment 2 is sent from the client port 1601 with a CC of 5000 and when it is received by the server the TAO test is OK (5000 is greater than 1), so the cached value for this client is updated to 5000, and the data is passed to the process. Segments 3 and 4 complete this transaction.

When segment 1 finally arrives at the server the TAO test fails (15 is less than 5000), so the server responds with a SYN and an ACK of the client's SYN, forcing the three-way handshake (3WHS) to complete before the data is passed to the server process. Segment 6 completes the three-way handshake and the queued data is passed to the process. (We don't show the remainder of this transaction.) But the server's cached CC for this client is *not* updated, even though the three-way handshake completes successfully, because the SYN with a CC of 15 is not an old duplicate (it was just received out of order). Updating the CC would move it backward from 5000 to 15, allowing the possibility of the server incorrectly accepting an old duplicate SYN from this client with a CC between 15 and 5000.

CC Values That Wrap Their Sign Bit

In Figure 4.11 we saw that when the TAO test fails, the server forces a three-way handshake, and even if this handshake completes successfully, the server's cached CC value for this client is not updated. While this is the right thing to do from a protocol perspective, it introduces an inefficiency.

It is possible for the TAO test to fail at the server because the CC values generated by the client, which are global to all connections on the client, "wrap their sign bit" with respect to this server. (CC values are unsigned 32-bit values, similar to TCP's sequence numbers. All comparisons of CC values use modular arithmetic, as described on pp. 810–812 of Volume 2. When we say the sign bit of the CC value *a* "wraps" with respect to *b*, we mean that *a* increases in value so that it is no longer greater than *b*, but is now less than *b*.) Consider Figure 4.12.

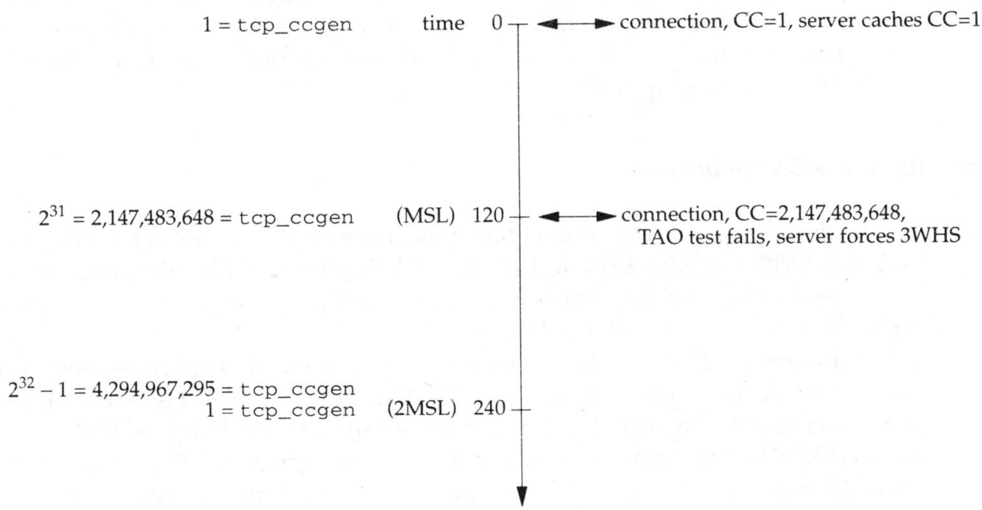

Figure 4.12 TAO test can fail because CC value wraps its sign bit.

The client establishes a connection with the server at time 0 with a CC of 1. The server's TAO test succeeds, and the server caches this CC for this client. The client then establishes 2,147,483,646 connections with other servers. At time 120 a connection is established with the same server as the connection at time 0, but now the CC value will be 2,147,483,648. When the server receives the SYN, the TAO test fails (2,147,483,648 is less than 1 when using modular arithmetic, as shown in Figure 24.26, p. 812 of Volume 2) and the three-way handshake validates the SYN, but the server's cached CC for this client remains at 1.

This means that any future SYN from this client to this server will force a three-way handshake until time 240. This assumes the `tcp_ccgen` counter keeps incrementing at its maximum possible rate. What is more likely is that this counter increments at a much slower rate, meaning that the time between the counter going from 2,147,483,648 and 4,294,967,295 will not be 120 seconds, but could be hours, or even days. But until the sign bit of this counter wraps again, all T/TCP connections between this client and server will require a three-way handshake.

The solution to this problem is twofold. First, not only does the server cache the most recent valid CC received from each client, but the client caches the most recent CC sent to each server. These two variables are shown as `tao_cc` and `tao_ccsent` in Figure 2.5.

Second, when the client detects that the value of `tcp_ccgen` that it is about to use is less than the most recent CC that it has sent to this server, the client sends the CCnew option instead of the CC option. The CCnew option forces the two hosts to resynchronize their cached CC values.

When the server receives a SYN with the CCnew option it marks the `tao_cc` for this client as 0 (undefined). When the three-way handshake completes successfully, if the cache entry for this client is undefined, it is updated with the received CC value.

The client sends the CCnew instead of the CC option in an initial SYN either when the client doesn't have a cached CC for this server (such as after a reboot or after the cache entry for the server has been flushed) or when the client detects that the CC value for this server has wrapped.

Duplicate SYN/ACK Segments

Up to this point our discussion has concentrated on the server being certain that a received SYN is a new SYN and not an old duplicate. This allows the server to avoid the three-way handshake. But how can the client be certain that the server's response (a SYN/ACK segment) is not an old duplicate?

With normal TCP the client sends no data with a SYN so the server's acknowledgment must ACK exactly 1 byte: the SYN. Furthermore, Berkeley-derived implementations increment the initial send sequence number (ISS) by 64,000 (`TCP_ISSINCR` divided by 2) each time a new connection is attempted (p. 1011 of Volume 2), so each successive client SYN has a higher sequence number than the previous connection. This makes it unlikely that an old duplicate SYN/ACK would ever have an acknowledgment field acceptable to the client.

With T/TCP, however, a SYN normally carries data, which increases the range of acceptable ACKs that the client can receive from the server. Figure 7 of RFC 1379 [Braden 1992b] shows an example of an old duplicate SYN/ACK being incorrectly accepted by the client. The problem with this example, however, is that the difference in the initial send sequence number between the two consecutive connections is only 100, which is less than the amount of data sent with the first SYN (300 bytes). As we mentioned, Berkeley-derived implementations increment the ISS by at least 64,000 for each connection, and 64,000 is greater than the default send window used by T/TCP (normally 4096). This makes it impossible for an old duplicate SYN/ACK to be acceptable to the client.

> 4.4BSD-Lite2 randomizes the ISS as we discussed in Section 3.2. The actual increment is now uniformly distributed between 31,232 and 96,767, with an average of 63,999. 31,232 is still greater than the default send window, and the CCecho option we're about to discuss makes this problem moot.

Nevertheless, T/TCP provides complete protection against old duplicate SYN/ACK segments: the CCecho option. The client knows the CC value that is sent with its SYN, and this value must be echoed by the server with the CCecho option. If the server's response does not have the expected CCecho value, it is ignored by the client (Figure 11.8). The monotonic increasing property of CC values, which cycle around in at most 2MSL seconds, guarantees that an old duplicate SYN/ACK will not be accepted by the client.

Notice that the client cannot perform a TAO test on the SYN/ACK from the server: it is too late. The client's SYN has already been accepted by the server, the server process has been passed the data, and the SYN/ACK received by the client contains the server's response. It is too late for the client to force a three-way handshake.

Retransmitted SYN segments

RFC 1644 and our discussion in this section have ignored the possibility of either the client SYN or the server's SYN being retransmitted. For example, in Figure 4.10 we assume that `tcp_ccgen` is 1 at time 0 and then all SYNs with a CC of 1 expire by time 120 (MSL). What can really happen is that the SYN with a CC of 1 can be retransmitted between time 0 and 75 so that all SYNs with a CC of 1 expire by time 195, not 120. (Berkeley-derived implementations set an upper limit of 75 seconds on the retransmission of either a client SYN or a server SYN, as discussed on p. 828 of Volume 2.)

This doesn't affect the correctness of the TAO test, but it does decrease the maximum rate at which the `tcp_ccgen` counter can increment. Earlier we showed the maximum rate of this variable as $2^{32}-1$ counts in 2MSL seconds, allowing a maximum transaction rate of almost 18 million per second. When the SYN retransmissions are considered the maximum rate becomes $2^{32}-1$ counts in 2MSL + 2MRX seconds, where MRX is the time limit on the SYN retransmission (75 seconds for Net/3). This decreases the transaction rate to about 11 million per second.

4.6 Summary

TCP's TIME_WAIT state performs two functions:

1. It implements the full-duplex closing of a connection.
2. It allows old duplicate segments to expire.

If the duration of a T/TCP connection is less than 120 seconds (1 MSL), the duration of the TIME_WAIT state is eight times the retransmission timeout, instead of 240 seconds. Also, the client can create a new incarnation of a connection that is in the TIME_WAIT state, further truncating the wait. We showed how this is OK, limited only by the maximum transaction rate supported by T/TCP (almost 18 million transactions per second). If a T/TCP client knows that it will perform lots of transactions with the same server, it can use the same local port number each time, which reduces the number of control blocks in the TIME_WAIT state.

TAO (TCP accelerated open) lets a T/TCP client–server avoid the three-way handshake. It works when the server receives a CC value from the client that is "greater than" the value cached by the server for this client. It is the monotonic property of the CC values and the two assumptions that

1. all segments have a finite lifetime of MSL seconds, and
2. the `tcp_ccgen` values increment no faster than $2^{32} - 1$ counts in 2MSL seconds

that guarantee the client's SYN is new, and allow T/TCP to avoid the three-way handshake.

5

T/TCP Implementation: Socket Layer

5.1 Introduction

This is the first of the chapters that describes the actual implementation of T/TCP within the Net/3 release. We follow the same order and style of presentation as Volume 2:

- Chapter 5: socket layer,
- Chapter 6: routing table,
- Chapter 7: protocol control blocks (PCBs),
- Chapter 8: TCP overview,
- Chapter 9: TCP output,
- Chapter 10: TCP functions,
- Chapter 11: TCP input, and
- Chapter 12: TCP user requests.

These chapters all assume the reader has a copy of Volume 2 or the source code described therein. This allows us to describe only the 1200 lines of new code required to implement T/TCP, instead of redescribing the 15,000 lines already presented in Volume 2.

The socket layer changes required by T/TCP are minimal: the `sosend` function needs to handle the `MSG_EOF` flag and allow a call to `sendto` or `sendmsg` for a protocol that allows an implied open–close.

5.2 Constants

Three new constants are required by T/TCP.

1. `MSG_EOF` is defined in `<sys/socket.h>`. If this flag is specified in a call to the `send`, `sendto`, or `sendmsg` functions, the sending of data on the connection is complete, combining the functionality of the `write` and `shutdown` functions. This flag should be added to Figure 16.12 (p. 482) of Volume 2.
2. A new protocol request, `PRU_SEND_EOF`, is defined in `<sys/protosw.h>`. This request should be added to Figure 15.17 (p. 450) of Volume 2. This request is issued by `sosend`, as we show later in Figure 5.2.
3. A new protocol flag, `PR_IMPLOPCL` (meaning "implied open–close"), is also defined in `<sys/protosw.h>`. This flag means two things: (a) the protocol allows a `sendto` or `sendmsg` that specifies the peer address without a prior `connect` (an implied open), and (b) the protocol understands the `MSG_EOF` flag (an implied close). Notice that (a) is required only for a connection-oriented protocol (such as TCP) since a connectionless protocol always allows a `sendto` or `sendmsg` without a `connect`. This flag should be added to Figure 7.9 (p. 189) of Volume 2.

   The protocol switch entry for TCP, `inetsw[2]` (lines 51–55 in Figure 7.13, p. 192 of Volume 2) should have `PR_IMPLOPCL` included in its `pr_flags` value.

5.3 sosend Function

Two changes are made to the `sosend` function. Figure 5.1 shows the replacement code for lines 314–321 on p. 495 of Volume 2.

> Notice that our replacement code starts at line 320, not 314. This is because other changes, unrelated to T/TCP, have been made earlier in this kernel file. Also, since we are replacing 8 lines from Volume 2 with 17 lines to support T/TCP, code fragments that we show later in this file will also have different line numbers from the corresponding code in Volume 2. In general, when we refer to code fragments in Volume 2 we specify the exact line numbers in Volume 2. Since code has been added and deleted from Volume 2 to Volume 3, the line numbers for similar code fragments will be close but not identical.

320–336 This code allows a `sendto` or `sendmsg` on a connection-oriented socket if the protocol's `PR_IMPLOPCL` flag is set (as it is for TCP with the changes described in this text) and if a destination address is supplied by the caller. If a destination address is not supplied, `ENOTCONN` is returned for a TCP socket, and `EDESTADDRREQ` is returned for a UDP socket.

330–331 This `if` allows a write consisting of control information and no data if the connection is in the `SS_ISCONFIRMING` state. This is used with OSI TP4 protocol, not with TCP/IP.

uipc_socket.c
```
        if ((so->so_state & SS_ISCONNECTED) == 0) {
            /*
             * sendto and sendmsg are allowed on a connection-
             * based socket only if it supports implied connect
             * (e.g., T/TCP).
             * Return ENOTCONN if not connected and no address is
             * supplied.
             */
            if ((so->so_proto->pr_flags & PR_CONNREQUIRED) &&
                (so->so_proto->pr_flags & PR_IMPLOPCL) == 0) {
                if ((so->so_state & SS_ISCONFIRMING) == 0 &&
                    !(resid == 0 && clen != 0))
                    snderr(ENOTCONN);
            } else if (addr == 0)
                snderr(so->so_proto->pr_flags & PR_CONNREQUIRED ?
                       ENOTCONN : EDESTADDRREQ);
        }
```
uipc_socket.c

Figure 5.1 sosend function: error checking.

The next change to sendto is shown in Figure 5.2 and replaces lines 399–403 on p. 499 of Volume 2.

uipc_socket.c
```
415         s = splnet();           /* XXX */
416         /*
417          * If the user specifies MSG_EOF, and the protocol
418          * understands this flag (e.g., T/TCP), and there's
419          * nothing left to send, then PRU_SEND_EOF instead
420          * of PRU_SEND.  MSG_OOB takes priority, however.
421          */
422         req = (flags & MSG_OOB) ? PRU_SENDOOB :
423             ((flags & MSG_EOF) &&
424              (so->so_proto->pr_flags & PR_IMPLOPCL) &&
425              (resid <= 0)) ? PRU_SEND_EOF : PRU_SEND;
426         error = (*so->so_proto->pr_usrreq) (so, req, top, addr, control);
427         splx(s);
```
uipc_socket.c

Figure 5.2 sosend function: protocol dispatch.

This is our first encounter with the comment XXX. It is a warning to the reader that the code is obscure, contains nonobvious side effects, or is a quick solution to a more difficult problem. In this case, the processor priority is being raised by splnet to prevent the protocol processing from executing. The processor priority is restored at the end of Figure 5.2 by splx. Section 1.12 of Volume 2 describes the various Net/3 interrupt levels.

416–427 If the MSG_OOB flag is specified, the PRU_SENDOOB request is issued. Otherwise, if the MSG_EOF flag is specified, and the protocol supports the PR_IMPLOPCL flag, and there is no more data to be sent to the protocol (resid is less than or equal to 0), then the PRU_SEND_EOF request is issued instead of the normal PRU_SEND request.

Recall our example in Section 3.6. The application calls sendto to write 3300 bytes, specifying the MSG_EOF flag. The first time around the loop in sosend the code in Figure 5.2 issues a PRU_SEND request for the first 2048 bytes of data (an mbuf cluster). The second time around the loop in sosend a request of PRU_SEND_EOF is issued for the remaining 1252 bytes of data (in another mbuf cluster).

5.4 Summary

T/TCP adds an implied open–close capability to TCP. The implied open means that instead of calling connect, an application can call sendto or sendmsg and specify the peer address. The implied close allows the application to specify the MSG_EOF flag in a call to send, sendto, or sendmsg, combining the output with the close. Our call to sendto in Figure 1.10 combines the open, write, and close in a single system call. The changes that we showed in this chapter add the implied open–close capability to the Net/3 socket layer.

6

T/TCP Implementation: Routing Table

6.1 Introduction

T/TCP needs to create a per-host cache entry for each host with which it communicates. The three variables, `tao_cc`, `tao_ccsent`, and `tao_mssopt`, shown in Figure 2.5 are stored in the per-host cache entry. A convenient place to store the per-host cache is in the existing IP routing table. With Net/3 it is easy to create a per-host routing table entry for each host with the "cloning" flag that we described in Chapter 19 of Volume 2.

In Volume 2 we saw that the Internet protocols (without T/TCP) use the generic routing table functions provided by Net/3. Figure 18.17 (p. 575) of Volume 2 shows that routes are added by calling `rn_addroute`, deleted by `rn_delete`, searched for by `rn_match`, and `rn_walktree` can walk through the entire tree. (Net/3 stores its routing tables using a binary tree, called a *radix tree*.) Nothing other than these generic functions are required by TCP/IP. With T/TCP, however, this changes.

Since a host can communicate with thousands of other hosts over a short period of time (say a few hours, or perhaps less than an hour for a busy WWW server, as we demonstrate in Section 14.10), some method is required to time out these per-host routing table entries so they don't take excessive amounts of kernel memory. In this chapter we examine the functions used with T/TCP to dynamically create and delete per-host routing table entries from the IP routing table.

> Exercise 19.2 of Volume 2 showed a trivial way to create a per-host routing table entry automatically for every peer with which a host communicates. What we describe in this chapter is similar in concept, but automatically done for most TCP/IP routes. The per-host entries created with this exercise never time out; they exist until the host reboots, or until the routes are manually deleted by the administrator. A better way is required to manage all the per-host routes automatically.

Not everyone agrees with the assumption that the existing routing table is the right place to store the T/TCP per-host cache. An alternate approach would be to store the T/TCP per-host cache as its own radix tree within the kernel. This technique (a separate radix tree) is easy to do, given the existing generic radix tree functions within the kernel, and is currently used with NFS mounts in Net/3.

6.2 Code Introduction

One C file, `netinet/in_rmx.c`, defines the functions added by T/TCP for TCP/IP routing. This file contains only the Internet-specific functions that we describe in this chapter. We do not describe all the routing functions presented in Chapters 18, 19, and 20 of Volume 2.

Figure 6.1 shows the relationship of the new Internet-specific routing functions (the shaded ellipses that we describe in this chapter, whose names begin with `in_`) to the generic routing functions (whose names usually begin with `rn_` or `rt`).

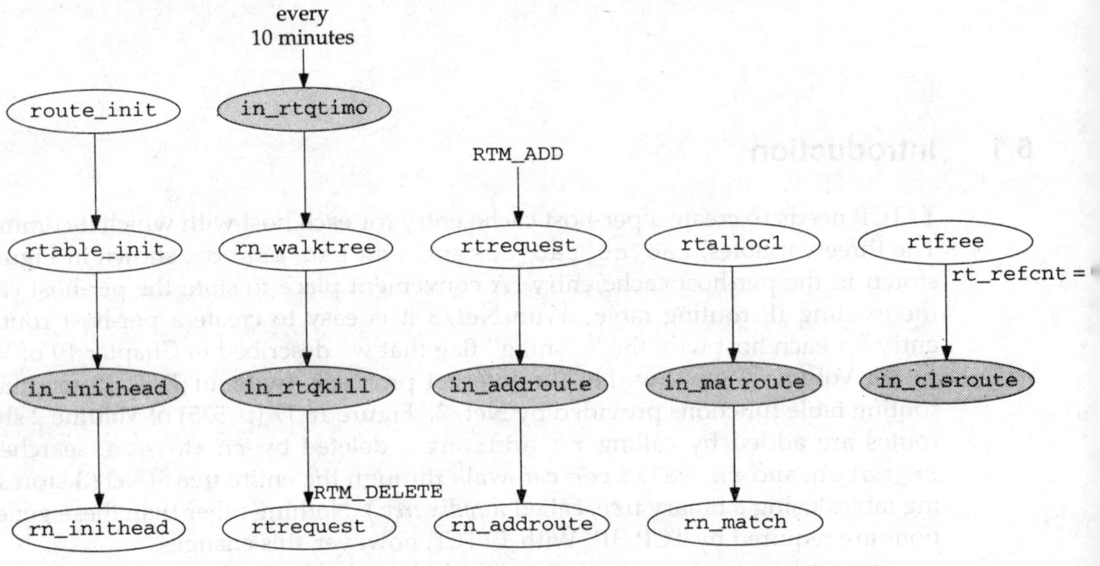

Figure 6.1 Relationship of Internet-specific routing functions.

Global Variables

The new Internet-specific global variables are shown in Figure 6.2.

The FreeBSD release allows the system administrator to modify the values of the last three variables in Figure 6.2 using the `sysctl` program with a prefix of `net.inet.ip`. We don't show the code to do this, because it is a trivial addition to the `ip_sysctl` function shown in Figure 8.35, p. 244 of Volume 2.

Variable	Datatype	Description
rtq_timeout	int	how often in_rtqtimo runs (default = every 10 min)
rtq_toomany	int	how many routes before dynamic deletion is started
rtq_reallyold	int	how long before route is considered really old
rtq_minreallyold	int	minimum value of rtq_reallyold

Figure 6.2 Internet-specific global routing variables.

6.3 radix_node_head Structure

One new pointer is added to the radix_node_head structure (Figure 18.16, p. 574 of Volume 2): rnh_close. Its value is always a null pointer except for the IP routing table, when it points to in_clsroute, which we show later in Figure 6.7.

This function pointer is used from the rtfree function. The following line is added between lines 108 and 109 in Figure 19.5, p. 605 of Volume 2, to declare and initialize the automatic variable rnh:

```
struct radix_node_head *rnh = rt_tables[rt_key(rt)->sa_family];
```

The following three lines are added between lines 112 and 113:

```
if(rnh->rnh_close && rt->rt_refcnt == 0) {
        rnh->rnh_close((struct radix_node *)rt, rnh);
}
```

If the function pointer is nonnull and the reference count reaches 0, the close function is called.

6.4 rtentry Structure

Two additional routing flags are required by T/TCP in the rtentry structure (p. 579 of Volume 2). But the existing rt_flags member is a short integer and 15 of the 16 bits are already used (p. 580 of Volume 2). A new flag member is therefore added to the rtentry structure, rt_prflags.

> Another solution is to change rt_flags from a short integer to a long integer, which may occur in a future release.

Two of the flag bits in rt_prflags are used with T/TCP.

- RTPRF_WASCLONED is set by rtrequest (between lines 335–336 on p. 609 of Volume 2) when a new entry is created from an entry with the RTF_CLONING flag set.
- RTPRF_OURS is set by in_clsroute (Figure 6.7) when the last reference to a cloned IP route is closed. When this happens a timer is set that will cause the route to be deleted at some time in the future.

6.5 rt_metrics Structure

The purpose of all the changes to the routing table for T/TCP is to store additional per-host information in each routing table entry, specifically the three variables tao_cc, tao_ccsent, and tao_mssopt. To accommodate this additional information, the rt_metrics structure (p. 580 of Volume 2) contains a new member:

```
u_long  rmx_filler[4]; /* protocol family specific metrics */
```

This allows for 16 bytes of protocol-specific metrics, which are used by T/TCP, as shown in Figure 6.3.

tcp_var.h

```
153 struct rmxp_tao {
154     tcp_cc  tao_cc;              /* latest CC in valid SYN from peer */
155     tcp_cc  tao_ccsent;          /* latest CC sent to peer */
156     u_short tao_mssopt;          /* latest MSS received from peer */
157 };
158 #define rmx_taop(r) ((struct rmxp_tao *)(r).rmx_filler)
```

tcp_var.h

Figure 6.3 rmxp_tao structure used by T/TCP as TAO cache.

153–157 The data type tcp_cc is used for connection counts, and this data type is typedefed to be an unsigned long (similar to TCP's sequence numbers). A value of 0 for a tcp_cc variable means undefined.

158 Given a pointer to an rtentry structure, the macro rmx_taop returns a pointer to the corresponding rmxp_tao structure.

6.6 in_inithead Function

Page 583 of Volume 2 details all the steps involved in the initialization of all the Net/3 routing tables. The first change made with T/TCP is to have the dom_rtattach member of the inetdomain structure (lines 78–81 on p. 192 of Volume 2) point to in_inithead instead of rn_inithead. We show the in_inithead function in Figure 6.4.

Perform initialization of routing table

222–225 rn_inithead allocates and initializes one radix_node_head structure. This was all that happened in Net/3. The remainder of the function is new with T/TCP and only when the "real" routing table is initialized. This function is also called to initialize a different routing table that is utilized with NFS mount points.

Change function pointers

226–229 Two of the function pointers in the radix_node_head structure are modified from the defaults set by rn_inithead: rnh_addaddr and rnh_matchaddr. This changes two of the four pointers in Figure 18.17, p. 575 of Volume 2. This allows the Internet-specific actions to be performed before calling the generic radix node functions. The rnh_close function pointer is new with T/TCP.

in_rmx.c

```
218 int
219 in_inithead(void **head, int off)
220 {
221     struct radix_node_head *rnh;

222     if (!rn_inithead(head, off))
223         return (0);

224     if (head != (void **) &rt_tables[AF_INET])
225         return (1);             /* only do this for the real routing table */

226     rnh = *head;
227     rnh->rnh_addaddr = in_addroute;
228     rnh->rnh_matchaddr = in_matroute;
229     rnh->rnh_close = in_clsroute;
230     in_rtqtimo(rnh);            /* kick off timeout first time */
231     return (1);
232 }
```

in_rmx.c

Figure 6.4 in_inithead function.

Initialize timeout function

230 The timeout function, in_rtqtimo, is called for the first time. Each time the function is called it arranges to be called again in the future.

6.7 in_addroute Function

When a new routing table entry is created by rtrequest, either as the result of an RTM_ADD command or the result of an RTM_RESOLVE command that creates a new entry from an existing entry with the cloning flag set (pp. 609–610 of Volume 2), the rnh_addaddr function is called, which we saw is in_addroute for the Internet protocols. Figure 6.5 shows this new function.

in_rmx.c

```
47 static struct radix_node *
48 in_addroute(void *v_arg, void *n_arg, struct radix_node_head *head,
49             struct radix_node *treenodes)
50 {
51     struct rtentry *rt = (struct rtentry *) treenodes;

52     /*
53      * For IP, all unicast non-host routes are automatically cloning.
54      */
55     if (!(rt->rt_flags & (RTF_HOST | RTF_CLONING))) {
56         struct sockaddr_in *sin = (struct sockaddr_in *) rt_key(rt);
57         if (!IN_MULTICAST(ntohl(sin->sin_addr.s_addr))) {
58             rt->rt_flags |= RTF_CLONING;
59         }
60     }
61     return (rn_addroute(v_arg, n_arg, head, treenodes));
62 }
```

in_rmx.c

Figure 6.5 in_addroute function.

52–61 If the route being added is not a host route and does not have the cloning flag set, the routing table key (the IP address) is examined. If the IP address is not a multicast address, the cloning flag is set for the new routing table entry being created. `rn_addroute` adds the entry to the routing table.

The effect of this function is to set the cloning flag for all nonmulticast network routes, which includes the default route. The effect of the cloning flag is to create a new host route for any destination that is looked up in the routing table when that destination matches either a nonmulticast network route or the default route. This new cloned host route is created the first time it is looked up.

6.8 `in_matroute` Function

`rtalloc1` (p. 603 of Volume 2) calls the function pointed to by the `rnh_matchaddr` pointer (i.e., the function `in_matroute` shown in Figure 6.6) when looking up a route.

in_rmx.c

```
68 static struct radix_node *
69 in_matroute(void *v_arg, struct radix_node_head *head)
70 {
71     struct radix_node *rn = rn_match(v_arg, head);
72     struct rtentry *rt = (struct rtentry *) rn;

73     if (rt && rt->rt_refcnt == 0) {      /* this is first reference */
74         if (rt->rt_prflags & RTPRF_OURS) {
75             rt->rt_prflags &= ~RTPRF_OURS;
76             rt->rt_rmx.rmx_expire = 0;
77         }
78     }
79     return (rn);
80 }
```

in_rmx.c

Figure 6.6 `in_matroute` function.

Call `rn_match` to look up route

71–78 `rn_match` looks up the route in the routing table. If the route is found and the reference count is 0, this is the first reference to the routing table entry. If the entry was being timed out, that is, if the `RTPRF_OURS` flag is set, that flag is turned off and the `rmx_expire` timer is set to 0. This occurs when a route is closed, but then reused before the route is deleted.

6.9 `in_clsroute` Function

We mentioned earlier that a new function pointer, `rnh_close`, is added to the `radix_node_head` structure with the T/TCP changes. This function is called by `rtfree` when the reference count reaches 0. This causes `in_clsroute`, shown in Figure 6.7, to be called.

in_rmx.c

```
 89 static void
 90 in_clsroute(struct radix_node *rn, struct radix_node_head *head)
 91 {
 92     struct rtentry *rt = (struct rtentry *) rn;

 93     if (!(rt->rt_flags & RTF_UP))
 94         return;
 95     if ((rt->rt_flags & (RTF_LLINFO | RTF_HOST)) != RTF_HOST)
 96         return;
 97     if ((rt->rt_prflags & (RTPRF_WASCLONED | RTPRF_OURS))
 98         != RTPRF_WASCLONED)
 99         return;

100     /*
101      * If rtq_reallyold is 0, just delete the route without
102      * waiting for a timeout cycle to kill it.
103      */
104     if (rtq_reallyold != 0) {
105         rt->rt_prflags |= RTPRF_OURS;
106         rt->rt_rmx.rmx_expire = time.tv_sec + rtq_reallyold;
107     } else {
108         rtrequest(RTM_DELETE,
109                   (struct sockaddr *) rt_key(rt),
110                   rt->rt_gateway, rt_mask(rt),
111                   rt->rt_flags, 0);
112     }
113 }
```

in_rmx.c

Figure 6.7 in_clsroute function.

Check flags

93–99 The following tests are made: the route must be up, the RTF_HOST flag must be on (i.e., this is not a network route), the RTF_LLINFO flag must be off (this flag is turned on for ARP entries), RTPRF_WASCLONED must be on (the entry was cloned), and RTPRF_OURS must be off (we are not currently timing out this entry). If any of these tests fail, the function returns.

Set expiration time for routing table entry

100–112 In the common case, rtq_reallyold is nonzero, causing the RTPRF_OURS flag to be turned on and the rmx_expire time to be set to the current time in seconds (time.tv_sec) plus rtq_reallyold (normally 3600 seconds, or 1 hour). If the administrator sets rtq_reallyold to 0 using the sysctl program, then the route is immediately deleted by rtrequest.

6.10 in_rtqtimo Function

The in_rtqtimo function was called for the first time by in_inithead in Figure 6.4. Each time in_rtqtimo is called, it schedules itself to be called again in rtq_timeout seconds in the future (whose default is 600 seconds or 10 minutes).

The purpose of in_rtqtimo is to walk the entire IP routing table (using the generic rn_walktree function), calling in_rtqkill for every entry. in_rtqkill makes the decision whether to delete the entry or not. Information needs to be passed from in_rtqtimo to in_rtqkill (recall Figure 6.1), and vice versa, and this is done through the third argument to rn_walktree. This argument is a pointer that is passed by rn_walktree to in_rtqkill. Since the argument is a pointer, information can be passed in either direction between in_rtqtimo and in_rtqkill.

The pointer passed by in_rtqtimo to rn_walktree is a pointer to an rtqk_arg structure, shown in Figure 6.8.

in_rmx.c

```
struct rtqk_arg {
    struct radix_node_head *rnh;     /* head of routing table */
    int     found;                  /* #entries found that we're timing out */
    int     killed;                 /* #entries deleted by in_rtqkill */
    int     updating;               /* set when deleting excess entries */
    int     draining;               /* normally 0 */
    time_t  nextstop;               /* time when to do it all again */
};
```

in_rmx.c

Figure 6.8 rtqk_arg structure: information from in_rtqtimo to in_rtqkill and vice versa.

We'll see how these members are used as we look at the in_rtqtimo function, shown in Figure 6.9.

Set rtqk_arg structure and call rn_walktree

167–172 The rtqk_arg structure is initialized by setting rnh to the head of the IP routing table, the counters found and killed to 0, the draining and update flags to 0, and nextstop to the current time (in seconds) plus rtq_timeout (600 seconds, or 10 minutes). rn_walktree walks the entire IP routing table, calling in_rtqkill (Figure 6.11) for every entry.

Check for too many routing table entries

173–189 There are too many routing tables entries if the following three conditions are all true:

1. The number of entries still in the routing table that we are timing out (found minus killed) exceeds rtq_toomany (which defaults to 128).
2. The number of seconds since we last performed this adjustment exceeds rtq_timeout (600 seconds, or 10 minutes).
3. rtq_reallyold exceeds rtq_minreallyold (which defaults to 10).

If these are all true, rtq_reallyold is set to two-thirds of its current value (using integer division). Since its value starts at 3600 seconds (60 minutes), it takes on the values 3600, 2400, 1600, 1066, 710, and so on. But this value is never allowed to go below rtq_minreallyold (which defaults to 10 seconds). The current time is saved in the static variable last_adjusted_timeout and a debug message is sent to the syslogd daemon. (Section 13.4.2 of [Stevens 1992] shows how the log function sends messages

in_rmx.c

```
159 static void
160 in_rtqtimo(void *rock)
161 {
162     struct radix_node_head *rnh = rock;
163     struct rtqk_arg arg;
164     struct timeval atv;
165     static time_t last_adjusted_timeout = 0;
166     int     s;

167     arg.rnh = rnh;
168     arg.found = arg.killed = arg.updating = arg.draining = 0;
169     arg.nextstop = time.tv_sec + rtq_timeout;
170     s = splnet();
171     rnh->rnh_walktree(rnh, in_rtqkill, &arg);
172     splx(s);

173     /*
174      * Attempt to be somewhat dynamic about this:
175      * If there are 'too many' routes sitting around taking up space,
176      * then crank down the timeout, and see if we can't make some more
177      * go away.  However, we make sure that we will never adjust more
178      * than once in rtq_timeout seconds, to keep from cranking down too
179      * hard.
180      */
181     if ((arg.found - arg.killed > rtq_toomany) &&
182         (time.tv_sec - last_adjusted_timeout >= rtq_timeout) &&
183         rtq_reallyold > rtq_minreallyold) {
184         rtq_reallyold = 2 * rtq_reallyold / 3;
185         if (rtq_reallyold < rtq_minreallyold)
186             rtq_reallyold = rtq_minreallyold;

187         last_adjusted_timeout = time.tv_sec;
188         log(LOG_DEBUG, "in_rtqtimo: adjusted rtq_reallyold to %d\n",
189             rtq_reallyold);
190         arg.found = arg.killed = 0;
191         arg.updating = 1;
192         s = splnet();
193         rnh->rnh_walktree(rnh, in_rtqkill, &arg);
194         splx(s);
195     }
196     atv.tv_usec = 0;
197     atv.tv_sec = arg.nextstop;
198     timeout(in_rtqtimo, rock, hzto(&atv));
199 }
```

in_rmx.c

Figure 6.9 in_rtqtimo function.

to the syslogd daemon.) The purpose of this code and the decreasing value of rtq_reallyold is to process the routing table more frequently, timing out old routes, as the routing table fills.

190–195 The counters found and killed in the rtqk_arg structure are initialized to 0 again, the updating flag is set to 1 this time, and rn_walktree is called again.

196–198 The `in_rtqkill` function sets the `nextstop` member of the `rtqk_arg` structure to the next time at which `in_rtqtimo` should be called again. The kernel's `timeout` function schedules this event in the future.

> How much overhead is involved in walking through the entire routing table every 10 minutes? Obviously this depends on the number of entries in the table. In Section 14.10 we simulate the size of the T/TCP routing table for a busy Web server and find that even though the server is contacted by over 5000 different clients over a 24-hour period, with a 1-hour expiration time on the host routes, the routing table never exceeds about 550 entries. Some backbone routers on the Internet have tens of thousands of routing table entries today, but these are routers, not hosts. We would not expect a backbone router to require T/TCP and then have to walk through such a large routing table on a regular basis, purging old entries.

6.11 `in_rtqkill` Function

`in_rtqkill` is called by `rn_walktree`, which is called by `in_rtqtimo`. The purpose of `in_rtqkill`, which we show in Figure 6.11, is to delete IP routing table entries when necessary.

Only process entries that we are timing out

134–135 This function only processes entries with the `RTPRF_OURS` flag set, that is, entries that have been closed by `in_clsroute` (i.e., their reference counts have reached 0), and then only after a timeout period (normally 1 hour) has expired. This function does not affect routes that are currently in use (since the route's `RTPRF_OURS` flag will not be set).

136–146 If either the `draining` flag is set (which it never is in the current implementation) or the timeout has expired (the `rmx_expire` time is less than the current time), the route is deleted by `rtrequest`. The `found` member of the `rtqk_arg` structure counts the number of entries in the routing table with the `RTPRF_OURS` flag set, and the `killed` member counts the number of these that are deleted.

147–151 This `else` clause is executed when the current entry has not timed out. If the `updating` flag is set (which we saw in Figure 6.9 occurs when there are too many routes being expired and the entire routing table is processed a second time), and if the expiration time (which must be in the future for the subtraction to yield a positive result) is too far in the future, the expiration time is reset to the current time plus `rtq_reallyold`. To understand this, consider the example shown in Figure 6.10.

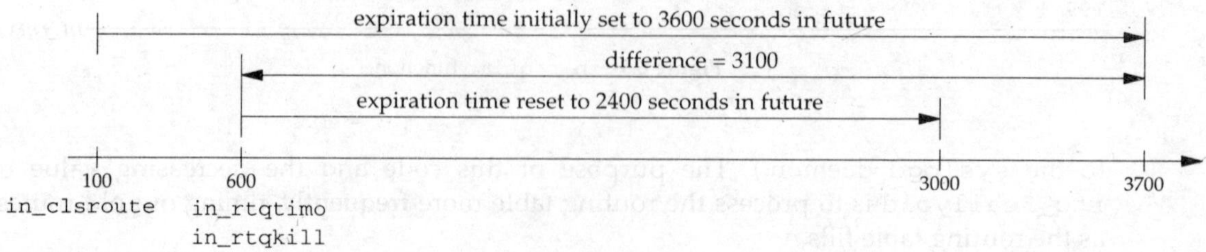

Figure 6.10 `in_rtqkill` resetting an expiration time in the future.

in_rmx.c
```
127 static int
128 in_rtqkill(struct radix_node *rn, void *rock)
129 {
130     struct rtqk_arg *ap = rock;
131     struct radix_node_head *rnh = ap->rnh;
132     struct rtentry *rt = (struct rtentry *) rn;
133     int     err;

134     if (rt->rt_prflags & RTPRF_OURS) {
135         ap->found++;

136         if (ap->draining || rt->rt_rmx.rmx_expire <= time.tv_sec) {
137             if (rt->rt_refcnt > 0)
138                 panic("rtqkill route really not free");

139             err = rtrequest(RTM_DELETE,
140                             (struct sockaddr *) rt_key(rt),
141                             rt->rt_gateway, rt_mask(rt),
142                             rt->rt_flags, 0);
143             if (err)
144                 log(LOG_WARNING, "in_rtqkill: error %d\n", err);
145             else
146                 ap->killed++;
147         } else {
148             if (ap->updating &&
149                 (rt->rt_rmx.rmx_expire - time.tv_sec > rtq_reallyold)) {
150                 rt->rt_rmx.rmx_expire = time.tv_sec + rtq_reallyold;
151             }
152             ap->nextstop = lmin(ap->nextstop, rt->rt_rmx.rmx_expire);
153         }
154     }
155     return (0);
156 }
```
in_rmx.c

Figure 6.11 in_rtqkill function.

The x-axis is time in seconds. A route is closed by in_clsroute at time 100 (when its reference count reaches 0) and rtq_reallyold has its initial value of 3600 (1 hour). The expiration time for the route is then 3700. But at time 600, in_rtqtimo executes and the route is not deleted (since its expiration time is 3100 seconds in the future), but there are too many entries, causing in_rtqtimo to reset rtq_reallyold to 2400, set updating to 1, and rn_walktree processes the entire IP routing table again. This time in_rtqkill finds updating set to 1 and the route will expire in 3100 seconds. Since 3100 is greater than 2400, the expiration time is reset to 2400 seconds in the future, namely, time 3000. As the routing table grows, the expiration times get shorter.

Calculate next timeout time

152–153 This code is executed every time an entry is found that is being expired but whose expiration time has not yet been reached. nextstop is set to the minimum of its current value and the expiration time of this routing table entry. Recall that the initial value of `nextstop` was set by `in_rtqtimo` to the current time plus `rtq_timeout` (i.e., 10 minutes in the future).

Consider the example shown in Figure 6.12. The *x*-axis is time in seconds and the large dots at times 0, 600, etc., are the times at which `in_rtqtimo` is called.

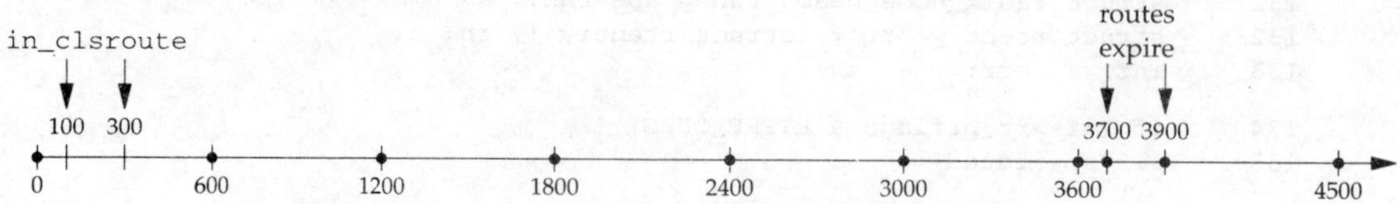

Figure 6.12 Execution of `in_rtqtimo` based on expiration of routes.

An IP route is created by `in_addroute` and then closed by `in_clsroute` at time 100. Its expiration time is set to 3700 (1 hour in the future). A second route is created and later closed at time 300, causing its expiration time to be set to 3900. `in_rtqtimo` executes every 10 minutes, at times 0, 600, 1200, 1800, 2400, 3000, and 3600. At times 0 through 3000 `nextstop` is set to the current time plus 600 so when `in_rtqkill` is called for each of the two routes at time 3000, `nextstop` is left at 3600 because 3600 is less than 3700 and less than 3900. But when `in_rtqkill` is called for each of these two routes at time 3600, `nextstop` becomes 3700 since 3700 is less than 3900 and less than 4200. This means `in_rtqtimo` will be called again at time 3700, instead of at time 4200. Furthermore, when `in_rtqkill` is called at time 3700, the other route that is due to expire at time 3900 causes `nextstop` to be set to 3900. Assuming there are no other IP routes expiring, after `in_rtqtimo` executes at time 3900, it will execute again at time 4500, 5100, and so on.

Interactions with Expiration Time

There are a few subtle interactions involving the expiration time of routing table entries and the `rmx_expire` member of the `rt_metrics` structure. First, this member is also used by ARP to time out ARP entries (Chapter 21 of Volume 2). This means the routing table entry for a host on the local subnet (along with its associated TAO information) is deleted when the ARP entry for that host is deleted, normally every 20 minutes. This is sooner than the default expiration time used by `in_rtqkill` (1 hour). Recall that `in_clsroute` explicitly ignored these ARP entries (Figure 6.7), which have the `RTM_LLINFO` flag set, allowing ARP to time them out, instead of `in_rtqkill`.

Second, executing the `route` program to fetch and print the metrics and expiration time for a cloned T/TCP routing table entry has the side effect of resetting the expiration time. This happens as follows. Assume a route is in use and then closed (its reference count becomes 0). When it is closed, its expiration time is set to 1 hour in the future. But 59 minutes later, 1 minute before it would have expired, the `route` program is used to print the metrics for the route. The following kernel functions execute as a result of the `route` program: `route_output` calls `rtalloc1`, which calls `in_matroute` (the Internet-specific `rnh_matchaddr` function), which increments the reference count, say, from 0 to 1. When this is complete, assuming the reference count goes from 1 to 0, `rtfree` calls `in_clsroute`, which resets the expiration time to 1 hour in the future.

6.12 Summary

With T/TCP we add 16 bytes to the `rt_metrics` structure. Ten of these bytes are used by T/TCP as the TAO cache:

- `tao_cc`, the latest CC received in a valid SYN from this peer,
- `tao_ccsent`, the latest CC sent to the peer, and
- `tao_mssopt`, the latest MSS received from the peer.

One new function pointer is added to the `radix_node_head` structure: the `rnh_close` member, which (if defined) is called when the reference count for a route reaches 0.

Four new functions are provided that are specific to the Internet protocols:

1. `in_inithead` initializes the Internet `radix_node_head` structure, setting the four function pointers that we're currently describing.
2. `in_addroute` is called when a new route is added to the IP routing table. It turns on the cloning flag for every IP route that is not a host route and is not a route to a multicast address.
3. `in_matroute` is called each time an IP route is looked up. If the route was currently being timed out by `in_clsroute`, its expiration time is reset to 0 since it is being used again.
4. `in_clsroute` is called when the last reference to an IP route is closed. It sets the expiration time for the route to be 1 hour in the future. We also saw that this time can be decreased if the routing table gets too large.

7

T/TCP Implementation: Protocol Control Blocks

7.1 Introduction

One small change is required to the PCB functions (Chapter 22 of Volume 2) for T/TCP. The function in pcbconnect (Section 22.8 of Volume 2) is now divided into two pieces: an inner routine named `in_pcbladdr`, which assigns the local interface address, and the function `in_pcbconnect`, which performs the same function as before (and which calls `in_pcbladdr`).

We split the functionality because it is possible with T/TCP to issue a `connect` when a previous incarnation of the same connection (i.e., the same socket pair) is still in the TIME_WAIT state. If the duration of the previous connection was less than the MSL, and if both sides used the CC options, then the existing connection in the TIME_WAIT state is closed, and the new connection is allowed to proceed. If we didn't make this change, and T/TCP used the unmodified `in_pcbconnect`, the application would receive an "address already in use" error when the existing PCB in the TIME_WAIT state was encountered.

`in_pcbconnect` is called not only for a TCP `connect`, but also when a new TCP connection request arrives, for a UDP `connect`, and for a UDP `sendto`. Figure 7.1 summarizes these Net/3 calls, before our modifications.

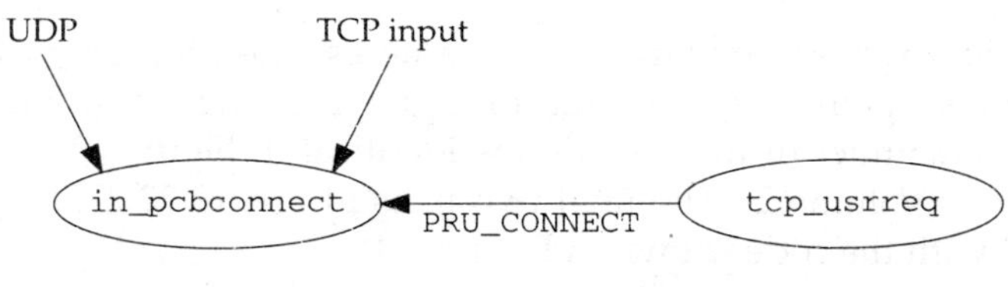

Figure 7.1 Summary of Net/3 calls to `in_pcbconnect`.

The calls by TCP input and UDP to `in_pcbconnect` remain the same, but the processing of a TCP `connect` (the `PRU_CONNECT` request) now calls the new function `tcp_connect` (Figures 12.2 and 12.3), which in turn calls the new function `in_pcbladdr`. Additionally, when a T/TCP client implicitly opens a connection using `sendto` or `sendmsg`, the resulting `PRU_SEND` or `PRU_SEND_EOF` request also calls `tcp_connect`. We show this new arrangement in Figure 7.2.

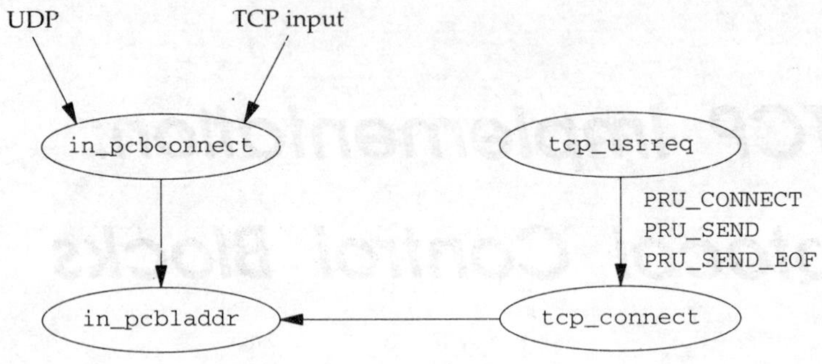

Figure 7.2 New arrangement of `in_pcbconnect` and `in_pcbladdr`.

7.2 `in_pcbladdr` Function

The first part of `in_pcbladdr` is shown in Figure 7.3. This portion shows only the arguments and the first two lines of code, which are identical to lines 138–139 on p. 736 of Volume 2.

in_pcb.c

```
136 int
137 in_pcbladdr(inp, nam, plocal_sin)
138 struct inpcb *inp;
139 struct mbuf *nam;
140 struct sockaddr_in **plocal_sin;
141 {
142     struct in_ifaddr *ia;
143     struct sockaddr_in *ifaddr;
144     struct sockaddr_in *sin = mtod(nam, struct sockaddr_in *);

145     if (nam->m_len != sizeof(*sin))
146         return (EINVAL);
```

in_pcb.c

Figure 7.3 `in_pcbladdr` function: first part.

136–140 The first two arguments are the same as those for `in_pcbconnect` and the third argument is a pointer to a pointer through which the local address is returned.

The remainder of this function is identical to Figures 22.25, 22.26, and most of Figure 22.27 of Volume 2. The final two lines in Figure 22.27, lines 225–226 on p. 739, are replaced with the code shown in Figure 7.4.

in_pcb.c

```
232         /*
233          * Don't call in_pcblookup here; return interface in
234          * plocal_sin and exit to caller, who will do the lookup.
235          */
236         *plocal_sin = &ia->ia_addr;

237     }
238     return (0);
239 }
```

in_pcb.c

Figure 7.4 in_pcbladdr function: final part.

232–236 If the caller specifies a wildcard local address, a pointer to the `sockaddr_in` structure is returned through the third argument.

Basically all that is done by `in_pcbladdr` is some error checking, special case handling of a destination address of 0.0.0.0 or 255.255.255.255, followed by an assignment of the local IP address (if the caller hasn't assigned one yet). The remainder of the processing required by a `connect` is handled by `in_pcbconnect`.

7.3 in_pcbconnect Function

Figure 7.5 shows the `in_pcbconnect` function. This function performs a call to `in_pcbladdr`, shown in the previous section, followed by the code from Figure 22.28, p. 739 of Volume 2.

Assign local address

255–259 The local IP address is calculated by `in_pcbladdr`, and returned through the `ifaddr` pointer, if the caller hasn't bound one to the socket yet.

Verify socket pair is unique

260–266 `in_pcblookup` verifies that the socket pair is unique. In the normal case of a TCP client calling `connect` (when the client has not bound a local port or a local address to the socket), the local port is 0, so `in_pcblookup` always returns 0, since a local port of 0 will not match any existing PCB.

Bind local address and local port, if not already bound

267–271 If a local address and a local port have not been bound to the socket, `in_pcbbind` assigns both. If a local address has not been bound, but the local port is nonzero, the local address returned by `in_pcbladdr` is stored in the PCB. It is not possible to bind a local address but still have a local port of 0, since the call to `in_pcbbind` to bind the local address also causes an ephemeral port to be assigned to the socket.

272–273 The foreign address and foreign port (arguments to `in_pcbconnect`) are stored in the PCB.

in_pcb.c

```
int
in_pcbconnect(inp, nam)
struct inpcb *inp;
struct mbuf *nam;
{
    struct sockaddr_in *ifaddr;
    struct sockaddr_in *sin = mtod(nam, struct sockaddr_in *);
    int     error;

    /*
     * Call inner function to assign local interface address.
     */
    if (error = in_pcbladdr(inp, nam, &ifaddr))
        return (error);

    if (in_pcblookup(inp->inp_head,
                     sin->sin_addr,
                     sin->sin_port,
                 inp->inp_laddr.s_addr ? inp->inp_laddr : ifaddr->sin_addr,
                     inp->inp_lport,
                     0))
        return (EADDRINUSE);
    if (inp->inp_laddr.s_addr == INADDR_ANY) {
        if (inp->inp_lport == 0)
            (void) in_pcbbind(inp, (struct mbuf *) 0);
        inp->inp_laddr = ifaddr->sin_addr;
    }
    inp->inp_faddr = sin->sin_addr;
    inp->inp_fport = sin->sin_port;
    return (0);
}
```

in_pcb.c

Figure 7.5 `in_pcbconnect` function.

7.4 Summary

The T/TCP modifications remove all the code from the `in_pcbconnect` function that calculates the local address and creates a new function named `in_pcbladdr` to perform this task. `in_pcbconnect` calls this function, and then completes the normal connection processing. This allows the processing of a T/TCP client connection request (either explicit using `connect` or implicit using `sendto`) to call `in_pcbladdr` to calculate the local address. The T/TCP client processing then duplicates the processing steps shown in Figure 7.5, but T/TCP allows a connection request to proceed even if there exists a previous incarnation of the same connection that is in the TIME_WAIT state. Normal TCP would not allow this to happen; instead `in_pcbconnect` would return `EADDRINUSE` from Figure 7.5.

8

T/TCP Implementation: TCP Overview

8.1 Introduction

This chapter covers the global changes that are made to the TCP data structures and functions for T/TCP. Two global variables are added: tcp_ccgen, the global CC counter, and tcp_do_rfc1644, a flag that specifies whether the CC options should be used. The protocol switch entry for TCP is modified to allow an implied open–close and four new variables are added to the TCP control block.

A simple change is made to the tcp_slowtimo function that measures the duration of every connection. Given the duration of a connection, T/TCP will truncate the TIME_WAIT state if the duration is less than MSL, as we described in Section 4.4.

8.2 Code Introduction

There are no new source files added with T/TCP, but some new variables are required.

Global Variables

Figure 8.1 shows the new global variables that are added with T/TCP, which we encounter throughout the TCP functions.

Variable	Datatype	Description
tcp_ccgen	tcp_cc	next CC value to send
tcp_do_rfc1644	int	if true (default), send CC or CCnew options

Figure 8.1 Global variables added with T/TCP.

We showed some examples of the `tcp_ccgen` variable in Chapter 3. We mentioned in Section 6.5 that the `tcp_cc` data type is `typedefed` to be an unsigned long. A value of 0 for a `tcp_cc` variable means undefined. The `tcp_ccgen` variable is always accessed as

```
tp->cc_send = CC_INC(tcp_ccgen);
```

where `cc_send` is a new member of the TCP control block (shown later in Figure 8.3). The macro `CC_INC` is defined in `<netinet/tcp_seq.h>` as

```
#define CC_INC(c)    (++(c) == 0 ? ++(c) : (c))
```

Since the value is incremented before it is used, `tcp_ccgen` is initialized to 0 and its first value is 1.

Four macros are defined to compare CC values using modular arithmetic: `CC_LT`, `CC_LEQ`, `CC_GT`, and `CC_GEQ`. These four macros are identical to the four `SEQ_`*xx* macros defined on p. 810 of Volume 2.

The variable `tcp_do_rfc1644` is similar to the variable `tcp_do_rfc1323` introduced in Volume 2. If `tcp_do_rfc1644` is 0, TCP will not send a CC or a CCnew option to the other end.

Statistics

Five new counters are added with T/TCP, which we show in Figure 8.2. These are added to the `tcpstat` structure, which is shown on p. 798 of Volume 2.

`tcpstat` member	Description
`tcps_taook`	#received SYNs with TAO OK
`tcps_taofail`	#received SYNs with CC option but fail TAO test
`tcps_badccecho`	#SYN/ACK segments with incorrect CCecho option
`tcps_impliedack`	#new SYNs that imply ACK of previous incarnation
`tcps_ccdrop`	#segments dropped because of invalid CC option

Figure 8.2 Additional T/TCP statistics maintained in the `tcpstat` structure.

The `netstat` program must be modified to print the values of these new members.

8.3 TCP `protosw` Structure

We mentioned in Chapter 5 that the `pr_flags` member of the TCP `protosw` entry, `inetsw[2]` (p. 801 of Volume 2) changes with T/TCP. The new socket-layer flag `PR_IMPLOPCL` must be included, along with the existing flags `PR_CONNREQUIRED` and `PR_WANTRCVD`. In `sosend`, this new flag allows a `sendto` on an unconnected socket if the caller specifies a destination address, and it causes the `PRU_SEND_EOF` request to be issued instead of the `PRU_SEND` request when the `MSG_EOF` flag is specified.

A related change to the `protosw` entry, which is not required by T/TCP, is to define the function named `tcp_sysctl` as the `pr_sysctl` member. This allows the system administrator to modify the values of some of the variables that control the operation of TCP by using the `sysctl` program with the prefix `net.inet.tcp`. (The Net/3 code in Volume 2 only provided `sysctl` control over some IP, ICMP, and UDP variables, through the functions `ip_sysctl`, `icmp_sysctl`, and `udp_sysctl`.) We show the `tcp_sysctl` function in Figure 12.6.

8.4 TCP Control Block

Four new variables are added to the TCP control block, the `tcpcb` structure shown on pp. 804–805 of Volume 2. Rather than showing the entire structure, we show only the new members in Figure 8.3.

Variable	Datatype	Description
`t_duration`	`u_long`	connection duration in 500-ms ticks
`t_maxopd`	`u_short`	MSS plus length of normal options
`cc_send`	`tcp_cc`	CC value to send to peer
`cc_recv`	`tcp_cc`	CC value received from peer

Figure 8.3 New members of `tcpcb` structure added with T/TCP.

`t_duration` is needed to determine if T/TCP can truncate the TIME_WAIT state, as we discussed in Section 4.4. Its value starts at 0 when a control block is created and is then incremented every 500 ms by `tcp_slowtimo` (Section 8.6).

`t_maxopd` is maintained for convenience in the code. It is the value of the existing `t_maxseg` member, plus the number of bytes normally occupied by TCP options. `t_maxseg` is the number of bytes of data per segment. For example, on an Ethernet with an MTU of 1500 bytes, if both timestamps and T/TCP are in use, `t_maxopd` will be 1460 and `t_maxseg` will be 1440. The difference of 20 bytes accounts for 12 bytes for the timestamp option plus 8 bytes for the CC option (Figure 2.4). `t_maxopd` and `t_maxseg` are both calculated and stored in the `tcp_mssrcvd` function.

The last two variables are taken from RFC 1644 and examples were shown of these three variables in Chapter 2. If the CC options were used by both hosts for a connection, `cc_recv` will be nonzero.

Six new flags are defined for the `t_flags` member of the TCP control block. These are shown in Figure 8.4 and are in addition to the nine flags shown in Figure 24.14, p. 805 of Volume 2.

`t_flags`	Description
TF_SENDSYN	send SYN (hidden state flag for half-synchronized connection)
TF_SENDFIN	send FIN (hidden state flag)
TF_SENDCCNEW	send CCnew option instead of CC option for active open
TF_NOPUSH	do not send segment just to empty send buffer
TF_RCVD_CC	set when other side sends CC option in SYN
TF_REQ_CC	have/will request CC option in SYN

Figure 8.4 New `t_flags` values with T/TCP.

Don't confuse the T/TCP flag `TF_SENDFIN`, which means TCP needs to send a FIN, with the existing flag `TF_SENTFIN`, which means a FIN has been sent.

> The names `TF_SENDSYN` and `TF_SENDFIN` are taken from Bob Braden's T/TCP implementation. The FreeBSD implementation changed these two names to `TF_NEEDSYN` and `TF_NEEDFIN`. We chose the former names, since the new flags specify that the control flags must be *sent*, whereas the latter have the incorrect implication of needing a SYN or a FIN to be received. Be careful, however, because with the chosen names there is only one character difference between the T/TCP `TF_SENDFIN` flag and the existing `TF_SENTFIN` flag (which indicates that TCP has already sent a FIN).

We describe the `TF_NOPUSH` and `TF_SENDCCNEW` flags in the next chapter, Figures 9.3 and 9.7 respectively.

8.5 `tcp_init` Function

No explicit initialization is required of any T/TCP variables, and the `tcp_init` function in Volume 2 is unchanged. The global `tcp_ccgen` is an uninitialized external that defaults to 0 by the rules of C. This is OK because the `CC_INC` macro defined in Section 8.2 increments the variable before using it, so the first value of `tcp_ccgen` after a reboot will be 1.

T/TCP also requires that the TAO cache be cleared on a reboot, but that is handled implicitly because the IP routing table is initialized on a reboot. Each time a new `rtentry` structure is added to the routing table, `rtrequest` initializes the structure to 0 (p. 610 of Volume 2). This means the three TAO variables in the `rmxp_tao` structure (Figure 6.3) default to 0. An initial value of 0 for `tao_cc` is required by T/TCP when a new TAO entry is created for a new host.

8.6 `tcp_slowtimo` Function

A one-line addition is made to one of the two TCP timing functions: for each TCP control block the `t_duration` member is incremented each time the 500-ms timer is processed, the `tcp_slowtimo` function shown on p. 823 of Volume 2. The following line

```
tp->t_duration++;
```

is added between lines 94 and 95 of this figure. The purpose of this variable is to measure the length of each connection in 500-ms ticks. If the connection duration is less than the MSL, the TIME_WAIT state can be truncated, as discussed in Section 4.4.

Related to this optimization is the addition of the following constant to the `<netinet/timer.h>` header:

```
#define TCPTV_TWTRUNC  8    /* RTO factor to truncate TIME_WAIT */
```

We'll see in Figures 11.17 and 11.19 that when a T/TCP connection is actively closed, and the value of `t_duration` is less than `TCPTV_MSL` (sixty 500-ms ticks, or 30 seconds), then the duration of the TIME_WAIT state is the current retransmission timeout

(RTO) times TCPTV_TWTRUNC. On a LAN, where the RTO is normally 3 clock ticks or 1.5 seconds, this decreases the TIME_WAIT state to 12 seconds.

8.7 Summary

T/TCP adds two new global variables (tcp_ccgen and tcp_do_rfc1644), four new members to the TCP control block, and five new counters to the TCP statistics structure.

The tcp_slowtimo function is also changed to count the duration of each TCP connection in 500-ms clock ticks. This duration determines whether T/TCP can truncate the TIME_WAIT state if the connection is actively closed.

9

T/TCP Implementation: TCP Output

9.1 Introduction

This chapter describes the changes made to the `tcp_output` function to support T/TCP. This function is called from numerous places within TCP to determine if a segment should be sent, and then to send one if necessary. The following changes are made with T/TCP:

- The two hidden state flags can turn on the `TH_SYN` and `TH_FIN` flags.
- T/TCP allows multiple segments to be sent in the SYN_SENT state, but only if we know that the peer understands T/TCP.
- Sender silly window avoidance must take into account the new `TF_NOPUSH` flag, which we described in Section 3.6.
- The new T/TCP options (CC, CCnew, and CCecho) can be sent.

9.2 `tcp_output` Function

New Automatic Variables

Two new automatic variables are declared within `tcp_output`:

```
struct rmxp_tao *taop;
struct rmxp_tao  tao_noncached;
```

The first is a pointer to the TAO cache for the peer. If no TAO cache entry exists (which shouldn't happen), `taop` points to `tao_noncached` and this latter structure is initialized to 0 (therefore its `tao_cc` value is undefined).

Add Hidden State Flags

At the beginning of `tcp_output` the TCP flags corresponding to the current connection state are fetched from the `tcp_outflags` array. Figure 2.7 shows the flags for each state. The code shown in Figure 9.1 logically ORs in the `TH_FIN` flag and the `TH_SYN` flag, if the corresponding hidden state flag is on.

tcp_output.c

```
again:
    sendalot = 0;
    off = tp->snd_nxt - tp->snd_una;
    win = min(tp->snd_wnd, tp->snd_cwnd);

    flags = tcp_outflags[tp->t_state];
    /*
     * Modify standard flags, adding SYN or FIN if requested by the
     * hidden state flags.
     */
    if (tp->t_flags & TF_SENDFIN)
        flags |= TH_FIN;
    if (tp->t_flags & TF_SENDSYN)
        flags |= TH_SYN;
```

tcp_output.c

Figure 9.1 `tcp_output`: add hidden state flags.

This code is located on pp. 853–854 of Volume 2.

Don't Resend SYN in SYN_SENT State

Figure 9.2 fetches the TAO cache for this peer and a check is made to determine whether a SYN has already been sent. This code is located at the beginning of Figure 26.3, p. 855 of Volume 2.

Fetch TAO cache entry

117–119 The TAO cache for the peer is fetched, and if one doesn't exist, the automatic variable `tao_noncached` is used, and is initialized to 0.

> If this all-zero entry is used, it is never modified. Therefore the `tao_noncached` structure could be statically allocated and initialized to 0, instead of being set to 0 by `bzero`.

Check if client request exceeds MSS

121–133 If the state indicates that a SYN is to be sent, and if a SYN has already been sent, then the `TH_SYN` flag is turned off. This can occur when the application sends more than one MSS of data to a peer using T/TCP (Section 3.6). If the peer understands T/TCP, then multiple segments can be sent, but only the first one should have the SYN flag set. If we don't know that the peer understands T/TCP (`tao_ccsent` is 0) then we do not send multiple segments of data until the three-way handshake is complete.

tcp_output.c

```
len = min(so->so_snd.sb_cc, win) - off;

if ((taop = tcp_gettaocache(tp->t_inpcb)) == NULL) {
    taop = &tao_noncached;
    bzero(taop, sizeof(*taop));
}
/*
 * Turn off SYN bit if it has already been sent.
 * Also, if the segment contains data, and if in the SYN-SENT state,
 * and if we don't know that foreign host supports TAO, suppress
 * sending segment.
 */
if ((flags & TH_SYN) && SEQ_GT(tp->snd_nxt, tp->snd_una)) {
    flags &= ~TH_SYN;
    off--, len++;
    if (len > 0 && tp->t_state == TCPS_SYN_SENT &&
        taop->tao_ccsent == 0)
        return (0);
}
if (len < 0) {
```

tcp_output.c

Figure 9.2 tcp_output: don't resend SYN in SYN_SENT state.

Sender Silly Window Avoidance

Two changes are made to the sender silly window avoidance (p. 859 of Volume 2), shown in Figure 9.3.

tcp_output.c

```
168    if (len) {
169        if (len == tp->t_maxseg)
170            goto send;
171        if ((idle || tp->t_flags & TF_NODELAY) &&
172            (tp->t_flags & TF_NOPUSH) == 0 &&
173            len + off >= so->so_snd.sb_cc)
174            goto send;
175        if (tp->t_force)
176            goto send;
177        if (len >= tp->max_sndwnd / 2 && tp->max_sndwnd > 0)
178            goto send;
179        if (SEQ_LT(tp->snd_nxt, tp->snd_max))
180            goto send;
181    }
```

tcp_output.c

Figure 9.3 tcp_output: determine whether to send segment, with silly window avoidance.

Send a full-sized segment

169–170 If a full-sized segment can be sent, it is sent.

Allow application to disable implied push

171–174 BSD implementations have always sent a segment if an ACK is not currently expected from the peer (`idle` is true), or if the Nagle algorithm is disabled (`TF_NODELAY` is true) *and* TCP is emptying the send buffer. This is sometimes called an *implied push* because each application write causes a segment to be sent, unless prevented by the Nagle algorithm. With T/TCP a new socket option is provided to disable the BSD implied push: `TCP_NOPUSH`, which gets turned into the `TF_NOPUSH` flag. We went through an example of this flag in Section 3.6. In this piece of code we see that a segment is sent only if all three of the following are true:

1. an ACK is not expected (`idle` is true), or if the Nagle algorithm is disabled (`TF_NODELAY` is true), and
2. the `TCP_NOPUSH` socket option is not enabled (the default), and
3. TCP is emptying the send buffer (i.e., all pending data can be sent in a single segment).

Check if receiver's window at least half open

177–178 With normal TCP this entire section of code is not executed for an initial SYN segment, since `len` would be 0. But with T/TCP it is possible to send data before receiving a SYN from the other end. This means the check for whether the receiver's window is now half open needs to be conditioned on `max_sndwnd` being greater than 0. This variable is the maximum window size advertised by the peer, but it is 0 until a window advertisement is received from the peer (i.e., until the peer's SYN is received).

Send if retransmission timer expires

179–180 `snd_nxt` is less than `snd_max` after the retransmission timer expires.

Force Segment with RST or SYN Flag

Lines 179–180 on p. 861 of Volume 2 always send a segment if the SYN flag or RST flag was set. These two lines are replaced with the code in Figure 9.4.

tcp_output.c

```
207     if ((flags & TH_RST) ||
208         ((flags & TH_SYN) && (tp->t_flags & TF_SENDSYN) == 0))
209         goto send;
```

tcp_output.c

Figure 9.4 `tcp_output`: check RST and SYN flags to determine if a segment should be sent.

207–209 If the RST flag is set, a segment is always sent. But if the SYN flag is set, a segment is sent only if the corresponding hidden state flag is off. The reason for this latter restriction can be seen in Figure 2.7. The `TF_SENDSYN` flag is on for the last five of the sever starred states (the half-synchronized states), causing the SYN flag to be turned on in Figure 9.1. But the purpose of this test in `tcp_output` is to send a segment only in the SYN_SENT, SYN_RCVD, SYN_SENT*, or SYN_RCVD* states.

Sending MSS Option

A minor change is made to this piece of code (p. 872 of Volume 2). The Net/3 function `tcp_mss` (with two arguments) is changed to `tcp_msssend` (with just `tp` as an argument). This is because we need to distinguish between calculating the MSS to send versus processing a received MSS option. The Net/3 `tcp_mss` function did both; with T/TCP we use two different functions, `tcp_msssend` and `tcp_mssrcvd`, both of which we describe in the next chapter.

Send a Timestamp Option?

On p. 873 of Volume 2, a timestamp option is sent if the following three conditions are all true: (1) TCP is configured to request the timestamp option, (2) the segment being formed does not contain the RST flag, and (3) either this is an active open or TCP has received a timestamp from the other end (`TF_RCVD_TSTMP`). The test for an active open is whether the SYN flag is on and the ACK flag is off. The T/TCP code for these three tests is shown in Figure 9.5.

tcp_output.c

```
283     /*
284      * Send a timestamp and echo-reply if this is a SYN and our side
285      * wants to use timestamps (TF_REQ_TSTMP is set) or both our side
286      * and our peer have sent timestamps in our SYN's.
287      */
288     if ((tp->t_flags & (TF_REQ_TSTMP | TF_NOOPT)) == TF_REQ_TSTMP &&
289         (flags & TH_RST) == 0 &&
290         ((flags & TH_ACK) == 0 ||
291          (tp->t_flags & TF_RCVD_TSTMP))) {
```

tcp_output.c

Figure 9.5 `tcp_output`: send a timestamp option?

283–291 With T/TCP the first half of the third test changes because we want to send the timestamp option on all initial segments from the client to the server (in the case of a multisegment request, as shown in Figure 3.9), not just the first segment that contains the SYN. The new test for all these initial segments is the absence of the ACK flag.

Send T/TCP CC options

The first test for sending one of the three new CC options is that the `TF_REQ_CC` flag is on (which is enabled by `tcp_newtcpcb` if the global `tcp_do_rfc1644` is nonzero), and the `TF_NOOPT` flag is off, and the RST flag is not on. Which CC option to send depends on the status of the SYN flag and the ACK flag in the outgoing segment. This gives four potential combinations, the first two of which are shown in Figure 9.6. (This code goes between lines 268–269 on p. 873 of Volume 2.)

> The `TF_NOOPT` flag is controlled by the new `TCP_NOOPT` socket option. This socket option appeared in Thomas Skibo's RFC 1323 code (Section 12.7). As noted in Volume 2, this flag (but not the socket option) has been in the Berkeley code since 4.2BSD, but there has normally been

no way to turn it on. If the option is set, TCP does not send any options with its SYN. The option was added to cope with nonconforming TCP implementations that do not ignore unknown TCP options (since the RFC 1323 changes added two new TCP options).

The T/TCP changes do not change the code that determines whether the MSS option should be sent (p. 872 of Volume 2). This code does not send an MSS option if the TF_NOOPT flag is set. But Bob Braden notes in his RFC 1323 code that there is really no reason to suppress sending an MSS option. The MSS option was part of the original RFC 793 specification.

tcp_output.c

```
299     /*
300      * Send CC-family options if our side wants to use them (TF_REQ_CC),
301      * options are allowed (!TF_NOOPT) and it's not a RST.
302      */
303     if ((tp->t_flags & (TF_REQ_CC | TF_NOOPT)) == TF_REQ_CC &&
304         (flags & TH_RST) == 0) {
305         switch (flags & (TH_SYN | TH_ACK)) {
306             /*
307              * This is a normal ACK (no SYN);
308              * send CC if we received CC from our peer.
309              */
310         case TH_ACK:
311             if (!(tp->t_flags & TF_RCVD_CC))
312                 break;
313             /* FALLTHROUGH */

314             /*
315              * We can only get here in T/TCP's SYN_SENT* state, when
316              * we're sending a non-SYN segment without waiting for
317              * the ACK of our SYN. A check earlier in this function
318              * assures that we only do this if our peer understands T/TCP.
319              */
320         case 0:
321             opt[optlen++] = TCPOPT_NOP;
322             opt[optlen++] = TCPOPT_NOP;
323             opt[optlen++] = TCPOPT_CC;
324             opt[optlen++] = TCPOLEN_CC;
325             *(u_int32_t *) & opt[optlen] = htonl(tp->cc_send);
326             optlen += 4;
327             break;
```

tcp_output.c

Figure 9.6 `tcp_output`: send one of the CC options, first part.

SYN off, ACK on

310–313 If the SYN flag is off but the ACK flag is on, this is a normal ACK (i.e., the connection is established). A CC option is sent only if we received one from our peer.

SYN off, ACK off

314–320 The only way both flags can be off is in the SYN_SENT* state when we're sending a non-SYN segment before the connection is established. That is, the client is sending more than one MSS of data. The code in Figure 9.2 ensures that this occurs only if the peer understands T/TCP. In this case a CC option is sent.

Build CC option

321–327 The CC option is built, preceded by two NOPs. The value of cc_send for this connection is sent as the CC option.

The remaining two cases for the SYN flag and the ACK flag are shown in Figure 9.7.

tcp_output.c

```
328            /*
329             * This is our initial SYN (i.e., client active open).
330             * Check whether to send CC or CCnew.
331             */
332        case TH_SYN:
333            opt[optlen++] = TCPOPT_NOP;
334            opt[optlen++] = TCPOPT_NOP;
335            opt[optlen++] =
336                (tp->t_flags & TF_SENDCCNEW) ? TCPOPT_CCNEW : TCPOPT_CC;
337            opt[optlen++] = TCPOLEN_CC;
338            *(u_int32_t *) & opt[optlen] = htonl(tp->cc_send);
339            optlen += 4;
340            break;

341            /*
342             * This is a SYN, ACK (server response to client active open).
343             * Send CC and CCecho if we received CC or CCnew from peer.
344             */
345        case (TH_SYN | TH_ACK):
346            if (tp->t_flags & TF_RCVD_CC) {
347                opt[optlen++] = TCPOPT_NOP;
348                opt[optlen++] = TCPOPT_NOP;
349                opt[optlen++] = TCPOPT_CC;
350                opt[optlen++] = TCPOLEN_CC;
351                *(u_int32_t *) & opt[optlen] = htonl(tp->cc_send);
352                optlen += 4;

353                opt[optlen++] = TCPOPT_NOP;
354                opt[optlen++] = TCPOPT_NOP;
355                opt[optlen++] = TCPOPT_CCECHO;
356                opt[optlen++] = TCPOLEN_CC;
357                *(u_int32_t *) & opt[optlen] = htonl(tp->cc_recv);
358                optlen += 4;
359            }
360            break;
361        }
362    }
363    hdrlen += optlen;
```

tcp_output.c

Figure 9.7 tcp_output: send one of the CC options, second part.

SYN on, ACK off (client active open)

328–340 The SYN flag is on and the ACK flag is off when the client performs an active open. The code in Figure 12.3 sets the flag TF_SENDCCNEW if a CCnew option should be sent instead of a CC option, and also sets the value of cc_send.

SYN on, ACK on (server response to client SYN)

341–360 If both the SYN flag and the ACK flag are on, this is a server's response to the peer's active open. If the peer sent either a CC or a CCnew option (`TF_RCVD_CC` is set), then we send both a CC option (`cc_send`) and a CCecho of the peer's CC value (`cc_recv`).

Adjust TCP header length for TCP options

363 The length of the TCP header is increased by all the TCP options (if any).

Adjust Data Length for TCP Options

`t_maxopd` is a new member of the `tcpcb` structure and is the maximum length of data *and* options in a normal TCP segment. It is possible for the options in a SYN segment (Figures 2.2 and 2.3) to require more room than the options in a non-SYN segment (Figure 2.4), since both the window scale option and the CCecho option appear only in SYN segments. The code in Figure 9.8 adjusts the amount of data to send, based on the size of the TCP options. This code replaces lines 270–277 on p. 873 of Volume 2.

tcp_output.c

```
364     /*
365      * Adjust data length if insertion of options will
366      * bump the packet length beyond the t_maxopd length.
367      * Clear the FIN bit because we cut off the tail of
368      * the segment.
369      */
370     if (len + optlen > tp->t_maxopd) {
371         /*
372          * If there is still more to send, don't close the connection.
373          */
374         flags &= ~TH_FIN;

375         len = tp->t_maxopd - optlen;
376         sendalot = 1;
377     }
```

tcp_output.c

Figure 9.8 `tcp_output`: adjust amount of data to send based on size of TCP options.

364–377 If the size of the data (`len`) plus the size of the options exceeds `t_maxopd`, the amount of data to send is adjusted downward, the FIN flag is turned off (in case it is on), and `sendalot` is turned on (which forces another loop through `tcp_output` after the current segment is sent).

> This code is not specific to T/TCP. It should be used with any TCP option that appears on a segment carrying data (e.g., the RFC 1323 timestamp option).

9.3 Summary

T/TCP adds about 100 lines to the 500-line `tcp_output` function. Most of this code involves sending the new T/TCP options, CC, CCnew, and CCecho.

Additionally, with T/TCP `tcp_output` allows multiple segments to be sent in the SYN_SENT state, if the peer understands T/TCP.

10

T/TCP Implementation: TCP Functions

10.1 Introduction

This chapter covers the miscellaneous TCP functions that change with T/TCP. That is, all the functions other than tcp_output (previous chapter), tcp_input, and tcp_usrreq (next two chapters). This chapter defines two new functions tcp_rtlookup and tcp_gettaocache lookup entries in the TAO cache.

The tcp_close function is modified to save the round-trip time estimators (smoothed estimators of the mean and mean deviation) in the routing table when a connection is closed that used T/TCP. Normally these estimators are saved only if at least 16 full-sized segments were sent on the connection. T/TCP, however, normally sends much less data, but these estimators should be maintained across different connections to the same peer.

The handling of the MSS option also changes with T/TCP. Some of this change is to clean up the overloaded tcp_mss function from Net/3, dividing it into one function that calculates the MSS to send (tcp_mssend) and another function that processes a received MSS option (tcp_mssrcvd). T/TCP also saves the last MSS value received from that peer in the TAO cache. This initializes the sending MSS when T/TCP sends data with a SYN, before receiving the server's SYN and MSS.

The tcp_dooptions function from Net/3 is changed to recognize the three new T/TCP options: CC, CCnew, and CCecho.

10.2 tcp_newtcpcb Function

This function is called when a new socket is created by the PRU_ATTACH request. The five lines of code in Figure 10.1 replace lines 177–178 on p. 833 of Volume 2.

tcp_subr.c

```
180     tp->t_maxseg = tp->t_maxopd = tcp_mssdflt;

181     if (tcp_do_rfc1323)
182         tp->t_flags = (TF_REQ_SCALE | TF_REQ_TSTMP);
183     if (tcp_do_rfc1644)
184         tp->t_flags |= TF_REQ_CC;
```

tcp_subr.c

Figure 10.1 `tcp_newtcpcb` function: T/TCP changes.

180 As mentioned with regard to Figure 8.3, `t_maxopd` is the maximum number of bytes of data plus TCP options that are sent in each segment. It, along with `t_maxseg`, both default to 512 (`tcp_mssdflt`). Since the two are equal, this assumes no TCP options will be sent in each segment. In Figures 10.13 and 10.14, shown later, `t_maxseg` is decreased if either the timestamp option or the CC option (or both) will be sent in each segment.

183–184 If the global `tcp_do_rfc1644` is nonzero (it defaults to 1), the `TF_REQ_CC` flag is set, which causes `tcp_output` to send a CC or a CCnew option with a SYN (Figure 9.6).

10.3 `tcp_rtlookup` Function

The first operation performed by `tcp_mss` (p. 898 of Volume 2) is to fetch the cached route for this connection (which is stored in the `inp_route` member of the Internet PCB), calling `rtalloc` to look up the route if one has not been cached yet for this connection. This operation is now placed into a separate function, `tcp_rtlookup`, which we show in Figure 10.3. This is done because the same operation is performed more often by T/TCP since the routing table entry for the connection contains the TAO information.

438–452 If a route is not yet cached for this connection, `rtalloc` calculates the route. But a route can only be calculated if the foreign address in the PCB is nonzero. Before `rtalloc` is called, the `sockaddr_in` structure within the `route` structure is filled in.

Figure 10.2 shows the `route` structure, one of which is contained within each Internet PCB.

route.h

```
struct route {
    struct rtentry *ro_rt;       /* pointer to struct with information */
    struct sockaddr ro_dst;      /* destination of this route */
};
```

route.h

Figure 10.2 `route` structure.

Figure 10.4 summarizes these structures, assuming the foreign address is 128.32.33.5.

tcp_subr.c

```
struct rtentry *
tcp_rtlookup(inp)
struct inpcb *inp;
{
    struct route *ro;
    struct rtentry *rt;

    ro = &inp->inp_route;
    rt = ro->ro_rt;
    if (rt == NULL) {
        /* No route yet, so try to acquire one */
        if (inp->inp_faddr.s_addr != INADDR_ANY) {
            ro->ro_dst.sa_family = AF_INET;
            ro->ro_dst.sa_len = sizeof(ro->ro_dst);
            ((struct sockaddr_in *) &ro->ro_dst)->sin_addr =
                inp->inp_faddr;
            rtalloc(ro);
            rt = ro->ro_rt;
        }
    }
    return (rt);
}
```

tcp_subr.c

Figure 10.3 `tcp_rtlookup` function.

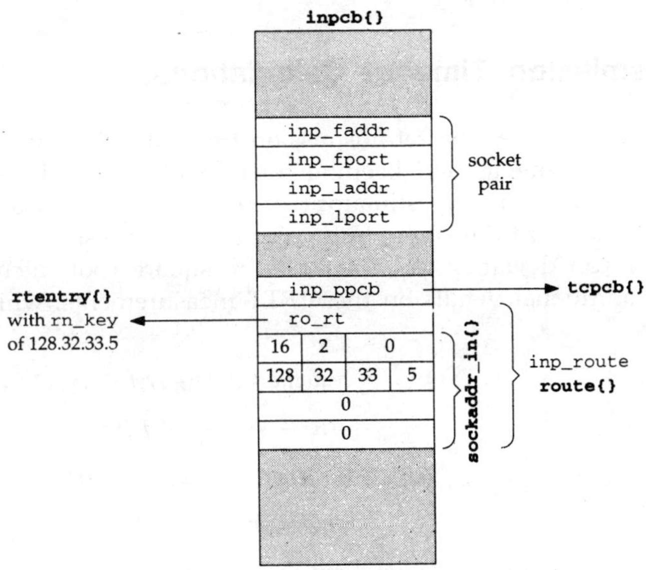

Figure 10.4 Summary of cached route within Internet PCB.

10.4 tcp_gettaocache Function

The TAO information for a given host is maintained in that host's routing table entry, specifically in the `rmx_filler` field of the `rt_metrics` structure (Section 6.5). The function `tcp_gettaocache`, shown in Figure 10.5, returns a pointer to the host's TAO cache.

tcp_subr.c

```
458 struct rmxp_tao *
459 tcp_gettaocache(inp)
460 struct inpcb *inp;
461 {
462     struct rtentry *rt = tcp_rtlookup(inp);

463     /* Make sure this is a host route and is up. */
464     if (rt == NULL ||
465         (rt->rt_flags & (RTF_UP | RTF_HOST)) != (RTF_UP | RTF_HOST))
466         return (NULL);

467     return (rmx_taop(rt->rt_rmx));
468 }
```

tcp_subr.c

Figure 10.5 `tcp_gettaocache` function.

460–468 `tcp_rtlookup` returns the pointer to the foreign host's `rtentry` structure. If that succeeds and if both the `RTF_UP` and `RTF_HOST` flags are on, the `rmx_taop` macro (Figure 6.3) returns a pointer to the `rmxp_tao` structure.

10.5 Retransmission Timeout Calculations

Net/3 TCP calculates the retransmission timeout (RTO) by measuring the round-trip time of data segments and keeping track of a smoothed RTT estimator (*srtt*) and a smoothed mean deviation estimator (*rttvar*). The mean deviation is a good approximation of the standard deviation, but easier to compute since, unlike the standard deviation, the mean deviation does not require square root calculations. [Jacobson 1988] provides additional details on these RTT measurements, which lead to the following equations:

$$delta = data - srtt$$

$$srtt \leftarrow srtt + g \times delta$$

$$rttvar \leftarrow rttvar + h(\,|\,delta\,|\, - rttvar)$$

$$RTO = srtt + 4 \times rttvar$$

where *delta* is the difference between the measured round-trip time just obtained (*data*) and the current smoothed RTT estimator (*srtt*); *g* is the gain applied to the RTT estimator and equals ⅛; and *h* is the gain applied to the mean deviation estimator and equals ¼. The two gains and the multiplier 4 in the RTO calculation are purposely powers of 2, so they can be calculated using shift operations instead of multiplying or dividing.

Chapter 25 of Volume 2 provides details on how these values are maintained using fixed-point integers.

On a normal TCP connection there are usually multiple RTTs to sample when calculating the two estimators *srtt* and *rttvar*, at least two samples given the minimal TCP connection shown in Figure 1.9. Furthermore under certain conditions Net/3 will maintain these two estimators over multiple connections between the same hosts. This is done by the `tcp_close` function, when a connection is closed, if at least 16 RTT samples were obtained and if the routing table entry for the peer is not the default route. The values are stored in the `rmx_rtt` and `rmx_rttvar` members of the `rt_metrics` structure in the routing table entry. The two estimators *srtt* and *rttvar* are initialized to the values from the routing table entry by `tcp_mssrcvd` (Section 10.8) when a new connection is initialized.

The problem that arises with T/TCP is that a minimal connection involves only one RTT measurement, and since fewer than 16 samples is the norm, nothing is maintained between successive T/TCP connections between the same peers. This means T/TCP never has a good estimate of what the RTO should be when the first segment is sent. Section 25.8 of Volume 2 discusses how the initialization done by `tcp_newtcpcb` causes the first RTO to be 6 seconds.

While it is not hard to have `tcp_close` save the smoothed estimators for a T/TCP connection even if fewer than 16 samples are collected (we'll see the changes in Section 10.6), the question is this: how are the new estimators merged with the previous estimators? Unfortunately, this is still a research problem [Paxson 1995a].

To understand the different possibilities, consider Figure 10.6. One hundred 400-byte UDP datagrams were sent from one of the author's hosts across the Internet (on a weekday afternoon, normally the most congested time on the Internet) to the echo server on another host. Ninety-three datagrams were returned (7 were lost somewhere on the Internet) and we show the first 91 of these in Figure 10.6. The samples were collected over a 30-minute period and the amount of time between each datagram was a uniformly distributed random number between 0 and 30 seconds. The actual RTTs were obtained by running Tcpdump on the client host. The bullets are the measured RTTs. The other three solid lines (RTO, *srtt*, and *rttvar*, from top to bottom) are calculated from the measured RTT using the formulas shown at the beginning in this section. The calculations were done using floating-point arithmetic, not with the fixed-point integers actually used in Net/3. The RTO that is shown is the value calculated using the corresponding data point. That is, the RTO for the first data point (about 2200 ms) is calculated using the first data point, and would be used as RTO for the next segment that is sent.

Although the measured RTTs average just under 800 ms (the author's client system is behind a dialup PPP link to the Internet and the server was across the country), the 26th sample has an RTT of almost 1400 ms and a few more after this point are around 1000 ms. As noted in [Jacobson 1994], "whenever there are competing connections sharing a path, transient RTT fluctuations of twice the minimum are completely normal (they just represent other connections starting or restarting after a loss) so it is never reasonable for RTO to be less than $2 \times$ RTT."

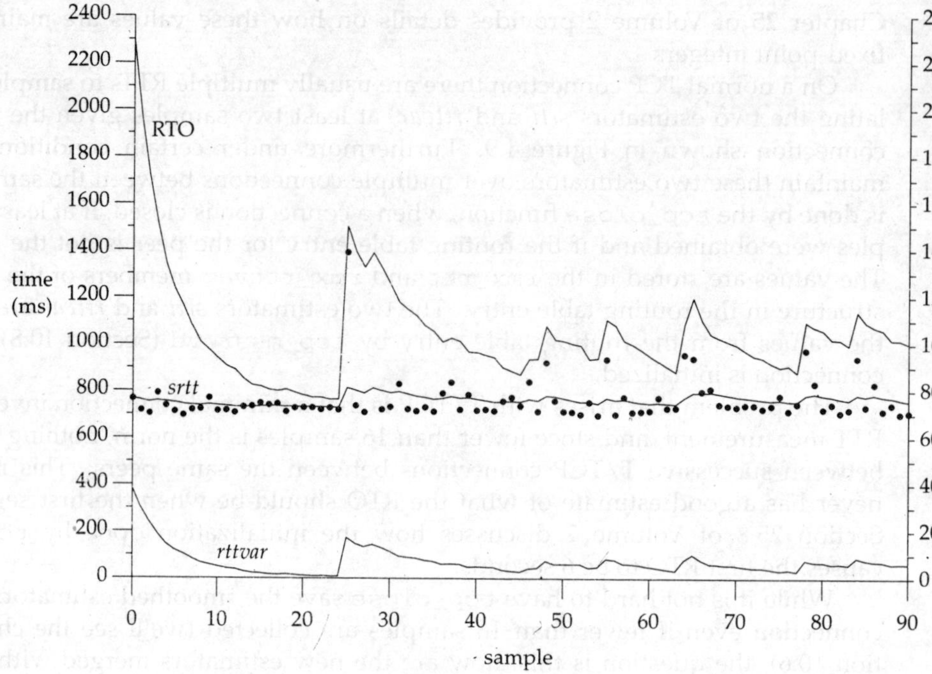

Figure 10.6 RTT measurements and corresponding *RTO*, *srtt*, and *rttvar*.

When new values of the estimators are stored in the routing table entry a decision must be made about how much of the new information is stored, versus the past history. That is, the formulas are

$$savesrtt = g \times savesrtt + (1 - g) \times srtt$$

$$saverttvar = g \times saverttvar + (1 - g) \times rttvar$$

This is a low-pass filter where g is a filter gain constant with a value between 0 and 1, and *savesrtt* and *saverttvar* are the values stored in the routing table entry. When Net/3 updates the routing table values using these equations (when a connection is closed, assuming 16 samples have been made), it uses a gain of 0.5: the new value stored in the routing table is one-half of the old value in the routing table plus one-half of the current estimator. Bob Braden's T/TCP code, however, uses a gain of 0.75.

Figure 10.7 provides a comparison of the normal TCP calculations from Figure 10.6 and the smoothing performed with a filter gain of 0.75. The three dotted lines are the three variables from Figure 10.6 (RTO on top, then *srtt* in the middle, and *rttvar* on the bottom). The three solid lines are the corresponding variables assuming that each data point is a separate T/TCP connection (one RTT measurement per connection) and that the value saved in the routing table between each connection uses a filter gain of 0.75. Realize the difference: the dotted lines assume a single TCP connection with 91 RTT samples over a 30-minute period, whereas the solid lines assume 91 separate T/TCP

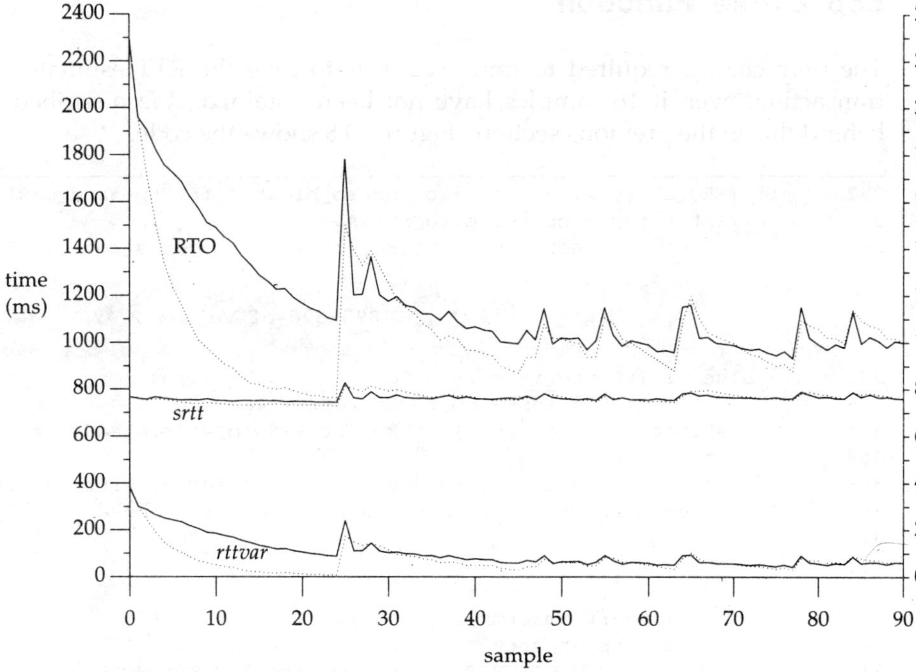

Figure 10.7 Comparison of TCP smoothing versus T/TCP smoothing.

connections, each with a single RTT measurement, over the same 30-minute period. The solid lines also assume that the two estimators are merged into the two routing table metrics between each of the 91 connections.

The solid and dotted lines for *srtt* do not differ greatly, but there is a larger difference between the solid and dotted lines for *rttvar*. The solid line for *rttvar* (the T/TCP case) is normally larger than the dotted line (the single TCP connection), giving a higher value for the T/TCP retransmission timeout.

Other factors affect the RTT measurements made by T/TCP. From the client's perspective the measured RTT normally includes either the server processing time or the server's delayed-ACK timer, since the server's reply is normally delayed until either of these events occurs. In Net/3 the delayed-ACK timer expires every 200 ms and the RTT measurements are in 500-ms clock ticks, so the delay of the reply shouldn't be a large factor. Also the processing of T/TCP segments normally involves the slow path through the TCP input processing (the segments are usually not candidates for header prediction, for example), which can add to the measured RTT values. (The difference between the slow path and the fast path, however, is probably negligible compared to the 200-ms delayed-ACK timer.) Finally, if the values stored in the routing table are "old" (say, they were last updated an hour ago), perhaps the current measurements should just replace the values in the routing table when the current transaction is complete, instead of merging in the new measurements with the existing values.

As noted in RFC 1644, more research is needed into the dynamics of TCP, and especially T/TCP, RTT estimation.

10.6 `tcp_close` Function

The only change required to `tcp_close` is to save the RTT estimators for a T/TCP transaction, even if 16 samples have not been obtained. We described the reasoning behind this in the previous section. Figure 10.8 shows the code.

tcp_subr.c

```
252     if (SEQ_LT(tp->iss + so->so_snd.sb_hiwat * 16, tp->snd_max) &&
253         (rt = inp->inp_route.ro_rt) &&
254       ((struct sockaddr_in *) rt_key(rt))->sin_addr.s_addr != INADDR_ANY) {

                      /* pp. 895-896 of Volume 2 */

304     } else if (tp->cc_recv != 0 &&
305                (rt = inp->inp_route.ro_rt) &&
306       ((struct sockaddr_in *) rt_key(rt))->sin_addr.s_addr != INADDR_ANY) {
307         /*
308          * For transactions we need to keep track of srtt and rttvar
309          * even if we don't have 'enough' data for above.
310          */
311         u_long  i;

312         if ((rt->rt_rmx.rmx_locks & RTV_RTT) == 0) {
313             i = tp->t_srtt *
314                 (RTM_RTTUNIT / (PR_SLOWHZ * TCP_RTT_SCALE));
315             if (rt->rt_rmx.rmx_rtt && i)
316                 /*
317                  * Filter this update to 3/4 the old plus
318                  * 1/4 the new values, converting scale.
319                  */
320                 rt->rt_rmx.rmx_rtt =
321                     (3 * rt->rt_rmx.rmx_rtt + i) / 4;
322             else
323                 rt->rt_rmx.rmx_rtt = i;
324         }
325         if ((rt->rt_rmx.rmx_locks & RTV_RTTVAR) == 0) {
326             i = tp->t_rttvar *
327                 (RTM_RTTUNIT / (PR_SLOWHZ * TCP_RTTVAR_SCALE));
328             if (rt->rt_rmx.rmx_rttvar && i)
329                 rt->rt_rmx.rmx_rttvar =
330                     (3 * rt->rt_rmx.rmx_rttvar + i) / 4;
331             else
332                 rt->rt_rmx.rmx_rttvar = i;
333         }
334     }
```

tcp_subr.c

Figure 10.8 `tcp_close` function: save RTT estimators for T/TCP transaction.

Update for T/TCP transactions only

304–311 The metrics in the routing table entry are updated only if T/TCP was used on the connection (`cc_recv` is nonzero), a routing table entry exists, and the route is not the default. Also, the two RTT estimators are updated only if they are not locked (the RTV_RTT and RTV_RTTVAR bits).

Update RTT

312–324 t_srtt is stored as 500-ms clock ticks × 8 and rmx_rtt is stored as microseconds. Therefore t_srtt is multiplied by 1,000,000 (RTM_RTTUNIT) and divided by 2 (ticks/second) times 8. If a value for rmx_rtt already exists, the new value is three-quarters the old value plus one-quarter of the new value. This is a filter gain of 0.75, as discussed in the previous section. Otherwise the new value is stored in rmx_rtt.

Update mean deviation

325–334 The same algorithm is applied to the mean deviation estimator. It too is stored as microseconds, requiring a conversion from the t_rttvar units of ticks × 4.

10.7 tcp_msssend Function

In Net/3 there is a single function, tcp_mss (Section 27.5 of Volume 2), which is called by tcp_input when an MSS option is processed, and by tcp_output when an MSS option is about to be sent. With T/TCP this function is renamed tcp_mssrcvd and it is called by tcp_input after a SYN is received (Figure 10.18, shown later, whether an MSS option is contained in the SYN or not), and by the PRU_SEND and PRU_SEND_EOF requests (Figure 12.4), when an implied connect is performed. A new function, tcp_msssend, which we show in Figure 10.9, is called only by tcp_output when an MSS option is sent.

tcp_input.c

```
int
tcp_msssend(tp)
struct tcpcb *tp;
{
    struct rtentry *rt;
    extern int tcp_mssdflt;

    rt = tcp_rtlookup(tp->t_inpcb);
    if (rt == NULL)
        return (tcp_mssdflt);

    /*
     * If there's an mtu associated with the route, use it,
     * else use the outgoing interface mtu.
     */
    if (rt->rt_rmx.rmx_mtu)
        return (rt->rt_rmx.rmx_mtu - sizeof(struct tcpiphdr));

    return (rt->rt_ifp->if_mtu - sizeof(struct tcpiphdr));
}
```

tcp_input.c

Figure 10.9 tcp_msssend function: return MSS value to send in MSS option.

Fetch routing table entry

1917–1919 The routing table is searched for the peer host, and if an entry is not found, the default of 512 (tcp_mssdflt) is returned. A routing table entry should always be found, unless the peer is unreachable.

Return MSS

1920–1926 If the routing table has an associated MTU (the rmx_mtu member of the rt_metrics structure, which can be stored by the system administrator using the route program), that value is returned. Otherwise the value returned is the outgoing interface MTU minus 40 (e.g., 1460 for an Ethernet). The outgoing interface is known, since the route has been determined by tcp_rtlookup.

> Another way for the MTU metric to be stored in the routing table entry is through path MTU discovery (Section 24.2 of Volume 1), although Net/3 does not yet support this.

This function differs from the normal BSD behavior. The Net/3 code (p. 900 of Volume 2) always announces an MSS of 512 (tcp_mssdflt) if the peer is nonlocal (as determined by the in_localaddr function) and if the rmx_mtu metric is 0.

The intent of the MSS option is to tell the other end how large a segment the sender of the option is prepared to receive. RFC 793 states that the MSS option "communicates the maximum receive segment size at the TCP which sends this segment." On some implementations this could be limited by the maximum size IP datagram that the host is capable of reassembling. On most current systems, however, the reasonable limit is based on the outgoing interface MTU, since TCP performance can degrade if fragmentation occurs and fragments are lost.

The following comments are from Bob Braden's T/TCP source code changes: "Using TCP options unfortunately requires considerable changes to BSD, because its handling of MSS was incorrect. BSD always sent an MSS option, and for a nonlocal network this option contained 536. This is a misunderstanding of the intent of the MSS option, which is to tell the sender what the receiver is prepared to handle. The sending host should then decide what MSS to use, considering both the MSS option it received and the path. When we have MTU discovery, the path is likely to have an MTU larger than 536; then the BSD usage will kill throughput. Hence, this routine only determines what MSS option should be SENT: the local interface MTU minus 40." (The values 536 in these comments should be 512.)

We'll see in the next section (Figure 10.12) that the receiver of the MSS option is the one that reduces the MSS to 512 if the peer is nonlocal.

10.8 tcp_mssrcvd Function

tcp_mssrcvd is called by tcp_input after a SYN is received, and by the PRU_SEND and PRU_SEND_EOF requests, when an implied connect is performed. It is similar to the tcp_mss function from Volume 2, but with enough differences that we need to present the entire function. The main goal of this function is to set the two variables t_maxseg (the maximum amount of data that we send per segment) and t_maxopd (the maximum amount of data plus options that we send per segment). Figure 10.10 shows the first part.

tcp_input.c

```
void
tcp_mssrcvd(tp, offer)
struct tcpcb *tp;
int     offer;
{
    struct rtentry *rt;
    struct ifnet *ifp;
    int     rtt, mss;
    u_long  bufsize;
    struct inpcb *inp;
    struct socket *so;
    struct rmxp_tao *taop;
    int     origoffer = offer;
    extern int tcp_mssdflt;
    extern int tcp_do_rfc1323;
    extern int tcp_do_rfc1644;

    inp = tp->t_inpcb;
    if ((rt = tcp_rtlookup(inp)) == NULL) {
        tp->t_maxopd = tp->t_maxseg = tcp_mssdflt;
        return;
    }
    ifp = rt->rt_ifp;
    so = inp->inp_socket;

    taop = rmx_taop(rt->rt_rmx);
    /*
     * Offer == -1 means we haven't received a SYN yet;
     * use cached value in that case.
     */
    if (offer == -1)
        offer = taop->tao_mssopt;
    /*
     * Offer == 0 means that there was no MSS on the SYN segment,
     * or no value in the TAO Cache.  We use tcp_mssdflt.
     */
    if (offer == 0)
        offer = tcp_mssdflt;
    else
        /*
         * Sanity check: make sure that maxopd will be large
         * enough to allow some data on segments even if all
         * the option space is used (40 bytes).  Otherwise
         * funny things may happen in tcp_output.
         */
        offer = max(offer, 64);
    taop->tao_mssopt = offer;
```

tcp_input.c

Figure 10.10 tcp_mssrcvd function: first part.

Get route to peer and its TAO cache

1771–1777 tcp_rtlookup finds the route to the peer. If for some reason this fails, t_maxseg and t_maxopd are both set to 512 (tcp_mssdflt).

1778–1799 taop points to the TAO cache for this peer that is contained in the routing table entry. If tcp_mssrcvd is called because the process has called sendto (an implied connect, as part of the PRU_SEND and PRU_SEND_EOF requests), offer is set to the value stored in the TAO cache. If this TAO value is 0, offer is set to 512. The value in the TAO cache is updated.

The next part of the function, shown in Figure 10.11, is identical to p. 899 of Volume 2.

tcp_input.c

```
1800        /*
1801         * While we're here, check if there's an initial rtt
1802         * or rttvar.  Convert from the route-table units
1803         * to scaled multiples of the slow timeout timer.
1804         */
1805        if (tp->t_srtt == 0 && (rtt = rt->rt_rmx.rmx_rtt)) {
1806            /*
1807             * XXX the lock bit for RTT indicates that the value
1808             * is also a minimum value; this is subject to time.
1809             */
1810            if (rt->rt_rmx.rmx_locks & RTV_RTT)
1811                tp->t_rttmin = rtt / (RTM_RTTUNIT / PR_SLOWHZ);
1812            tp->t_srtt = rtt / (RTM_RTTUNIT / (PR_SLOWHZ * TCP_RTT_SCALE));
1813            if (rt->rt_rmx.rmx_rttvar)
1814                tp->t_rttvar = rt->rt_rmx.rmx_rttvar /
1815                    (RTM_RTTUNIT / (PR_SLOWHZ * TCP_RTTVAR_SCALE));
1816            else
1817                /* default variation is +- 1 rtt */
1818                tp->t_rttvar =
1819                    tp->t_srtt * TCP_RTTVAR_SCALE / TCP_RTT_SCALE;
1820            TCPT_RANGESET(tp->t_rxtcur,
1821                          ((tp->t_srtt >> 2) + tp->t_rttvar) >> 1,
1822                          tp->t_rttmin, TCPTV_REXMTMAX);
1823        }
```

tcp_input.c

Figure 10.11 tcp_mssrcvd function: initialize RTT variables from routing table metrics.

1800–1823 If there are no RTT measurements yet for the connection (t_srtt is 0) and the rmx_rtt metric is nonzero, then the variables t_srtt, t_rttvar, and t_rxtcur are initialized from the metrics stored in the routing table entry.

1806–1811 If the RTV_RTT bit in the routing metric lock flag is set, it indicates that rmx_rtt should also be used to initialize the minimum RTT for this connection (t_rttmin). By default t_rttmin is initialized to two ticks, so this provides a way for the system administrator to override this default.

The next part of tcp_mssrcvd, shown in Figure 10.12, sets the value of the automatic variable mss.

tcp_input.c

```
1824     /*
1825      * If there's an mtu associated with the route, use it.
1826      */
1827     if (rt->rt_rmx.rmx_mtu)
1828         mss = rt->rt_rmx.rmx_mtu - sizeof(struct tcpiphdr);
1829     else {
1830         mss = ifp->if_mtu - sizeof(struct tcpiphdr);
1831         if (!in_localaddr(inp->inp_faddr))
1832             mss = min(mss, tcp_mssdflt);
1833     }
1834     mss = min(mss, offer);

1835     /*
1836      * t_maxopd contains the maximum length of data AND options
1837      * in a segment; t_maxseg is the amount of data in a normal
1838      * segment.  We need to store this value (t_maxopd) apart
1839      * from t_maxseg, because now every segment can contain options
1840      * therefore we normally have somewhat less data in segments.
1841      */
1842     tp->t_maxopd = mss;
```

tcp_input.c

Figure 10.12 tcp_mssrcvd function: calculate value of mss variable.

1824–1834 If there is an MTU associated with the route (the rmx_mtu metric) then that value is used. Otherwise mss is calculated as the outgoing interface MTU minus 40. Additionally, if the peer is on a different network or perhaps a different subnet (as determined by the in_localaddr function), then the maximum value of mss is 512 (tcp_mssdflt). When an MTU is stored in the routing table entry, the local–nonlocal test is not performed.

Set t_maxopd

1835–1842 t_maxopd is set to mss, the maximum segment size, including data and options.

The next piece of code, shown in Figure 10.13, reduces mss by the size of the options that will appear in every segment.

Decrease mss if timestamp option to be used

1843–1856 mss is decreased by the size of the timestamp option (TCPOLEN_TSTAMP_APPA, or 12 bytes) if either of the following is true:

1. our end will request the timestamp option (TF_REQ_TSTAMP) and we have not received an MSS option from the other end yet (origoffer equals –1), or
2. we have received a timestamp option from the other end.

As the comment in the code notes, since tcp_mssrcvd is called at the end of tcp_dooptions (Figure 10.18), after all the options have been processed, the second test is OK.

tcp_input.c

```
1843     /*
1844      * Adjust mss to leave space for the usual options.  We're
1845      * called from the end of tcp_dooptions so we can use the
1846      * REQ/RCVD flags to see if options will be used.
1847      */
1848     /*
1849      * In case of T/TCP, origoffer == -1 indicates that no segments
1850      * were received yet (i.e., client has called sendto).  In this
1851      * case we just guess, otherwise we do the same as before T/TCP.
1852      */
1853     if ((tp->t_flags & (TF_REQ_TSTMP | TF_NOOPT)) == TF_REQ_TSTMP &&
1854         (origoffer == -1 ||
1855          (tp->t_flags & TF_RCVD_TSTMP) == TF_RCVD_TSTMP))
1856         mss -= TCPOLEN_TSTAMP_APPA;
1857     if ((tp->t_flags & (TF_REQ_CC | TF_NOOPT)) == TF_REQ_CC &&
1858         (origoffer == -1 ||
1859          (tp->t_flags & TF_RCVD_CC) == TF_RCVD_CC))
1860         mss -= TCPOLEN_CC_APPA;

1861 #if (MCLBYTES & (MCLBYTES - 1)) == 0
1862     if (mss > MCLBYTES)
1863         mss &= ~(MCLBYTES - 1);
1864 #else
1865     if (mss > MCLBYTES)
1866         mss = mss / MCLBYTES * MCLBYTES;
1867 #endif
```

tcp_input.c

Figure 10.13 `tcp_mssrcvd` function: decrease `mss` based on options.

Decrease mss if CC option to be used

1857–1860 Similar logic can reduce the value of `mss` by 8 bytes (`TCPOLEN_CC_APPA`).

> The term APPA in the names of the two lengths is because Appendix A of RFC 1323 contained the suggestion that the timestamp option be preceded by two NOPs, to align the two 4-byte timestamp values on 4-byte boundaries. While there is an Appendix A to RFC 1644, it says nothing about alignment of the options. Nevertheless, it makes sense for the code to precede each of the three CC options with two NOPs, as is done in Figure 9.6.

Round MSS down to multiple of MCLBYTES

1861–1867 `mss` is rounded down to a multiple of `MCLBYTES`, the size in bytes of an mbuf cluster (often 1024 or 2048).

> This code is an awful attempt to optimize by using logical operations, instead of a divide and multiply, if `MCLBYTES` is a power of 2. It has been around since Net/1 and should be cleaned up.

Figure 10.14 shows the final part of `tcp_mssrcvd`, which sets the send buffer size and the receive buffer size.

tcp_input.c

```
1868     /*
1869      * If there's a pipesize, change the socket buffer
1870      * to that size.  Make the socket buffers an integral
1871      * number of mss units; if the mss is larger than
1872      * the socket buffer, decrease the mss.
1873      */
1874     if ((bufsize = rt->rt_rmx.rmx_sendpipe) == 0)
1875         bufsize = so->so_snd.sb_hiwat;
1876     if (bufsize < mss)
1877         mss = bufsize;
1878     else {
1879         bufsize = roundup(bufsize, mss);
1880         if (bufsize > sb_max)
1881             bufsize = sb_max;
1882         (void) sbreserve(&so->so_snd, bufsize);
1883     }
1884     tp->t_maxseg = mss;

1885     if ((bufsize = rt->rt_rmx.rmx_recvpipe) == 0)
1886         bufsize = so->so_rcv.sb_hiwat;
1887     if (bufsize > mss) {
1888         bufsize = roundup(bufsize, mss);
1889         if (bufsize > sb_max)
1890             bufsize = sb_max;
1891         (void) sbreserve(&so->so_rcv, bufsize);
1892     }
1893     /*
1894      * Don't force slow-start on local network.
1895      */
1896     if (!in_localaddr(inp->inp_faddr))
1897         tp->snd_cwnd = mss;

1898     if (rt->rt_rmx.rmx_ssthresh) {
1899         /*
1900          * There's some sort of gateway or interface
1901          * buffer limit on the path.  Use this to set
1902          * the slow start threshhold, but set the
1903          * threshold to no less than 2*mss.
1904          */
1905         tp->snd_ssthresh = max(2 * mss, rt->rt_rmx.rmx_ssthresh);
1906     }
1907 }
```

tcp_input.c

Figure 10.14 tcp_mssrcvd function: set send and receive buffer sizes.

Modify socket send buffer size

1868–1883 The rmx_sendpipe and rmx_recvpipe metrics can be set by the system administrator using the route program. bufsize is set to the value of the rmx_sendpipe metric (if defined) or the current value of the socket send buffer's high-water mark. If the value of bufsize is less than mss, then mss is reduced to the value of bufsize.

(This is a way to force a smaller MSS than the default for a given destination.) Otherwise the value of bufsize is rounded up to the next multiple of mss. (The socket buffers should always be a multiple of the segment size.) The upper bound is sb_max, which is 262,144 in Net/3. The socket buffer's high-water mark is set by sbreserve.

Set t_maxseg

1884 t_maxseg is set to the maximum amount of data (excluding normal options) that TCP will send to the peer.

Modify socket receive buffer size

1885–1892 Similar logic is applied to the socket receive buffer high-water mark. For a local connection on an Ethernet, for example, assuming both timestamps and the CC option are in use, t_maxopd will be 1460 and t_maxseg will be 1440 (Figure 2.4). The socket's send buffer size and receive buffer size will both be rounded up from their defaults of 8192 (Figure 16.4, p. 477 of Volume 2) to 8640 (1440×6).

Slow start for nonlocal peer only

1893–1897 If the peer is not on a local network (in_localaddr is false) slow start is initiated by setting the congestion window (snd_cwnd) to one segment.

> Forcing slow start only if the peer is nonlocal is a change with T/TCP. This allows a T/TCP client or server to send multiple segments to a local peer, without incurring the additional RTT latencies required by slow start (Section 3.6). In Net/3, slow start was always performed (p. 902 of Volume 2).

Set slow start threshold

1898–1906 If the slow start threshold metric (rmx_ssthresh) is nonzero, snd_ssthresh is set to that value.

We can see the interaction of the receive buffer size with the MSS and the TAO cache in Figures 3.1 and 3.3. In the first figure the client performs an implied connect, the PRU_SEND_EOF request calls tcp_mssrcvd with an offer of –1, and the function finds a tao_mssopt of 0 for the server (since the client just rebooted). The default of 512 is used, and with only the CC option in use (we disabled timestamps for the examples in Chapter 2) this value is decreased by 8 bytes (the options) to become 504. Note that 8192 rounded up to a multiple of 504 becomes 8568, which is the window advertised by the client's SYN. When the server calls tcp_mssrcvd, however, it has received the client's SYN with an MSS of 1460. This value is decremented by 8 bytes (the options) to 1452 and 8192 rounded up to a multiple of 1452 is 8712. This is the window advertised in the server's SYN. When the server's SYN is processed by the client (the third segment in the figure), tcp_mssrcvd is called again by the client, this time with an offer of 1460. This increases the client's t_maxopd to 1460 and the client's t_maxseg to 1452, and the client's receive buffer is rounded up to 8712. This is the window advertised by the client in its ACK of the server's SYN.

In Figure 3.3, when the client performs the implied connect, the value of tao_mssopt is now 1460—the last value received from this peer. The client advertises a window of 8712, the multiple of 1452 greater than 8192.

10.9 tcp_dooptions Function

In the Net/1 and Net/2 releases, tcp_dooptions recognized only the NOP, EOL, and MSS options, and the function had three arguments. When support was added for the window scale and timestamp options in Net/3, the number of arguments increased to seven (p. 933 of Volume 2), three of which are just for the timestamp option. With support now required for the CC, CCnew, and CCecho options, instead of adding even more arguments, the number of arguments was decreased to five, and a different technique is used to return information about which options are present, and their respective values.

Figure 10.15 shows the tcpopt structure. One of these structures is allocated in tcp_input (the only function that calls tcp_dooptions) and a pointer to the structure is passed to tcp_dooptions, which fills in the structure. tcp_input uses the values stored in the structure as it is processing the received segment.

tcp_var.h

```
struct tcpopt {
    u_long  to_flag;            /* TOF_xxx flags */
    u_long  to_tsval;           /* timestamp value */
    u_long  to_tsecr;           /* timestamp echo reply */
    tcp_cc  to_cc;              /* CC or CCnew value */
    tcp_cc  to_ccecho;          /* CCecho value */
};
```

tcp_var.h

Figure 10.15 tcpopt structure, which is filled in by tcp_dooptions.

Figure 10.16 shows the four values that can be combined in the to_flag member.

to_flag	Description
TOF_CC	CC option present
TOF_CCNEW	CCnew option present
TOF_CCECHO	CCecho option present
TOF_TS	timestamp option present

Figure 10.16 to_flag values.

Figure 10.17 shows the declaration of the function with its arguments. The first four arguments are the same as in Net/3, but the fifth argument replaces the final three arguments from the Net/3 version.

tcp_input.c

```
void
tcp_dooptions(tp, cp, cnt, ti, to)
struct tcpcb *tp;
u_char *cp;
int     cnt;
struct tcpiphdr *ti;
struct tcpopt *to;
{
```

tcp_input.c

Figure 10.17 tcp_dooptions function: arguments.

We will not show the processing of the EOL, NOP, MSS, window scale, and time stamp options, because the code is nearly the same as that on pp. 933–935 of Volume 2. (The differences deal with the new arguments that we just discussed.) Figure 10.18 shows the final part of the function, which processes the three new options with T/TCP.

Check length and whether to process option

1580–1584 The option length is verified (it must be 6 for all three of the CC options). To process a received CC option, we must be sending the option (the `TF_REQ_CC` flag is set by `tcp_newtcpcb` if the kernel's `tcp_do_rfc1644` flag is set) and the `TF_NOOPT` flag must not be set. (This latter flag prevents TCP from sending any options with its SYN.)

Set corresponding flag and copy 4-byte value

1585–1588 The corresponding `to_flag` value is set. The 4-byte value of the option is stored in the `to_cc` member of the `tcpopt` structure and converted to host byte order.

1589–1595 If this is a SYN segment, the `TF_RCVD_CC` flag is set for the connection, since we have received a CC option.

CCnew and CCecho options

1596–1623 The processing steps for the CCnew and CCecho options are similar to those for the CC option. But an additional check is made that the received segment contains the SYN flag, since the CCnew and CCecho options are valid only on SYN segments.

> Although the `TOF_CCNEW` flag is correctly set, it is never examined. This is because in Figure 11.6 the cached CC value is invalidated (i.e., set to 0) if a CC option is not present. If a CCnew option is present, `cc_recv` is still set correctly (notice that both the CC and CCnew options in Figure 10.18 store the value in `to_cc`) and when the three-way handshake completes (Figure 11.14), the cached value, `tao_cc`, is copied from `cc_recv`.

Process received MSS

625–1626 The local variable `mss` is either the value of the MSS option (if present) or 0 if the option was not present. In either case `tcp_mssrcvd` sets the variables `t_maxseg` and `t_maxopd`. This function must be called at the end of `tcp_dooptions`, since `tcp_mssrcvd` uses the `TF_RCVD_TSTMP` and `TF_RCVD_CC` flags, as noted in Figure 10.13.

10.10 `tcp_reass` Function

When a server receives a SYN that contains data, assuming either the TAO test fails or the segment doesn't contain a CC option, `tcp_input` queues the data, waiting for the three-way handshake to complete. In Figure 11.6 the state is set to SYN_RCVD, a branch is made to `trimthenstep6`, and at the label `dodata` (p. 988 of Volume 2), the macro `TCP_REASS` finds that the state is not ESTABLISHED, calling `tcp_reass` to add the segment to the out-of-order queue for the connection. (The data isn't really out of order; it just arrived before the three-way handshake is complete. Nevertheless, the two statistics counters `tcps_rcvoopack` and `tcps_rcvoobyte` at the bottom of Figure 27.19, p. 912 of Volume 2, are incorrectly incremented.)

tcp_input.c

```
        case TCPOPT_CC:
            if (optlen != TCPOLEN_CC)
                continue;
            if ((tp->t_flags & (TF_REQ_CC | TF_NOOPT)) != TF_REQ_CC)
                continue;       /* we're not sending CC opts */
            to->to_flag |= TOF_CC;
            bcopy((char *) cp + 2, (char *) &to->to_cc,
                  sizeof(to->to_cc));
            NTOHL(to->to_cc);
            /*
             * A CC or CCnew option received in a SYN makes
             * it OK to send CC in subsequent segments.
             */
            if (ti->ti_flags & TH_SYN)
                tp->t_flags |= TF_RCVD_CC;
            break;

        case TCPOPT_CCNEW:
            if (optlen != TCPOLEN_CC)
                continue;
            if ((tp->t_flags & (TF_REQ_CC | TF_NOOPT)) != TF_REQ_CC)
                continue;       /* we're not sending CC opts */
            if (!(ti->ti_flags & TH_SYN))
                continue;
            to->to_flag |= TOF_CCNEW;
            bcopy((char *) cp + 2, (char *) &to->to_cc,
                  sizeof(to->to_cc));
            NTOHL(to->to_cc);
            /*
             * A CC or CCnew option received in a SYN makes
             * it OK to send CC in subsequent segments.
             */
            tp->t_flags |= TF_RCVD_CC;
            break;

        case TCPOPT_CCECHO:
            if (optlen != TCPOLEN_CC)
                continue;
            if (!(ti->ti_flags & TH_SYN))
                continue;
            to->to_flag |= TOF_CCECHO;
            bcopy((char *) cp + 2, (char *) &to->to_ccecho,
                  sizeof(to->to_ccecho));
            NTOHL(to->to_ccecho);
            break;
        }
    }
    if (ti->ti_flags & TH_SYN)
        tcp_mssrcvd(tp, mss);   /* sets t_maxseg */
}
```

tcp_input.c

Figure 10.18 `tcp_dooptions` function: processing of new T/TCP options.

When the ACK of the server's SYN arrives later (normally the third segment of the three-way handshake), the case TCPS_SYN_RECEIVED on p. 969 of Volume 2 is executed, moving the connection to the ESTABLISHED state and calling tcp_reass with a second argument of 0, to present the queued data to the process. But in Figure 11.14 we'll see that this call to tcp_reass is skipped if there is data in the new segment or if the FIN flag is set, since either condition causes a call to TCP_REASS at the label dodata. The problem is that this call to TCP_REASS won't force queued data to be presented to the process if the new segment completely overlaps a previous segment

The fix to tcp_reass is trivial: replace the return at line 106 on p. 912 of Volume 2 with a branch to the label present.

10.11 Summary

The TAO information for a given host is maintained in the routing table entry. The function tcp_gettaocache fetches the cache value for a host, and it calls tcp_rtlookup to look up the host, if the route is not already in the PCB's route cache.

T/TCP modifies the tcp_close function to save the two estimators *srtt* and *rttvar* in the routing table for T/TCP connections, even if fewer than 16 full-sized segments were sent on the connection. This allows the next T/TCP connection to that host to start with the values of these two estimators (assuming the routing table entry does not time out before the next connection).

The Net/3 function tcp_mss is split into two functions with T/TCP: tcp_mssrcvd and tcp_msssend. The former is called when an MSS option is received, and the latter when an MSS option is sent. The latter differs from the normal BSD behavior in that it normally announces an MSS equal to the outgoing interface MTU minus the size of the TCP and IP headers. BSD systems would announce an MSS of 512 for a nonlocal peer.

The Net/3 tcp_dooptions function changes with T/TCP. Numerous function arguments are removed and placed in a structure instead. This allows the function to process new options (such as the three new ones added with T/TCP) without adding more function arguments.

11

T/TCP Implementation: TCP Input

11.1 Introduction

Most of the changes required by T/TCP are in the tcp_input function. One change that occurs throughout this function is the new arguments and return values for tcp_dooptions (Section 10.9). We do not show every piece of code that is affected by this change.

Figure 11.1 is a redo of Figure 28.1, pp. 924–925 of Volume 2, with the T/TCP changes shown in a bolder font.

Our presentation of the changes to tcp_input follows the same order as the flow through the function.

11.2 Preliminary Processing

Three new automatic variables are defined, one of which is the tcpopt structure used by tcp_dooptions. The following lines replace line 190 on p. 926 of Volume 2.

```
struct tcpopt to;               /* options in this segment */
struct rmxp_tao *taop;          /* pointer to our TAO cache entry */
struct rmxp_tao tao_noncached;  /* in case there's no cached entry */

bzero((char *)&to, sizeof(to));
tcpstat.tcps_rcvtotal++;
```

The initialization of the tcpopt structure to 0 is important: this sets the to_cc member (the received CC value) to 0, which means it is undefined.

```
void
tcp_input()
{
    checksum TCP header and data;
    skip over IP/TCP headers in mbuf;
findpcb:
    locate PCB for segment;
    if (not found)
        goto dropwithreset;
    reset idle time to 0 and keepalive timer to 2 hours;
    process options if not LISTEN state;
    if (packet matched by header prediction) {
        completely process received segment;
        return;
    }

    switch (tp->t_state) {
    case TCPS_LISTEN:
        if SYN flag set, accept new connection request;
        perform TAO test;
        goto trimthenstep6;

    case TCPS_SYN_SENT:
        check CCecho option;
        if ACK of our SYN, connection completed;
trimthenstep6:
        trim any data not within window;
        if (ACK flag set)
            goto processack;
        goto step6;

    case TCPS_LAST_ACK:
    case TCPS_CLOSING:
    case TCPS_TIME_WAIT:
        check for new SYN as implied ACK of previous incarnation;
    }

    process RFC 1323 timestamp;
    check CC option;
    check if some data bytes are within the receive window;
    trim data segment to fit within window;
    if (RST flag set) {
        process depending on state;
        goto drop;
    }
```

```
    if (ACK flag off)
        if (SYN_RCVD || half-synchronized)
            goto step6;
        else
            goto drop;

    if (ACK flag set) {
        if (SYN_RCVD state)
            passive open or simultaneous open complete;
        if (duplicate ACK)
            fast recovery algorithm;
processack:
        update RTT estimators if segment timed;
        if (no data was ACKed)
            goto step6;
        open congestion window;
        remove ACKed data from send buffer;
        change state if in FIN_WAIT_1, CLOSING, or LAST_ACK state;
    }

step6:
    update window information;
    process URG flag;
dodata:
    process data in segment, add to reassembly queue;

    if (FIN flag is set)
        process depending on state;

    if (SO_DEBUG socket option)
        tcp_trace(TA_INPUT);

    if (need output || ACK now)
        tcp_output();
    return;

dropafterack:
    tcp_output() to generate ACK;
    return;
dropwithreset:
    tcp_respond() to generate RST;
    return;

drop:
    if (SO_DEBUG socket option)
        tcp_trace(TA_DROP);
    return;
}
```

Figure 11.1 Summary of TCP input processing steps: T/TCP changes are shown in a bold font.

In Net/3 the only branch back to the label `findpcb` is when a new SYN is processed for a connection that is still in the TIME_WAIT state (p. 958 of Volume 2). But there's a bug because the two lines of code

```
m->m_data += sizeof(struct tcpiphdr) + off - sizeof(struct tcphdr);
m->m_len  -= sizeof(struct tcpiphdr) + off - sizeof(struct tcphdr);
```

which occur twice after `findpcb`, are executed a second time after the `goto`. (The two lines of code appear once in p. 940 and again on p. 941 of Volume 2; only one of the two instances is executed, depending on whether or not the segment is matched by header prediction.) This has never been a problem prior to T/TCP, because SYNs rarely carried data and the bug shows up only if a new SYN carrying data arrives for a connection that is in the TIME_WAIT state. With T/TCP, however, there will be a second branch back to `findpcb` (Figure 11.11, shown later, which handles the implied ACK that we showed in Figure 4.7) and the SYN being processed will probably carry data. Therefore the two lines of code must be moved before `findpcb`, as shown in Figure 11.2.

tcp_input.c

```
    /*
     * Skip over TCP, IP headers, and TCP options in mbuf.
     * optp & ti still point into TCP header, but that's OK.
     */
    m->m_data += sizeof(struct tcpiphdr) + off - sizeof(struct tcphdr);
    m->m_len -= sizeof(struct tcpiphdr) + off - sizeof(struct tcphdr);

    /*
     * Locate pcb for segment.
     */
  findpcb:
```

tcp_input.c

Figure 11.2 `tcp_input`: modify mbuf pointer and length before `findpcb`.

These two lines are then removed from pp. 940 and 941 of Volume 2.

The next change occurs at line 327 on p. 931 of Volume 2, the creation of a new socket when a segment arrives for a listening socket. After `t_state` is set to `TCPS_LISTEN`, the two flags `TF_NOPUSH` and `TF_NOOPT` must be carried over from the listening socket to the new socket:

```
tp->t_flags |= tp0->t_flags & (TF_NOPUSH|TF_NOOPT);
```

where `tp0` is an automatic variable that points to the `tcpcb` for the listening socket.

The call to `tcp_dooptions` at lines 344–345 on p. 932 of Volume 2 is changed to use the new calling sequence (Section 10.9):

```
if (optp && tp->t_state != TCPS_LISTEN)
    tcp_dooptions(tp, optp, optlen, ti, &to);
```

11.3 Header Prediction

The initial test for whether header prediction can be applied (p. 936 of Volume 2) needs to check that the hidden state flags are off. If either of these flags is on, they may need to be turned off by the slow path processing in `tcp_input`. Figure 11.3 shows the new test.

tcp_input.c

```
398     if (tp->t_state == TCPS_ESTABLISHED &&
399         (tiflags & (TH_SYN | TH_FIN | TH_RST | TH_URG | TH_ACK)) == TH_ACK &&
400           ((tp->t_flags & (TF_SENDSYN | TF_SENDFIN)) == 0) &&
401           ((to.to_flag & TOF_TS) == 0 ||
402            TSTMP_GEQ(to.to_tsval, tp->ts_recent)) &&
403     /*
404      * Using the CC option is compulsory if once started:
405      *   the segment is OK if no T/TCP was negotiated or
406      *   if the segment has a CC option equal to CCrecv
407      */
408     ((tp->t_flags & (TF_REQ_CC | TF_RCVD_CC)) != (TF_REQ_CC | TF_RCVD_CC)
409      (to.to_flag & TOF_CC) != 0 && to.to_cc == tp->cc_recv) &&
410          ti->ti_seq == tp->rcv_nxt &&
411          tiwin && tiwin == tp->snd_wnd &&
412          tp->snd_nxt == tp->snd_max) {

413          /*
414           * If last ACK falls within this segment's sequence numbers,
415           * record the timestamp.
416           * NOTE that the test is modified according to the latest
417           * proposal of the tcplw@cray.com list (Braden 1993/04/26).
418           */
419          if ((to.to_flag & TOF_TS) != 0 &&
420              SEQ_LEQ(ti->ti_seq, tp->last_ack_sent)) {
421              tp->ts_recent_age = tcp_now;
422              tp->ts_recent = to.to_tsval;
423          }
```

tcp_input.c

Figure 11.3 `tcp_input`: can header prediction be applied?

Verify hidden state flags are off

400 The first change here is to verify that the `TF_SENDSYN` and `TF_SENDFIN` flags are both off.

Check timestamp option (if present)

401–402 The next change deals with the modified `tcp_dooptions` function: instead of testing `ts_present`, the `TOF_TS` bit in `to_flag` is tested, and if a timestamp is present, its value is in `to_tsval` and not `ts_val`.

Verify CC if T/TCP is being used

403–409 Finally, if T/TCP was not negotiated (we requested the CC option but didn't receive it from the other end, or we didn't even request it) the `if` tests continue. If T/TCP is being used then the received segment must contain a CC option and the CC value must equal `cc_recv` for the `if` tests to continue.

We expect header prediction to be used infrequently for short T/TCP transactions. This is because in the minimal T/TCP exchange the first two segments have control flags set (SYN and FIN) that fail the second test in Figure 11.3. These T/TCP segments are processed by the slow path through `tcp_input`. But longer connections (e.g., bulk data transfer) between two hosts that support T/TCP will use the CC option and can benefit from header prediction.

Update `ts_recent` from received timestamp

413–423 The test for whether `ts_recent` should be updated differs from the one on lines 371–372 on p. 936 of Volume 2. The reason for the newer test in Figure 11.3 is detailed on pp. 868–870 of Volume 2.

11.4 Initiation of Passive Open

We now replace all the code on p. 945 of Volume 2: the final part of processing a received SYN for a socket in the LISTEN state. This is the initiation of a passive open when the server receives a SYN from a client. (We do not duplicate the code on pp. 942–943 of Volume 2, which performs the initial processing in this state.) Figure 11.4 shows the first part of this code.

Get TAO entry for client

551–554 `tcp_gettaocache` looks up the TAO entry for this client. If an entry is not found, the automatic variable is used after being set to all zero.

Process options and initialize sequence numbers

555–564 `tcp_dooptions` processes any options (this function was not called earlier because the connection is in the LISTEN state). The initial send sequence number (`iss`) and the initial receive sequence number (`irs`) are initialized. All the sequence number variables in the control block are initialized by `tcp_sendseqinit` and `tcp_rcvseqinit`.

Update send window

565–570 `tiwin` is the window advertised by the client in the received SYN (p. 930 of Volume 2). It is the initial send window for the new socket. Normally the send window is not updated until a segment is received with an ACK (p. 982 of Volume 2). But T/TCP needs to use the value in the received SYN, even though the segment does not contain an ACK. This window affects how much data the server can immediately send to the client in the reply (the second segment of the minimal three-segment T/TCP exchange).

Set `cc_send` and `cc_recv`

571–572 `cc_send` is set from `tcp_ccgen` and `cc_recv` is set to the CC value if a CC option was present. If a CC option was not present, since `to` is initialized to 0 at the beginning of this function, `cc_recv` will be 0 (undefined).

tcp_input.c

```
        tp->t_template = tcp_template(tp);
        if (tp->t_template == 0) {
            tp = tcp_drop(tp, ENOBUFS);
            dropsocket = 0; /* socket is already gone */
            goto drop;
        }
        if ((taop = tcp_gettaocache(inp)) == NULL) {
            taop = &tao_noncached;
            bzero(taop, sizeof(*taop));
        }
        if (optp)
            tcp_dooptions(tp, optp, optlen, ti, &to);
        if (iss)
            tp->iss = iss;
        else
            tp->iss = tcp_iss;
        tcp_iss += TCP_ISSINCR / 4;
        tp->irs = ti->ti_seq;
        tcp_sendseqinit(tp);
        tcp_rcvseqinit(tp);
        /*
         * Initialization of the tcpcb for transaction:
         *   set SND.WND = SEG.WND,
         *   initialize CCsend and CCrecv.
         */
        tp->snd_wnd = tiwin;     /* initial send-window */
        tp->cc_send = CC_INC(tcp_ccgen);
        tp->cc_recv = to.to_cc;
```

tcp_input.c

Figure 11.4 `tcp_input`: get TAO entry, initialize control block for transaction.

Figure 11.5 performs the TAO test on the received segment.

Perform TAO test

573–587 The TAO test is performed only if the segment contains a CC option. The TAO test succeeds if the received CC value is nonzero and if it is greater than the cached value for this client (`tao_cc`).

TAO test succeeded; update TAO cache for client

588–594 The cached value for this client is updated and the connection state is set to ESTABLISHED*. (The hidden state variable is set a few lines later, which makes this the half-synchronized starred state.)

Determine whether to delay ACK or not

595–606 If the segment contains a FIN or if the segment contains data, then the client application must be coded to use T/TCP (i.e., it called `sendto` specifying `MSG_EOF` and could not have called `connect`, `write`, and `shutdown`). In this case the ACK is delayed, to try to let the server's response piggyback on the server's SYN/ACK.

tcp_input.c

```
    /*
     * Perform TAO test on incoming CC (SEG.CC) option, if any.
     * - compare SEG.CC against cached CC from the same host,
     *  if any.
     * - if SEG.CC > cached value, SYN must be new and is accepted
     *  immediately: save new CC in the cache, mark the socket
     *  connected, enter ESTABLISHED state, turn on flag to
     *  send a SYN in the next segment.
     *  A virtual advertised window is set in rcv_adv to
     *  initialize SWS prevention.  Then enter normal segment
     *  processing: drop SYN, process data and FIN.
     * - otherwise do a normal 3-way handshake.
     */
    if ((to.to_flag & TOF_CC) != 0) {
        if (taop->tao_cc != 0 && CC_GT(to.to_cc, taop->tao_cc)) {
            /*
             * There was a CC option on the received SYN
             * and the TAO test succeeded.
             */
            tcpstat.tcps_taook++;
            taop->tao_cc = to.to_cc;
            tp->t_state = TCPS_ESTABLISHED;

            /*
             * If there is a FIN, or if there is data and the
             * connection is local, then delay SYN,ACK(SYN) in
             * the hope of piggybacking it on a response
             * segment.  Otherwise must send ACK now in case
             * the other side is slow starting.
             */
            if ((tiflags & TH_FIN) ||
                (ti->ti_len != 0 && in_localaddr(inp->inp_faddr)))
                tp->t_flags |= (TF_DELACK | TF_SENDSYN);
            else
                tp->t_flags |= (TF_ACKNOW | TF_SENDSYN);
            tp->rcv_adv += tp->rcv_wnd;
            tcpstat.tcps_connects++;
            soisconnected(so);
            tp->t_timer[TCPT_KEEP] = TCPTV_KEEP_INIT;
            dropsocket = 0;     /* committed to socket */
            tcpstat.tcps_accepts++;
            goto trimthenstep6;
        } else if (taop->tao_cc != 0)
            tcpstat.tcps_taofail++;
```

tcp_input.c

Figure 11.5 `tcp_input`: perform TAO test on received segment.

If the FIN flag is not set, but the segment contains data, then since the segment also contains the SYN flag, this is probably the first segment of multiple segments of data from the client. In this case, if the client is not on a local subnet (`in_localaddr` returns 0), then the acknowledgment is not delayed because the client is probably in slow start.

Set `rcv_adv`

607 `rcv_adv` is defined as the highest advertised sequence number plus one (Figure 24.18, p. 809 of Volume 2). But the `tcp_rcvseqinit` macro in Figure 11.4 initialized it to the received sequence number plus one. At this point in the processing, `rcv_wnd` will be the size of the socket's receive buffer, from p. 941 of Volume 2. Therefore, by adding `rcv_wnd` to `rcv_adv`, the latter points just beyond the current receive window. `rcv_adv` must be initialized here because its value is used in the silly window avoidance in `tcp_output` (p. 879 of Volume 2). `rcv_adv` is set at the end of `tcp_output`, normally when the first segment is sent (which in this case would be the server SYN/ACK in response to the client's SYN). But with T/TCP `rcv_adv` needs to be set the first time through `tcp_output`, since we may be sending data with the first segment that we send.

Complete connection

608–609 The incrementing of `tcps_connects` and calling of `soisconnected` are normally done when the third segment of the three-way handshake is received (p. 969 of Volume 2). Both are done now with T/TCP since the connection is complete.

610–613 The connection-establishment timer is set to 75 seconds, the `dropsocket` flag is set to 0, and a branch is made to the label `trimthenstep6`.

Figure 11.6 shows the remainder of the processing for a SYN received for a socket in the LISTEN state.

tcp_input.c

```
616             } else {
617                 /*
618                  * No CC option, but maybe CCnew:
619                  * invalidate cached value.
620                  */
621                 taop->tao_cc = 0;
622             }
623             /*
624              * TAO test failed or there was no CC option,
625              * do a standard 3-way handshake.
626              */
627             tp->t_flags |= TF_ACKNOW;
628             tp->t_state = TCPS_SYN_RECEIVED;
629             tp->t_timer[TCPT_KEEP] = TCPTV_KEEP_INIT;
630             dropsocket = 0;        /* committed to socket */
631             tcpstat.tcps_accepts++;
632             goto trimthenstep6;
633         }
```

tcp_input.c

Figure 11.6 `tcp_input`: LISTEN processing: no CC option or TAO test failed.

No CC option; set cached CC to undefined

616–622 The `else` clause is when a CC option is not present (the first `if` in Figure 11.5). The cached CC value is set to 0 (undefined). If it turns out that the segment contains a

CCnew option, the cached value is updated when the three-way handshake competes (Figure 11.14).

Three-way handshake required

623–633 At this point either there was no CC option in the segment, or a CC option was present but the TAO test failed. In either case, a three-way handshake is required. The remaining lines are identical to the end of Figure 28.17, p. 945 of Volume 2: the `TF_ACKNOW` flag is set and the state is set to SYN_RCVD, which will cause a SYN/ACK to be sent immediately.

11.5 Initiation of Active Open

The next `case` is for the SYN_SENT state. TCP previously sent a SYN (an active open) and is now processing the server's reply. Figure 11.7 shows the first portion of the processing. The corresponding Net/3 code starts on p. 947 of Volume 2.

Get TAO cache entry

647–650 The TAO cache entry for the server is fetched. Since we recently sent the SYN, there should be an entry.

Handle incorrect ACK

651–666 If the segment contains an ACK but the acknowledgment field is incorrect (see Figure 28.19, p. 947 of Volume 2, for a description of the fields being compared), our reply depends on whether we have a cached `tao_ccsent` for this host. If `tao_ccsent` is nonzero, we just drop the segment, instead of sending an RST. This is the processing step labeled "discard" in Figure 4.7. But if `tao_ccsent` is 0, we drop the segment and send an RST, which is the normal TCP response to an incorrect ACK in this state.

Check for RST

667–671 If the RST flag is set in the received segment, it is dropped. Additionally, if the ACK flag is set, the server TCP actively refused the connection and the error `ECONNREFUSED` is returned to the calling process.

SYN must be set

672–673 If the SYN flag is not set, the segment is dropped.

674–677 The initial send window is set to the window advertised in the segment and `cc_recv` is set to the received CC value (which is 0 if a CC option was not present). `irs` is the initial receive sequence number and the `tcp_rcvseqinit` macro initializes the receive variables in the control block.

The code now separates depending on whether the segment contains an ACK that acknowledges our SYN (the normal case) or whether the ACK flag is not on (a simultaneous open, the less frequent case). Figure 11.8 shows the normal case.

tcp_input.c

```
        /*
         * If the state is SYN_SENT:
         *  if seg contains an ACK, but not for our SYN, drop the input.
         *  if seg contains a RST, then drop the connection.
         *  if seg does not contain SYN, then drop it.
         * Otherwise this is an acceptable SYN segment
         *  initialize tp->rcv_nxt and tp->irs
         *  if seg contains ack then advance tp->snd_una
         *  if SYN has been acked change to ESTABLISHED else SYN_RCVD state
         *  arrange for segment to be acked (eventually)
         *  continue processing rest of data/controls, beginning with URG
         */
    case TCPS_SYN_SENT:
        if ((taop = tcp_gettaocache(inp)) == NULL) {
            taop = &tao_noncached;
            bzero(taop, sizeof(*taop));
        }
        if ((tiflags & TH_ACK) &&
            (SEQ_LEQ(ti->ti_ack, tp->iss) ||
             SEQ_GT(ti->ti_ack, tp->snd_max))) {
            /*
             * If we have a cached CCsent for the remote host,
             * hence we haven't just crashed and restarted,
             * do not send a RST.  This may be a retransmission
             * from the other side after our earlier ACK was lost.
             * Our new SYN, when it arrives, will serve as the
             * needed ACK.
             */
            if (taop->tao_ccsent != 0)
                goto drop;
            else
                goto dropwithreset;
        }
        if (tiflags & TH_RST) {
            if (tiflags & TH_ACK)
                tp = tcp_drop(tp, ECONNREFUSED);
            goto drop;
        }
        if ((tiflags & TH_SYN) == 0)
            goto drop;
        tp->snd_wnd = ti->ti_win;   /* initial send window */
        tp->cc_recv = to.to_cc; /* foreign CC */

        tp->irs = ti->ti_seq;
        tcp_rcvseqinit(tp);
```

tcp_input.c

Figure 11.7 `tcp_input`: initial processing of SYN_SENT state.

tcp_input.c

```
    if (tiflags & TH_ACK) {
        /*
         * Our SYN was acked.  If segment contains CCecho
         * option, check it to make sure this segment really
         * matches our SYN.  If not, just drop it as old
         * duplicate, but send an RST if we're still playing
         * by the old rules.
         */
        if ((to.to_flag & TOF_CCECHO) &&
            tp->cc_send != to.to_ccecho) {
            if (taop->tao_ccsent != 0) {
                tcpstat.tcps_badccecho++;
                goto drop;
            } else
                goto dropwithreset;
        }
        tcpstat.tcps_connects++;
        soisconnected(so);

        /* Do window scaling on this connection? */
        if ((tp->t_flags & (TF_RCVD_SCALE | TF_REQ_SCALE)) ==
            (TF_RCVD_SCALE | TF_REQ_SCALE)) {
            tp->snd_scale = tp->requested_s_scale;
            tp->rcv_scale = tp->request_r_scale;
        }
        /* Segment is acceptable, update cache if undefined. */
        if (taop->tao_ccsent == 0)
            taop->tao_ccsent = to.to_ccecho;

        tp->rcv_adv += tp->rcv_wnd;
        tp->snd_una++;      /* SYN is acked */
        /*
         * If there's data, delay ACK; if there's also a FIN
         * ACKNOW will be turned on later.
         */
        if (ti->ti_len != 0)
            tp->t_flags |= TF_DELACK;
        else
            tp->t_flags |= TF_ACKNOW;
        /*
         * Received <SYN,ACK> in SYN_SENT[*] state.
         * Transitions:
         *  SYN_SENT  --> ESTABLISHED
         *  SYN_SENT* --> FIN_WAIT_1
         */
        if (tp->t_flags & TF_SENDFIN) {
            tp->t_state = TCPS_FIN_WAIT_1;
            tp->t_flags &= ~TF_SENDFIN;
            tiflags &= ~TH_SYN;
        } else
            tp->t_state = TCPS_ESTABLISHED;
```

tcp_input.c

Figure 11.8 tcp_input: processing of SYN/ACK response in SYN_SENT state.

ACK flag is on

678 If the ACK flag is on, we know from the tests of `ti_ack` in Figure 11.7 that the ACK acknowledges our SYN.

Check CCecho value, if present

679–693 If the segment contains a CCecho option but the CCecho value does not equal the CC value that we sent, the segment is dropped. (This "should never happen" unless the other end is broken, since the received ACK acknowledges our SYN.) If we didn't even send a CC option (`tao_ccsent` is 0) then an RST is sent also.

Mark socket connected and process window scale option

694–701 The socket is marked as connected and the window scale option is processed (if present).

> Bob Braden's T/TCP implementation incorrectly had these two lines of code before the test of the CCecho value.

Update TAO cache if undefined

702–704 The segment is acceptable, so if our TAO cache is undefined for this server (i.e., after the client host reboots and sends a CCnew option), we update it with the received CCecho value (which is 0 if a CCecho option is not present).

Set `rcv_adv`

705–706 `rcv_adv` is updated, as described with Figure 11.4. `snd_una` (the oldest unacknowledged sequence number) is incremented by one since our SYN was ACKed.

Determine whether to delay ACK or not

707–714 If the server sent data with its SYN, we delay our ACK; otherwise we send our ACK immediately (since this is probably the second segment of the three-way handshake). The ACK is delayed because if the server's SYN contains data, the server is probably using T/TCP and there's no need to send an immediate ACK in case we receive additional segments containing the rest of the reply. But if it turns out that this segment also contains the server's FIN (the second segment of the minimal three-segment T/TCP exchange), the code in Figure 11.18 will turn on the `TF_ACKNOW` flag, to send the ACK immediately.

715–726 We know `t_state` equals `TCPS_SYN_SENT`, but if the hidden state flag `TF_SENDFIN` is also set, our state was really SYN_SENT*. In this case we transition to the FIN_WAIT_1 state. (This is really a combination of two state transitions if you look at the state transition diagram in RFC 1644. The receipt of the SYN in the SYN_SENT* moves to the FIN_WAIT_1* state, and the ACK of our SYN then moves to the FIN_WAIT_1 state.)

The `else` clause corresponding to the `if` at the beginning of Figure 11.8 is shown in Figure 11.9. It corresponds to a simultaneous open: we sent a SYN and then received a SYN without an ACK. This figure replaces lines 581–582 on p. 949 of Volume 2.

tcp_input.c

```
727         } else {
728             /*
729              * Simultaneous open.
730              * Received initial SYN in SYN-SENT[*] state.
731              * If segment contains CC option and there is a
732              * cached CC, apply TAO test; if it succeeds,
733              * connection is half-synchronized.
734              * Otherwise, do 3-way handshake:
735              *        SYN-SENT -> SYN-RECEIVED
736              *        SYN-SENT* -> SYN-RECEIVED*
737              * If there was no CC option, clear cached CC value.
738              */
739             tp->t_flags |= TF_ACKNOW;
740             tp->t_timer[TCPT_REXMT] = 0;
741             if (to.to_flag & TOF_CC) {
742                 if (taop->tao_cc != 0 && CC_GT(to.to_cc, taop->tao_cc)) {
743                     /*
744                      * update cache and make transition:
745                      *          SYN-SENT -> ESTABLISHED*
746                      *          SYN-SENT* -> FIN-WAIT-1*
747                      */
748                     tcpstat.tcps_taook++;
749                     taop->tao_cc = to.to_cc;
750                     if (tp->t_flags & TF_SENDFIN) {
751                         tp->t_state = TCPS_FIN_WAIT_1;
752                         tp->t_flags &= ~TF_SENDFIN;
753                     } else
754                         tp->t_state = TCPS_ESTABLISHED;
755                     tp->t_flags |= TF_SENDSYN;
756                 } else {
757                     tp->t_state = TCPS_SYN_RECEIVED;
758                     if (taop->tao_cc != 0)
759                         tcpstat.tcps_taofail++;
760                 }
761             } else {
762                 /* CCnew or no option => invalidate cache */
763                 taop->tao_cc = 0;
764                 tp->t_state = TCPS_SYN_RECEIVED;
765             }
766         }
```

tcp_input.c

Figure 11.9 `tcp_input`: simultaneous open.

Immediate ACK and turn off retransmission timer

739–740 An ACK is sent immediately and the retransmission timer is turned off. Even though the timer is turned off, since the `TF_ACKNOW` flag is set, `tcp_output` is called at the end of `tcp_input`. When the ACK is sent, the retransmission timer is restarted since at least one data byte (the SYN) is outstanding.

Perform TAO test

741–755 If the segment contains a CC option then the TAO test is applied: the cached value (`tao_cc`) must be nonzero and the received CC value must be greater than the cached value. If the TAO test passes, the cached value is updated with the received CC value, and a transition is made from either the SYN_SENT state to the ESTABLISHED* state, or from the SYN_SENT* state to the FIN_WAIT_1* state.

Tao test fails or no CC option

756–765 If the TAO test fails, the new state is SYN_RCVD. If there was no CC option, the TAO cache is set to 0 (undefined) and the new state is SYN_RCVD.

Figure 11.10 contains the label `trimthenstep6`, which was branched to at the end of processing for the LISTEN state (Figure 11.5). Most of the code in this figure is copied from p. 950 of Volume 2.

tcp_input.c

```
767     trimthenstep6:
768         /*
769          * Advance ti->ti_seq to correspond to first data byte.
770          * If data, trim to stay within window,
771          * dropping FIN if necessary.
772          */
773         ti->ti_seq++;
774         if (ti->ti_len > tp->rcv_wnd) {
775             todrop = ti->ti_len - tp->rcv_wnd;
776             m_adj(m, -todrop);
777             ti->ti_len = tp->rcv_wnd;
778             tiflags &= ~TH_FIN;
779             tcpstat.tcps_rcvpackafterwin++;
780             tcpstat.tcps_rcvbyteafterwin += todrop;
781         }
782         tp->snd_wl1 = ti->ti_seq - 1;
783         tp->rcv_up = ti->ti_seq;
784         /*
785          *  Client side of transaction: already sent SYN and data.
786          *  If the remote host used T/TCP to validate the SYN,
787          *  our data will be ACK'd; if so, enter normal data segment
788          *  processing in the middle of step 5, ack processing.
789          *  Otherwise, goto step 6.
790          */
791         if (tiflags & TH_ACK)
792             goto processack;
793         goto step6;
```

tcp_input.c

Figure 11.10 `tcp_input`: `trimthenstep6` processing after active or passive open processing.

Do not skip ACK processing if client

784–793 If the ACK flag is on, we are the client side of a transaction. That is, our SYN was ACKed and we got here from the SYN_SENT state, not the LISTEN state. In this case we cannot branch to `step6` because that would skip the ACK processing (see Figure 11.1), and if we sent data with our SYN, we need to process the possible ACK of our data. (Normal TCP can skip the ACK processing here, because it never sends data with its SYN.)

The next step in processing is new with T/TCP. Normally the `switch` that begins on p. 942 of Volume 2 only has `case`s for the LISTEN and SYN_SENT states (both of which we've just described). T/TCP also adds `case`s for the LAST_ACK, CLOSING, and TIME_WAIT states, shown in Figure 11.11.

tcp_input.c

```
794        /*
795         * If the state is LAST_ACK or CLOSING or TIME_WAIT:
796         *   if segment contains a SYN and CC [not CCnew] option
797         *   and peer understands T/TCP (cc_recv != 0):
798         *              if state == TIME_WAIT and connection duration > MSL,
799         *                  drop packet and send RST;
800         *
801         *        if SEG.CC > CCrecv then is new SYN, and can implicitly
802         *            ack the FIN (and data) in retransmission queue.
803         *                  Complete close and delete TCPCB.  Then reprocess
804         *                  segment, hoping to find new TCPCB in LISTEN state;
805         *
806         *        else must be old SYN; drop it.
807         *        else do normal processing.
808         */
809    case TCPS_LAST_ACK:
810    case TCPS_CLOSING:
811    case TCPS_TIME_WAIT:
812        if ((tiflags & TH_SYN) &&
813            (to.to_flag & TOF_CC) && tp->cc_recv != 0) {
814            if (tp->t_state == TCPS_TIME_WAIT &&
815                tp->t_duration > TCPTV_MSL)
816                goto dropwithreset;
817            if (CC_GT(to.to_cc, tp->cc_recv)) {
818                tp = tcp_close(tp);
819                tcpstat.tcps_impliedack++;
820                goto findpcb;
821            } else
822                goto drop;
823        }
824        break;                      /* continue normal processing */
825    }
```

tcp_input.c

Figure 11.11 `tcp_input`: initial processing for LAST_ACK, CLOSING, and TIME_WAIT states.

812–813 The following special tests are performed only if the received segment contains a SYN and a CC option and if we have a cached CC value for this host (`cc_recv` is nonzero). Also realize that to be in any of these three states, TCP has sent a FIN and received a FIN (Figure 2.6). In the LAST_ACK and CLOSING states, TCP is awaiting the ACK of the FIN that it sent. So the tests being performed are whether a new SYN in the TIME_WAIT state can safely truncate the TIME_WAIT state, or whether a new SYN in the LAST_ACK or CLOSING states implicitly ACKs the FIN that we sent.

Do not allow truncation of TIME_WAIT state if duration > MSL

814–816 Normally the receipt of a new SYN for a connection that is in the TIME_WAIT state is allowed (p. 958 of Volume 2). This is an implicit truncation of the TIME_WAIT state that Berkeley-derived systems have allowed, at least since Net/1. (The solution to Exercise 18.5 in Volume 1 talks about this feature.) But with T/TCP this is not allowed if the duration of the connection that is in the TIME_WAIT state is greater than the MSL, in which case an RST is sent. We talked about this limitation in Section 4.4.

New SYN is an implied ACK of existing connection

817–820 If the received CC value is greater than the cached CC value, the TAO test is OK (i.e., this is a new SYN). The existing connection is closed and a branch is made back to `findpcb`, hopefully to find a socket in the LISTEN state to process the new SYN. Figure 4.7 showed an example of a server socket that would be in the LAST_ACK state when an implied ACK is processed.

11.6 PAWS: Protection Against Wrapped Sequence Numbers

The PAWS test from p. 952 of Volume 2 remains the same—the code dealing with the timestamp option. The test shown in Figure 11.12 comes after these timestamp tests and verifies the received CC.

tcp_input.c

```
860     /*
861      * T/TCP mechanism:
862      *   If T/TCP was negotiated, and the segment doesn't have CC
863      *   or if its CC is wrong, then drop the segment.
864      *   RST segments do not have to comply with this.
865      */
866     if ((tp->t_flags & (TF_REQ_CC | TF_RCVD_CC)) == (TF_REQ_CC | TF_RCVD_CC) &&
867         ((to.to_flag & TOF_CC) == 0 || tp->cc_recv != to.to_cc) &&
868         (tiflags & TH_RST) == 0) {
869         tcpstat.tcps_ccdrop++;
870         goto dropafterack;
871     }
```

tcp_input.c

Figure 11.12 `tcp_input`: verification of received CC.

860–871 If T/TCP is being used (both of the flags `TF_REQ_CC` and `TF_RCVD_CC` are on) then the received segment must contain a CC option and the CC value must equal the value being used for this connection (`cc_recv`), or the segment is dropped as an old duplicate (but acknowledged, since all duplicate segments are acknowledged). If the segment contains an RST it is not dropped, allowing the RST processing later in the function to handle the segment.

11.7 ACK Processing

On p. 965 of Volume 2, after the RST processing, if the ACK flag is not on, the segment is dropped. This is normal TCP processing. T/TCP changes this, as shown in Figure 11.13.

tcp_input.c

```
1024     /*
1025      * If the ACK bit is off: if in SYN-RECEIVED state or SENDSYN
1026      * flag is on (half-synchronized state), then queue data for
1027      * later processing; else drop segment and return.
1028      */
1029     if ((tiflags & TH_ACK) == 0) {
1030         if (tp->t_state == TCPS_SYN_RECEIVED ||
1031             (tp->t_flags & TF_SENDSYN))
1032             goto step6;
1033         else
1034             goto drop;
1035     }
```

tcp_input.c

Figure 11.13 `tcp_input`: handle segments without ACK flag.

1024–1035 If the ACK flag is off and the state is SYN_RCVD or the `TF_SENDSYN` flag is on (i.e., half-synchronized), a branch is made to `step6`, instead of dropping the segment. This handles the case of a data segment arriving without an ACK before the connection is established, but after the initial SYN (examples of which are segments 2 and 3 in Figure 3.9).

11.8 Completion of Passive Opens and Simultaneous Opens

ACK processing continues as in Chapter 29 of Volume 2. Most of the code on p. 969 remains the same (line 806 is deleted), and the code in Figure 11.14 replaces lines 813–815. At this point we are in the SYN_RCVD state and processing the ACK that completes the three-way handshake. This is the normal processing on the server end of a connection.

Update cached CC value if undefined

1057–1064 The TAO entry for this peer is fetched and if the cached CC value is 0 (undefined), it is updated from the received CC value. Notice that this happens only if the cached value is undefined. Recall that Figure 11.6 explicitly set `tao_cc` to 0 if a CC option was not present (so that this update would occur when the three-way handshake completed) but it did not modify `tao_cc` if the TAO test failed. This latter action is so that an out-of-order SYN does not cause the cached `tao_cc` to change, as we discussed with Figure 4.11.

Transition to new state

1065–1074 The SYN_RCVD state moves to the ESTABLISHED state, the normal TCP state transition for a server completing the three-way handshake. The SYN_RCVD* state moves

tcp_input.c

```
1057        /*
1058         * Upon successful completion of 3-way handshake,
1059         * update cache.CC if it was undefined, pass any queued
1060         * data to the user, and advance state appropriately.
1061         */
1062        if ((taop = tcp_gettaocache(inp)) != NULL &&
1063            taop->tao_cc == 0)
1064            taop->tao_cc = tp->cc_recv;

1065        /*
1066         * Make transitions:
1067         *      SYN-RECEIVED  -> ESTABLISHED
1068         *      SYN-RECEIVED* -> FIN-WAIT-1
1069         */
1070        if (tp->t_flags & TF_SENDFIN) {
1071            tp->t_state = TCPS_FIN_WAIT_1;
1072            tp->t_flags &= ~TF_SENDFIN;
1073        } else
1074            tp->t_state = TCPS_ESTABLISHED;

1075        /*
1076         * If segment contains data or FIN, will call tcp_reass()
1077         * later; if not, do so now to pass queued data to user.
1078         */
1079        if (ti->ti_len == 0 && (tiflags & TH_FIN) == 0)
1080            (void) tcp_reass(tp, (struct tcpiphdr *) 0,
1081                             (struct mbuf *) 0);
1082        tp->snd_wl1 = ti->ti_seq - 1;
1083        /* fall into ... */
```

tcp_input.c

Figure 11.14 `tcp_input`: completion of passive open or simultaneous open.

to the FIN_WAIT_1 state, since the process has closed the sending half of the connection with the `MSG_EOF` flag.

Check for data or FIN

1075–1081 If the segment contains either data or the FIN flag then the macro `TCP_REASS` will be called at the label `dodata` (recall Figure 11.1) to pass any data to the process. Page 988 of Volume 2 shows the call to this macro at the label `dodata` and that code does not change with T/TCP. Otherwise `tcp_reass` is called here with a second argument of 0, to pass any queued data to the process.

11.9 ACK Processing (Continued)

The fast retransmit and fast recovery algorithms (Section 29.4 of Volume 2) remain the same. The code in Figure 11.15 goes between lines 899 and 900 on p. 974 of Volume 2.

tcp_input.c

```
1168        /*
1169         *  If we reach this point, ACK is not a duplicate,
1170         *     i.e., it ACKs something we sent.
1171         */
1172        if (tp->t_flags & TF_SENDSYN) {
1173            /*
1174             *   T/TCP: Connection was half-synchronized, and our
1175             *   SYN has been ACK'd (so connection is now fully
1176             *   synchronized).  Go to non-starred state and
1177             *   increment snd_una for ACK of SYN.
1178             */
1179            tp->t_flags &= ~TF_SENDSYN;
1180            tp->snd_una++;
1181        }
1182    processack:
```

tcp_input.c

Figure 11.15 `tcp_input`: turn off `TF_SENDSYN` if it is on.

Turn off `TF_SENDSYN` hidden state flag

1168–1181 The `TF_SENDSYN` hidden state flag is turned off if it is on. This is because the received ACK acknowledges something we sent, so the connection is no longer half-synchronized. `snd_una` is incremented since the SYN has been ACKed and since the SYN occupies 1 byte of sequence number space.

Figure 11.16 goes between lines 926 and 927 on pp. 976–977 of Volume 2.

tcp_input.c

```
1210        /*
1211         * If no data (only SYN) was ACK'd,
1212         *    skip rest of ACK processing.
1213         */
1214        if (acked == 0)
1215            goto step6;
```

tcp_input.c

Figure 11.16 `tcp_input`: skip remainder of ACK processing if no data ACKed.

Skip remainder of ACK processing if no data ACKed

1210–1215 If no data was acknowledged (only our SYN was ACKed), the remainder of the ACK processing is skipped. This skips over the code that opens the congestion window and removes the ACKed data from the send buffer.

> This test and branch is performed regardless of T/TCP. It corrects the bug discussed at the end of Section 14.12, where the server side of the connection slow starts by sending two back-to-back segments instead of one.

The next change is shown in Figure 11.17, which replaces Figure 29.12, p. 980 of Volume 2. We are in the CLOSING state and processing the ACK that moves the connection to the TIME_WAIT state. T/TCP might allow the TIME_WAIT state to be truncated (Section 4.4).

tcp_input.c

```
1266         /*
1267          * In CLOSING STATE in addition to the processing for
1268          * the ESTABLISHED state if the ACK acknowledges our FIN
1269          * then enter the TIME-WAIT state, otherwise ignore
1270          * the segment.
1271          */
1272     case TCPS_CLOSING:
1273         if (ourfinisacked) {
1274             tp->t_state = TCPS_TIME_WAIT;
1275             tcp_canceltimers(tp);
1276             /* Shorten TIME_WAIT [RFC 1644, p.28] */
1277             if (tp->cc_recv != 0 && tp->t_duration < TCPTV_MSL)
1278                 tp->t_timer[TCPT_2MSL] = tp->t_rxtcur * TCPTV_TWTRUNC;
1279             else
1280                 tp->t_timer[TCPT_2MSL] = 2 * TCPTV_MSL;
1281             soisdisconnected(so);
1282         }
1283         break;
```

tcp_input.c

Figure 11.17 `tcp_input`: receipt of ACK in CLOSING state: set TIME_WAIT timer.

1276–1280 If we received a CC value from the peer and the duration of the connection was less than MSL, the TIME_WAIT timer is set to `TCPTV_TWTRUNC` (8) times the current retransmission timeout. Otherwise the TIME_WAIT timer is set to the normal 2MSL.

11.10 FIN Processing

The next three sections of TCP input processing—updating the window information, urgent mode processing, and the processing of received data—are all unchanged with T/TCP (recall Figure 11.1). Also recall from Section 29.9 of Volume 2 that if the FIN flag is set, but it cannot be acknowledged because of a hole in the sequence space, the code in that section clears the FIN flag. Therefore at this point in the processing we know that the FIN is to be acknowledged.

The next change occurs in FIN processing, which we show in Figure 11.18. The changes replace line 1123 on p. 990 of Volume 2.

Determine whether to delay ACK or not

1414–1424 If the connection is half-synchronized (the `TF_SENDSYN` hidden state flag is on), the ACK is delayed, to try to piggyback the ACK with data. This is typical for a T/TCP server that receives a SYN in the LISTEN state, which causes the `TF_SENDSYN` flag to be set in Figure 11.5. Notice that the delayed-ACK flag was already set in that figure, but here TCP is deciding what to do based on the FIN flag that is also set. If the `TF_SENDSYN` flag is not on, the ACK is not delayed.

The normal transition to the TIME_WAIT state is from the FIN_WAIT_2 state, and this also needs to be modified for T/TCP to allow possible truncation of the TIME_WAIT state (Section 4.4). Figure 11.19 shows this, which replaces lines 1142–1152 on p. 991 of Volume 2.

tcp_input.c

```
    /*
     * If FIN is received ACK the FIN and let the user know
     * that the connection is closing.
     */
    if (tiflags & TH_FIN) {
        if (TCPS_HAVERCVDFIN(tp->t_state) == 0) {
            socantrcvmore(so);
            /*
             *  If connection is half-synchronized
             *  (i.e., TF_SENDSYN flag on) then delay the ACK
             *  so it may be piggybacked when SYN is sent.
             *  Else, since we received a FIN, no more
             *  input can be received, so we send the ACK now.
             */
            if (tp->t_flags & TF_SENDSYN)
                tp->t_flags |= TF_DELACK;
            else
                tp->t_flags |= TF_ACKNOW;
            tp->rcv_nxt++;
        }
```

tcp_input.c

Figure 11.18 tcp_input: decide whether to delay ACK of FIN.

tcp_input.c

```
1443            /*
1444             * In FIN_WAIT_2 state enter the TIME_WAIT state,
1445             * starting the time-wait timer, turning off the other
1446             * standard timers.
1447             */
1448        case TCPS_FIN_WAIT_2:
1449            tp->t_state = TCPS_TIME_WAIT;
1450            tcp_canceltimers(tp);
1451            /* Shorten TIME_WAIT [RFC 1644, p.28] */
1452            if (tp->cc_recv != 0 && tp->t_duration < TCPTV_MSL) {
1453                tp->t_timer[TCPT_2MSL] = tp->t_rxtcur * TCPTV_TWTRUNC;
1454                /* For transaction client, force ACK now. */
1455                tp->t_flags |= TF_ACKNOW;
1456            } else
1457                tp->t_timer[TCPT_2MSL] = 2 * TCPTV_MSL;
1458            soisdisconnected(so);
1459            break;
```

tcp_input.c

Figure 11.19 tcp_input: transition to TIME_WAIT state, possibly truncating the timeout.

Set TIME_WAIT timeout

1451–1453 As in Figure 11.17, the TIME_WAIT state is truncated only if we received a CC option from the peer and the connection duration is less than MSL.

Force immediate ACK of FIN

1454–1455 This transition is normally made in the T/TCP client when the server's response is received along with the server's SYN and FIN. The server's FIN should be ACKed immediately because both ends have sent a FIN so there's no reason to delay the ACK.

> There are two places where the TIME_WAIT timer is restarted: the receipt of an ACK in the TIME_WAIT state and the receipt of a FIN in the TIME_WAIT state (pages 981 and 991 of Volume 2). T/TCP does not change this code. This means that even if the TIME_WAIT state was truncated, if a duplicate ACK or a FIN is received while in that state, the timer is restarted at 2MSL, not at the truncated value. The information required to restart the timer at the truncated value is still available (i.e., the control block), but since the peer had to retransmit, it is more conservative to not truncate the TIME_WAIT state.

11.11 Summary

Most of the T/TCP changes occur in `tcp_input` and most of these changes deal with the opening of new connections.

When a SYN is received in the LISTEN state the TAO test is performed. If the segment passes this test, the segment is not an old duplicate and the three-way handshake is not required. When a SYN is received in the SYN_SENT state, the CCecho option (if present) verifies that the SYN is not an old duplicate. When a SYN is received in the LAST_ACK, CLOSING, or TIME_WAIT state, it is possible for the SYN to be an implicit ACK that completes the closing of the existing incarnation of the connection.

When a connection is closed actively, the TIME_WAIT state is truncated if the duration was less than the MSL.

12

T/TCP Implementation: TCP User Requests

12.1 Introduction

The `tcp_usrreq` function handles all the `PRU_xxx` requests from the socket layer. In this chapter we describe only the `PRU_CONNECT`, `PRU_SEND`, and `PRU_SEND_EOF` requests, because they are the only ones that change with T/TCP. We also describe the `tcp_usrclosed` function, which is called when the process is done sending data, and the `tcp_sysctl` function, which handles the new TCP `sysctl` variables.

We do not describe the changes required to the `tcp_ctloutput` function (Section 30.6 of Volume 2) to handle the setting and fetching of the two new socket options: `TCP_NOPUSH` and `TCP_NOOPT`. The changes required are trivial and self-evident from the source code.

12.2 `PRU_CONNECT` Request

In Net/3 the processing of the `PRU_CONNECT` request by `tcp_usrreq` required about 25 lines of code (p. 1011 of Volume 2). With T/TCP most of the code moves into the `tcp_connect` function (which we show in the next section), leaving only the code shown in Figure 12.1.

tcp_usrreq.c

```
    case PRU_CONNECT:
        if ((error = tcp_connect(tp, nam)) != 0)
            break;
        error = tcp_output(tp);
        break;
```

tcp_usrreq.c

Figure 12.1 `PRU_CONNECT` request.

137–141 tcp_connect performs the steps required for the connection and tcp_output sends the SYN segment (the active open).

When a process calls connect, even if the local host and the host being connected both support T/TCP, the normal three-way handshake still takes place. This is because it is not possible to pass data along with the connect function, causing tcp_output to send only a SYN. To bypass the three-way handshake, the application must avoid connect and use either sendto or sendmsg specifying both data and the peer address of the server.

12.3 tcp_connect Function

The new function tcp_connect performs the processing steps required for an active open. It is called when the process calls connect (the PRU_CONNECT request) or when the process calls either sendto or sendmsg, specifying a peer address to connect to (the PRU_SEND and PRU_SEND_EOF requests). The first part of tcp_connect is shown in Figure 12.2.

Bind local port

308–312 nam points to an Internet socket address structure containing the IP address and port number of the server to which to connect. If a local port has not yet been assigned to the socket (the normal case), in_pcbbind assigns one (p. 732 of Volume 2).

Assign local address, check for uniqueness of socket pair

313–323 in_pcbladdr assigns the local IP address, if one has not yet been bound to the socket (the normal case). in_pcblookup searches for a matching PCB, returning a nonnull pointer if one is found. A match should be found only if the process bound a specific local port, because if in_pcbbind chooses the local port, it chooses one that is not currently in use. But with T/TCP it is more likely for a client to bind the same local port for a set of transactions (Section 4.2).

Existing incarnation exists; check if TIME_WAIT can be truncated

324–332 If a matching PCB was found, the following three tests are made:

1. if the PCB is in the TIME_WAIT state, and
2. if the duration of that connection was less than the MSL, and
3. if the connection used T/TCP (that is, if a CC option or a CCnew option was received from the peer).

If all three are true, the existing PCB is closed by tcp_close. This is the truncation of the TIME_WAIT state that we discuss in Section 4.4, when a new connection reuses the same socket pair and performs an active open.

Complete socket pair in Internet PCB

333–336 If the local address is still the wildcard, the value calculated by in_pcbladdr is saved in the PCB. The foreign address and foreign port are also saved in the PCB.

tcp_usrreq.c

```
int
tcp_connect(tp, nam)
struct tcpcb *tp;
struct mbuf *nam;
{
    struct inpcb *inp = tp->t_inpcb, *oinp;
    struct socket *so = inp->inp_socket;
    struct tcpcb *otp;
    struct sockaddr_in *sin = mtod(nam, struct sockaddr_in *);
    struct sockaddr_in *ifaddr;
    int     error;
    struct rmxp_tao *taop;
    struct rmxp_tao tao_noncached;

    if (inp->inp_lport == 0) {
        error = in_pcbbind(inp, NULL);
        if (error)
            return (error);
    }
    /*
     * Cannot simply call in_pcbconnect, because there might be an
     * earlier incarnation of this same connection still in
     * TIME_WAIT state, creating an ADDRINUSE error.
     */
    error = in_pcbladdr(inp, nam, &ifaddr);
    oinp = in_pcblookup(inp->inp_head,
                        sin->sin_addr, sin->sin_port,
                        inp->inp_laddr.s_addr != INADDR_ANY ?
                            inp->inp_laddr : ifaddr->sin_addr,
                        inp->inp_lport, 0);

    if (oinp) {
        if (oinp != inp && (otp = intotcpcb(oinp)) != NULL &&
            otp->t_state == TCPS_TIME_WAIT &&
            otp->t_duration < TCPTV_MSL &&
            (otp->t_flags & TF_RCVD_CC))
            otp = tcp_close(otp);
        else
            return (EADDRINUSE);
    }
    if (inp->inp_laddr.s_addr == INADDR_ANY)
        inp->inp_laddr = ifaddr->sin_addr;
    inp->inp_faddr = sin->sin_addr;
    inp->inp_fport = sin->sin_port;
```

tcp_usrreq.c

Figure 12.2 tcp_connect function: first part.

The steps in Figure 12.2 are similar to those in the final part of Figure 7.5. The final part of tcp_connect is shown in Figure 12.3. This code is similar to the final part of the PRU_CONNECT request on p. 1011 of Volume 2.

tcp_usrreq.c

```
337        tp->t_template = tcp_template(tp);
338        if (tp->t_template == 0) {
339            in_pcbdisconnect(inp);
340            return (ENOBUFS);
341        }
342        /* Compute window scaling to request.  */
343        while (tp->request_r_scale < TCP_MAX_WINSHIFT &&
344               (TCP_MAXWIN << tp->request_r_scale) < so->so_rcv.sb_hiwat)
345            tp->request_r_scale++;

346        soisconnecting(so);
347        tcpstat.tcps_connattempt++;
348        tp->t_state = TCPS_SYN_SENT;
349        tp->t_timer[TCPT_KEEP] = TCPTV_KEEP_INIT;
350        tp->iss = tcp_iss;
351        tcp_iss += TCP_ISSINCR / 4;
352        tcp_sendseqinit(tp);

353        /*
354         * Generate a CC value for this connection and
355         * check whether CC or CCnew should be used.
356         */
357        if ((taop = tcp_gettaocache(tp->t_inpcb)) == NULL) {
358            taop = &tao_noncached;
359            bzero(taop, sizeof(*taop));
360        }
361        tp->cc_send = CC_INC(tcp_ccgen);
362        if (taop->tao_ccsent != 0 &&
363            CC_GEQ(tp->cc_send, taop->tao_ccsent)) {
364            taop->tao_ccsent = tp->cc_send;
365        } else {
366            taop->tao_ccsent = 0;
367            tp->t_flags |= TF_SENDCCNEW;
368        }

369        return (0);
370 }
```

tcp_usrreq.c

Figure 12.3 `tcp_connect` function: second part.

Initialize IP and TCP headers

337–341 `tcp_template` allocates an mbuf for a copy of the IP and TCP headers, and initializes both headers with as much information as possible.

Calculate window scale factor

342–345 The window scale value for the receive buffer is calculated.

Set socket and connection state

346–349 `soisconnecting` sets the appropriate bits in the socket's state variable, and the state of the TCP connection is set to SYN_SENT. (If the process called `sendto` or sendmsg with a flag of MSG_EOF, instead of connect, we'll see shortly that tcp_usrclosed sets the TF_SENDSYN hidden state flag, moving the connection to the SYN_SENT* state.) The connection-establishment timer is initialized to 75 seconds.

Initialize sequence numbers

350–352 The initial send sequence number is copied from the global tcp_iss and the global is then incremented by TCP_ISSINCR divided by 4. The send sequence numbers are initialized by tcp_sendseqinit.

> The randomization of the ISS that we discussed in Section 3.2 occurs in the macro TCP_ISSINCR.

Generate CC value

353–361 The TAO cache entry for the peer is fetched. The value of the global tcp_ccgen is incremented by CC_INC (Section 8.2) and stored in the T/TCP variable tcp_ccgen. As we noted earlier, the value of tcp_ccgen is incremented for every connection made by the host, regardless of whether the CC options are used or not.

Determine whether CC or CCnew option is to be used

362–368 If the TAO cache for this host (tao_ccsent) is nonzero (this is not the first connection to this host) and the value of cc_send is greater than or equal to tao_ccsent (the CC value has not wrapped), then a CC option is sent and the TAO cache is updated with the new CC value. Otherwise a CCnew option is sent and tao_ccsent is set to 0 (undefined).

Recall Figure 4.12 as an example of how the second part of the if statement can be false: the last CC sent to this host is 1 (tao_ccsent), but the current value of tcp_ccgen (which becomes cc_send for the connection) is 2,147,483,648. T/TCP must send a CCnew option instead of a CC option, because if we sent a CC option with a value of 2,147,483,648 and the other host still has our last CC value (1) in its cache, that host will force a three-way handshake since the CC value has wrapped around. The other host cannot tell whether the SYN with a CC of 2,147,483,648 is an old duplicate or not. Also, if we send a CC option, even if the three-way handshake completes successfully, the other end will not update its cache entry for us (recall Figure 4.12 again). By sending the CCnew option, the client forces the three-way handshake, *and* causes the server to update its cached value for us when the three-way handshake completes.

> Bob Braden's T/TCP implementation performs the test of whether to send a CC option or a CCnew option in tcp_output instead of here. That leads to a subtle bug that can be seen as follows [Olah 1995]. Consider Figure 4.11 but assume that segment 1 is discarded by some intermediate router. Segments 2–4 are as shown, and that connection from the client port 1601 completes successfully. The next segment from the client is a retransmission of segment 1, but contains a CCnew option with a value of 15. Assuming that segment is successfully received, it forces a three-way handshake by the server and, when complete, the server updates its cache for this client with a cached CC of 15. If the network then delivers an old duplicate of segment 2, with a CC of 5000, it will be accepted by the server. The solution is to make the determination of whether to send a CC option or a CCnew option when the client performs the active open, not when the segment is sent by tcp_output.

12.4 PRU_SEND and PRU_SEND_EOF Requests

On p. 1014 of Volume 2 the processing of the PRU_SEND request is just a call to sbappend followed by a call to tcp_output. With T/TCP this request is handled exactly the same, but the code is now intermixed with the new PRU_SEND_EOF request, which we show in Figure 12.4. We saw that the PRU_SEND_EOF request is generated for TCP by sosend when the MSG_EOF flag is specified (Figure 5.2) and when the final mbuf is sent to the protocol.

tcp_usrreq.c

```
189        case PRU_SEND_EOF:
190        case PRU_SEND:
191            sbappend(&so->so_snd, m);
192            if (nam && tp->t_state < TCPS_SYN_SENT) {
193                /*
194                 * Do implied connect if not yet connected,
195                 * initialize window to default value, and
196                 * initialize maxseg/maxopd using peer's cached
197                 * MSS.
198                 */
199                error = tcp_connect(tp, nam);
200                if (error)
201                    break;
202                tp->snd_wnd = TTCP_CLIENT_SND_WND;
203                tcp_mssrcvd(tp, -1);
204            }
205            if (req == PRU_SEND_EOF) {
206                /*
207                 * Close the send side of the connection after
208                 * the data is sent.
209                 */
210                socantsendmore(so);
211                tp = tcp_usrclosed(tp);
212            }
213            if (tp != NULL)
214                error = tcp_output(tp);
215            break;
```

tcp_usrreq.c

Figure 12.4 PRU_SEND and PRU_SEND_EOF requests.

Implied connect

192–202 If the nam argument is nonnull, the process called sendto or sendmsg and specified a peer address. If the connection state is either CLOSED or LISTEN then tcp_connect performs the implied connect. The initial send window is set to 4096 (TTCP_CLIENT_SND_WND) because with T/TCP the client can send data before receiving a window advertisement from the server (Section 3.6).

Set initial MSS for connection

203–204 Calling tcp_mssrcvd with a second argument of –1 means that we have not received a SYN yet, so the cached value for this host (tao_mssopt) is used as the initial MSS. When tcp_mssrcvd returns, the variables t_maxseg and t_maxopd are set, based on the cached tao_mssopt value, or based on the value stored by the system administrator in the routing table entry (the rmx_mtu member of the rt_metrics structure). tcp_mssrcvd will be called again, by tcp_dooptions, if and when a SYN is received from the server with an MSS option. But T/TCP needs to set the MSS variables in the TCP control block now, before receiving a SYN, since data is being sent before receiving an MSS option from the peer.

Process MSG_EOF flag

205–212 If the MSG_EOF flag was specified by the process, socantsendmore sets the socket's SS_CANTSENDMORE flag. tcp_usrclosed then moves the connection from the SYN_SENT state (set by tcp_connect) to the SYN_SENT* state.

Send first segment

213–214 tcp_output checks if a segment should be sent. In the case of a T/TCP client that just calls sendto with the MSG_EOF flag (Figure 1.10), this call sends the segment containing the SYN, data, and FIN.

12.5 tcp_usrclosed Function

In Net/3 this function was called by tcp_disconnect and when the PRU_SHUTDOWN request was processed. With T/TCP we saw in Figure 12.4 that this function is also called by the PRU_SEND_EOF request. Figure 12.5 shows the function, which replaces the code on p. 1021 of Volume 2.

543–546 With T/TCP a user-initiated close in the SYN_SENT or SYN_RCVD states moves to the corresponding starred state, by setting the TF_SENDFIN state flag. The remaining state transitions are unchanged by T/TCP.

12.6 tcp_sysctl Function

The ability to modify TCP variables using the sysctl program was also added when the T/TCP changes were made. While not strictly required by T/TCP, this functionality provides an easier way to modify the values of certain TCP variables, instead of patching the kernel with a debugger. The TCP variables are accessed using the prefix net.inet.tcp. A pointer to this function is stored in the pr_sysctl member of the TCP protosw structure (p. 801 of Volume 2). Figure 12.6 shows the function.

570–572 Only three variables are currently supported, but more can easily be added.

tcp_usrreq.c

```
struct tcpcb *
tcp_usrclosed(tp)
struct tcpcb *tp;
{

    switch (tp->t_state) {

    case TCPS_CLOSED:
    case TCPS_LISTEN:
        tp->t_state = TCPS_CLOSED;
        tp = tcp_close(tp);
        break;

    case TCPS_SYN_SENT:
    case TCPS_SYN_RECEIVED:
        tp->t_flags |= TF_SENDFIN;
        break;

    case TCPS_ESTABLISHED:
        tp->t_state = TCPS_FIN_WAIT_1;
        break;

    case TCPS_CLOSE_WAIT:
        tp->t_state = TCPS_LAST_ACK;
        break;
    }
    if (tp && tp->t_state >= TCPS_FIN_WAIT_2)
        soisdisconnected(tp->t_inpcb->inp_socket);
    return (tp);
}
```

tcp_usrreq.c

Figure 12.5 `tcp_usrclosed` function.

12.7 T/TCP Futures

It is interesting to look at the propagation of the TCP changes defined in RFC 1323, the window scale and timestamp options. These changes were driven by the increasing speed of networks (T3 phone lines and FDDI), and the potential for long-delay paths (satellite links). One of the first implementations was done by Thomas Skibo for SGI workstations. He then put these changes into the Berkeley Net/2 release and made the changes publicly available in May 1992. (Figure 1.16 details the differences and time frames of the various BSD releases.) About one year later (April 1993) Bob Braden and Liming Wei made available similar RFC 1323 source code changes for SunOS 4.1.1. Berkeley added Skibo's changes to the 4.4BSD release in August 1993 and this was made publicly available with the 4.4BSD-Lite release in April 1994. As of 1995 some vendors have added RFC 1323 support, and some have announced intentions to add the support. But RFC 1323 is not universal, especially in PC implementations. (Indeed, in Section 14.6 we see that less than 2% of the clients contacting a particular WWW server sent the window scale or timestamp options.)

tcp_usrreq.c

```
int
tcp_sysctl(name, namelen, oldp, oldlenp, newp, newlen)
int     *name;
u_int   namelen;
void    *oldp;
size_t *oldlenp;
void    *newp;
size_t  newlen;
{
    extern int tcp_do_rfc1323;
    extern int tcp_do_rfc1644;
    extern int tcp_mssdflt;

    /* All sysctl names at this level are terminal. */
    if (namelen != 1)
        return (ENOTDIR);

    switch (name[0]) {
    case TCPCTL_DO_RFC1323:
        return (sysctl_int(oldp, oldlenp, newp, newlen, &tcp_do_rfc1323));
    case TCPCTL_DO_RFC1644:
        return (sysctl_int(oldp, oldlenp, newp, newlen, &tcp_do_rfc1644));
    case TCPCTL_MSSDFLT:
        return (sysctl_int(oldp, oldlenp, newp, newlen, &tcp_mssdflt));
    default:
        return (ENOPROTOOPT);
    }
    /* NOTREACHED */
}
```

tcp_usrreq.c

Figure 12.6 `tcp_sysctl` function.

T/TCP will probably follow a similar path. The first implementation in September 1994 (Section 1.9) contained source code differences for SunOS 4.1.3, which was of little interest to most users unless they had the SunOS source code. Nevertheless, this is the reference implementation by the designer of T/TCP. The FreeBSD implementation (taken from the SunOS source code differences), which was made publicly available in early 1995 on the ubiquitous 80x86 hardware platform, should spread T/TCP to many users.

The goal of this part of the text has been to provide examples of T/TCP to show why it is a worthwhile enhancement to TCP, and to document in detail and explain the source code changes. Like the RFC 1323 changes, T/TCP implementations interoperate with non-T/TCP implementations, and the CC options are used only if both ends understand the options.

12.8 Summary

The `tcp_connect` function is new with the T/TCP changes and is called for both an explicit `connect` and for an implicit connect (a `sendto` or `sendmsg` that specifies a destination address). It allows a new incarnation of a connection that is in the TIME_WAIT state if that connection used T/TCP and if its duration was less than the MSL.

The `PRU_SEND_EOF` request is new and is generated by the socket layer when the final call to the protocol output occurs and if the application specifies the `MSG_EOF` flag. This request allows an implicit connect and also calls `tcp_usrclosed` if the `MSG_EOF` flag is specified.

The only change to the `tcp_usrclosed` function is to allow a process to close a connection that is still in either the SYN_SENT or the SYN_RCVD state. Doing this sets the hidden `TF_SENDFIN` flag.

Part 2

Additional TCP Applications

13

HTTP: Hypertext Transfer Protocol

13.1 Introduction

HTTP, the Hypertext Transfer Protocol, is the basis for the World Wide Web (WWW), which we simply refer to as the Web. In this chapter we examine this protocol and in the next chapter we examine the operation of a real Web server, bringing together many topics from Volumes 1 and 2 in the context of a real-world application. This chapter is not an introduction to the Web or how to use a Web browser.

Statistics from the NSFnet backbone (Figure 13.1) show the incredible growth in HTTP usage since January 1994.

Month	HTTP	NNTP	FTP (data)	Telnet	SMTP	DNS	#Packets $\times 10^9$
1994 Jan.	1.5 %	8.8 %	21.4 %	15.4 %	7.4 %	5.8 %	55
1994 Apr.	2.8	9.0	20.0	13.2	8.4	5.0	71
1994 Jul.	4.5	10.6	19.8	13.9	7.5	5.3	74
1994 Oct.	7.0	9.8	19.7	12.6	8.1	5.3	100
1995 Jan.	13.1	10.0	18.8	10.4	7.4	5.4	87
1995 Apr.	21.4	8.1	14.0	7.5	6.4	5.4	59

Figure 13.1 Packet count percentages for various protocols on NSFnet backbone.

These percentages are based on packet counts, not byte counts. (All these statistics are available from `ftp://ftp.merit.edu/statistics`.) As the HTTP percentage increases, both FTP and Telnet percentages decrease. We also note that the total number of packets increased through 1994, and then started to decrease in 1995. This is because other backbone networks started replacing the NSFnet backbone in December 1994. Nevertheless, the packet percentages are still valid, and show the growth in HTTP traffic.

A simplified organization of the Web is shown in Figure 13.2.

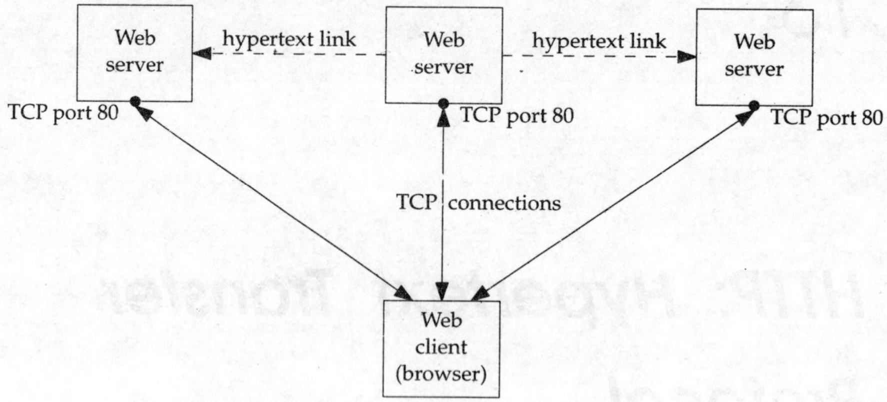

Figure 13.2 Organization of a Web client–server.

The Web client (commonly called a *browser*) communicates with a Web server using one or more TCP connections. The well-known port for the Web server is TCP port 80. The protocol used by the client and server to communicate over the TCP connection is called HTTP, the *Hypertext Transfer Protocol*, which we describe in this chapter. We also show how a given Web server can "point to" other Web servers with *hypertext links*. These links are not restricted to pointing only to other Web servers: a Web server can point to an FTP server or a Telnet server, for example.

Although HTTP has been in use since 1990, the first available documentation appeared in 1993 ([Berners-Lee 1993] approximately describes HTTP version 1.0), but this Internet Draft expired long ago. As of this writing newer documentation is available ([Berners-Lee, Fielding, and Nielsen 1995]), though still as an Internet Draft.

One type of document returned by a Web server to a client is called an HTML document (*hypertext markup language*), described in [Berners-Lee and Connolly 1995]. Other types of documents are also returned by the servers (images, PostScript files, plain text files, etc.), and we'll see some examples later in the chapter.

The next section is a brief introduction to the HTTP protocol and HTML documents, followed by a more detailed examination of the protocol. We then look at how a popular browser (Netscape) uses the protocol, some statistics regarding HTTP's use of TCP, and some of the performance problems with HTTP. [Stein 1995] discusses many of the day-to-day details involved in running a Web site.

13.2 Introduction to HTTP and HTML

HTTP is a simple protocol. The client establishes a TCP connection to the server, issues a request, and reads back the server's response. The server denotes the end of its response by closing the connection. The file returned by the server normally contains pointers (hypertext links) to other files that can reside on other servers. The simplicity seen by the user is the apparent ease of following these links from server to server.

It is the client (the browser) that provides this simplicity to the user, along with a fancy graphical interface. HTTP servers just return the documents requested by the clients. HTTP servers are therefore simpler than HTTP clients. For example, the NCSA version 1.3 Unix server is about 6500 lines of C code, while the Mosaic 2.5 Unix client that runs under the X Window System is about 80,000 lines of C.

As with many of the Internet protocols, an easy way to see what's going on is to run a Telnet client and communicate with the appropriate server. This is possible with HTTP because the client sends lines containing ASCII commands to the server (terminated with a carriage return followed by a linefeed, called CR/LF), and the server's response begins with ASCII lines. HTTP uses the 8-bit ISO Latin 1 character set, which is ASCII with extensions for Western European languages. (Information on various character sets can be found at `http://unicode.org`.)

In the following example we fetch the Addison-Wesley home page.

```
sun % telnet www.aw.com 80                connect to port 80 on server
Trying 192.207.117.2..                    output by Telnet client
Connected to aw.com.                      output by Telnet client
Escape character is  ^]                   output by Telnet client
GET /                                     we type only this line
<HTML>                                    first line of output from Web server
<HEAD>
<TITLE>AW's HomePage</TITLE>
</HEAD>
<BODY>
<CENTER><IMG SRC  = "awplogob.gif" ALT=" "><BR></CENTER>
<P><CENTER><H1>Addison-Wesley Longman</H1></CENTER>
Welcome to our Web server.
 ...                                      we omit 33 lines of output here
<DD><IMG ALIGN=bottom SRC="ball_whi.gif" ALT=" ">
Information Resource
<A HREF = "http://www.ncsa.uiuc.edu/SDG/Software/Mosaic/MetaIndex.html">
Meta-Index</A>
 ...                                      we omit 4 lines of output here
</BODY>
</HTML>
Connection closed by foreign host.        output by Telnet client
```

All we type is the line `GET /` and the server returns 51 lines comprising 3611 bytes. This fetches the server's *home page* from the root directory of the Web server. The final line of output from the Telnet client indicates that the server closes the TCP connection after writing the final line of output.

A complete HTML document begins with `<HTML>` and ends with `</HTML>`. Most HTML commands are paired like this. The document then contains a head and a body, the former bounded by `<HEAD>` and `</HEAD>`, and the latter bounded by `<BODY>` and `</BODY>`. The title is normally displayed by the client at the top of the window. [Raggett, Lam, and Alexander 1996] discuss HTML in more detail.

The next line specifies an image (in this case the corporate logo).

```
<CENTER><IMG SRC = "awplogob.gif" ALT=" "><BR></CENTER>
```

The `<CENTER>` tag tells the client to center the image and the `<IMG>` tag contains information about the image. `SRC` specifies the name that the client must use to fetch the image and ALT gives a text string to display for a text-only client (in this case just a blank).
 forces a line break. When the server returns this home page it does not return this image file. It only returns the name of the file, and the client must open another TCP connection to the server to fetch this file. (We'll see later in this chapter that requiring separate connections for each referenced image increases the overhead of the Web.)

The next line

```
<P><CENTER><H1>Addison-Wesley Longman</H1></CENTER>
```

starts a new paragraph (<P>), is centered in the window, and is a level 1 heading (<H1>). The client chooses how to display a level 1 heading (versus the other headings, levels 2 through 7), usually displaying it in a larger and bolder font than normal.

This shows one of the differences between a *markup language* such as HTML and a *formatting language* such as Troff, TeX, or PostScript. HTML is derived from SGML, the Standard Generalized Markup Language. (http://www.sgmlopen.org contains more information on SGML.) HTML specifies the data and structure of the document (a level 1 heading in this example) but does not specify how the browser should format the document.

We then omit much of the home page that follows the "Welcome" greeting, until we encounter the lines

```
<DD><IMG ALIGN=bottom SRC="ball_whi.gif" ALT=" ">
Information Resource
<A HREF = "http://www.ncsa.uiuc.edu/SDG/Software/Mosaic/MetaIndex.html">
Meta-Index</A>
```

<DD> specifies an entry in a definition list. This entry begins with an image (a white ball), followed by the text "Information Resource Meta-Index," with the last word specifying a hypertext link (the <A> tag) with a hypertext reference (the HREF attribute) that begins with http://www.ncsa.uiuc.edu. Hypertext links such as this are normally underlined by the client or displayed in a different color. As with the previous image that we encountered (the corporate logo), the server does not return this image or the HTML document referenced by the hypertext link. The client will normally fetch the image immediately (to display on the home page) but does nothing with the hypertext link until the user selects it (i.e., moves the cursor over the link and clicks a mouse button). When selected by the user, the client will open an HTTP connection to the site www.ncsa.uiuc.edu and perform a GET of the specified document.

http://www.ncsa.uiuc.edu/SDG/Software/Mosaic/MetaIndex.html is called an URL: a *Uniform Resource Locator*. The specification and meaning of URLs is given in RFC 1738 [Berners-Lee, Masinter, and McCahill 1994] and RFC 1808 [Fielding 1995]. URLs are part of a grander scheme called URIs (*Uniform Resource Identifiers*), which also includes URNs (*Universal Resource Names*). URIs are described in RFC 1630 [Berners-Lee 1994]. URNs are intended to be more persistent than URLs but are not yet defined.

Most browsers also provide the ability of viewing the HTML source for a Web page. For example, both Netscape and Mosaic provide a "View Source" feature.

13.3 HTTP Protocol

The example in the previous section, with the client issuing the command `GET /`, is an HTTP version 0.9 command. Most servers support this version (for backward compatibility) but the current version of HTTP is 1.0. The server can tell the difference because starting with 1.0 the client specifies the version as part of the request line, for example

```
GET  /  HTTP/1.0
```

In this section we look at the HTTP/1.0 protocol in more detail.

Message Types: Requests and Responses

There are two HTTP/1.0 message types: requests and responses. The format of an HTTP/1.0 request is

request-line
headers (0 or more)
<blank line>
body (only for a `POST` request)

The format of the *request-line* is

request request-URI HTTP-version

Three *requests* are supported.

1. The `GET` request, which returns whatever information is identified by the *request-URI*.
2. The `HEAD` request is similar to the `GET` request, but only the server's header information is returned, not the actual contents (the body) of the specified document. This request is often used to test a hypertext link for validity, accessibility, and recent modification.
3. The `POST` request is used for posting electronic mail, news, or sending forms that can be filled in by an interactive user. This is the only request that sends a body with the request. A valid `Content-Length` header field (described later) is required to specify the length of the body.

In a sample of 500,000 client requests on a busy Web server, 99.68% were `GET`, 0.25% were `HEAD`, and 0.07% were `POST`. On a server that accepted pizza orders, however, we would expect a much higher percentage of `POST` requests.

The format of an HTTP/1.0 response is

status-line
headers (0 or more)
<blank line>
body

The format of the *status-line* is

HTTP-version response-code response-phrase

We'll discuss these fields shortly.

Header Fields

With HTTP/1.0 both the request and response can contain a variable number of header fields. A blank line separates the header fields from the body. A header field consists of a field name (Figure 13.3), followed by a colon, a single space, and the field value. Field names are case insensitive.

Headers can be divided into three categories: those that apply to requests, those that apply to responses, and those that describe the body. Some headers apply to both requests and responses (e.g., `Date`). Those that describe the body can appear in a `POST` request or any response. Figure 13.3 shows the 17 different headers that are described in [Berners-Lee, Fielding, and Nielsen 1995]. Unknown header fields should be ignored by a recipient. We'll look at some common header examples after discussing the response codes.

Header name	Request?	Response?	Body?
`Allow`			•
`Authorization`	•		
`Content-Encoding`			•
`Content-Length`			•
`Content-Type`			•
`Date`	•	•	
`Expires`			•
`From`	•		
`If-Modified-Since`	•		
`Last-Modified`			•
`Location`		•	
`MIME-Version`	•	•	
`Pragma`	•	•	
`Referer`	•		
`Server`		•	
`User-Agent`	•		
`WWW-Authenticate`		•	

Figure 13.3 HTTP header names.

Response Codes

The first line of the server's response is called the status line. It begins with the HTTP version, followed by a 3-digit numeric response code, followed by a human-readable response phrase. The meanings of the numeric 3-digit response codes are shown in Figure 13.4. The first of the three digits divides the code into one of five general categories.

Using a 3-digit response code of this type is not an arbitrary choice. We'll see that NNTP also uses these types of response codes (Figure 15.2), as do other Internet applications such as FTP and SMTP.

Response	Description
1yz	Informational. Not currently used.
	Success.
200	OK, request succeeded.
201	OK, new resource created (POST command).
202	Request accepted but processing not completed.
204	OK, but no content to return.
	Redirection; further action need be taken by user agent.
301	Requested resource has been assigned a new permanent URL.
302	Requested resource resides temporarily under a different URL.
304	Document has not been modified (conditional GET).
	Client error.
400	Bad request.
401	Unauthorized; request requires user authentication.
403	Forbidden for unspecified reason.
404	Not found.
	Server error.
500	Internal server error.
501	Not implemented.
502	Bad gateway; invalid response response from gateway or upstream server.
503	Service temporarily unavailable.

Figure 13.4 HTTP 3-digit response codes.

Example of Various Headers

If we retrieve the logo image referred to in the home page shown in the previous section using HTTP version 1.0, we have the following exchange:

```
sun % telnet www.aw.com 80
Trying 192.207.117.2...
Connected to aw.com.
Escape character is '^]'.
GET /awplogob.gif HTTP/1.0                    we type this line
From: rstevens@noao.edu                       and this line
                                              then we type a blank line to terminate the request
HTTP/1.0 200 OK                               first line of server response
Date: Saturday, 19-Aug-95 20:23:52 GMT
Server: NCSA/1.3
MIME-version: 1.0
Content-type: image/gif
Last-modified: Monday, 13-Mar-95 01:47:51 GMT
Content-length: 2859
                                              blank line terminates the server's response headers
                                              ← the 2859-byte binary GIF image is received here
Connection closed by foreign host.            output by Telnet client
```

- We specify version 1.0 with the GET request.
- We send a single header, From, which can be logged by the server.
- The server's status line indicates the version, a response code of 200, and a response phrase of "OK."
- The Date header specifies the time and date on the server, always in Universal Time. This server returns an obsolete date string. The recommended header is

  ```
  Date: Sat, 19 Aug 1995 20:23:52 GMT
  ```

  with an abbreviated day, no hyphens in the date, and a 4-digit year.
- The server program type and version is version 1.3 of the NCSA server.
- The MIME version is 1.0. Section 28.4 of Volume 1 and [Rose 1993] talk more about MIME.
- The data type of the body is specified by the Content-Type and Content-Encoding fields. The former is specified as a *type*, followed by a slash, followed by a *subtype*. In this example the type is image and the subtype is gif. HTTP uses the Internet media types, specified in the latest Assigned Numbers RFC ([Reynolds and Postel 1994] is current as of this writing).

  Other typical values are

  ```
  Content-Type: text/html
  Content-Type: text/plain
  Content-Type: application/postscript
  ```

  If the body is encoded, the Content-Encoding header also appears. For example, the following two headers could appear with a PostScript file that has been compressed with the Unix compress program (commonly stored in a file with a .ps.Z suffix).

  ```
  Content-Type: application/postscript
  Content-Encoding: x-compress
  ```

- Last-Modified specifies the time of last modification of the resource.
- The length of the image (2859 bytes) is given by the Content-Length header.

Following the final response header, the server sends a blank line (a CR/LF pair) followed immediately by the image. The sending of binary data across the TCP connection is OK since 8-bit bytes are exchanged with HTTP. This differs from some Internet applications, notably SMTP (Chapter 28 of Volume 1), which transmits 7-bit ASCII across the TCP connection, explicitly setting the high-order bit of each byte to 0, preventing binary data from being exchanged.

A common client header is User-Agent to identify the type of client program. Some common examples are

```
User-Agent: Mozilla/1.1N (Windows; I; 16bit)
User-Agent: NCSA Mosaic/2.6b1 (X11;SunOS 5.4 sun4m)  libwww/2.12 modified
```

Example: Client Caching

Many clients cache HTTP documents on disk along with the time and date at which the file was fetched. If the document being fetched is in the client's cache, the `If-Modified-Since` header can be sent by the client to prevent the server from sending another copy if the document has not changed. This is called a conditional `GET` request.

```
sun % telnet www.aw.com 80
Trying 192.207.117.2...
Connected to aw.com.
Escape character is '^]'.
GET /awplogob.gif HTTP/1.0
If-Modified-Since: Saturday, 08-Aug-95 20:20:14 GMT
                                        blank line terminates the client request
HTTP/1.0 304 Not modified
Date: Saturday, 19-Aug-95 20:25:26 GMT
Server: NCSA/1.3
MIME-version: 1.0
                                        blank line terminates the server's response headers
Connection closed by foreign host.
```

This time the response code is 304, which indicates that the document has not changed. From a TCP protocol perspective, this avoids transmitting the body from the server to the client, 2859 bytes comprising a GIF image in this example. The remainder of the TCP connection overhead—the three-way handshake and the four packets to terminate the connection—is still required.

Example: Server Redirect

The following example shows a server redirect. We try to fetch the author's home page, but purposely omit the ending slash (which is a required part of an URL specifying a directory).

```
sun % telnet www.noao.edu 80
Trying 140.252.1.11...
Connected to gemini.tuc.noao.edu.
Escape character is '^]'.
GET /~rstevens HTTP/1.0
                                        blank line terminates the client request
HTTP/1.0 302 Found
Date: Wed, 18 Oct 1995 16:37:23 GMT
Server: NCSA/1.4
Location: http://www.noao.edu/~rstevens/
Content-type: text/html
                                        blank line terminates the server's response headers
<HEAD><TITLE>Document moved</TITLE></HEAD>
<BODY><H1>Document moved</H1>
This document has moved <A HREF="http://www.noao.edu/~rstevens/">here</A>.<P>
</BODY>
Connection closed by foreign host.
```

The response-code is 302 indicating that the request-URI has moved. The `Location` header specifies the new location, which contains the ending slash. Most browsers automatically fetch this new URL. The server also returns an HTML file that the browser can display if it does not want to automatically fetch the new URL.

13.4 An Example

We'll now go through a detailed example using a popular Web client (Netscape 1.1N) and look specifically at its use of HTTP and TCP. We'll start with the Addison-Wesley home page (`http://www.aw.com`) and follow three links from there (all to `www.aw.com`), ending up at the page containing the description for Volume 1. Seventeen TCP connections are used and 3132 bytes are sent by the client host to the server, with a total of 47,483 bytes returned by the server. Of the 17 connections, 4 are for HTML documents (28,159 bytes) and 13 are for GIF images (19,324 bytes). Before starting this session the cache used by the Netscape client was erased from disk, forcing the client to go to the server for all the files. Tcpdump was run on the client host, to log all the TCP segments sent or received by the client.

As we expect, the first TCP connection is for the home page (`GET /`) and this HTML document refers to seven GIF images. As soon as this home page is received by the client, four TCP connections are opened in parallel for the first four images. This is a feature of the Netscape client to reduce the overall time. (Most Web clients are not this aggressive and fetch one image at a time.) The number of simultaneous connections is configurable by the user and defaults to four. As soon as one of these connections terminates, another connection is immediately established to fetch the next image. This continues until all seven images are fetched by the client. Figure 13.5 shows a time line for these eight TCP connections. The y-axis is time in seconds.

The eight connections are all initiated by the client and use sequential port numbers from 1114 through 1121. All eight connections are also closed by the server. We consider a connection as starting when the client sends the initial SYN (the client `connect`) and terminating when the client sends its FIN (the client `close`) after receiving the server's FIN. A total time of about 12 seconds is required to fetch the home page and all seven images referenced from that page.

In the next chapter, in Figure 14.22, we show the Tcpdump packet trace for the first connection initiated by the client (port 1114).

> Notice that the connections using ports 1115, 1116, and 1117 start before the first connection (port 1114) terminates. This is because the Netscape client initiates these three nonblocking connects after it reads the end-of-file on the first connection, but before it closes the first connection. Indeed, in Figure 14.22 we notice a delay of just over one-half second between the client receiving the FIN and the client sending its FIN.

Do multiple connections help the client, that is, does this technique reduce the transaction time for the interactive user? To test this, the Netscape client was run from the host `sun` (Figure 1.13), fetching the Addison-Wesley home page. This host is connected to the Internet through a dialup modem at a speed of 28,800 bits/sec, which is common for Web access these days. The number of connections for the client to use can

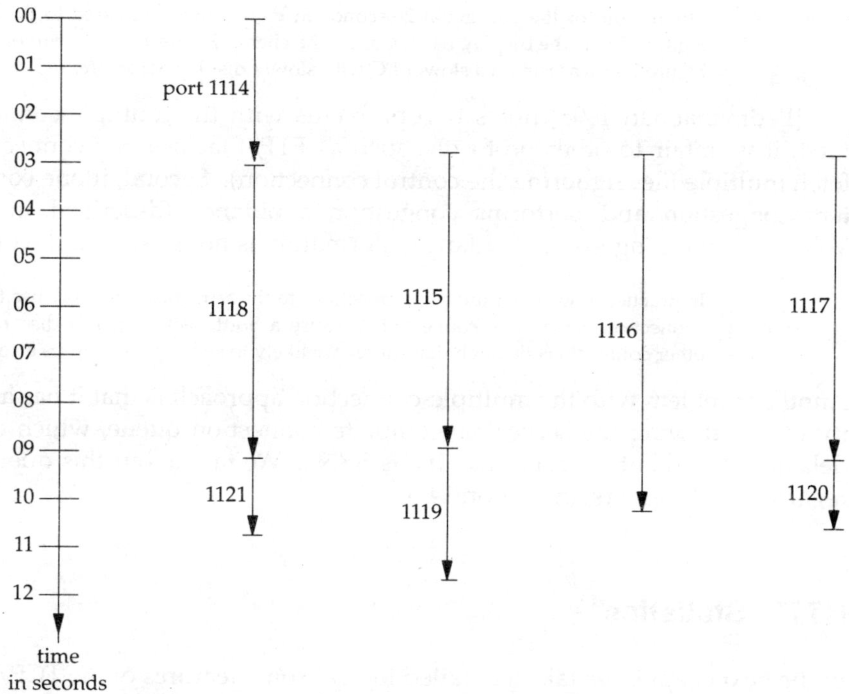

Figure 13.5 Time line of eight TCP connections for a home page and seven GIF images.

be changed in the user's preference file, and the values 1 through 7 were tested. The disk caching feature was disabled. The client was run three times for each value, and the results averaged. Figure 13.6 shows the results.

#Simultaneous connections	Total time (seconds)
1	14.5
2	11.4
3	10.5
4	10.2
5	10.2
6	10.2
7	10.2

Figure 13.6 Total Web client time versus number of simultaneous connections.

Additional connections do decrease the total time, up to 4 connections. But when the exchanges were watched using Tcpdump it was seen that even though the user can specify more than 4 connections, the program's limit is 4. Regardless, given the decreasing differences from 1 to 2, 2 to 3, and then 3 to 4, increasing the number of connections beyond 4 would probably have little, if any, effect on the total time.

The reason for the additional 2 seconds in Figure 13.5, compared to the best value of 10.2 in Figure 13.6, is the display hardware on the client. Figure 13.6 was run on a workstation while Figure 13.5 was run on a slower PC with slower display hardware.

[Padmanabhan 1995] notes two problems with the multiple-connection approach. First, it is unfair to other protocols, such as FTP, that use one connection at a time to fetch multiple files (ignoring the control connection). Second, if one connection encounters congestion and performs congestion avoidance (described in Section 21.6 of Volume 1), the congestion avoidance information is not passed to the other connections.

In practice, however, multiple connections to the same host probably use the same path. If one connection encounters congestion because a bottleneck router is discarding its packets, the other connections through that router are likely to suffer packet drops also.

Another problem with the multiple-connection approach is that it has a higher probability of overflowing the server's incomplete connection queue, which can lead to large delays as the client host retransmits its SYNs. We talk about this queue in detail, with regard to Web servers, in Section 14.5.

13.5 HTTP Statistics

In the next chapter we take a detailed look at some features of the TCP/IP protocol suite and how they're used (and misused) on a busy HTTP server. Our interest in this section is to examine what a typical HTTP connection looks like. We'll use the 24-hour Tcpdump data set described at the beginning of the next chapter.

Figure 13.7 shows the statistics for approximately 130,000 individual HTTP connections. If the client terminated the connection abnormally, such as hanging up the phone line, we may not be able to determine one or both of the byte counts from the Tcpdump output. The mean of the connection duration can also be skewed toward a higher than normal value by connections that are timed out by the server.

	Median	Mean
client bytes/connection	224	266
server bytes/connection	3,093	7,900
connection duration (sec)	3.4	22.3

Figure 13.7 Statistics for individual HTTP connections.

Most references to the statistics of an HTTP connection specify the median and the mean, since the median is often the better indicator of the "normal" connection. The mean is often higher, caused by a few very long files. [Mogul 1995b] measured 200,000 HTTP connections and found that the amount of data returned by the server had a median of 1770 bytes and a mean of 12,925 bytes. Another measurement in [Mogul 1995b] for almost 1.5 million retrievals from a different server found a median of 958 bytes and a mean of 2394 bytes. For the NCSA server, [Braun and Claffy 1994] measured a median of about 3000 bytes and a mean of about 17,000 bytes. One obvious point is that the size of the server's response depends on the files provided by the server, and can vary greatly between different servers.

The numbers discussed so far in this section deal with a single HTTP connection using TCP. Most users running a Web browser access multiple files from a given server during what is called an *HTTP session*. Measuring the session characteristics is harder because all that is available at the server is the client's IP address. Multiple users on the same client host can access the same server at the same time. Furthermore, many organizations funnel all HTTP client requests through a few servers (sometimes in conjunction with firewall gateways) causing many users to appear from only a few client IP addresses. (These servers are commonly called *proxy servers* and are discussed in Chapter 4 of [Stein 1995].) Nevertheless, [Kwan, McGrath, and Reed 1995] attempt to measure the session characteristics at the NCSA server, defining a session to be at most 30 minutes. During this 30-minute session each client performed an average of six HTTP requests causing a total of 95,000 bytes to be returned by the server.

All of the statistics mentioned in this section were measured at the server. They are all affected by the types of HTTP documents the server provides. The average number of bytes transmitted by a server providing large weather maps. for example, will be much higher than at a server providing mainly textual information. Better statistics on the Web in general would be seen in tracing client requests from numerous clients to numerous servers. [Cunha, Bestavros, and Crovella 1995] provide one set of measurements. They measured HTTP sessions and collected 4700 sessions involving 591 different users for a total of 575,772 file accesses. They measured an average file size of 11,500 bytes, but also provide the averages for different document types (HTML, image, sound, video, text, etc.). As with other measurements, they found the distribution of the file size has a large tail, with numerous large files skewing the mean. They found a strong preference for small files.

13.6 Performance Problems

Given the increasing usage of HTTP (Figure 13.1), its impact on the Internet is of wide interest. General usage patterns at the NCSA server are given in [Kwan, McGrath, and Reed 1995]. This is done by examining the server log files for different weeks across a five-month period in 1994. For example, they note that 58% of the requests originate from personal computers, and that the request rate is increasing between 11 and 14% per month. They also provide statistics on the number of requests per day of the week, average connection length, and so on. Another analysis of the NCSA server is provided in [Braun and Claffy 1994]. This paper also describes the performance improvement obtained when the HTTP server caches the most commonly referenced documents.

The biggest factor affecting the response time seen by the interactive user is the usage of TCP connections by HTTP. As we've seen, one TCP connection is used for *each* document. This is described in [Spero 1994a], which begins "HTTP/1.0 interacts badly with TCP." Other factors are the RTT between the client and server, and the server load.

[Spero 1994a] also notes that each connection involves slow start (described in Section 20.6 of Volume 1), adding to the delay. The effect of slow start depends on the size of the client request and the MSS announced by the server (typically 512 or 536 for client connections arriving from across the Internet). Assuming an MSS of 512, if the client request is less than or equal to 512 bytes, slow start will not be a factor. (But beware of a common interaction with mbufs in many Berkeley-derived implementations, which we describe in Section 14.11, which can invoke slow start.) Slow start adds additional RTTs when the client request exceeds the server's MSS. The size of the client request depends on the browser software. In [Spero 1994a] the Xmosaic client issued a 1130-byte request, which required three TCP segments. (This request consisted of 42 lines, 41 of which were `Accept` headers.) In the example from Section 13.4 the Netscape 1.1N client issued 17 requests, ranging in size from 150 to 197 bytes, hence slow start was not an issue. The median and mean client request sizes from Figure 13.7 show that most client requests to that server do not invoke slow start, but most server replies will invoke slow start.

We just mentioned that the Mosaic client sends many `Accept` headers, but this header is not listed in Figure 13.3 (because it doesn't appear in [Berners-Lee, Fielding, and Nielsen 1995]). The reason this header is omitted from this Internet Draft is because few servers do anything with the header. The intent of the header is for the client to tell the server the data formats that the client is willing to accept (GIF images, PostScript files, etc.). But few servers maintain multiple copies of a given document in different formats, and currently there is no method for the client and server to negotiate the document content.

Another significant item is that the connection is normally closed by the HTTP server, causing the connection to go through the TIME_WAIT delay on the server, which can lead to many control blocks in this state on a busy server.

[Padmanabhan 1995] and [Mogul 1995b] propose having the client and server keep a TCP connection open instead of the server closing the connection after sending the response. This is done when the server knows the size of the response that it is generating (recall the `Content-Length` header from our earlier example on p. 167 that specified the size of the GIF image). Otherwise the server must close the connection to denote the end of the response for the client. This protocol modification requires changes in both the client and server. To provide backward compatibility, the client specifies the `Pragma: hold-connection` header. A server that doesn't understand this pragma ignores it and closes the connection after sending the document. This pragma allows new clients communicating with new servers to keep the connection open when possible, but allows interoperation with all existing clients and servers.

Persistent connections will probably be supported in the next release of the protocol, HTTP/1.1, although the syntax of how to do this may change.

There are actually three currently defined ways for the server to terminate its response. The first preference is with the `Content-Length` header. The next preference is for the server to send a `Content-Type` header with a `boundary=` attribute. (An example of this attribute and how it is used is given in Section 6.1.1 of [Rose 1993]. Not all clients support this feature.) The lowest preference (but the most widely used) is for the server to close the connection.

Padmanabhan and Mogul also propose two new client requests to allow pipelining of server responses: `GETALL` (causing the server to return an HTML document and all of its inline images in a single response) and `GETLIST` (similar to a client issuing a series of GET requests). GETALL would be used when the client knows it doesn't have any files from this server in its cache. The intent of the latter command is for the client to issue a GET of an HTML file and then a GETLIST for all referenced files that are not in the client's cache.

A fundamental problem with HTTP is a mismatch between the byte-oriented TCP stream and the message-oriented HTTP service. An ideal solution is a session-layer protocol on top of TCP that provides a message-oriented interface between an HTTP client and server over a single TCP connection. [Spero 1994b] describes such an approach. Called HTTP-NG, this approach uses a single TCP connection with the connection divided into multiple sessions. One session carries control information—client requests and response codes from the server—and other sessions return requested files from the server. The data exchanged across the TCP connection consists of an 8-byte session header (containing some flag bits, a session ID, and the length of the data that follows) followed by data for that session.

13.7 Summary

HTTP is a simple protocol. The client establishes a TCP connection to the server, issues a request, and reads back the server's response. The server denotes the end of its response by closing the connection. The file returned by the server normally contains pointers (hypertext links) to other files that can reside on other servers. The simplicity seen by the user is the apparent ease of following these links from server to server.

The client requests are simple ASCII lines and the server's response begins with ASCII lines (headers) followed by the data (which can be ASCII or binary). It is the client software (the browser) that parses the server's response, formatting the output and highlighting links to other documents.

The amount of data transferred across an HTTP connection is small. The client requests are a few hundred bytes and the server's response typically between a few hundred to 10,000 bytes. Since a few large documents (i.e., images or big PostScript files) can skew the mean, HTTP statistics normally report the median size of the server's response. Numerous studies show a median of less than 3000 bytes for the server's response.

The biggest performance problem associated with HTTP is its use of one TCP connection per file. In the example we looked at in Section 13.4, one home page caused the client to create eight TCP connections. When the size of the client request exceeds the MSS announced by the server, slow start adds additional delays to each TCP connection. Another problem is that the server normally closes the connection, causing the TIME_WAIT delay to take place on the server host, and a busy server can collect lots of these terminating connections.

For historical comparisons, the Gopher protocol was developed around the same time as HTTP. The Gopher protocol is documented in RFC 1436 [Anklesaria et al. 1993]. From a networking perspective HTTP and Gopher are similar. The client opens a TCP connection to a server (port 70 is used by Gopher) and issues a request. The server responds with a reply and closes the connection. The main difference is in the contents of what the server sends back to the client. Although the Gopher protocol allows for nontextual information such as GIF files returned by the server, most Gopher clients are designed for ASCII terminals. Therefore most documents returned by a Gopher server are ASCII text files. As of this writing many sites on the Internet are shutting down their Gopher servers, since HTTP is clearly the winner. Many Web browsers understand the Gopher protocol and communicate with these servers when the URL is of the form `gopher://`*hostname*.

The next version of the HTTP protocol, HTTP/1.1, should be announced in December 1995, and will appear first as an Internet Draft. Features that may be enhanced include authentication (MD5 signatures), persistent TCP connections, and content negotiation.

14

Packets Found on an HTTP Server

14.1 Introduction

This chapter provides a different look at the HTTP protocol, and some features of the Internet protocol suite in general, by analyzing the packets processed by a busy HTTP server. This lets us tie together some real-world TCP/IP features from both Volumes 1 and 2. This chapter also shows how varied, and sometimes downright weird, TCP behavior and implementations can be. There are numerous topics in this chapter and we'll cover them in approximately the order of a TCP connection: establishment, data transfer, and connection termination.

The system on which the data was collected is a commercial Internet service provider. The system provides HTTP service for 22 organizations, running 22 copies of the NCSA `httpd` server. (We talk more about running multiple servers in the next section.) The CPU is an Intel Pentium processor running BSD/OS V1.1.

Three collections of data were made.

1. Once an hour for 5 days the `netstat` program was run with the `-s` option to collect all the counters maintained by the Internet protocols. These counters are the ones shown in Volume 2, p. 208 (IP) and p. 799 (TCP), for example.
2. Tcpdump (Appendix A of Volume 1) was run for 24 hours during this 5-day period, recording every TCP packet to or from port 80 that contained a SYN, FIN, or RST flag. This lets us take a detailed look at the resulting HTTP connection statistics. Tcpdump collected 686,755 packets during this period, which reduced into 147,103 TCP connection attempts.

3. For a 2.5-hour period following the 5-day measurement, every packet to or from TCP port 80 was recorded. This lets us look at a few special cases in more detail, for which we need to examine more segments than just those containing the SYN, FIN, or RST flags. During this period 1,039,235 packets were recorded, for an average of about 115 packets per second.

The Tcpdump command for the 24-hour SYN/FIN/RST collection was

```
$ tcpdump -p -w data.out 'tcp and port 80 and tcp[13:1] & 0x7 != 0'
```

The `-p` flag does not put the interface into promiscuous mode, so only packets received or sent by the host on which Tcpdump is running are captured. This is what we want. It also reduces the volume of data collected from the local network, and reduces the chance of the program losing packets.

> This flag does not guarantee nonpromiscuous mode. Someone else can put the interface into promiscuous mode.
>
> For various long runs of Tcpdump on this host the reported packet loss was between 1 packet lost out of 16,000 to 1 packet lost out of 22,000.

The `-w` flag collects the output in a binary format in a file, instead of a textual representation on the terminal. This file is later processed with the `-r` flag to convert the binary data to the textual format we expect.

Only TCP packets to or from port 80 are collected. Furthermore the single byte at offset 13 from the start of the TCP header logically ANDed with 7 must be nonzero. This is the test for any of the SYN, FIN, or RST flags being on (p. 225 of Volume 1). By collecting only these packets, and then examining the TCP sequence numbers on the SYN and FIN, we can determine how many bytes were transferred in each direction of the connection. Vern Paxson's `tcpdump-reduce` software was used for this reduction (`http://town.hall.org/Archives/pub/ITA/`).

The first graph we show, Figure 14.1, is the total number of connection attempts, both active and passive, during the 5-day period. These are the two TCP counters `tcps_connattempt` and `tcps_accepts`, respectively, from p. 799 of Volume 2. The first counter is incremented when a SYN is sent for an active open and the second is incremented when a SYN is received for a listening socket. These counters are for all TCP connections on the host, not just HTTP connections. We expect a system that is primarily a Web server to receive many more connection requests than it initiates. (The system is also used for other purposes, but most of its TCP/IP traffic is made up of HTTP packets.)

The two dashed lines around Friday noon and Saturday noon delineate the 24-hour period during which the SYN/FIN/RST trace was also collected. Looking at just the number of passive connection attempts, we note that each day the slope is higher from before noon until before midnight, as we expect. We can also see the slope decrease from midnight Friday through the weekend. This daily periodicity is easier to see if we plot the rate of the passive connection attempts, which we show in Figure 14.2.

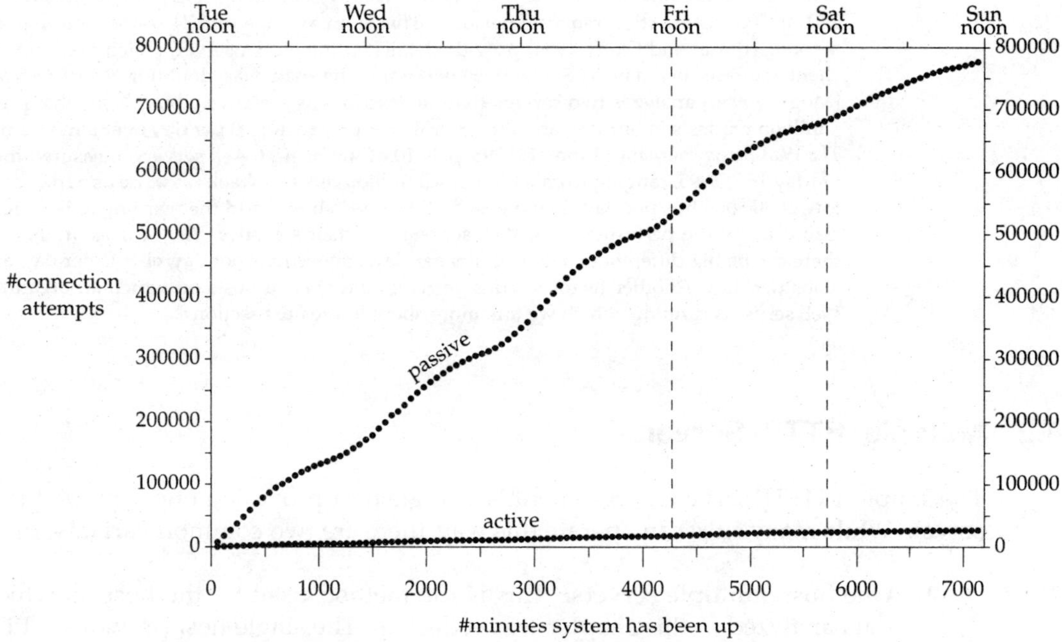

Figure 14.1 Cumulative number of connection attempts, active and passive.

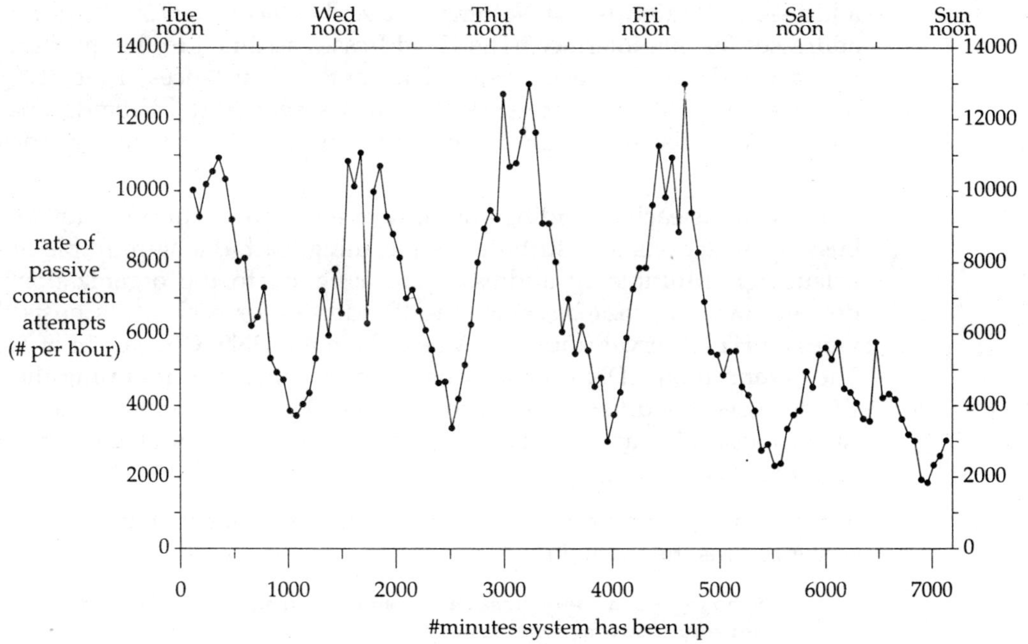

Figure 14.2 Rate of passive connection attempts.

What is the definition of a "busy" server? The system being analyzed received just over 150,000 TCP connection requests per day. This is an average of 1.74 connection requests per second. [Braun and Claffy 1994] provide details on the NCSA server, which averaged 360,000 client requests per day in September 1994 (and the load was doubling every 6–8 weeks). [Mogul 1995b] analyzes two servers that he describes as "relatively busy," one that processed 1 million requests in one day and the other that averaged 40,000 per day over almost 3 months. *The Wall Street Journal* of June 21, 1995, lists 10 of the busiest Web servers, measured the week of May 1–7, 1995, ranging from a high of 4.3 million hits in a week (`www.netscape.com`), to a low of 300,000 hits per day. Having said all this, we should add the warning to beware of any claims about the performance of Web servers and their statistics. As we'll see in this chapter, there can be big differences between hits per day, connections per day, clients per day, and sessions per day. Another factor to consider is the number of hosts on which an organization's Web server is running, which we talk more about in the next section.

14.2 Multiple HTTP Servers

The simplest HTTP server arrangement is a single host providing one copy of the HTTP server. While many sites can operate this way, there are two common variants.

1. One host, multiple servers. This is the method used by the host on which the data analyzed in this chapter was collected. The single host provides HTTP service for multiple organizations. Each organization's WWW domain (`www.`*organization*`.com`) maps to a different IP address (all on the same subnet), and the single Ethernet interface is aliased to each of these different IP addresses. (Section 6.6 of Volume 2 describes how Net/3 allows multiple IP addresses for one interface. The IP addresses assigned to the interface after its primary address are called *aliases*.) Each of the 22 instances of the `httpd` server handles only one IP address. When each server starts, it binds one local IP address to its listening TCP socket, so it only receives connections destined to that IP address.
2. Multiple hosts each providing one copy of the server. This technique is used by busy organizations to distribute the incoming load among multiple hosts (load balancing). Multiple IP addresses are assigned to the organization's WWW domain, `www.`*organization*`.com`, one IP address for each of its hosts that provides an HTTP server (multiple A records in the DNS, Chapter 14 of Volume 1). The organization's DNS server must then be capable of returning the multiple IP addresses in a different order for each DNS client request. In the DNS this is called *round-robin* and is supported by current versions of the common DNS server (BIND), for example.

   For example, NCSA provides nine HTTP servers. Our first query of their name server returns the following:

```
$ host -t a www.ncsa.uiuc.edu newton.ncsa.uiuc.edu
Server: newton.ncsa.uiuc.edu
Address: 141.142.6.6 141.142.2.2
```

```
www.ncsa.uiuc.edu       A       141.142.3.129
www.ncsa.uiuc.edu       A       141.142.3.131
www.ncsa.uiuc.edu       A       141.142.3.132
www.ncsa.uiuc.edu       A       141.142.3.134
www.ncsa.uiuc.edu       A       141.142.3.76
www.ncsa.uiuc.edu       A       141.142.3.70
www.ncsa.uiuc.edu       A       141.142.3.74
www.ncsa.uiuc.edu       A       141.142.3.30
www.ncsa.uiuc.edu       A       141.142.3.130
```

(The `host` program was described and used in Chapter 14 of Volume 1.) The final argument is the name of the NCSA DNS server to query, because by default the program will contact the local DNS server, which will probably have the nine A records in its cache, and might return them in the same order each time.

The next time we run the program we see that the ordering is different:

```
$ host  -t a  www.ncsa.uiuc.edu  newton.ncsa.uiuc.edu
Server: newton.ncsa.uiuc.edu
Address: 141.142.6.6 141.142.2.2

www.ncsa.uiuc.edu       A       141.142.3.132
www.ncsa.uiuc.edu       A       141.142.3.134
www.ncsa.uiuc.edu       A       141.142.3.76
www.ncsa.uiuc.edu       A       141.142.3.70
www.ncsa.uiuc.edu       A       141.142.3.74
www.ncsa.uiuc.edu       A       141.142.3.30
www.ncsa.uiuc.edu       A       141.142.3.130
www.ncsa.uiuc.edu       A       141.142.3.129
www.ncsa.uiuc.edu       A       141.142.3.131
```

14.3 Client SYN Interarrival Time

It is interesting to look at the arrivals of the client SYNs to see what difference there is between the average request rate and the maximum request rate. A server should be capable of servicing the peak load, not the average load.

We can examine the interarrival time of the client SYNs from the 24-hour SYN/FIN/RST trace. There are 160,948 arriving SYNs for the HTTP servers in the 24-hour trace period. (At the beginning of this chapter we noted that 147,103 connection attempts arrived in this period. The difference is caused by retransmitted SYNs. Notice that almost 10% of the SYNs are retransmitted.) The minimum interarrival time is 0.1 ms and the maximum is 44.5 seconds. The mean is 538 ms and the median is 222 ms. Of the interarrival times, 91% are less than 1.5 seconds and we show this histogram in Figure 14.3.

While this graph is interesting, it doesn't provide the peak arrival rate. To determine the peak rate we divide the 24-hour time period into 1-second intervals and compute the number of arriving SYNs in each second. (The actual measurement period

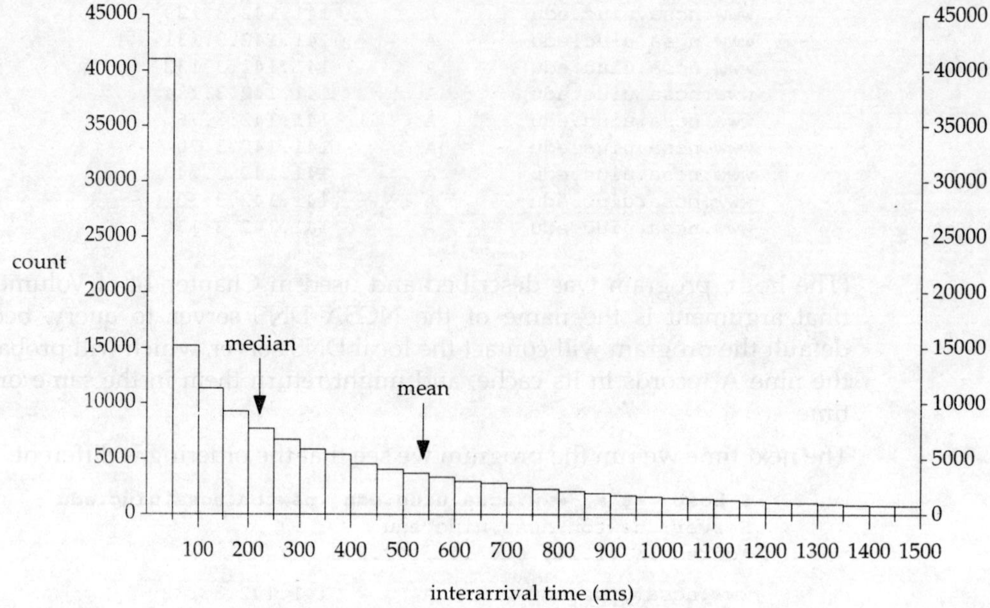

Figure 14.3 Distribution of interarrival times of client SYNs.

#SYNs arriving in 1 second	Counter for all SYNs	Counter for new SYNs
0	27,868	30,565
1	22,471	22,695
2	13,036	12,374
3	7,906	7,316
4	5,499	5,125
5	3,752	3,441
6	2,525	2,197
7	1,456	1,240
8	823	693
9	536	437
10	323	266
11	163	130
12	90	66
13	50	32
14	22	18
15	14	10
16	12	9
17	4	3
18	5	2
19	2	1
20	3	0
	86,560	86,620

Figure 14.4 Number of SYNs arriving in a given second.

consisted of 86,622 seconds, a few minutes longer than 24 hours.) Figure 14.4 shows the first 20 counters. In this figure the second column shows the 20 counters when all arriving SYNs are considered and the third column shows the counters when we ignore retransmitted SYNs. We'll use the final column at the end of this section.

For example, considering all arriving SYNs, there were 27,868 seconds (32% of the day) with no arriving SYNs, 22,471 seconds (26% of the day) with 1 arriving SYN, and so on. The maximum number of SYNs arriving in any second was 73 and there were two of these seconds during the day. If we look at all the seconds with 50 or more arriving SYNs we find that they are all within a 3-minute period. This is the peak that we are looking for.

Figure 14.6 is a summary of the hour containing this peak. For this graph we combine 30 of the 1-second counters, and scale the y-axis to be the count of arriving SYNs per second. The average arrival rate is about 3.5 per second, so this entire hour is already processing arriving SYNs at almost double the mean rate.

Figure 14.7 is a more detailed look at the 3 minutes containing the peak.

The variation during these 3 minutes appears counterintuitive and suggests pathological behavior of some client. If we look at the Tcpdump output for these 3 minutes, we can see that the problem is indeed one particular client. For the 30 seconds containing the leftmost spike in Figure 14.7 this client sent 1024 SYNs from two different ports, for an average of about 30 SYNs per second. A few seconds had peaks around 60–65, which, when added to other clients, accounts for the spikes near 70 in the figure. The middle spike in Figure 14.7 was also caused by this client.

Figure 14.5 shows a portion of the Tcpdump output related to this client.

```
1  0.0                client.1537 > server.80: S 1317079:1317079(0)
                                                  win 2048 <mss 1460>
2  0.001650 (0.0016)  server.80 > client.1537: S 2104019969:2104019969(0)
                                                  ack 1317080 win 4096 <mss 512>
3  0.020060 (0.0184)  client.1537 > server.80: S 1317092:1317092(0)
                                                  win 2048 <mss 1460>
4  0.020332 (0.0003)  server.80 > client.1537: R 2104019970:2104019970(0)
                                                  ack 1317080 win 4096
5  0.020702 (0.0004)  server.80 > client.1537: R 0:0(0)
                                                  ack 1317093 win 0
6  1.938627 (1.9179)  client.1537 > server.80: R 1317080:1317080(0) win 2048

7  1.958848 (0.0202)  client.1537 > server.80: S 1319042:1319042(0)
                                                  win 2048 <mss 1460>
8  1.959802 (0.0010)  server.80 > client.1537: S 2105107969:2105107969(0)
                                                  ack 1319043 win 4096 <mss 512>
9  2.026194 (0.0664)  client.1537 > server.80: S 1319083:1319083(0)
                                                  win 2048 <mss 1460>
10 2.027382 (0.0012)  server.80 > client.1537: R 2105107970:2105107970(0)
                                                  ack 1319043 win 4096
11 2.027998 (0.0006)  server.80 > client.1537: R 0:0(0)
                                                  ack 1319084 win 0
```

Figure 14.5 Broken client sending invalid SYNs at a high rate.

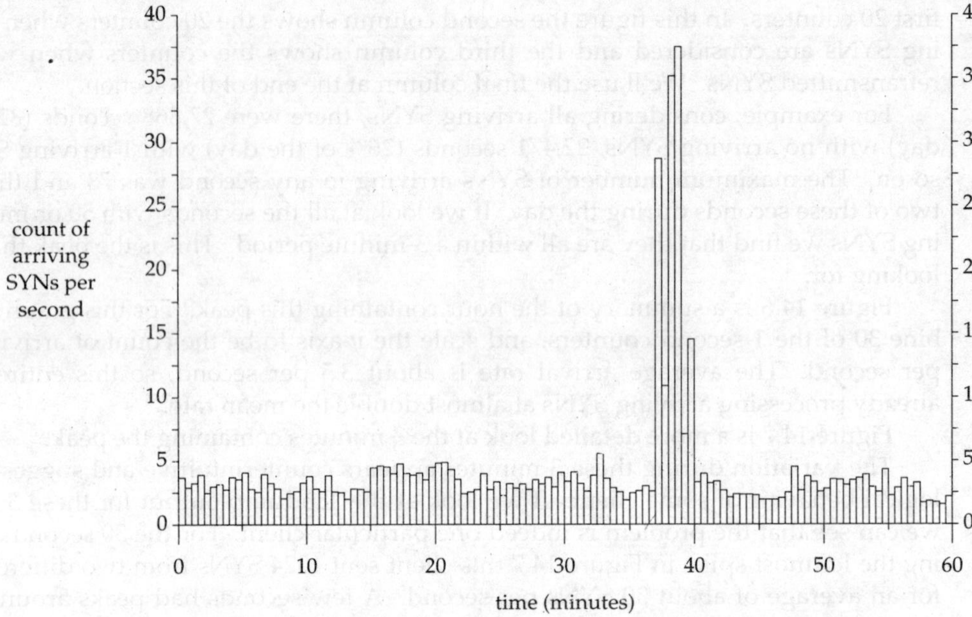

Figure 14.6 Graph of arriving SYNs per second over 60 minutes.

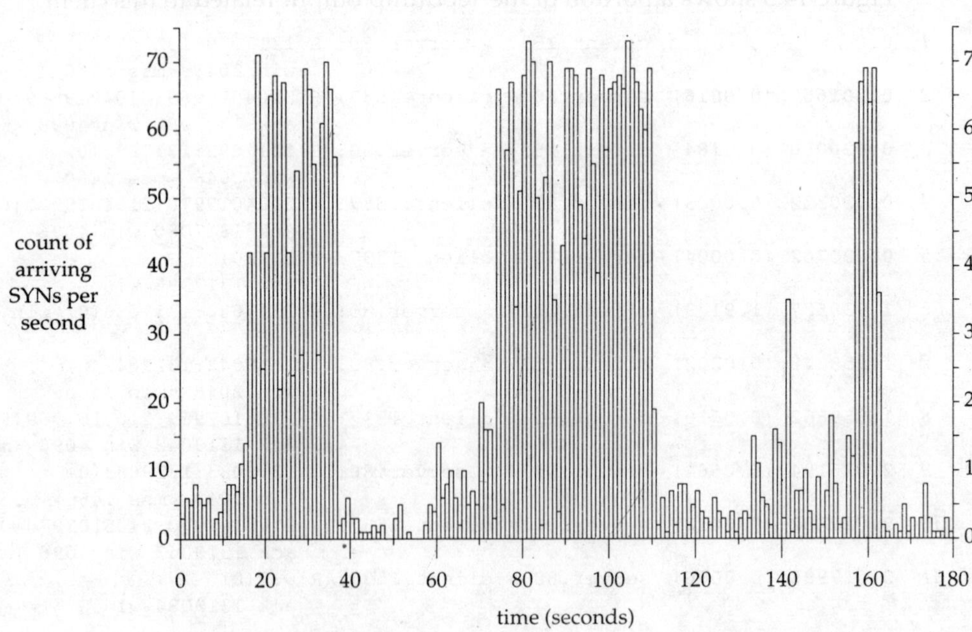

Figure 14.7 Count of arriving SYNs per second over a 3-minute peak.

Line 1 is the client SYN and line 2 is the server's SYN/ACK. But line 3 is another SYN from the same port on the same client but with a starting sequence number that is 13 higher than the sequence number on line 1. The server sends an RST in line 4 and another RST in line 5, and the client sends an RST in line 6. The scenario starts over again with line 7.

Why does the server send two RSTs in a row to the client (lines 4 and 5)? This is probably caused by some data segments that are not shown, since unfortunately this Tcpdump trace contains only the segments with the SYN, FIN, or RST flags set. Nevertheless, this client is clearly broken, sending SYNs at such a high rate from the same port with a small increment in the sequence number from one SYN to the next.

Recalculations Ignoring Retransmitted SYNs

We need to reexamine the client SYN interarrival time, ignoring retransmitted SYNs, since we just saw that one broken client can skew the peak noticeably. As we mentioned at the beginning of this section, this removes about 10% of the SYNs. Also, by looking at only the new SYNs we examine the arrival rate of new connections to the server. While the arrival rate of all SYNs affects the TCP/IP protocol processing (since each SYN is processed by the device driver, IP input, and then TCP input), the arrival rate of connections affects the HTTP server (which handles a new client request for each connection).

In Figure 14.3 the mean increases from 538 to 600 ms and the median increases from 222 to 251 ms. We already showed the distribution of the SYNs arriving per second in Figure 14.4. The peaks such as the one discussed with Figure 14.6 are much smaller. The 3 seconds during the day with the greatest number of arriving SYNs contain 19, 21, and 33 SYNs in each second. This gives us a range from 4 SYNs per second (using the median interarrival time of 251 ms) to 33 SYNs per second, for a factor of about 8. This means when designing a Web server we should accommodate peaks of this magnitude above the average. We'll see the effect of these peak arrival rates on the queue of incoming connection requests in Section 14.5.

14.4 RTT Measurements

The next item of interest is the round-trip time between the various clients and the server. Unfortunately we are not able to measure this on the server from the SYN/FIN/RST trace. Figure 14.8 shows the TCP three-way handshake and the four segments that terminate a connection (with the first FIN from the server). The bolder lines are the ones available in the SYN/FIN/RST trace.

The client can measure the RTT as the difference between sending its SYN and receiving the server's SYN, but our measurements are on the server. We might consider measuring the RTT at the server by measuring the time between sending the server's FIN and receiving the client's FIN, but this measurement contains a variable delay at the client end: the time between the client application receiving an end-of-file and closing its end of the connection.

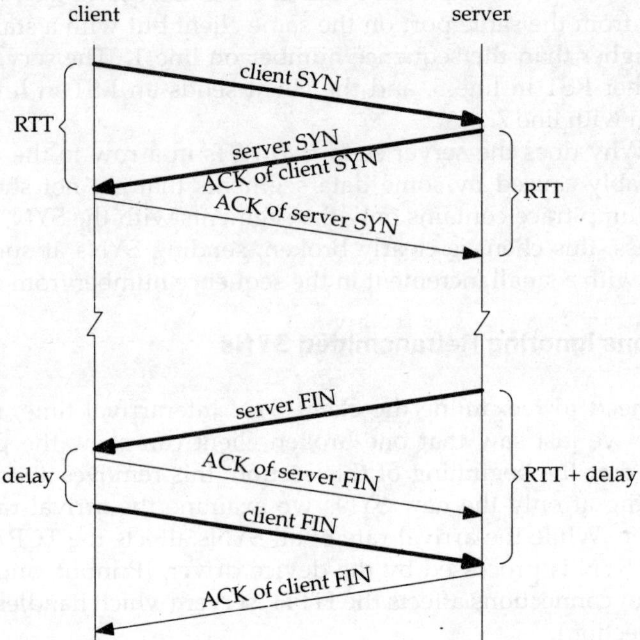

Figure 14.8 TCP three-way handshake and connection termination.

We need a trace containing all the packets to measure the RTT on the server, so we'll use the 2.5-hour trace and measure the difference between the server sending its SYN/ACK and the server receiving the client's ACK. The client's ACK of the server's SYN is normally not delayed (p. 949 of Volume 2) so this measurement should not include a delayed ACK. The segment sizes are normally the smallest possible (44 bytes for the server's SYN, which always includes an MSS option on the server being used, and 40 bytes for the client's ACK) so they should not involve appreciable delays on slow SLIP or PPP links.

During this 2.5-hour period 19,195 RTT measurements were made involving 810 unique client IP addresses. The minimum RTT was 0 (from a client on the same host), the maximum was 12.3 seconds, the mean was 445 ms, and the median was 187 ms. Figure 14.9 shows the distribution of the RTTs up to 3 seconds. This accounts for 98.5% of the measurements. From these measurements we see that even with a best-case coast-to-coast RTT around 60 ms, typical clients are at least three times this value.

Why is the median (178 ms) so much higher than the coast-to-coast RTT (60 ms)? One possibility is that lots of clients are using dialup lines today, and even a fast modem (28,800 bps) adds about 100–200 ms to any RTT. Another possibility is that some client implementations do delay the third segment of the three-way handshake: the client's ACK of the server's SYN.

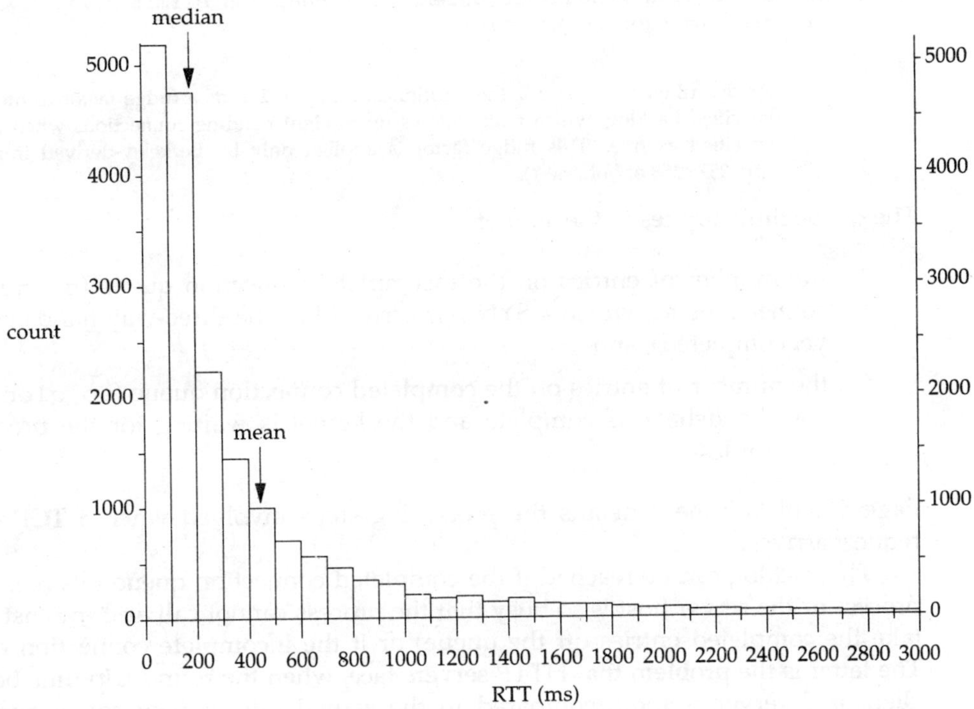

Figure 14.9 Distribution of round-trip times to clients.

14.5 `listen` Backlog Queue

To prepare a socket for receiving incoming connection requests, servers traditionally perform the call

```
listen(sockfd, 5);
```

The second argument is called the *backlog*, and manuals call it the limit for the queue of incoming connections. BSD kernels have historically enforced an upper value of 5 for this limit, the SOMAXCONN constant in the <sys/socket.h> header. If the application specifies a larger value, it is silently truncated to SOMAXCONN by the kernel. Newer kernels have increased SOMAXCONN, say, to 10 or higher, for reasons that we are about to show.

The backlog argument becomes the `so_qlimit` value for the socket (p. 456 of Volume 2). When an incoming TCP connection request arrives (the client's SYN), TCP calls `sonewconn` and the following test is applied (lines 130–131 on p. 462 of Volume 2):

```
if (head->so_qlen + head->so_q0len > 3 * head->so_qlimit / 2)
    return ((struct socket *)0);
```

As described in Volume 2, the multiplication by 3/2 adds a fudge factor to the application's specified backlog, which really allows up to eight pending connections when the backlog is specified as five. This fudge factor is applied only by Berkeley-derived implementations (pp. 257–258 of Volume 1).

The queue limit applies to the sum of

1. the number of entries on the incomplete connection queue (`so_q0len`, those connections for which a SYN has arrived but the three-way handshake has not yet completed), and
2. the number of entries on the completed connection queue (`so_qlen`, the three-way handshake is complete and the kernel is waiting for the process to call `accept`).

Page 461 of Volume 2 details the processing steps involved when a TCP connection request arrives.

The backlog can be reached if the completed connection queue fills (i.e., the server process or the server host is so busy that the process cannot call `accept` fast enough to take the completed entries off the queue) or if the incomplete connection queue fills. The latter is the problem that HTTP servers face, when the round-trip time between the client and server is long, compared to the arrival rate of new connection requests, because a new SYN occupies an entry on this queue for one round-trip time. Figure 14.10 shows this time on the incomplete connection queue.

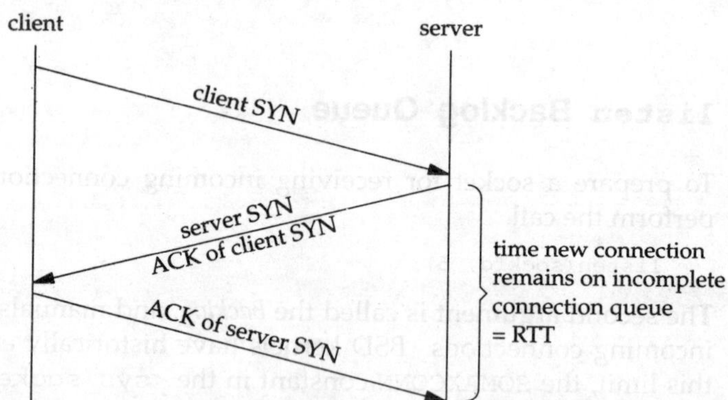

Figure 14.10 Packets showing the time an entry exists on the incomplete connection queue.

To verify that the incomplete connection queue is filling, and not the completed queue, a version of the `netstat` program was modified to print the two variables `so_q0len` and `so_qlen` continually for the busiest of the listening HTTP servers. This program was run for 2 hours, collecting 379,076 samples, or about one sample every 19 ms. Figure 14.11 shows the result.

Queue length	Count for incomplete connection queue	Count for complete connection queue
0	167,123	379,075
1	116,175	1
2	42,185	
3	18,842	
4	12,871	
5	14,581	
6	6,346	
7	708	
8	245	
	379,076	379,076

Figure 14.11 Distribution of connection queue lengths for busy HTTP server.

As we mentioned earlier, a backlog of five allows eight queued connections. The completed connection queue is almost always empty because when an entry is placed on this queue, the server's call to `accept` returns, and the server takes the completed connection off the queue.

TCP ignores incoming connection requests when its queue fills (p. 931 of Volume 2), on the assumption that the client will time out and retransmit its SYN, hopefully finding room on the queue in a few seconds. But the Net/3 code doesn't count these missed SYNs in its kernel statistics, so the system administrator has no way of finding out how often this happens. We modified the code on the system to be the following:

```
if (so->so_options & SO_ACCEPTCONN) {
    so = sonewconn(so, 0);
    if (so == 0) {
        tcpstat.tcps_listendrop++;     /* new counter */
        goto drop;
    }
```

All that changes is the addition of the new counter.

Figure 14.12 shows the value of this counter, monitored once an hour over the 5-day period. The counter applies to all servers on the host, but given that this host is mainly a Web server, most of the overflows are sure to occur on the `httpd` listening sockets. On the average this host is missing just over three incoming connections per minute (22,918 overflows divided by 7139 minutes) but there are a few noticeable jumps where the loss is greater. Around time 4500 (4:00 Friday afternoon) 1964 incoming SYNs are discarded in 1 hour, for a rate of 32 discards per minute (one every 2 seconds). The other two noticeable jumps occur early on Thursday afternoon.

On kernels that support busy servers, the maximum allowable value of the backlog argument must be increased, and busy server applications (such as `httpd`) must be modified to specify a larger backlog. For example, version 1.3 of `httpd` suffers from this problem because it hard codes the backlog as

```
listen(sd, 5);
```

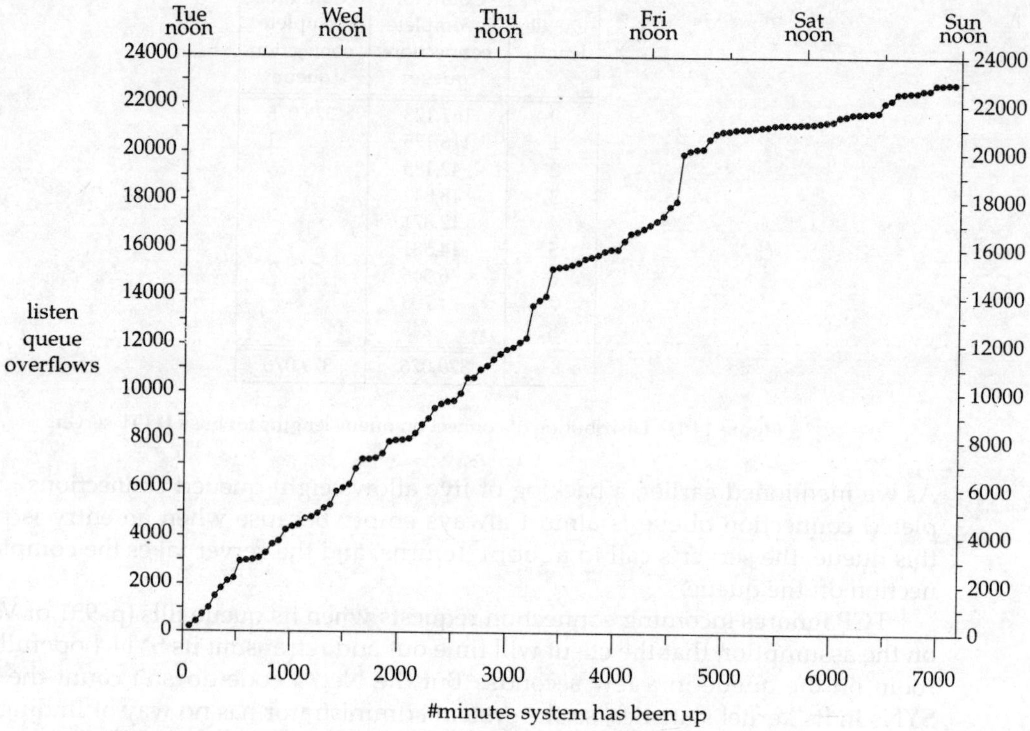

Figure 14.12 Overflow of server's listen queue.

Version 1.4 increases the backlog to 35, but even this may be inadequate for busy servers.

Different vendors have different methods of increasing the kernel's backlog limit. With BSD/OS V2.0, for example, the kernel global `somaxconn` is initialized to 16 but can be modified by the system administrator to a larger value. Solaris 2.4 allows the system administrator to change the TCP parameter `tcp_conn_req_max` using the `ndd` program. The default is 5 and the maximum the parameter can be set to is 32. Solaris 2.5 increases the default to 32 and the maximum to 1024. Unfortunately there is no easy way for an application to determine the value of the kernel's current limit, to use in the call to `listen`, so the best the application can do is code a large value (because a value that is too large does not cause `listen` to return an error) or let the user specify the limit as a command-line argument. One idea [Mogul 1995c] is that the backlog argument to `listen` should be ignored and the kernel should just set it to the maximum value.

> Some applications intentionally specify a low backlog argument to limit the server's load, so there would have to be a way to avoid increasing the value for some applications.

SYN_RCVD Bug

When examining the `netstat` output, it was noticed that one socket remained in the SYN_RCVD state for many minutes. Net/3 limits this state to 75 seconds with its connection-establishment timer (pp. 828 and 945 of Volume 2), so this was unexpected. Figure 14.13 shows the Tcpdump output.

```
1    0.0                  client.4821 > server.80: S 32320000:32320000(0)
                                                   win 61440 <mss 512>
2    0.001045 ( 0.0010) server.80 > client.4821: S 365777409:365777409(0)
                                                   ack 32320001 win 4096 <mss 512>

3    5.791575 ( 5.7905) server.80 > client.4821: S 365777409:365777409(0)
                                                   ack 32320001 win 4096 <mss 512>
4    5.827420 ( 0.0358) client.4821 > server.80: S 32320000:32320000(0)
                                                   win 61440 <mss 512>
5    5.827730 ( 0.0003) server.80 > client.4821: S 365777409:365777409(0)
                                                   ack 32320001 win 4096 <mss 512>

6   29.801493 (23.9738) server.80 > client.4821: S 365777409:365777409(0)
                                                   ack 32320001 win 4096 <mss 512>
7   29.828256 ( 0.0268) client.4821 > server.80: S 32320000:32320000(0)
                                                   win 61440 <mss 512>
8   29.828600 ( 0.0003) server.80 > client.4821: S 365777409:365777409(0)
                                                   ack 32320001 win 4096 <mss 512>

9   77.811791 (47.9832) server.80 > client.4821: S 365777409:365777409(0)
                                                   ack 32320001 win 4096 <mss 512>
10 141.821740 (64.0099) server.80 > client.4821: S 365777409:365777409(0)
                                                   ack 32320001 win 4096 <mss 512>

                    server retransmits its SYN/ACK every 64 seconds

18 654.197350 (64.1911) server.80 > client.4821: S 365777409:365777409(0)
                                                   ack 32320001 win 4096 <mss 512>
```

Figure 14.13 Server socket stuck in SYN_RCVD state for almost 11 minutes.

The client's SYN arrives in segment 1 and the server's SYN/ACK is sent in segment 2. The server sets the connection-establishment timer to 75 seconds and the retransmission timer to 6 seconds. The retransmission timer expires on line 3 and the server retransmits its SYN/ACK. This is what we expect.

The client responds in line 4, but the response is a retransmission of its original SYN from line 1, not the expected ACK of the server's SYN. The client appears to be broken. The server responds with a retransmission of its SYN/ACK, which is correct. The receipt of segment 4 causes TCP input to set the keepalive timer for this connection to 2 hours (p. 932 of Volume 2). But the keepalive timer and the connection-establishment timer share the same counter in the connection control block (Figure 25.2, p. 819 of Volume 2), so this wipes out the remaining 69 seconds in this counter, setting it to 2 hours instead. Normally the client completes the three-way handshake with an ACK of the server's SYN. When this ACK is processed the keepalive timer is set to 2 hours and the retransmission timer is turned off.

Lines 6, 7, and 8 are similar. The server's retransmission timer expires after 24 seconds, it resends its SYN/ACK, but the client incorrectly responds with its original SYN once again, so the server correctly resends its SYN/ACK. On line 9 the server's retransmission timer expires again after 48 seconds, and the SYN/ACK is resent. The retransmission timer then reaches its maximum value of 64 seconds and 12 retransmissions occur (12 is the constant `TCP_MAXRXTSHIFT` on p. 842 of Volume 2) before the connection is dropped.

The fix to this bug is not to reset the keepalive timer to 2 hours when the connection is not established (p. 932 of Volume 2), since the `TCPT_KEEP` counter is shared between the keepalive timer and the connection-establishment timer. But applying this fix then requires that the keepalive timer be set to its initial value of 2 hours when the connection moves to the established state.

14.6 Client SYN Options

Since we collect every SYN segment in the 24-hour trace, we can look at some of the different values and options that can accompany a SYN.

Client Port Numbers

Berkeley-derived systems assign client ephemeral ports in the range of 1024 through 5000 (p. 732 of Volume 2). As we might expect, 93.5% of the more than 160,000 client ports are in this range. Fourteen client requests arrived with a port number of less than 1024, normally considered reserved ports in Net/3, and the remaining 6.5% were between 5001 and 65535. Some systems, notably Solaris 2.x, assign client ports starting at 32768.

Figure 14.14 shows a plot of the client ports, collected into ranges of 1000. Notice that the *y*-axis is logarithmic. Also notice that not only are most client ports in the range of 1024–5000, but two-thirds of these are between 1024 and 2000.

Maximum Segment Size (MSS)

The advertised MSS can be based on the attached network's MTU (see our earlier discussion for Figure 10.9) or certain fixed values can be used (512 or 536 for nonlocal peers, 1024 for older BSD systems, etc.). RFC 1191 [Mogul and Deering 1990] lists 16 different MTUs that are typical. We therefore expected to find a dozen or more different MSS values announced by the Web clients. Instead we found 117 different values, ranging from 128 to 17,520.

Figure 14.15 shows the counts of the 13 most common MSS values announced by the clients. These 5071 clients account for 94% of the 5386 different clients that contacted the Web servers. The first entry labeled "none" means that client's SYN did not announce an MSS.

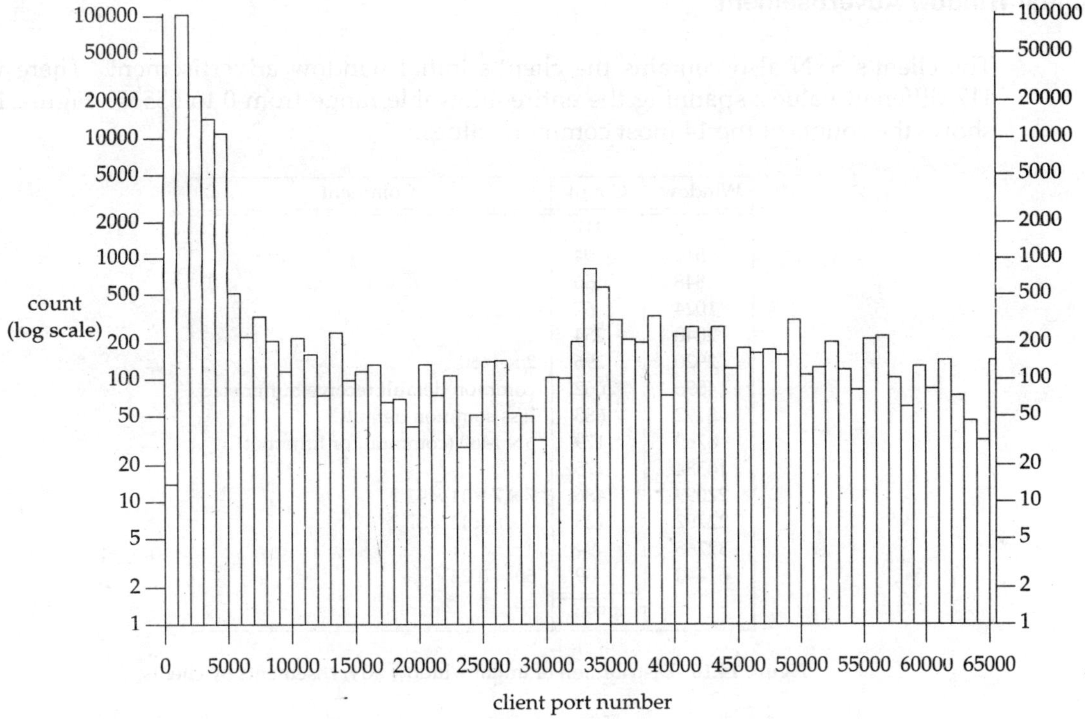

Figure 14.14 Range of client port numbers.

MSS	Count	Comment
none	703	RFC 1122 says 536 must be assumed when option not used
212	53	
216	47	256 – 40
256	516	SLIP or PPP link with MTU of 296
408	24	
472	21	512 – 40
512	465	common default for nonlocal host
536	1097	common default for nonlocal host
966	123	ARPANET MTU (1006) – 40
1024	31	older BSD default for local host
1396	117	
1440	248	
1460	1626	Ethernet MTU (1500) – 40
	5071	

Figure 14.15 Distribution of MSS values announced by clients.

Initial Window Advertisement

The client's SYN also contains the client's initial window advertisement. There were 117 different values, spanning the entire allowable range from 0 to 65535. Figure 14.16 shows the counts of the 14 most common values.

Window	Count	Comment
0	317	
512	94	
848	66	
1024	67	
2048	254	
2920	296	2×1460
4096	2062	common default receive buffer size
8192	683	less common default
8760	179	6×1460 (common for Ethernet)
16384	175	
22099	486	$7 \times 7 \times 11 \times 41$?
22792	128	$7 \times 8 \times 11 \times 37$?
32768	94	
61440	89	60×1024
	4,990	

Figure 14.16 Distribution of initial window advertisements by clients.

These 4990 values account for 93% of the 5386 different clients. Some of the values makes sense, while others such as 22099 are a puzzle.

Apparently there are some PC Web browsers that allow the user to specify values such as the MSS and initial window advertisement. One reason for some of the bizarre values that we've seen is that users might set these values without understanding what they affect.

Despite the fact that we found 117 different MSS values and 117 different initial windows, examining the 267 different combinations of MSS and initial window did not show any obvious correlation.

Window Scale and Timestamp Options

RFC 1323 specifies the window scale and timestamp options (Figure 2.1). Of the 5386 different clients, 78 sent only a window scale option, 23 sent both a window scale and a timestamp option, and none sent only a timestamp option. Of all the window scale options, all announced a shift factor of 0 (implying a scaling factor of 1 or just the announced TCP window size).

Sending Data with a SYN

Five clients sent data with a SYN, but the SYNs did not contain any of the new T/TCP options. Examination of the actual packets showed that each connection followed the same pattern. The client sent a normal SYN without any data. The server responded with the second segment of the three-way handshake, but this appeared to be lost, so the client retransmitted its SYN. But in each case when the client SYN was retransmitted, it contained data (between 200 and 300 bytes, a normal HTTP client request).

Path MTU Discovery

Path MTU discovery is described in RFC 1191 [Mogul and Deering 1990] and in Section 24.2 of Volume 1. We can see how many clients support this option by looking at how many SYN segments are sent with the DF bit set (don't fragment). In our sample, 679 clients (12.6%) appear to support path MTU discovery.

Client Initial Sequence Number

An astounding number of clients (just over 10%) use an initial sequence number of 0, a clear violation of the TCP specification. It appears these client TCP/IP implementations use the value of 0 for *all* active connections, because the traces show multiple connections from different ports from the same client within seconds of each other, each with a starting sequence number of 0. Figure 14.19 (p. 199) shows one of these clients.

14.7 Client SYN Retransmissions

Berkeley-derived systems retransmit a SYN 6 seconds after the initial SYN, and then again 24 seconds later if a response is still not received (p. 828 of Volume 2). Since we have all SYN segments in the 24-hour trace (all those that were not dropped by the network or by Tcpdump), we can see how often the client's retransmit their SYN and the time between each retransmission.

During the 24-hour trace there were 160,948 arriving SYNs (Section 14.3) of which 17,680 (11%) were duplicates. (The count of true duplicates is smaller since some of the time differences between the consecutive SYNs from a given IP address and port were quite large, implying that the second SYN was not a duplicate but was to initiate another incarnation of the connection at a later time. We didn't try to remove these multiple incarnations because they were a small fraction of the 11%.)

For SYNs that were only retransmitted once (the most common case) the retransmission times were typically 3, 4, or 5 seconds after the first SYN. When the SYN was retransmitted multiple times, many of the client's used the BSD algorithm: the first retransmission was after 6 seconds, followed by another 24 seconds later. We'll denote this sequence as {6, 24}. Other observed sequences were

- {3, 6, 12, 24},
- {5, 10, 20, 40, 60, 60},
- {4, 4, 4, 4} (a violation of RFC 1122's requirement for an exponential backoff),
- {0.7, 1.3} (overly aggressive retransmission by a host that is actually 20 hops away; indeed there were 20 connections from this host with a retransmitted SYN and all showed a retransmission interval of less than 500 ms!),

- {3, 6.5, 13, 26, 3, 6.5, 13, 26, 3, 6.5, 13, 26} (this host resets its exponential backoff after four retransmissions),
- {2.75, 5.5, 11, 22, 44},
- {21, 17, 106},
- {5, 0.1, 0.2, 0.4, 0.8, 1.4, 3.2, 6.4} (far too aggressive after first timeout),
- {0.4, 0.9, 2, 4} (another overly aggressive client that is 19 hops away),
- {3, 18, 168, 120, 120, 240}.

As we can see, some of these are bizarre. Some of these SYNs that were retransmitted many times are probably from clients with routing problems: they can send to the server but they never receive any of the server replies. Also, there is a possibility that some of these are requests for a new incarnation of a previous connection (p. 958 of Volume 2 describes how BSD servers will accept a new connection request for a connection in the TIME_WAIT state if the new SYN has a sequence number that is greater than the final sequence number of the connection in the TIME_WAIT state) but the timing (obvious multiples of 3 or 6 seconds, for example) make this unlikely.

14.8 Domain Names

During the 24-hour period, 5386 different IP addresses connected to the Web servers. Since Tcpdump (with the -w flag) just records the packet header with the IP address, we must look up the corresponding domain name later.

Our first attempt to map the IP addresses to their domain name using the DNS found names for only 4052 (75%) of the IP addresses. We then ran the remaining 1334 IP addresses through the DNS a day later, finding another 62 names. This means that 23.6% of the clients do not have a correct inverse mapping from their IP address to their name. (Section 14.5 of Volume 1 talks about these pointer queries.) While many of these clients may be behind a dialup line that is down most of the time, they should still have their name service provided by a name server and a secondary that are connected to the Internet full time.

To see whether these clients without an address-to-name mapping were temporarily unreachable, the Ping program was run to the remaining 1272 clients, immediately after the DNS failed to find the name. Ping reached 520 of the hosts (41%).

Looking at the distribution of the top level domains for the IP addresses that did map into a domain name, there were 57 different top level domains. Fifty of these were the two-letter domains for countries other than the United States, which means the adjective "world wide" is appropriate for the Web.

14.9 Timing Out Persist Probes

Net/3 never gives up sending persist probes. That is, when Net/3 receives a window advertisement of 0 from its peer, it sends persist probes indefinitely, regardless of whether it ever receives *anything* from the other end. This is a problem when the other end disappears completely (i.e., hangs up the phone line on a SLIP or PPP connection). Recall from p. 905 of Volume 2 that even if some intermediate router sends an ICMP host unreachable error when the client disappears, TCP ignores these errors once the connection is established.

If these connections are not dropped, TCP will send a persist probe every 60 seconds to the host that has disappeared (wasting Internet resources), and each of these connections also ties up memory on the host with its TCP and associated control blocks.

The code in Figure 14.17 appears in 4.4BSD-Lite2 to fix this problem, and replaces the code on p. 827 of Volume 2.

tcp_timer.c

```
case TCPT_PERSIST:
    tcpstat.tcps_persisttimeo++;
    /*
     * Hack: if the peer is dead/unreachable, we do not
     * time out if the window is closed.  After a full
     * backoff, drop the connection if the idle time
     * (no responses to probes) reaches the maximum
     * backoff that we would use if retransmitting.
     */
    if (tp->t_rxtshift == TCP_MAXRXTSHIFT &&
        (tp->t_idle >= tcp_maxpersistidle ||
         tp->t_idle >= TCP_REXMTVAL(tp) * tcp_totbackoff)) {
            tcpstat.tcps_persistdrop++;
            tp = tcp_drop(tp, ETIMEDOUT);
            break;
    }
    tcp_setpersist(tp);
    tp->t_force = 1;
    (void) tcp_output(tp);
    tp->t_force = 0;
    break;
```

tcp_timer.c

Figure 14.17 Corrected code for handling persist timeout.

The `if` statement is the new code. The variable `tcp_maxpersistidle` is new and is initialized to `TCPTV_KEEP_IDLE` (14,400 500-ms clock ticks, or 2 hours). The `tcp_totbackoff` variable is also new and its value is 511, the sum of all the elements in the `tcp_backoff` array (p. 836 of Volume 2). Finally, `tcps_persistdrop` is a new counter in the `tcpstat` structure (p. 798 of Volume 2) that counts these dropped connections.

`TCP_MAXRXTSHIFT` is 12 and specifies the maximum number of retransmissions while TCP is waiting for an ACK. After 12 retransmissions the connection is dropped if nothing has been received from the peer in either 2 hours, or 511 times the current RTO for the peer, whichever is smaller. For example, if the RTO is 2.5 seconds (5 clock ticks, a reasonable value), the second half of the OR test causes the connection to be dropped after 22 minutes (2640 clock ticks), since 2640 is greater than 2555 (5×511).

The comment "Hack" in the code is not required. RFC 1122 states that TCP must keep a connection open indefinitely even if the offered receive window is zero "as long as the receiving

> TCP continues to send acknowledgments in response to the probe segments." Dropping the connection after a long duration of no response to the probes is fine.

This code was added to the system to see how frequently this scenario happened. Figure 14.18 shows the value of the new counter over the 5-day period. This system averaged 90 of these dropped connections per day, almost 4 per hour.

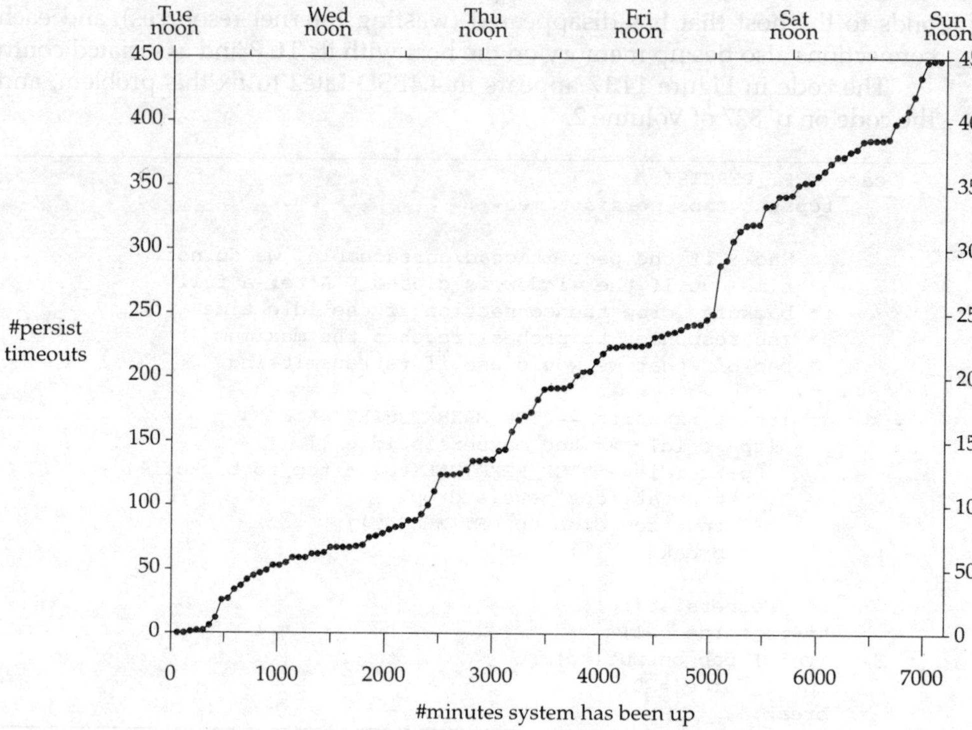

Figure 14.18 Number of connections dropped after time out of persist probes.

Let's look at one of these connections in detail. Figure 14.19 shows the detailed Tcpdump packet trace.

```
 1  0.0                  client.1464 > serv.80: S 0:0(0) win 4096 <mss 1396>
 2  0.001212  (0.0012)   serv.80 > client.1464: S 323930113:323930113(0)
                                               ack 1 win 4096 <mss 512>
 3  0.364841  (0.3636)   client.1464 > serv.80: P ack 1 win 4096
 4  0.481275  (0.1164)   client.1464 > serv.80: P 1:183(182) ack 1 win 4096
 5  0.546304  (0.0650)   serv.80 > client.1464: . 1:513(512) ack 183 win 4096
 6  0.546761  (0.0005)   serv.80 > client.1464: P 513:1025(512) ack 183 win 4096
 7  1.393139  (0.8464)   client.1464 > serv.80: FP 183:183(0) ack 513 win 3584
 8  1.394103  (0.0010)   serv.80 > client.1464: . 1025:1537(512) ack 184 win 4096
 9  1.394587  (0.0005)   serv.80 > client.1464: . 1537:2049(512) ack 184 win 4096
10  1.582501  (0.1879)   client.1464 > serv.80: FP 183:183(0) ack 1025 win 3072
11  1.583139  (0.0006)   serv.80 > client.1464: . 2049:2561(512) ack 184 win 4096
12  1.583608  (0.0005)   serv.80 > client.1464: . 2561:3073(512) ack 184 win 4096
```

```
13     2.851548  (1.2679) client.1464 > serv.80: P ack 2049 win 2048
14     2.852214  (0.0007) serv.80 > client.1464: . 3073:3585(512) ack 184 win 4096
15     2.852672  (0.0005) serv.80 > client.1464: . 3585:4097(512) ack 184 win 4096

16     3.812675  (0.9600) client.1464 > serv.80: P ack 3073 win 1024
17     5.257997  (1.4453) client.1464 > serv.80: P ack 4097 win 0

18    10.024936  (4.7669) serv.80 > client.1464: . 4097:4098(1) ack 184 win 4096
19    16.035379  (6.0104) serv.80 > client.1464: . 4097:4098(1) ack 184 win 4096
20    28.055130 (12.0198) serv.80 > client.1464: . 4097:4098(1) ack 184 win 4096
21    52.086026 (24.0309) serv.80 > client.1464: . 4097:4098(1) ack 184 win 4096
22   100.135380 (48.0494) serv.80 > client.1464: . 4097:4098(1) ack 184 win 4096
23   160.195529 (60.0601) serv.80 > client.1464: . 4097:4098(1) ack 184 win 4096
24   220.255059 (60.0595) serv.80 > client.1464: . 4097:4098(1) ack 184 win 4096

                          persist probes continue

140 7187.603975 (60.0501) serv.80 > client.1464: . 4097:4098(1) ack 184 win 4096
141 7247.643905 (60.0399) serv.80 > client.1464: R 4098:4098(0) ack 184 win 4096
```

Figure 14.19 Tcpdump trace of persist timeout.

Lines 1–3 are the normal TCP three-way handshake, except for the bad initial sequence number (0) and the weird MSS. The client sends a 182-byte request in line 4. The server acknowledges the request in line 5 and this segment also contains the first 512 bytes of the reply. Line 6 contains the next 512 bytes of the reply.

The client sends a FIN in line 7 and the server ACKs the FIN and continues with the next 1024 bytes of the reply in lines 8 and 9. The client acknowledges another 512 bytes of the server's reply in line 10 and resends its FIN. Lines 11 and 12 contain the next 1024 bytes of the server's reply. This scenario continues in lines 13–15.

Notice that as the server sends data, the client's advertised window decreases in lines 7, 10, 13, and 16, until the window is 0 in line 17. The client TCP has received the server's 4096 bytes of reply in line 17, but the 4096-byte receive buffer is full, so the client advertises a window of 0. The client application has not read any data from the receive buffer.

Line 18 is the first persist probe from the server, sent about 5 seconds after the zero-window advertisement. The timing of the persist probes then follows the typical scenario shown in Figure 25.14, p. 827 of Volume 2. It appears that the client host left the Internet between lines 17 and 18. A total of 124 persist probes are sent over a period of just over 2 hours before the server gives up on line 141 and sends an RST. (The RST is sent by `tcp_drop`, p. 893 of Volume 2.)

> Why does this example continue sending persist probes for 2 hours, given our explanation of the second half of the OR test in the 4.4BSD-Lite2 source code that we examined at the beginning of this section? The BSD/OS V2.0 persist timeout code; which was used in the system being monitored, only had the test for `t_idle` being greater than or equal to `tcp_maxpersistidle`. The second half of the OR test is newer with 4.4BSD-Lite2. We can see the reason for this part of the OR test in our example: there is no need to keep probing for 2 hours when it is obvious that the other end has disappeared.

We said that the system averaged 90 of these persist timeouts per day, which means that if the kernel did not time these out, after 4 days we would have 360 of these "stuck" connections, causing about 6 wasted TCP segments to be sent every second. Additionally, since the HTTP server is trying to send data to the client, there are mbufs on the connection's send queue waiting to be sent. [Mogul 1995a] notes "when clients abort their TCP connections prematurely, this can trigger lurking server bugs that really hurt performance."

In line 7 of Figure 14.19 the server receives a FIN from the client. This moves the server's endpoint to the CLOSE_WAIT state. We cannot tell from the Tcpdump output, but the server called `close` at some time during the trace, moving to the LAST_ACK state. Indeed, most of these connections that are stuck sending persist probes are in the LAST_ACK state.

> When this problem of sockets stuck in the LAST_ACK state was originally discussed on Usenet in early 1995, one proposal was to set the `SO_KEEPALIVE` socket option to detect when the client disappears and terminate the connection. (Chapter 23 of Volume 1 discusses how this socket option works and Section 25.6 of Volume 2 provides details on its implementation.) Unfortunately, this doesn't help. Notice on p. 829 of Volume 2 that the keepalive option does not terminate a connection in the FIN_WAIT_1, FIN_WAIT_2, CLOSING, or LAST_ACK states. Some vendors have reportedly changed this.

14.10 Simulation of T/TCP Routing Table Size

A host that implements T/TCP maintains a routing table entry for *every* host with which it communicates (Chapter 6). Since most hosts today maintain a routing table with just a default route and perhaps a few other explicit routes, the T/TCP implementation has the potential of creating a much larger than normal routing table. We'll use the data from the HTTP server to simulate the T/TCP routing table, and see how its size changes over time.

Our simulation is simple. We use the 24-hour packet trace to build a routing table for every one of the 5386 different IP addresses that communicate with the Web servers on this host. Each entry remains in the routing table for a specified expiration time after it is last referenced. We'll run the simulation with expiration times of 30 minutes, 60 minutes, and 2 hours. Every 10 minutes the routing table is scanned and all routes older than the expiration time are deleted (similar to what `in_rtqtimo` does in Section 6.10), and a count is produced of the number of entries left in the table. These counts are shown in Figure 14.20.

In Exercise 18.2 of Volume 2 we noted that each Net/3 routing table entry requires 152 bytes. With T/TCP this becomes 168 bytes, with 16 bytes added for the `rt_metrics` structure (Section 6.5) used for the TAO cache, although 256 bytes are actually allocated, given the BSD memory allocation policy. With the largest expiration time of 2 hours the number of entries reaches almost 1000, which equals about 256,000 bytes. Halving the expiration time reduces the memory by about one-half.

With an expiration time of 30 minutes the maximum size of the routing table is about 300 entries, out of the 5386 different IP addresses that contact this server. This is not at all unreasonable for the size of a routing table.

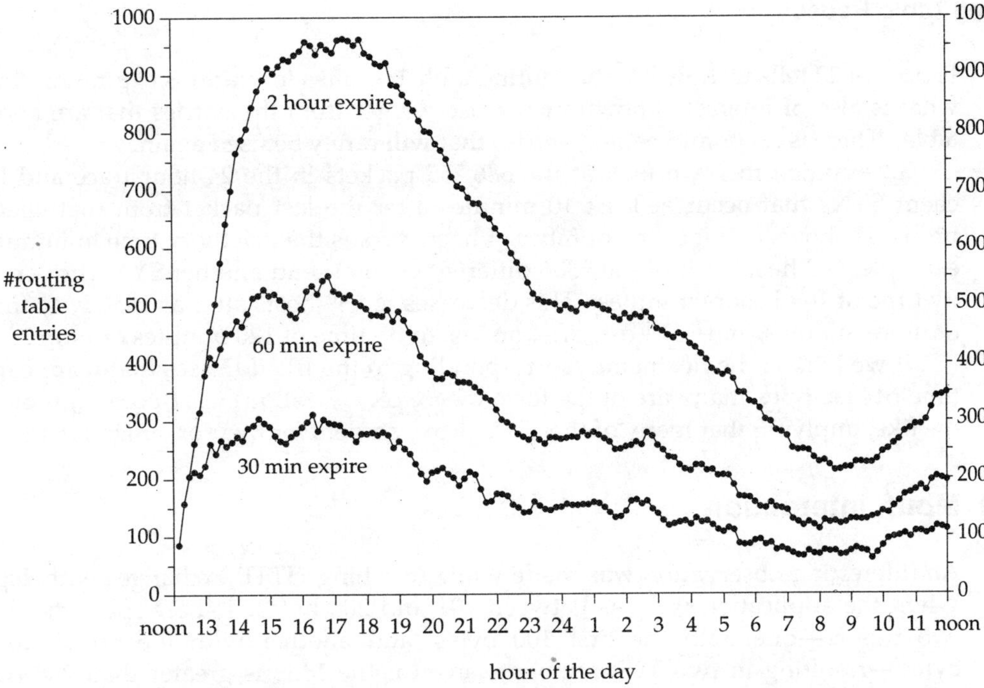

Figure 14.20 Simulation of T/TCP routing table: number of entries over time.

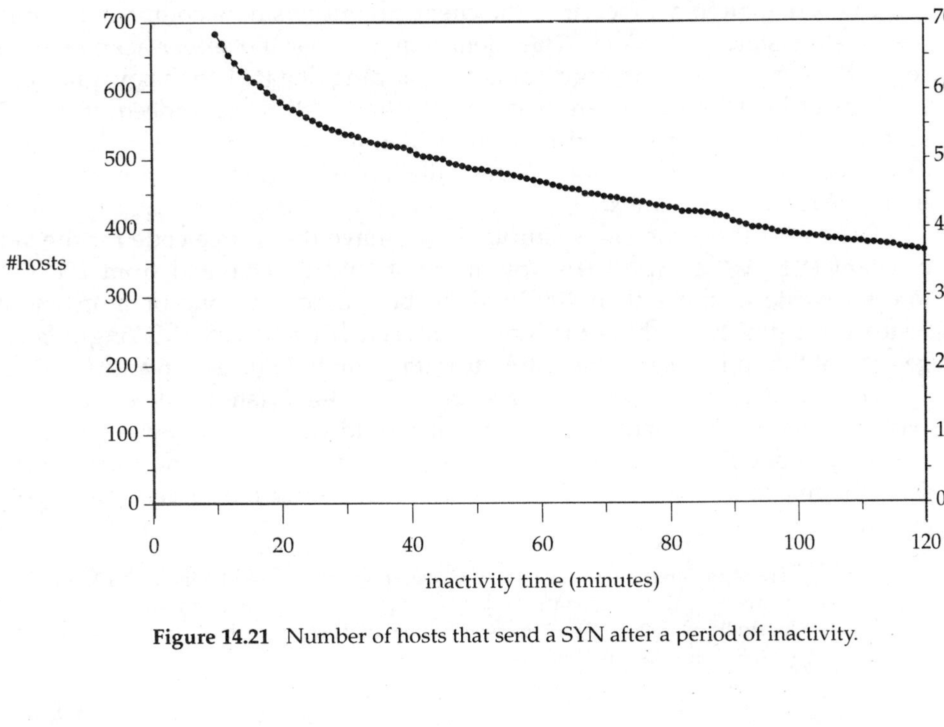

Figure 14.21 Number of hosts that send a SYN after a period of inactivity.

Routing Table Reuse

Figure 14.20 tells us how big the routing table becomes for various expiration times, but what is also of interest is how much reuse we get from the entries that are kept in the table. There is no point keeping entries that will rarely be used again.

To examine this, we look at the 686,755 packets in the 24-hour trace and look for client SYNs that occur at least 10 minutes after the last packet from that client. Figure 14.21 shows a plot of the number of hosts versus the inactivity time in minutes. For example, 683 hosts (out of the 5386 different clients) send another SYN after an inactivity time of 10 or more minutes. This decreases to 669 hosts after an inactivity time of 11 or more minutes, and 367 hosts after an inactivity time of 120 minutes or more.

If we look at the hostnames corresponding to the IP addresses that reappear after a time of inactivity, many are of the form `wwwproxy1`, `webgate1`, `proxy`, `gateway`, and the like, implying that many of these are proxy servers for their organizations.

14.11 Mbuf Interaction

An interesting observation was made while watching HTTP exchanges with Tcpdump. When the application write is between 101 and 208 bytes, 4.4BSD splits the data into two mbufs—one with the first 100 bytes, and another with the remaining 1–108 bytes—resulting in two TCP segments, even if the MSS is greater than 208 (which it normally is). The reason for this anomaly is in the `sosend` function, pp. 497 and 499 of Volume 2. Since TCP is not an atomic protocol, each time an mbuf is filled, the protocol's output function is called.

To make matters worse, since the client's request is now comprised of multiple segments, slow start is invoked. The client requires that the server acknowledge this first segment before the second segment is sent, adding one RTT to the overall time.

Lots of HTTP requests are between 101 and 208 bytes. Indeed, in the 17 requests sent in the example discussed in Section 13.4, all 17 were between 152 and 197 bytes. This is because the client request is basically a fixed format with only the URL changing from one request to the next.

The fix for this problem is simple (if you have the source code for the kernel). The constant `MINCLSIZE` (p. 37 of Volume 2) should be changed from 208 to 101. This forces a write of more than 100 bytes to be placed into one or more mbuf clusters, instead of using two mbufs for writes between 101 and 208. Making this change also gets rid of the spike seen at the 200-byte data point in Figures A.6 and A.7.

The client in the Tcpdump trace in Figure 14.22 (shown later) contains this fix. Without this fix the client's first segment would contain 100 bytes of data, the client would wait one RTT for an ACK of this segment (slow start), and then the client would send the remaining 52 bytes of data. Only then would the server's first reply segment be sent.

> There are alternate fixes. First, the size of an mbuf could be increased from 128 to 256 bytes. Some systems based on the Berkeley code have already done this (e.g., AIX). Second, changes could be made to `sosend` to avoid calling TCP output multiple times when mbufs (as opposed to mbuf clusters) are being used.

14.12 TCP PCB Cache and Header Prediction

When Net/3 TCP receives a segment, it saves the pointer to the corresponding Internet PCB (the `tcp_last_inpcb` pointer to the `inpcb` structure on p. 929 of Volume 2) in the hope that the next time a segment is received, it might be for the same connection. This saves the costly lookup through the TCP linked list of PCBs. Each time this cache comparison fails, the counter `tcps_pcbcachemiss` is incremented. In the sample statistics on p. 799 of Volume 2 the cache hit rate is almost 80%, but the system on which those statistics were collected is a general time-sharing system, not an HTTP server.

TCP input also performs header prediction (Section 28.4 of Volume 2), when the next received segment on a given connection is either the next expected ACK (the data sending side) or the next expected data segment (the data receiving side).

On the HTTP server used in this chapter the following percentages were observed:

- 20% PCB cache hit rate (18–20%),
- 15% header prediction rate for next ACK (14–15%),
- 30% header prediction rate for next data segment (20–35%).

All three rates are low. The variations in these percentages were small when measured every hour across two days: the number range in parentheses shows the low and high values.

The PCB cache hit rate is low, but this is not surprising given the large number of different clients using TCP at the same time on a busy HTTP server. This low rate is consistent with the fact that HTTP is really a transaction protocol, and [McKenney and Dove 1992] show that the Net/3 PCB cache performs poorly for a transaction protocol.

An HTTP server normally sends more data segments than it receives. Figure 14.22 is a time line of the first HTTP request from the client in Figure 13.5 (client port 1114). The client request is sent in segment 4 and the server's reply in segments 5, 6, 8, 9, 11, 13, and 14. There is only one potential next-data prediction for the server, segment 4. The potential next-ACK predictions for the server are segments 7, 10, 12, 15, and 16. (The connection is not established when segment 3 arrives, and the FIN in segment 17 disqualifies it from the header prediction code.) Whether any of these ACKs qualify for header prediction depends on the advertised window, which depends on how the HTTP client is reading the data returned by the server and when the client sends the ACKs. In segment 7, for example, TCP acknowledges the 1024 bytes that have been received, but the HTTP client application has read only 260 bytes from its socket buffer $(1024 - 8192 + 7428)$.

> This ACK with the funny window advertisement is a delayed ACK sent when the TCP 200-ms timer expires. The time difference between segments 7 and 12, both delayed ACKs, is 799 ms: 4 of TCP's 200-ms clock interrupts. This is the clue that both are delayed ACKs, sent because of a clock interrupt and not because the process had performed another read from its socket buffer. Segment 10 also appears to be a delayed ACK since the time between segments 7 and 10 is 603 ms.

The ACKs sent with the smaller advertised window defeat header prediction on the other end, because header prediction is performed only when the advertised window equals the current send window.

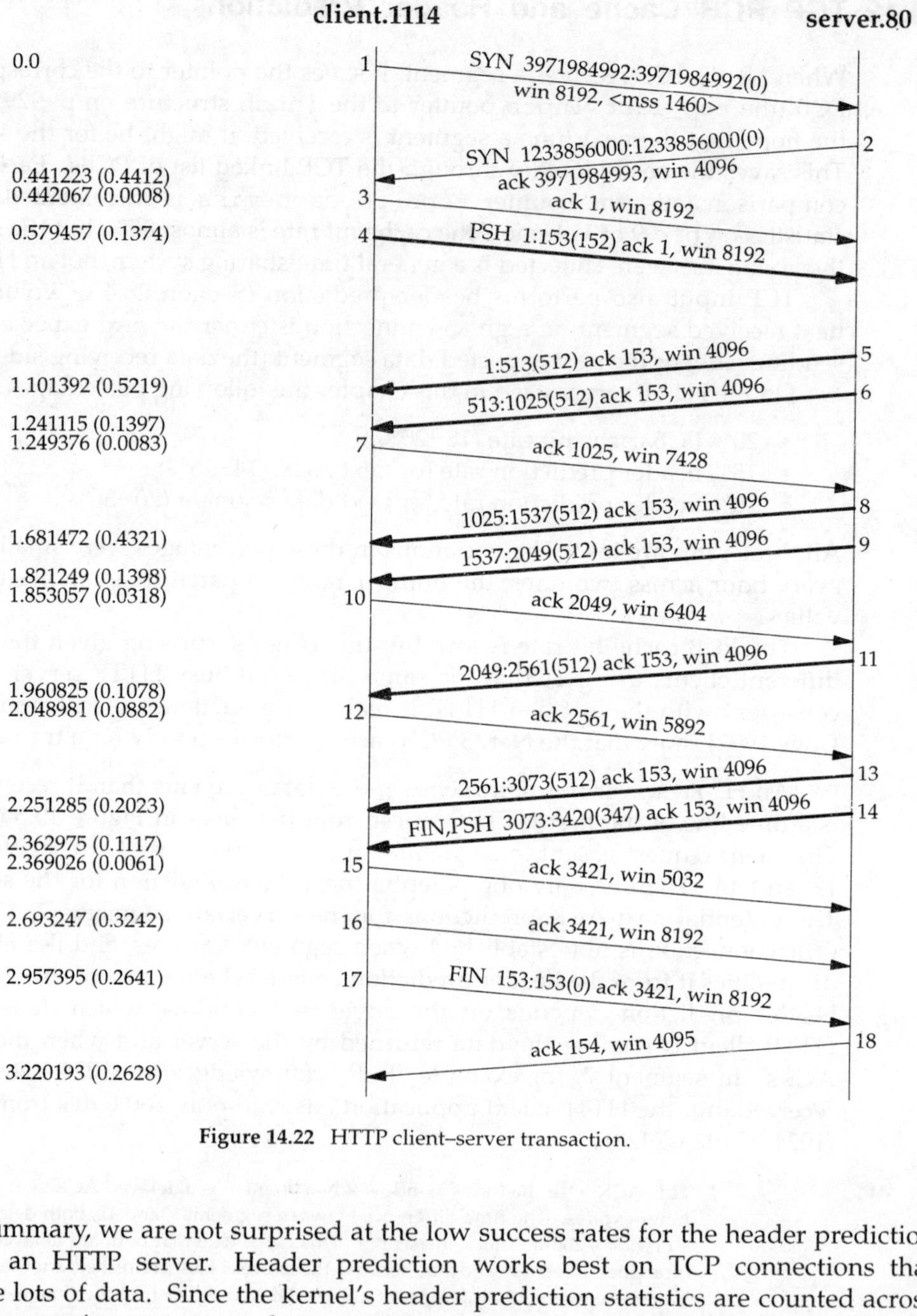

Figure 14.22 HTTP client–server transaction.

In summary, we are not surprised at the low success rates for the header prediction code on an HTTP server. Header prediction works best on TCP connections that exchange lots of data. Since the kernel's header prediction statistics are counted across all TCP connections, we can only guess that the higher percentage on this host for the next-data prediction (compared to the next-ACK prediction) is from the very long NNTP connections (Figure 15.3), which receive an average of 13 million bytes per TCP connection.

Slow Start Bug

Notice in Figure 14.22 that when the server sends its reply it does not slow start as expected. We expect the server to send its first 512-byte segment, wait for the client's ACK, and then send the next two 512-byte segments. Instead the server sends two 512-byte segments immediately (segments 5 and 6) without waiting for an ACK. Indeed, this is an anomaly found in most Berkeley-derived systems that is rarely noticed, since many applications have the client sending most data to the server. Even with FTP, for example, when fetching a file from an FTP server, the FTP server opens the data connection, effectively becoming the client for the data transfer. (Page 429 of Volume 1 shows an example of this.)

The bug is in the `tcp_input` function. New connections start with a congestion window of one segment. When the client's end of the connection establishment completes (pp. 949–950 of Volume 2), the code branches to `step6`, which bypasses the ACK processing. When the first data segment is sent by the client, its congestion window will be one segment, which is correct. But when the server's end of the connection establishment completes (p. 969 of Volume 2) control falls into the ACK processing code and the congestion window increases by one segment for the received ACK (p. 977 of Volume 2). This is why the server starts off sending two back-to-back segments. The correction for this bug is to include the code in Figure 11.16, regardless of whether or not the implementation supports T/TCP.

When the server receives the ACK in segment 7, its congestion window increases to three segments, but the server appears to send only two segments (8 and 9). What we cannot tell from Figure 14.22, since we only recorded the segments on one end of the connection (running Tcpdump on the client), is that segments 10 and 11 probably crossed somewhere in the network between the client and server. If this did indeed happen, then the server did have a congestion window of three segments as we expect.

The clues that the segments crossed are the RTT values from the packet trace. The RTT measured by the client between segments 1 and 2 is 441 ms, between segments 4 and 5 is 521 ms, and between segments 7 and 8 is 432 ms. These are reasonable and using Ping on the client (specifying a packet size of 300 bytes) also shows an RTT of about 461 ms to this server. But the RTT between segments 10 and 11 is 107 ms, which is too small.

14.13 Summary

Running a busy Web server stresses a TCP/IP implementation. We've seen that some bizarre packets can be received from the wide variety of clients existing on the Internet.

In this chapter we've examined packet traces from a busy Web server, looking at a variety of implementation features. We found the following items:

- The peak arrival rate of client SYNs can exceed the mean rate by a factor of 8 (when we ignore pathological clients).

- The RTT between the client and server had a mean of 445 ms and a median of 187 ms.
- The queue of incomplete connection requests can easily overflow with typical backlog limits of 5 or 10. The problem is not that the server process is busy, but that client SYNs sit on this queue for one RTT. Much larger limits for this queue are required for busy Web servers. Kernels should also provide a counter for the number of times this queue overflows to allow the system administrator to determine how often this occurs.
- Systems must provide a way to time out connections that are stuck in the LAST_ACK state sending persist probes, since this occurs regularly.
- Many Berkeley-derived systems have an mbuf feature that interacts poorly with Web clients when requests are issued of size 101–208 bytes (common for many clients).
- The TCP PCB cache found in many Berkeley-derived implementations and the TCP header prediction found in most implementations provide little help for a busy Web server.

A similar analysis of another busy Web server is provided in [Mogul 1995d].

15

NNTP: Network News Transfer Protocol

15.1 Introduction

NNTP, the Network News Transfer Protocol, distributes news articles between cooperating hosts. NNTP is an application protocol that uses TCP and it is described in RFC 977 [Kantor and Lapsley 1986]. Commonly implemented extensions are documented in [Barber 1995]. RFC 1036 [Horton and Adams 1987] documents the contents of the various header fields in the news articles.

Network news started as mailing lists on the ARPANET and then grew into the Usenet news system. Mailing lists are still popular today, but in terms of sheer volume, network news has shown large growth over the past decade. Figure 13.1 shows that NNTP accounts for as many packets as electronic mail. [Paxson 1994a] notes that since 1984 network news traffic has sustained a growth of about 75% per year.

Usenet is not a physical network, but a logical network that is implemented on top of many different types of physical networks. Years ago the popular way to exchange network news on Usenet was with dialup phone lines (normally after hours to save money), while today the Internet is the basis for most news distribution. Chapter 15 of [Salus 1995] details the history of Usenet.

Figure 15.1 is an overview of a typical news setup. One host is the organization's news server and maintains all the news articles on disk. This news server communicates with other news servers across the Internet, each feeding news to the other. NNTP is used for communication between the news servers. There are a variety of different implementations of news servers, with INN (InterNetNews) being the popular Unix server.

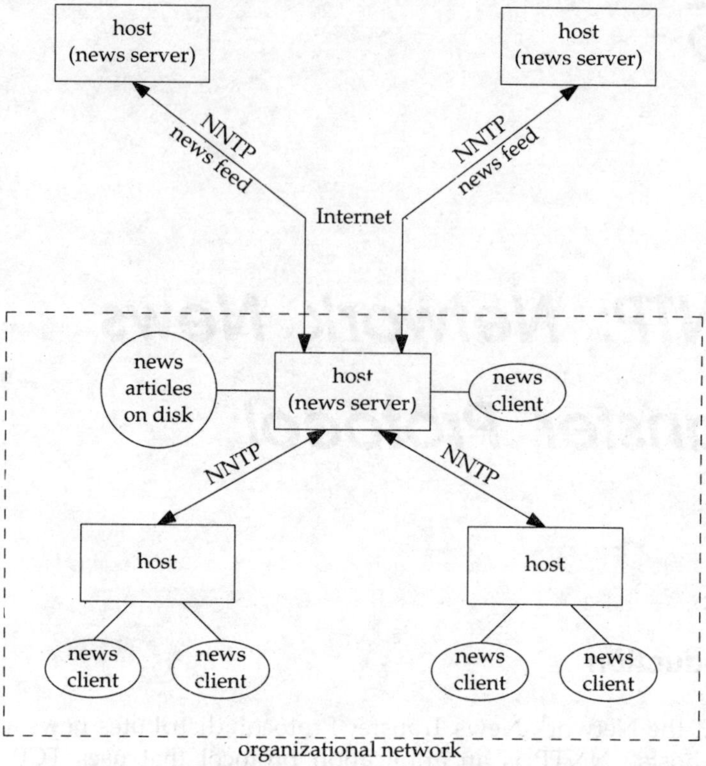

Figure 15.1 Typical news setup.

Other hosts within the organization access the news server to read news articles and post new articles to selected newsgroups. We label these client programs as "news clients." These client programs communicate with the news server using NNTP. Additionally, news clients on the same host as the news server normally use NNTP to read and post articles also.

There are dozens of news readers (clients), depending on the client operating system. The original Unix client was Readnews, followed by Rn and its many variations: Rrn is the remote version, allowing the client and server to be on different hosts; Trn stands for "threaded Rn" and it follows the various threads of discussion within a newsgroup; Xrn is a version of Rn for the X11 window system. GNUS is a popular news reader within the Emacs editor. It has also become common for Web browsers, such as Netscape, to provide an interface to news within the browser, obviating the need for a separate news client. Each news client presents a different user interface, similar to the multitude of different user interfaces presented by various email client programs.

Regardless of the client program, the common feature that binds the various clients to the server is the NNTP protocol, which is what we describe in this chapter.

15.2 NNTP Protocol

NNTP uses TCP, and the well-known port for the NNTP server is 119. NNTP is similar to other Internet applications (HTTP, FTP, SMTP, etc.) in that the client sends ASCII commands to the server and the server responds with a numeric response code followed by optional ASCII data (depending on the command). The command and response lines are terminated with a carriage return followed by a linefeed.

The easiest way to examine the protocol is to use the Telnet client and connect to the NNTP port on a host running an NNTP server. But normally we must connect from a client host that is known to the server, typically one from the same organizational network. For example, if we connect to a server from a host on another network across the Internet, we receive the following error:

```
vangogh.cs.berkeley.edu % telnet noao.edu nntp
Trying 140.252.1.54...                            output by Telnet client
Connected to noao.edu.                            output by Telnet client
Escape character is '^]'.                         output by Telnet client
502 You have no permission to talk.  Goodbye.
Connection closed by foreign host.                output by Telnet client
```

The fourth line of output, with the response code 502, is output by the NNTP server. The NNTP server receives the client's IP address when the TCP connection is established, and compares this address with its configured list of allowable client IP addresses.

In the next example we connect from a "local" client.

```
sun.tuc.noao.edu % telnet noao.edu nntp
Trying 140.252.1.54...
Connected to noao.edu.
Escape character is '^]'
200 noao InterNetNews NNRP server INN 1.4 22-Dec-93 ready (posting ok).
```

This time the response code from the server is 200 (command OK) and the remainder of the line is information about the server. The end of the message contains either "posting ok" or "no posting," depending on whether the client is allowed to post articles or not. (This is controlled by the system administrator depending on the client's IP address.)

One thing we notice in the server's response line is that the server is the NNRP server (Network News Reading Protocol), not the INND server (InterNetNews daemon). It turns out that the INND server accepts the client's connection request and then looks at the client's IP address. If the client's IP address is OK but the client is not one of the known news feeds, the NNRP server is invoked instead, assuming the client is one that wants to read news, and not one that will feed news to the server. This allows the implementation to separate the news feed server (about 10,000 lines of C code) from the news reading server (about 5000 lines of C code).

The meanings of the first and second digits of the numeric reply codes are shown in Figure 15.2. These are similar to the ones used by FTP (p. 424 of Volume 1).

Reply	Description
1yz	Informative message.
2yz	Command OK.
3yz	Command OK so far; send the rest of the command.
4yz	Command was correct but it could not be performed for some reason.
5yz	Command unimplemented, or incorrect, or a serious program error occurred.
x0z	Connection, setup, and miscellaneous messages.
x1z	Newsgroup selection.
x2z	Article selection.
x3z	Distribution functions.
x4z	Posting
x8z	Nonstandard extensions.
x9z	Debugging output.

Figure 15.2 Meanings of first and second digits of 3-digit reply codes.

Our first command to the news server is `help`, which lists all the commands supported by the server.

```
help
100 Legal commands                                    100 is reply code
  authinfo user Name|pass Password
  article [MessageID|Number]
  body [MessageID|Number]
  date
  group newsgroup
  head [MessageID|Number]
  help
  ihave
  last
  list [active|newsgroups|distributions|schema]
  listgroup newsgroup
  mode reader
  newgroups yymmdd hhmmss ["GMT"] [<distributions>]
  newnews newsgroups yymmdd hhmmss ["GMT"] [<distributions>]
  next
  post
  slave
  stat [MessageID|Number]
  xgtitle [group_pattern]
  xhdr header [range|MessageID]
  xover [range]
  xpat header range|MessageID pat [morepat...]
  xpath xpath MessageID
Report problems to <usenet@noao.edu>
                                   line with just a period terminates server reply
```

Since the client has no knowledge of how many lines of data will be returned by the server, the protocol requires the server to terminate its response with a line consisting of just a period. If any line actually begins with a period, the server prepends another period to the line before it is sent, and the client removes the period after the line is received.

Our next command is `list`, which when executed without any arguments lists each newsgroup name followed by the number of the last article in the group, the number of the first article in the group, and a "y" or "m" depending on whether posting to this newsgroup is allowed or whether the group is moderated.

```
list
215 Newsgroups in form "group high low flags".          215 is reply code
alt.activism 0000113976 13444 y
alt.aquaria 0000050114 44782 y
                                         many more lines that are not shown

comp.protocols.tcp-ip 0000043831 41289 y
comp.security.announce 0000000141 00117 m
                                         many more lines that are not shown

rec.skiing.alpine 0000025451 03612 y
rec.skiing.nordic 0000007641 01507 y
                           line with just a period terminates server reply
```

Again, 215 is the reply code, not the number of newsgroups. This example returned 4238 newsgroups comprising 175,833 bytes of TCP data from the server to the client. We have omitted all but 6 of the newsgroup lines. The returned listing of newsgroups is not normally in alphabetical order.

Fetching this listing from the server across a slow dialup link can often slow down the start-up of a news client. For example, assuming a data rate of 28,800 bits/sec this takes about 1 minute. (The actual measured time using a modem of this speed, which also compresses the data that is sent, was about 50 seconds.) On an Ethernet this takes less than 1 second.

The `group` command specifies the newsgroup to become the "current" newsgroup for this client. The following command selects `comp.protocols.tcp-ip` as the current group.

```
group comp.protocols.tcp-ip
211 181 41289 43831 comp.protocols.tcp-ip
```

The server responds with the code 211 (command OK) followed by an estimate of the number of articles in the group (181), the first article number in the group (41289), the last article number in the group (43831), and the name of the group. The difference between the ending and starting article numbers (43831 – 41289 = 2542) is often greater than the number of articles (181). One reason is that some articles, notably the FAQ for the group (Frequently Asked Questions), have a longer expiration time (perhaps one month) than most articles (often a few days, depending on the server's disk capacity). Another reason is that articles can be explicitly deleted.

We now ask the server for only the header lines for one particular article (number 43814) using the `head` command.

```
head 43814
221 43814 <3vtrje$ote@noao.edu> head
Path: noao!rstevens
From: rstevens@noao.edu (W. Richard Stevens)
Newsgroups: comp.protocols.tcp-ip
```

```
Subject: Re: IP Mapper: Using RAW sockets?
Date: 4 Aug 1995 19:14:54 GMT
Organization: National Optical Astronomy Observatories, Tucson, AZ, USA
Lines: 29
Message-ID: <3vtrje$ote@noao.edu>
References: <3vtdhb$jnf@oclc.org>
NNTP-Posting-Host: gemini.tuc.noao.edu
```

The first line of the reply begins with the reply code 221 (command OK), followed by 10 lines of header, followed by the line consisting of just a period.

Most of the header fields are self-explanatory, but the message IDs look bizarre. INN attempts to generate unique message IDs in the following format: the current time, a dollar sign, the process ID, an at-sign, and the fully qualified domain name of the local host. The time and process ID are numeric values that are printed as radix-32 strings: the numeric value is converted into 5-bit nibbles and each nibble printed using the alphabet `0..9a..v`.

We follow this with the `body` command for the same article number, which returns the body of the article.

```
body 43814
222 43814 <3vtrje$ote@noao.edu> body
> My group is looking at implementing an IP address mapper on a UNIX
                                        28 lines of the article not shown
```

Both the header lines and the body can be returned with a single command (`article`), but most news clients fetch the headers first, allowing the user to select articles based on the subject, and then fetch the body only for the articles chosen by the user.

We terminate the connection to the server with the `quit` command.

```
quit
205
Connection closed by foreign host.
```

The server's response is the numeric reply of 205. Our Telnet client indicates that the server closed the TCP connection.

This entire client–server exchange used a single TCP connection, which was initiated by the client. But most data across the connection is from the server to the client. The duration of the connection, and the amount of data exchanged, depends on how long the user reads news.

15.3 A Simple News Client

We now watch the exchange of NNTP commands and replies during a brief news session using a simple news client. We use the Rn client, one of the oldest news readers, because it is simple and easy to watch, and because it provides a debug option (the `-D16` command-line option, assuming the client was compiled with the debug option enabled). This lets us see the NNTP commands that are issued, along with the server's responses. We show the client commands in a bolder font.

1. The first command is `list`, which we saw in the previous section returned about 175,000 bytes from the server, one line per newsgroup.

   Rn also saves in the file `.newsrc` (in the user's home directory) a listing of the newsgroups that the user wants to read, with a list of the article numbers that have been read. For example, one line contains

   ```
   comp.protocols.tcp-ip: 1-43815
   ```

   By comparing the final article number for the newsgroup in the file with the final article number returned by the `list` command for that group, the client knows whether there are unread articles in the group.

2. The client then checks whether new newsgroups have been created.

   ```
   NEWGROUPS 950803 192708 GMT
   231 New newsgroups follow.                    231 is reply code
   ```

   Rn saves the time at which it was last notified of a new newsgroup in the file `.rnlast` in the user's home directory. That time becomes the argument to the `newgroups` command. (NNTP commands and command arguments are not case sensitive.) In this example the date saved is August 3, 1995, 19:27:08 GMT. The server's reply is empty (there are no lines between the line with the 231 reply code and the line consisting of just a period), indicating no new newsgroups. If there were new newsgroups, the client could ask the user whether to join the group or not.

3. Rn then displays the number of unread articles in the first 5 newsgroups and asks if we want to read the first newsgroup, `comp.protocols.tcp-ip`. We respond with an equals sign, directing Rn to display a one-line summary of all the articles in the group, so we can select which articles (if any) we want to read. (We can configure Rn with our `.rninit` file to display any type of per-article summary that we desire. The author displays the article number, subject, number of lines in the article, and the article's author.) The `group` command is issued by Rn, making this the current group.

   ```
   GROUP comp.protocols.tcp-ip
   211 182 41289 43832 comp.protocols.tcp-ip
   ```

   The header and body of the first unread article of the group are fetched with

   ```
   ARTICLE 43815
   220 43815 <3vtq8o$5p1@newsflash.concordia.ca> article
                                                 article not shown
   ```

   A one-line summary of the first unread article is displayed on the terminal.

4. For each of the remaining 17 unread articles in this newsgroup an `xhdr` command, followed by a `head` command, is issued. For example,

```
XHDR subject 43816
221 subject fields follow
43816 Re: RIP-2 and messy sub-nets

HEAD 43816
221 43816 <3vtqe3$cgb@xap.xyplex.com> head
```
14 lines of headers that are not shown

The xhdr command can accept a range of article numbers, not just a single number, which is why the server's return is a variable number of lines terminated with a line containing a period. A one-line summary of each article is displayed on the terminal.

5. We type the space bar, selecting the first unread article, and a head command is issued, followed by an article command. The article is displayed on the terminal. These two commands continue as we go sequentially through the articles.

6. When we are done with this newsgroup and move on to the next, another group command is sent by the client. We ask for a one-line summary of all the unread articles, and the same sequence of commands that we just described occurs again for the new group.

The first thing we notice is that the Rn client issues too many commands. For example, to produce the one-line summary of all the unread articles it issues an xhdr command to fetch the subject, followed by a head command, to fetch the entire header. The first of these two could be omitted. One reason for these extraneous commands is that the client was originally written to work on a host that is also the news server, without using NNTP, so these extra commands were "faster," not requiring a network round trip. The ability to access a remote server using NNTP was added later.

15.4 A More Sophisticated News Client

We now examine a more sophisticated news client, the Netscape version 1.1N Web browser, which has a built-in news reader. This client does not have a debug option, so we determined what it does by tracing the TCP packets that are exchanged between it and the news server.

1. When we start the client and select its news reader feature, it reads our .newsrc file and only asks the server about the newsgroups to which we subscribe. For each subscribed newsgroup a group command is issued to determine the starting and ending article numbers, which are compared to the last-read article number in our .newsrc file. In this example the author only subscribes to 77 of the over 4000 newsgroups, so 77 group commands are issued to the server. This takes only 23 seconds on a dialup PPP link, compared to 50 seconds for the list command used by Rn.

Reducing the number of newsgroups from 4000 to 77 should take much less than 23 seconds. Indeed, sending the same 77 group commands to the server using the sock (Appendix C of Volume 1) requires about 3 seconds. It would appear that the browser is overlapping these 77 commands with other startup processing.

2. We select one newsgroup with unread articles, comp.protocols.tcp-ip, and the following two commands are issued.

```
group comp.protocols.tcp-ip
211 181 41289 43831 comp.protocols.tcp-ip
xover 43815-43831
224 data follows
43815\tping works but netscape is flaky\troot@PROBLEM_WITH_INEWS
_DOMAIN_FILE (root)\t4 Aug 1995 18:52:08 GMT\t<3vtq8o$5p1@newsfl
ash.concordia.ca>\t\t1202\t13
43816\tRe: help me to select a terminal server\tgvcnet@hntp2.hin
et.net (gvcnet)\t5 Aug 1995 09:35:08 GMT\t<3vve0c$gq5@serv.hinet
.net>\t<claude.807537607@bauv111>\t1503\t23
```
one-line summary of remaining articles in range

The first command establishes the current newsgroup and the second asks the server for an overview of the specified articles. Article 43815 is the first unread article and 43831 is the last article number in the group. The one-line summary for each article consists of the article number, subject, author, date and time, message ID, message ID that the article references, number of bytes, and number of lines. (Notice that each one-line summary is long, so we have wrapped each line. We have also replaced the tab characters that separate the fields with \t so they can be seen.)

The Netscape client organizes the returned overview by subject and displays a listing of the unread subjects along with the article's author and the number of lines. An article and its replies are grouped together, which is called *threading*, since the threads of a discussion are grouped together.

3. For each article that we select to read, an article command is issued and the article is displayed.

From this brief overview it appears that the Netscape news client uses two optimizations to reduce the user's latency. First it only asks about newsgroups that the user reads, instead of issuing the list command. Second, it provides the per-newsgroup summary using the xover command, instead of issuing the head or xhdr commands for each article in the group.

15.5 NNTP Statistics

To understand the typical NNTP usage, Tcpdump was run to collect all the SYN, FIN, and RST segments used by NNTP on the same host used in Chapter 14. This host obtains its news from one NNTP news feed (there are additional backup news feeds, but all the segments observed were from a single feed) and in turn feeds 10 other sites. Of these 10 sites, only two use NNTP and the other 8 use UUCP, so our Tcpdump trace records only the two NNTP feeds. These two outgoing news feeds receive only a small portion of the arriving news. Finally, since the host is an Internet service provider, numerous clients read news using the host as an NNTP server. All the readers use NNTP—both the news reading processes on the same host and news readers on other hosts (typically connected using PPP or SLIP). Tcpdump was run continuously for 113 hours (4.7 days) and 1250 connections were collected. Figure 15.3 summarizes the information.

	1 Incoming news feed	2 Outgoing news feeds	News readers	Total
# connections	67	32	1,151	1,250
total bytes incoming	875,345,619	4,499	593,731	875,943,849
total bytes outgoing	4,071,785	1,194,086	56,488,715	61,754,586
total duration (min)	6,686	407	21,758	28,851
bytes incoming per conn.	13,064,860	141	516	
bytes outgoing per conn.	60,773	37,315	49,078	
average conn. duration (min)	100	13	19	

Figure 15.3 NNTP statistics on a single host for 4.7 days.

We first notice from the incoming news feed that this host receives about 186 million bytes of news per day, or an average of almost 8 million bytes per hour. We also notice that the NNTP connection to the primary news feed remains up for a long time: 100 minutes, exchanging 13 million bytes. After a period of inactivity across the TCP connection between this host and its incoming news feed, the TCP connection is closed by the news server. The connection is established again later, when needed.

The typical news reader uses the NNTP connection for about 19 minutes, reading almost 50,000 bytes of news. Most NNTP traffic is unidirectional: from the primary news feed to the server, and from the server to the news readers.

There is a huge site-to-site variation in the volume of NNTP traffic. These statistics should be viewed as one example—there is no typical value for these statistics.

15.6 Summary

NNTP is another simple protocol that uses TCP. The client issues ASCII commands (servers support over 20 different commands) and the server responds with a numeric response code, followed by one or more lines of reply, followed by a line consisting of just a period (if the reply can be variable length). As with many Internet protocols, the protocol itself has not changed for many years, but the interface presented by the client to the interactive user has been changing rapidly.

Much of the difference between different news readers depends on how the application uses the protocol. We saw differences between the Rn client and the Netscape client, in how they determine which articles are unread and in how they fetch the unread articles.

NNTP uses a single TCP connection for the duration of a client–server exchange. This differs from HTTP, which used one TCP connection for each file fetched from the server. One reason for this difference is that an NNTP client communicates with just one server, while an HTTP client can communicate with many different servers. We also saw that most data flow across the TCP connection with NNTP is unidirectional.

Part 3

The Unix Domain Protocols

16

Unix Domain Protocols: Introduction

16.1 Introduction

The Unix domain protocols are a form of interprocess communication (IPC) that are accessed using the same sockets API that is used for network communication. The left half of Figure 16.1 shows a client and server written using sockets and communicating on the same host using the Internet protocols. The right half shows a client and server written using sockets with the Unix domain protocols.

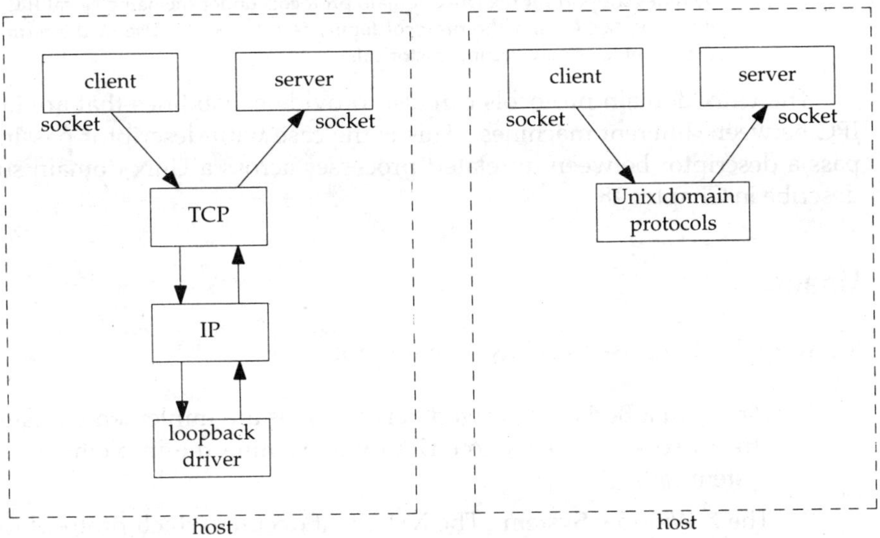

Figure 16.1 Client and server using the Internet protocols or the Unix domain protocols.

When the client sends data to the server using TCP, the data is processed by TCP output, then by IP output, sent to the loopback driver (Section 5.4 of Volume 2) where it is placed onto IP's input queue, then processed by IP input, then TCP input, and finally passed to the server. This works fine and it is transparent to the client and server that the peer is on the same host. Nevertheless, a fair amount of processing takes place in the TCP/IP protocol stack, processing that is not required when the data never leaves the host.

The Unix domain protocols provide less processing (i.e., they are faster) since they know that the data never leaves the host. There is no checksum to calculate or verify, there is no potential for data to arrive out of order, flow control is simplified because the kernel can control the execution of both processes, and so on. While other forms of IPC can also provide these same advantages (message queues, shared memory, named pipes, etc.) the advantage of the Unix domain protocols is that they use the same, identical sockets interface that networked applications use: clients call `connect`, servers calls `listen` and `accept`, both use `read` and `write`, and so on. The other forms of IPC use completely different APIs, some of which do not interact nicely with sockets and other forms of I/O (e.g., we cannot use the `select` function with System V message queues).

> Some TCP/IP implementations attempt to improve performance with optimizations, such as omitting the TCP checksum calculation and verification, when the destination is the loopback interface.

The Unix domain protocols provide both a stream socket (`SOCK_STREAM`, similar to a TCP byte stream) and a datagram socket (`SOCK_DGRAM`, similar to UDP datagrams). The address family for a Unix domain socket is `AF_UNIX`. The names used to identify sockets in the Unix domain are pathnames in the filesystem. (The Internet protocols use the combination of an IP address and a port number to identify TCP and UDP sockets.)

> The IEEE POSIX 1003.1g standard that is being developed for the network programming APIs includes support for the Unix domain protocols under the name "local IPC." The address family is `AF_LOCAL` and the protocol family is `PF_LOCAL`. Use of the term "Unix" to describe these protocols may become historical.

The Unix domain protocols can also provide capabilities that are not possible with IPC between different machines. This is the case with descriptor passing, the ability to pass a descriptor between unrelated processes across a Unix domain socket, which we describe in Chapter 18.

16.2 Usage

Many applications use the Unix domain protocols:

1. Pipes. In a Berkeley-derived kernel, pipes are implemented using Unix domain stream sockets. In Section 17.13 we examine the implementation of the `pipe` system call.
2. The X Window System. The X11 client decides which protocol to use when connecting with the X11 server, normally based on the value of the `DISPLAY`

environment variable, or on the value of the `-display` command-line argument. The value is of the form *hostname*:*display*.*screen*. The *hostname* is optional. Its default is the current host and the protocol used is the most efficient form of communication, typically the Unix domain stream protocol. A value of `unix` forces the Unix domain stream protocol. The name bound to the Unix socket by the server is something like `/tmp/.X11-unix/X0`.

Since an X server normally handles clients on either the same host or across a network, this implies that the server is waiting for a connection request to arrive on either a TCP socket or on a Unix stream socket.

3. The BSD print spooler (the `lpr` client and the `lpd` server, described in detail in Chapter 13 of [Stevens 1990]) communicates on the same host using a Unix domain stream socket named `/dev/lp`. Like the X server, the `lpd` server handles connections from clients on the same host using a Unix socket and connections from clients on the network using a TCP socket.
4. The BSD system logger—the `syslog` library function that can be called by any application and the `syslogd` server—communicate on the same host using a Unix domain datagram socket named `/dev/log`. The client writes a message to this socket, which the server reads and processes. The server also handles messages from clients on other hosts using a UDP socket. More details on this facility are in Section 13.4.2 of [Stevens 1992].
5. The InterNetNews daemon (`innd`) creates a Unix datagram socket on which it reads control messages and a Unix stream socket on which it reads articles from local news readers. The two sockets are named `control` and `nntpin`, and are normally in the `/var/news/run` directory.

This list is not exhaustive: there are other applications that use Unix domain sockets.

16.3 Performance

It is interesting to compare the performance of Unix domain sockets versus TCP sockets. A version of the public domain `ttcp` program was modified to use a Unix domain stream socket, in addition to TCP and UDP sockets. We sent 16,777,216 bytes between two copies of the program running on the same host and the results are summarized in Figure 16.2.

Kernel	Fastest TCP (bytes/sec)	Unix domain (bytes/sec)	% increase TCP → Unix
DEC OSF/1 V3.0	14,980,000	32,109,000	114 %
SunOS 4.1.3	4,877,000	11,570,000	137
BSD/OS V1.1	3,459,000	7,626,000	120
Solaris 2.4	2,829,000	3,570,000	26
AIX 3.2.2	1,592,000	3,948,000	148

Figure 16.2 Comparison of Unix domain socket throughput versus TCP.

What is interesting is the percent increase in speed from a TCP socket to a Unix domain socket, not the absolute speeds. (These tests were run on five different systems, covering a wide range of processor speeds. Speed comparisons between the different rows are meaningless.) All the kernels are Berkeley derived, other than Solaris 2.4. We see that Unix domain sockets are more than twice as fast as a TCP socket on a Berkeley-derived kernel. The percent increase is less under Solaris.

> Solaris, and SVR4 from which it is derived, have a completely different implementation of Unix domain sockets. Section 7.5 of [Rago 1993] provides a overview of the streams-based SVR4 implementation of Unix domain sockets.

In these tests the term "Fastest TCP" means the tests were run with the send buffer and receive buffer set to 32768 (which is larger than the defaults on some systems), and the loopback address was explicitly specified instead of the host's own IP address. On earlier BSD implementations if the host's own IP address is specified, the packet is not sent to the loopback interface until the ARP code is executed (p. 28 of Volume 1). This degrades performance slightly (which is why the timing tests were run specifying the loopback address). These hosts have a network entry for the local subnet whose interface is the network's device driver. The entry for network 140.252.13.32 at the top of p. 117 in Volume 1 is an example (SunOS 4.1.3). Newer BSD kernels have an explicit route to the host's own IP address whose interface is the loopback driver. The entry for 140.252.13.35 in Figure 18.2, p. 560 of Volume 2, is an example (BSD/OS V2.0).

We return to the topic of performance in Section 18.11 after examining the implementation of the Unix domain protocols.

16.4 Coding Examples

To show how minimal the differences are between a TCP client–server and a Unix domain client–server, we have modified Figures 1.5 and 1.7 to work with the Unix domain protocols. Figure 16.3 shows the Unix domain client. We show the differences from Figure 1.5 in a bolder font.

2–6 We include the `<sys/un.h>` header, and the client and server socket address structures are now of type `sockaddr_un`.

11–15 The protocol family for the call to `socket` is `PF_UNIX`. The socket address structure is filled in with the pathname associated with the server (from the command-line argument) using `strncpy`.

We'll see the reasons for these differences when we examine the implementation in the next chapter.

Figure 16.4 (p. 226) shows the Unix domain server. We identify the differences from Figure 1.7 with a bolder font.

2–7 We include the `<sys/un.h>` header and also `#define` the pathname associated with this server. (Normally this pathname would be defined in a header that is included by both the client and server; we define it here for simplicity.) The socket address structures are now of type `sockaddr_un`.

13–14 The server's socket address structure is filled in with the pathname using `strncpy`.

unixcli.c

```
#include    "cliserv.h"
#include    <sys/un.h>

int
main(int argc, char *argv[])
{                                   /* simple Unix domain client */
    struct sockaddr_un serv;
    char    request[REQUEST], reply[REPLY];
    int     sockfd, n;

    if (argc != 2)
        err_quit("usage: unixcli <pathname of server>");

    if ((sockfd = socket(PF_UNIX, SOCK_STREAM, 0)) < 0)
        err_sys("socket error");

    memset(&serv, 0, sizeof(serv));
    serv.sun_family = AF_UNIX;
    strncpy(serv.sun_path, argv[1], sizeof(serv.sun_path));

    if (connect(sockfd, (SA) &serv, sizeof(serv)) < 0)
        err_sys("connect error");

    /* form request[] ... */

    if (write(sockfd, request, REQUEST) != REQUEST)
        err_sys("write error");
    if (shutdown(sockfd, 1) < 0)
        err_sys("shutdown error");

    if ((n = read_stream(sockfd, reply, REPLY)) < 0)
        err_sys("read error");

    /* process "n" bytes of reply[] ... */

    exit(0);
}
```

unixcli.c

Figure 16.3 Unix domain transaction client.

16.5 Summary

The Unix domain protocols provide a form of interprocess communication using the same programming interface (sockets) as used for networked communication. The Unix domain protocols provide both a stream socket that is similar to TCP and a datagram socket that is similar to UDP. The advantage gained with the Unix domain is speed: on a Berkeley-derived kernel the Unix domain protocols are about twice as fast as TCP/IP.

The biggest users of the Unix domain protocols are pipes and the X Window System. If the X client finds that the X server is on the same host as the client, a Unix

unixserv.c

```
#include    "cliserv.h"
#include    <sys/un.h>

#define SERV_PATH   "/tmp/tcpipiv3.serv"

int
main()
{                               /* simple Unix domain server */
    struct sockaddr_un serv, cli;
    char    request[REQUEST], reply[REPLY];
    int     listenfd, sockfd, n, clilen;

    if ((listenfd = socket(PF_UNIX, SOCK_STREAM, 0)) < 0)
        err_sys("socket error");

    memset(&serv, 0, sizeof(serv));
    serv.sun_family = AF_UNIX;
    strncpy(serv.sun_path, SERV_PATH, sizeof(serv.sun_path));

    if (bind(listenfd, (SA) &serv, sizeof(serv)) < 0)
        err_sys("bind error");

    if (listen(listenfd, SOMAXCONN) < 0)
        err_sys("listen error");

    for (;;) {
        clilen = sizeof(cli);
        if ((sockfd = accept(listenfd, (SA) &cli, &clilen)) < 0)
            err_sys("accept error");

        if ((n = read_stream(sockfd, request, REQUEST)) < 0)
            err_sys("read error");

        /* process "n" bytes of request[] and create reply[] ... */

        if (write(sockfd, reply, REPLY) != REPLY)
            err_sys("write error");

        close(sockfd);
    }
}
```

unixserv.c

Figure 16.4 Unix domain transaction server.

domain stream connection is used instead of a TCP connection. The coding changes are minimal between a TCP client–server and a Unix domain client–server.

The following two chapters describe the implementation of Unix domain sockets in the Net/3 kernel.

17

Unix Domain Protocols: Implementation

17.1 Introduction

The source code to implement the Unix domain protocols consists of 16 functions in the file `uipc_usrreq.c`. This totals about 1000 lines of C code, which is similar in size to the 800 lines required to implement UDP in Volume 2, but far less than the 4500 lines required to implement TCP.

We divide our presentation of the Unix domain protocol implementation into two chapters. This chapter covers everything other than I/O and descriptor passing, both of which we describe in the next chapter.

17.2 Code Introduction

There are 16 Unix domain functions in a single C file and various definitions in another C file and two headers, as shown in Figure 17.1.

File	Description
`sys/un.h`	`sockaddr_un` structure definition
`sys/unpcb.h`	`unpcb` structure definition
`kern/uipc_proto.c`	Unix domain `protosw{}` and `domain{}` definitions
`kern/uipc_usrreq.c`	Unix domain functions
`kern/uipc_syscalls.c`	`pipe` and `socketpair` system calls

Figure 17.1 Files discussed in this chapter.

We also include in this chapter a presentation of the `pipe` and `socketpair` system calls, both of which use the Unix domain functions described in this chapter.

Global Variables

Figure 17.2 shows 11 global variables that are introduced in this chapter and the next.

Variable	Datatype	Description
unixdomain	struct domain	domain definitions (Figure 17.4)
unixsw	struct protosw	protocol definitions (Figure 17.5)
sun_noname	struct sockaddr	socket address structure containing null pathname
unp_defer	int	garbage collection counter of deferred entries
unp_gcing	int	set if currently performing garbage collection
unp_ino	ino_t	value of next fake i-node number to assign
unp_rights	int	count of file descriptors currently in flight
unpdg_recvspace	u_long	default size of datagram socket receive buffer, 4096 bytes
unpdg_sendspace	u_long	default size of datagram socket send buffer, 2048 bytes
unpst_recvspace	u_long	default size of stream socket receive buffer, 4096 bytes
unpst_sendspace	u_long	default size of stream socket send buffer, 4096 bytes

Figure 17.2 Global variables introduced in this chapter.

17.3 Unix `domain` and `protosw` Structures

Figure 17.3 shows the three `domain` structures normally found in a Net/3 system, along with their corresponding `protosw` arrays.

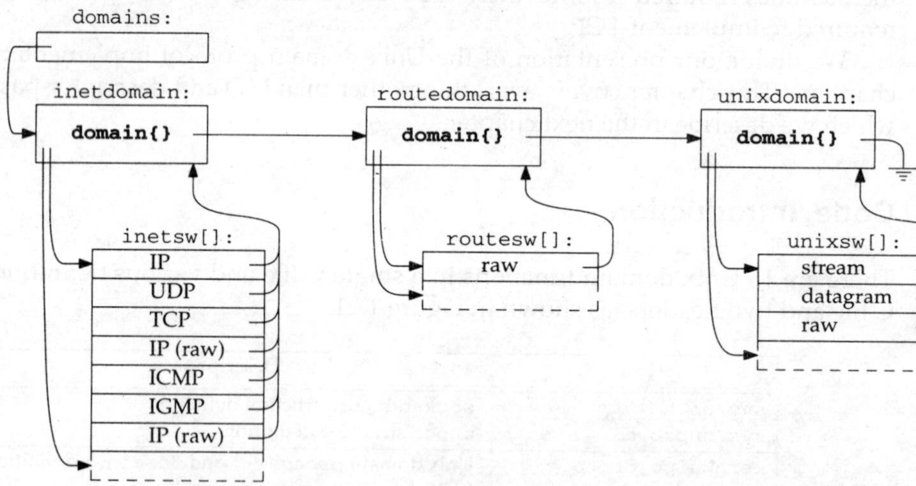

Figure 17.3 The `domain` list and `protosw` arrays.

Volume 2 described the Internet and routing domains. Figure 17.4 shows the fields in the `domain` structure (p. 187 of Volume 2) for the Unix domain protocols.

> The historical reasons for two raw IP entries are described on p. 191 of Volume 2.

Member	Value	Description
dom_family	*PF_UNIX*	protocol family for domain
dom_name	*unix*	name
dom_init	*0*	not used in Unix domain
dom_externalize	*unp_externalize*	externalize access rights (Figure 18.12)
dom_dispose	*unp_dispose*	dispose of internalized rights (Figure 18.14)
dom_protosw	*unixsw*	array of protocol switch structures (Figure 17.5)
dom_protoswNPROTOSW		pointer past end of protocol switch structure
dom_next		filled in by domaininit, p. 194 of Volume 2
dom_rtattach	*0*	not used in Unix domain
dom_rtoffset	*0*	not used in Unix domain
dom_maxrtkey	*0*	not used in Unix domain

Figure 17.4 unixdomain structure.

The Unix domain is the only one that defines dom_externalize and dom_dispose functions. We describe these in Chapter 18 when we discuss the passing of descriptors. The final three members of the structure are not defined since the Unix domain does not maintain a routing table.

Figure 17.5 shows the initialization of the unixsw structure. (Page 192 of Volume 2 shows the corresponding structure for the Internet protocols.)

uipc_proto.c

```
struct protosw unixsw[] =
{
    {SOCK_STREAM, &unixdomain, 0, PR_CONNREQUIRED | PR_WANTRCVD | PR_RIGHTS,
     0, 0, 0, 0,
     uipc_usrreq,
     0, 0, 0, 0,
    },
    {SOCK_DGRAM, &unixdomain, 0, PR_ATOMIC | PR_ADDR | PR_RIGHTS,
     0, 0, 0, 0,
     uipc_usrreq,
     0, 0, 0, 0,
    },
    {0, 0, 0, 0,
     raw_input, 0, raw_ctlinput, 0,
     raw_usrreq,
     raw_init, 0, 0, 0,
    },
};
```

uipc_proto.c

Figure 17.5 Initialization of unixsw array.

Three protocols are defined:

- a stream protocol similar to TCP,
- a datagram protocol similar to UDP, and
- a raw protocol similar to raw IP.

The Unix domain stream and datagram protocols both specify the PR_RIGHTS flag, since the domain supports access rights (the passing of descriptors, which we describe in the next chapter). The other two flags for the stream protocol, PR_CONNREQUIRED and PR_WANTRCVD, are identical to the TCP flags, and the other two flags for the datagram protocol, PR_ATOMIC and PR_ADDR, are identical to the UDP flags. Notice that the only function pointer defined for the stream and datagram protocols is uipc_usrreq, which handles all user requests.

The four function pointers in the raw protocol's protosw structure, all beginning with raw_, are the same ones used with the PF_ROUTE domain, which is described in Chapter 20 of Volume 2.

> The author has never heard of an application that uses the raw Unix domain protocol.

17.4 Unix Domain Socket Address Structures

Figure 17.6 shows the definition of a Unix domain socket address structure, a sockaddr_un structure occupying 106 bytes.

un.h

```
struct sockaddr_un {
    u_char  sun_len;          /* sockaddr length including null */
    u_char  sun_family;       /* AF_UNIX */
    char    sun_path[104];    /* path name (gag) */
};
```

un.h

Figure 17.6 Unix domain socket address structure.

The first two fields are the same as all other socket address structures: a length byte followed by the address family (AF_UNIX).

> The comment "gag" has existed since 4.2BSD. Either the original author did not like using pathnames to identify Unix domain sockets, or the comment is because there is not enough room in the mbuf for a complete pathname (whose length can be up to 1024 bytes).

We'll see that Unix domain sockets use pathnames in the filesystem to identify sockets and the pathname is stored in the sun_path member. The size of this member is 104 to allow room for the socket address structure in a 128-byte mbuf, along with a terminating null byte. We show this in Figure 17.7.

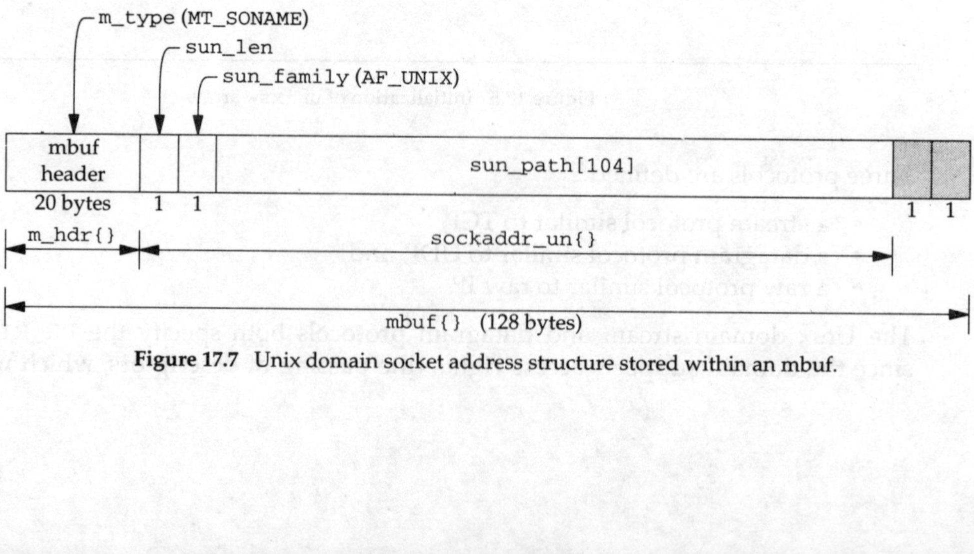

Figure 17.7 Unix domain socket address structure stored within an mbuf.

We show the `m_type` field of the mbuf set to `MT_SONAME`, because that is the normal value when the mbuf contains a socket address structure. Although it appears that the final 2 bytes are unused, and that the maximum length pathname that can be associated with these sockets is 104 bytes, we'll see that the `unp_bind` and `unp_connect` functions allow a pathname up to 105 bytes, followed by a null byte.

Unix domain sockets need a *name space* somewhere, and pathnames were chosen since the filesystem name space already existed. As other examples, the Internet protocols use IP addresses and port numbers for their name space, and System V IPC (Chapter 14 of [Stevens 1992]) uses 32-bit keys. Since pathnames are used by Unix domain clients to rendezvous with servers, absolute pathnames are normally used (those that begin with /). If relative pathnames are used, the client and server must be in the same directory or the server's bound pathname will not be found by the client's `connect` or `sendto`.

17.5 Unix Domain Protocol Control Blocks

Sockets in the Unix domain have an associated protocol control block (PCB), a `unpcb` structure. We show this 36-byte structure in Figure 17.8.

unpcb.h

```
struct unpcb {
    struct socket *unp_socket;   /* pointer back to socket structure */
    struct vnode *unp_vnode;     /* nonnull if associated with file */
    ino_t   unp_ino;             /* fake inode number */
    struct unpcb *unp_conn;      /* control block of connected socket */
    struct unpcb *unp_refs;      /* referencing socket linked list */
    struct unpcb *unp_nextref;   /* link in unp_refs list */
    struct mbuf *unp_addr;       /* bound address of socket */
    int     unp_cc;              /* copy of rcv.sb_cc */
    int     unp_mbcnt;           /* copy of rcv.sb_mbcnt */
};

#define sotounpcb(so)   ((struct unpcb *)((so)->so_pcb))
```

unpcb.h

Figure 17.8 Unix domain protocol control block.

Unlike Internet PCBs and the control blocks used in the route domain, both of which are allocated by the kernel's `MALLOC` function (pp. 665 and 718 of Volume 2), the `unpcb` structures are stored in mbufs. This is probably an historical artifact.

Another difference is that all control blocks other than the Unix domain control blocks are maintained on a doubly linked circular list that can be searched when data arrives that must be demultiplexed to the appropriate socket. There is no need for such a list of all Unix domain control blocks because the equivalent operation, say, finding the server's control block when the client calls `connect`, is performed by the existing pathname lookup functions in the kernel. Once the server's `unpcb` is located, its address is stored in the client's `unpcb`, since the client and server are on the same host with Unix domain sockets.

Figure 17.9 shows the arrangement of the various data structures dealing with Unix domain sockets. In this figure we show two Unix domain datagram sockets. We assume that the socket on the right (the server) has bound a pathname to its socket and the socket on the left (the client) has connected to the server's pathname.

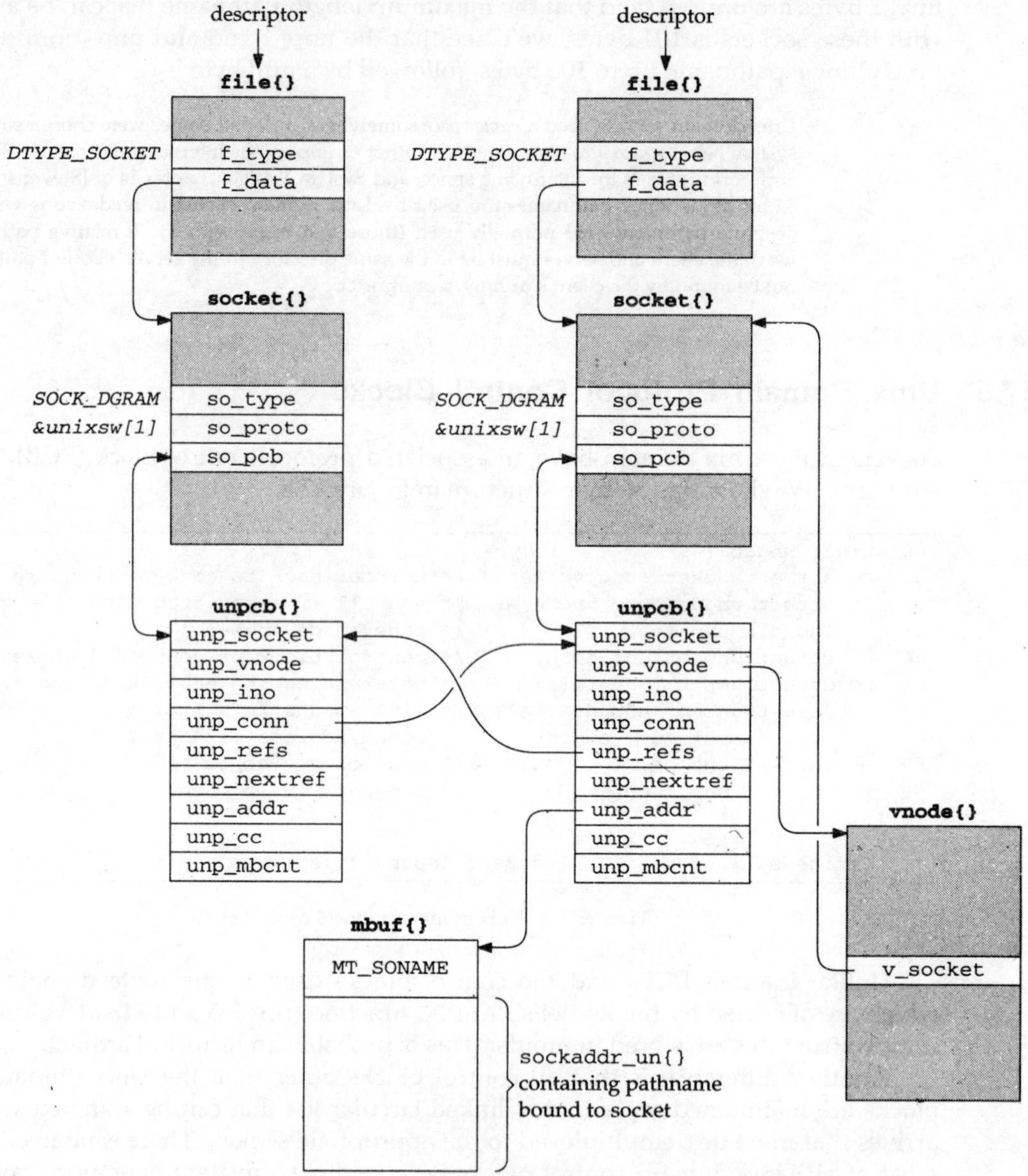

Figure 17.9 Two Unix domain datagram sockets connected to each other.

The unp_conn member of the client PCB points to the server's PCB. The server's unp_refs points to the first client that has connected to this PCB. (Unlike stream sockets, multiple datagram clients can connect to a single server. We discuss the connection of Unix domain datagram sockets in detail in Section 17.11.)

The unp_vnode member of the server socket points to the vnode associated with the pathname that the server socket was bound to and the v_socket member of the vnode points to the server's socket. This is the link required to locate a unpcb that has been bound to a pathname. For example, when the server binds a pathname to its Unix domain socket, a vnode structure is created and the pointer to the unpcb is stored in the v_socket member of the v-node. When the client connects to this server, the pathname lookup code in the kernel locates the v-node and then obtains the pointer to the server's unpcb from the v_socket pointer.

The name that was bound to the server's socket is contained in a sockaddr_un structure, which is itself contained in an mbuf structure, pointed to by the unp_addr member. Unix v-nodes never contain the pathname that led to the v-node, because in a Unix filesystem a given file (i.e., v-node) can be pointed to by multiple names (i.e., directory entries).

Figure 17.9 shows two connected datagram sockets. We'll see in Figure 17.26 that some things differ when we deal with stream sockets.

17.6 uipc_usrreq Function

We saw in Figure 17.5 that the only function referenced in the unixsw structure for the stream and datagram protocols is uipc_usrreq. Figure 17.10 shows the outline of the function.

PRU_CONTROL requests invalid

57–58 The PRU_CONTROL request is from the ioctl system call and is not supported in the Unix domain.

Control information supported only for PRU_SEND

59–62 If control information was passed by the process (using the sendmsg system call) the request must be PRU_SEND, or an error is returned. Descriptors are passed between processes using control information with this request, as we describe in Chapter 18.

Socket must have a control block

63–66 If the socket structure doesn't point to a Unix domain control block, the request must be PRU_ATTACH; otherwise an error is returned.

67–248 We discuss the individual case statements from this function in the following sections, along with the various unp_*xxx* functions that are called.

249–255 Any control information and data mbufs are released and the function returns.

17.7 PRU_ATTACH Request and unp_attach Function

The PRU_ATTACH request, shown in Figure 17.11, is issued by the socket system call and the sonewconn function (p. 462 of Volume 2) when a connection request arrives for a listening stream socket.

uipc_usrreq.c

```
47 int
48 uipc_usrreq(so, req, m, nam, control)
49 struct socket *so;
50 int     req;
51 struct mbuf *m, *nam, *control;
52 {
53     struct unpcb *unp = sotounpcb(so);
54     struct socket *so2;
55     int     error = 0;
56     struct proc *p = curproc;     /* XXX */

57     if (req == PRU_CONTROL)
58         return (EOPNOTSUPP);
59     if (req != PRU_SEND && control && control->m_len) {
60         error = EOPNOTSUPP;
61         goto release;
62     }
63     if (unp == 0 && req != PRU_ATTACH) {
64         error = EINVAL;
65         goto release;
66     }
67     switch (req) {

            /* switch cases (discussed in following sections) */

246     default:
247         panic("piusrreq");
248     }
249   release:
250     if (control)
251         m_freem(control);
252     if (m)
253         m_freem(m);
254     return (error);
255 }
```

uipc_usrreq.c

Figure 17.10 Body of `uipc_usrreq` function.

uipc_usrreq.c

```
68     case PRU_ATTACH:
69         if (unp) {
70             error = EISCONN;
71             break;
72         }
73         error = unp_attach(so);
74         break;
```

uipc_usrreq.c

Figure 17.11 `PRU_ATTACH` request.

68–74 The `unp_attach` function, shown in Figure 17.12, does all the work for this request. The `socket` structure has already been allocated and initialized by the socket layer and it is now up to the protocol layer to allocate and initialize its own protocol control block, a unpcb structure in this case.

uipc_usrreq.c

```
270 int
271 unp_attach(so)
272 struct socket *so;
273 {
274     struct mbuf *m;
275     struct unpcb *unp;
276     int     error;

277     if (so->so_snd.sb_hiwat == 0 || so->so_rcv.sb_hiwat == 0) {
278         switch (so->so_type) {

279         case SOCK_STREAM:
280             error = soreserve(so, unpst_sendspace, unpst_recvspace);
281             break;

282         case SOCK_DGRAM:
283             error = soreserve(so, unpdg_sendspace, unpdg_recvspace);
284             break;

285         default:
286             panic("unp_attach");
287         }
288         if (error)
289             return (error);
290     }
291     m = m_getclr(M_DONTWAIT, MT_PCB);
292     if (m == NULL)
293         return (ENOBUFS);
294     unp = mtod(m, struct unpcb *);
295     so->so_pcb = (caddr_t) unp;
296     unp->unp_socket = so;
297     return (0);
298 }
```

uipc_usrreq.c

Figure 17.12 unp_attach function.

Set socket high-water marks

277–290 If the socket's send high-water mark or receive high-water mark is 0, soreserve sets the values to the defaults shown in Figure 17.2. The high-water marks limit the amount of data that can be in a socket's send or receive buffer. These two high-water marks are both 0 when unp_attach is called through the socket system call, but they contain the values for the listening socket when called through sonewconn.

Allocate and initialize PCB

291–296 m_getclr obtains an mbuf that is used for the unpcb structure, zeros out the mbuf, and sets the type to MT_PCB. Notice that all the members of the PCB are initialized to 0. The socket and unpcb structures are linked through the so_pcb and unp_socket pointers.

17.8 PRU_DETACH Request and unp_detach Function

The PRU_DETACH request, shown in Figure 17.13, is issued when a socket is closed (p. 472 of Volume 2), following the PRU_DISCONNECT request (which is issued for connected sockets only).

uipc_usrreq.c

```
75      case PRU_DETACH:
76          unp_detach(unp);
77          break;
```

uipc_usrreq.c

Figure 17.13 PRU_DETACH request.

75–77 The unp_detach function, shown in Figure 17.14, does all the work for the PRU_DETACH request.

uipc_usrreq.c

```
299 void
300 unp_detach(unp)
301 struct unpcb *unp;
302 {
303     if (unp->unp_vnode) {
304         unp->unp_vnode->v_socket = 0;
305         vrele(unp->unp_vnode);
306         unp->unp_vnode = 0;
307     }
308     if (unp->unp_conn)
309         unp_disconnect(unp);
310     while (unp->unp_refs)
311         unp_drop(unp->unp_refs, ECONNRESET);
312     soisdisconnected(unp->unp_socket);
313     unp->unp_socket->so_pcb = 0;
314     m_freem(unp->unp_addr);
315     (void) m_free(dtom(unp));
316     if (unp_rights) {
317         /*
318          * Normally the receive buffer is flushed later,
319          * in sofree, but if our receive buffer holds references
320          * to descriptors that are now garbage, we will dispose
321          * of those descriptor references after the garbage collector
322          * gets them (resulting in a "panic: closef: count < 0").
323          */
324         sorflush(unp->unp_socket);
325         unp_gc();
326     }
327 }
```

uipc_usrreq.c

Figure 17.14 unp_detach function.

Release v-node

303–307 If the socket is associated with a v-node, that structure's pointer to this PCB is set to 0 and vrele releases the v-node.

Disconnect if closing socket is connected

308–309 If the socket being closed is connected to another socket, unp_disconnect disconnects the sockets. This can happen with both stream and datagram sockets.

Disconnect sockets connected to closing socket

310–311 If other datagram sockets are connected to this socket, those connections are dropped by unp_drop and those sockets receive the ECONNRESET error. This while loop goes through the linked list of all unpcb structures connected to this unpcb. The function unp_drop calls unp_disconnect, which changes this PCB's unp_refs member to point to the next member of the list. When the entire list has been processed, this PCB's unp_refs pointer will be 0.

312–313 The socket being closed is disconnected by soisdisconnected and the pointer from the socket structure to the PCB is set to 0.

Free address and PCB mbufs

314–315 If the socket has bound an address, the mbuf containing the address is released by m_freem. Notice that the code does not check whether the unp_addr pointer is nonnull, since that is checked by m_freem. The unpcb structure is released by m_free.

> This call to m_free should be moved to the end of the function, since the pointer unp may be used in the next piece of code.

Check for descriptors being passed

316–326 If there are descriptors currently being passed by any process in the kernel, unp_rights is nonzero, which causes sorflush and unp_gc (the garbage collector) to be called. We describe the passing of descriptors in Chapter 18.

17.9 PRU_BIND Request and unp_bind Function

Stream and datagram sockets in the Unix domain can be bound to pathnames in the filesystem with bind. The bind system call issues the PRU_BIND request, which we show in Figure 17.15.

uipc_usrreq.c

```
78      case PRU_BIND:
79          error = unp_bind(unp, nam, p);
80          break;
```

uipc_usrreq.c

Figure 17.15 PRU_BIND request.

78–80 All the work is done by the unp_bind function, shown in Figure 17.16.

Initialize nameidata structure

338–339 unp_bind allocates a nameidata structure, which encapsulates all the arguments to the namei function, and initializes the structure using the NDINIT macro. The CREATE argument specifies that the pathname will be created, FOLLOW allows symbolic links to be followed, and LOCKPARENT specifies that the parent's v-node must be locked on return (to prevent another process from modifying the v-node until we're done).

uipc_usrreq.c

```
int
unp_bind(unp, nam, p)
struct unpcb *unp;
struct mbuf *nam;
struct proc *p;
{
    struct sockaddr_un *soun = mtod(nam, struct sockaddr_un *);
    struct vnode *vp;
    struct vattr vattr;
    int     error;
    struct nameidata nd;

    NDINIT(&nd, CREATE, FOLLOW | LOCKPARENT, UIO_SYSSPACE, soun->sun_path, p);
    if (unp->unp_vnode != NULL)
        return (EINVAL);
    if (nam->m_len == MLEN) {
        if (*(mtod(nam, caddr_t) + nam->m_len - 1) != 0)
            return (EINVAL);
    } else
        *(mtod(nam, caddr_t) + nam->m_len) = 0;
/* SHOULD BE ABLE TO ADOPT EXISTING AND wakeup() ALA FIFO's */
    if (error = namei(&nd))
        return (error);
    vp = nd.ni_vp;
    if (vp != NULL) {
        VOP_ABORTOP(nd.ni_dvp, &nd.ni_cnd);
        if (nd.ni_dvp == vp)
            vrele(nd.ni_dvp);
        else
            vput(nd.ni_dvp);
        vrele(vp);
        return (EADDRINUSE);
    }
    VATTR_NULL(&vattr);
    vattr.va_type = VSOCK;
    vattr.va_mode = ACCESSPERMS;
    if (error = VOP_CREATE(nd.ni_dvp, &nd.ni_vp, &nd.ni_cnd, &vattr))
        return (error);
    vp = nd.ni_vp;
    vp->v_socket = unp->unp_socket;
    unp->unp_vnode = vp;
    unp->unp_addr = m_copy(nam, 0, (int) M_COPYALL);
    VOP_UNLOCK(vp, 0, p);
    return (0);
}
```

uipc_usrreq.c

Figure 17.16 unp_bind function.

UIO_SYSSPACE specifies that the pathname is in the kernel (since the bind system call processing copies it from the user space into an mbuf). soun->sun_path is the starting address of the pathname (which is passed to unp_bind as its nam argument).

Finally, p is the pointer to the proc structure for the process that issued the bind system call. This structure contains all the information about a process that the kernel needs to keep in memory at all times. The NDINIT macro only initializes the structure; the call to namei is later in this function.

> Historically the name of the function that looks up pathnames in the filesystem has been namei, which stands for "name-to-inode." This function would go through the filesystem searching for the specified name and, if successful, initialize an inode structure in the kernel that contained a copy of the file's i-node information from disk. Although i-nodes have been superseded by v-nodes, the term namei remains.

> This is our first major encounter with the filesystem code in the BSD kernel. The kernel supports many different types of filesystems: the standard disk filesystem (sometimes called the "fast file system"), network filesystems (NFS), CD-ROM filesystems, MS-DOS filesystems, memory-based filesystems (for directories such as /tmp), and so on. [Kleiman 1986] describes an early implementation of v-nodes. The functions with names beginning with VOP_ are generic v-node operation functions. There are about 40 of these functions and when called, each invokes a filesystem-defined function to perform that operation. The functions beginning with a lowercase v are kernel functions that may call one or more of the VOP_ functions. For example, vput calls VOP_UNLOCK and then calls vrele. The function vrele releases a v-node: the v-node's reference count is decremented and if it reaches 0, VOP_INACTIVE is called.

Check if socket is already bound

340–341 If the unp_vnode member of the socket's PCB is nonnull, the socket is already bound, which is an error.

Null terminate pathname

342–346 If the length of the mbuf containing the sockaddr_un structure is 108 (MLEN), which is copied from the third argument to the bind system call, then the final byte of the mbuf must be a null byte. This ensures that the pathname is null terminated, which is required when the pathname is looked up in the filesystem. (The sockargs function, p. 452 of Volume 2, ensures that the length of the socket address structure passed by the process is not greater than 108.) If the length of the mbuf is less than 108, a null byte is stored at the end of the pathname, in case the process did not null-terminate the pathname.

Lookup pathname in filesystem

347–349 namei looks up the pathname in the filesystem and tries to create an entry for the specified filename in the appropriate directory. For example, if the pathname being bound to the socket is /tmp/.X11-unix/X0, the filename X0 must be added to the directory /tmp/.X11-unix. This directory containing the entry for X0 is called the parent directory. If the directory /tmp/.X11-unix does not exist, or if the directory exists but already contains a file named X0, an error is returned. Another possible error is that the calling process does not have permission to create a new file in the parent directory. The desired return from namei is a value of 0 from the function and nd.ni_vp a null pointer (the file does not already exist). If both of these conditions are true, then nd.ni_dvp contains the locked directory of the parent in which the new filename will be created.

> The comment about adopting an existing pathname refers to `bind` returning an error if the pathname already exists. Therefore most applications that `bind` a Unix domain socket precede the `bind` with a call to `unlink`, to remove the pathname if it already exists.

Pathname already exists

350–359 If `nd.ni_vp` is nonnull, the pathname already exists. The v-node references are released and `EADDRINUSE` is returned to the process.

Create v-node

360–365 A `vattr` structure is initialized by the `VATTR_NULL` macro. The type is set to `VSOCK` (a socket) and the access mode is set to octal 777 (`ACCESSPERMS`). These nine permission bits allow read, write, and execute for the owner, group, and other (i.e., everyone). The file is created in the specified directory by the filesystem's create function, referenced indirectly through the `VOP_CREATE` function. The arguments to the create function are `nd.ni_dvp` (the pointer to the parent directory v-node), `nd.ni_cnd` (additional information from the `namei` function that needs to be passed to the `VOP` function), and the `vattr` structure. The return information is pointed to by the second argument, `nd.ni_vp`, which is set to point to the newly created v-node (if successful).

Link structures

365–367 The `vnode` and `socket` are set to point to each other through the `v_socket` and `unp_vnode` members.

Save pathname

368–371 A copy is made of the mbuf containing the pathname that was just bound to the socket by `m_copy` and the `unp_addr` member of the PCB points to this new mbuf. The v-node is unlocked.

17.10 `PRU_CONNECT` Request and `unp_connect` Function

Figure 17.17 shows the `PRU_LISTEN` and `PRU_CONNECT` requests.

uipc_usrreq.c

```
81     case PRU_LISTEN:
82         if (unp->unp_vnode == 0)
83             error = EINVAL;
84         break;

85     case PRU_CONNECT:
86         error = unp_connect(so, nam, p);
87         break;
```

uipc_usrreq.c

Figure 17.17 `PRU_LISTEN` and `PRU_CONNECT` requests.

Verify listening socket is already bound

81–84 The `listen` system call can only be issued on a socket that has been bound to a pathname. TCP does not have this requirement, and on p. 1010 of Volume 2 we saw that when `listen` is called for an unbound TCP socket, an ephemeral port is chosen by TCP and assigned to the socket.

85–87 All the work for the PRU_CONNECT request is performed by the unp_connect function, the first part of which is shown in Figure 17.18. This function is called by the PRU_CONNECT request, for both stream and datagram sockets, and by the PRU_SEND request, when temporarily connecting an unconnected datagram socket.

uipc_usrreq.c

```
372 int
373 unp_connect(so, nam, p)
374 struct socket *so;
375 struct mbuf *nam;
376 struct proc *p;
377 {
378     struct sockaddr_un *soun = mtod(nam, struct sockaddr_un *);
379     struct vnode *vp;
380     struct socket *so2, *so3;
381     struct unpcb *unp2, *unp3;
382     int     error;
383     struct nameidata nd;

384     NDINIT(&nd, LOOKUP, FOLLOW | LOCKLEAF, UIO_SYSSPACE, soun->sun_path, p);
385     if (nam->m_data + nam->m_len == &nam->m_dat[MLEN]) {     /* XXX */
386         if (*(mtod(nam, caddr_t) + nam->m_len - 1) != 0)
387             return (EMSGSIZE);
388     } else
389         *(mtod(nam, caddr_t) + nam->m_len) = 0;
390     if (error = namei(&nd))
391         return (error);
392     vp = nd.ni_vp;
393     if (vp->v_type != VSOCK) {
394         error = ENOTSOCK;
395         goto bad;
396     }
397     if (error = VOP_ACCESS(vp, VWRITE, p->p_ucred, p))
398         goto bad;
399     so2 = vp->v_socket;
400     if (so2 == 0) {
401         error = ECONNREFUSED;
402         goto bad;
403     }
404     if (so->so_type != so2->so_type) {
405         error = EPROTOTYPE;
406         goto bad;
407     }
```

uipc_usrreq.c

Figure 17.18 unp_connect function: first part.

Initialize nameidata structure for pathname lookup

383–384 The nameidata structure is initialized by the NDINIT macro. The LOOKUP argument specifies that the pathname should be looked up, FOLLOW allows symbolic links to be followed, and LOCKLEAF specifies that the v-node must be locked on return (to prevent another process from modifying the v-node until we're done). UIO_SYSSPACE specifies that the pathname is in the kernel, and soun->sun_path is the starting address of the pathname (which is passed to unp_connect as its nam argument). p is the pointer to the proc structure for the process that issued the connect or sendto system call.

Null terminate pathname

385–389 If the length of the socket address structure is 108 bytes, the final byte must be a null. Otherwise a null is stored at the end of the pathname.

> This section of code is similar to that in Figure 17.16, but different. Not only is the first if coded differently, but the error returned if the final byte is nonnull also differs: EMSGSIZE here and EINVAL in Figure 17.16. Also, this test has the side effect of verifying that the data is not contained in a cluster, although this is probably accidental since the function sockargs will never place the socket address structure into a cluster.

Lookup pathname and verify

390–398 namei looks up the pathname in the filesystem. If the return is OK, the pointer to the vnode structure is returned in nd.ni_vp. The v-node type must be VSOCK and the current process must have write permission for the socket.

Verify socket is bound to pathname

399–403 A socket must currently be bound to the pathname, that is, the v_socket pointer in the v-node must be nonnull. If not, the connection is refused. This can happen if the server is not running but the pathname was left in the filesystem the last time the server ran.

Verify socket type

404–407 The type of the connecting client socket (so) must be the same as the type of the server socket being connected to (so2). That is, a stream socket cannot connect to a datagram socket or vice versa.

Figure 17.19 shows the remainder of the unp_connect, which first deals with connecting stream sockets, and then calls unp_connect2 to link the two unpcb structures.

uipc_usrreq.c

```
    if (so->so_proto->pr_flags & PR_CONNREQUIRED) {
        if ((so2->so_options & SO_ACCEPTCONN) == 0 ||
            (so3 = sonewconn(so2, 0)) == 0) {
            error = ECONNREFUSED;
            goto bad;
        }
        unp2 = sotounpcb(so2);
        unp3 = sotounpcb(so3);
        if (unp2->unp_addr)
            unp3->unp_addr =
                m_copy(unp2->unp_addr, 0, (int) M_COPYALL);
        so2 = so3;
    }
    error = unp_connect2(so, so2);
  bad:
    vput(vp);
    return (error);
}
```

uipc_usrreq.c

Figure 17.19 unp_connect function: second part.

Connect stream sockets

408–415 Stream sockets are handled specially because a new socket must be created from the listening socket. First, the server socket must be a listening socket: the SO_ACCEPTCONN flag must be set. (The solisten function does this on p. 456 of Volume 2.) sonewconn is then called to create a new socket from the listening socket. sonewconn also places this new socket on the listening socket's incomplete connection queue (so_q0).

Make copy of name bound to listening socket

416–418 If the listening socket contains a pointer to an mbuf containing a sockaddr_un with the name that was bound to the socket (which should always be true), a copy is made of that mbuf by m_copy for the newly created socket.

Figure 17.20 shows the status of the various structures immediately before the assignment so2 = so3. The following steps take place.

- The rightmost file, socket, and unpcb structures are created when the server calls socket. The server then calls bind, which creates the reference to the vnode and to the associated mbuf containing the pathname. The server then calls listen, enabling client connections.
- The leftmost file, socket, and unpcb structures are created when the client calls socket. The client then calls connect, which calls unp_connect.
- The middle socket structure, which we call the "connected server socket," is created by sonewconn, which then issues the PRU_ATTACH request, creating the corresponding unpcb structure.
- sonewconn also calls soqinsque to insert the newly created socket on the incomplete connection queue for the listening socket (which we assume was previously empty). We also show the completed connection queue for the listening socket (so_q and so_qlen) as empty. The so_head member of the newly created socket points back to the listening socket.
- unp_connect calls m_copy to create a copy of the mbuf containing the pathname that was bound to the listening socket, which is pointed to by the middle unpcb. We'll see that this copy is needed for the getpeername system call.
- Finally, notice that the newly created socket is not yet pointed to by a file structure (and indeed, its SS_NOFDREF flag was set by sonewconn to indicate this). The allocation of a file structure for this socket, along with a corresponding file descriptor, will be done when the listening server process calls accept.

The pointer to the vnode is not copied from the listening socket to the connected server socket. The only purpose of this vnode structure is to allow clients calling connect to locate the appropriate server socket structure, through the v_socket pointer.

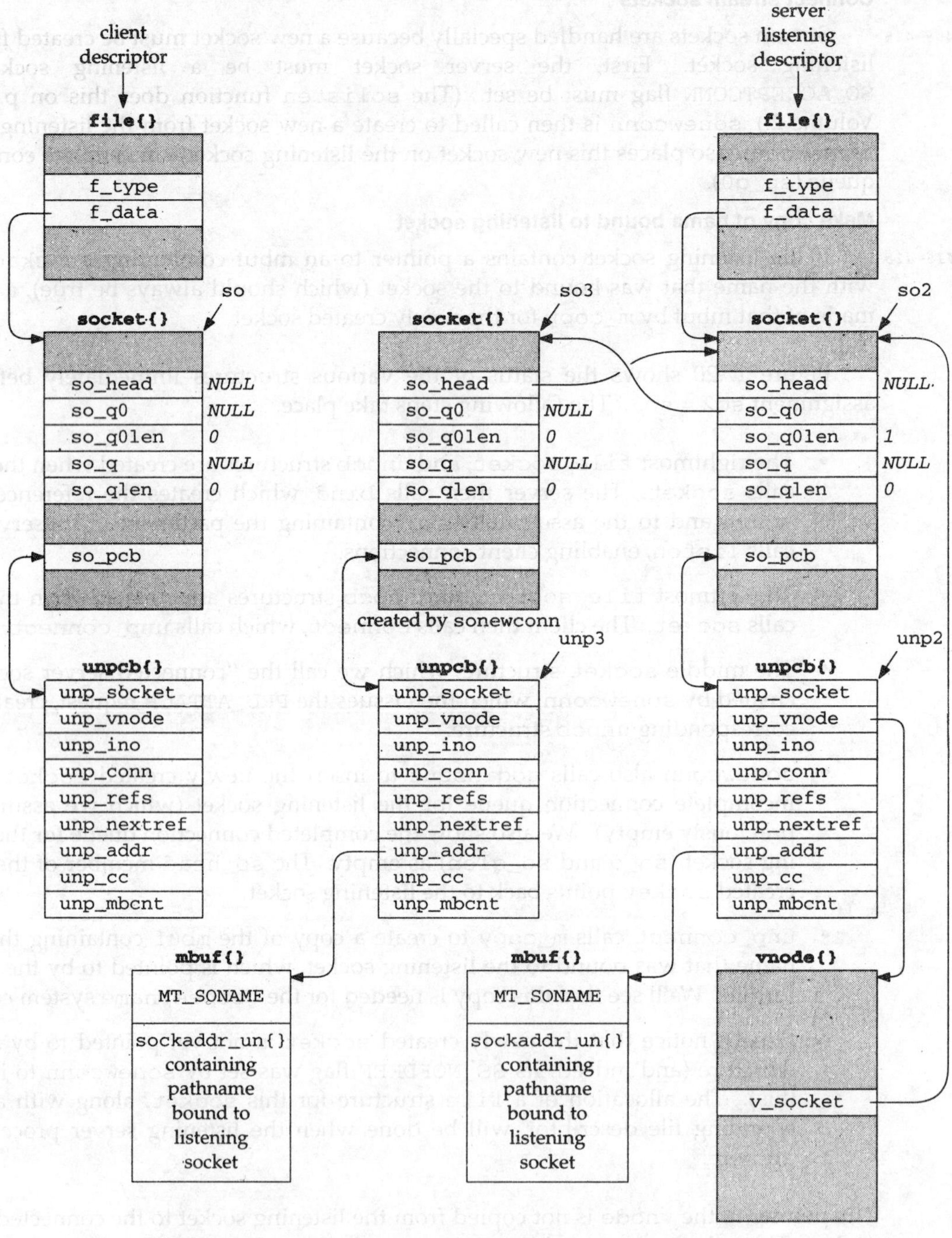

Figure 17.20 Various structures during stream socket connect.

Connect the two stream or datagram sockets

421 The final step in unp_connect is to call unp_connect2 (shown in the next section), which is done for both stream and datagram sockets. With regard to Figure 17.20, this will link the unp_conn members of the leftmost two unpcb structures and move the newly created socket from the incomplete connection queue to the completed connection queue for the listening server's socket. We show the resulting data structures in a later section (Figure 17.26).

17.11 PRU_CONNECT2 Request and unp_connect2 Function

The PRU_CONNECT2 request, shown in Figure 17.21, is issued only as a result of the socketpair system call. This request is supported only in the Unix domain.

uipc_usrreq.c

```
88      case PRU_CONNECT2:
89          error = unp_connect2(so, (struct socket *) nam);
90          break;
```

uipc_usrreq.c

Figure 17.21 PRU_CONNECT2 request.

88–90 All the work for this request is done by the unp_connect2 function. This function is also called from two other places within the kernel, as we show in Figure 17.22.

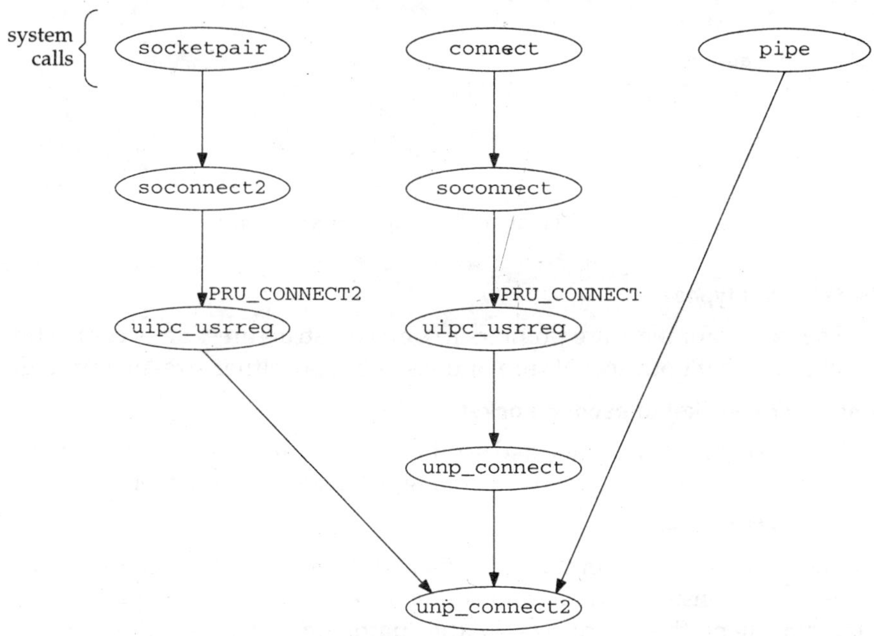

Figure 17.22 Callers of the unp_connect2 function.

We describe the socketpair system call and the soconnect2 function in Section 17.12 and the pipe system call in Section 17.13. Figure 17.23 shows the unp_connect2 function.

uipc_usrreq.c

```
426 int
427 unp_connect2(so, so2)
428 struct socket *so;
429 struct socket *so2;
430 {
431     struct unpcb *unp = sotounpcb(so);
432     struct unpcb *unp2;

433     if (so2->so_type != so->so_type)
434         return (EPROTOTYPE);
435     unp2 = sotounpcb(so2);
436     unp->unp_conn = unp2;
437     switch (so->so_type) {

438     case SOCK_DGRAM:
439         unp->unp_nextref = unp2->unp_refs;
440         unp2->unp_refs = unp;
441         soisconnected(so);
442         break;

443     case SOCK_STREAM:
444         unp2->unp_conn = unp;
445         soisconnected(so);
446         soisconnected(so2);
447         break;

448     default:
449         panic("unp_connect2");
450     }
451     return (0);
452 }
```

uipc_usrreq.c

Figure 17.23 unp_connect2 function.

Check socket types

426–434 The two arguments are pointers to socket structures: so is connecting to so2. The first check is that both sockets are of the same type: either stream or datagram.

Connect first socket to second socket

435–436 The first unpcb is connected to the second through the unp_conn member. The next steps, however, differ between datagram and stream sockets.

Connect datagram sockets

438–442 The unp_nextref and unp_refs members of the PCB connect datagram sockets. For example, consider a datagram server socket that binds the pathname /tmp/foo. A datagram client then connects to this pathname. Figure 17.24 shows the resulting unpcb structures, after unp_connect2 returns. (For simplicity, we do not show the corresponding file or socket structures, or the vnode associated with the rightmost socket.) We show the two pointers unp and unp2 that are used within unp_connect2.

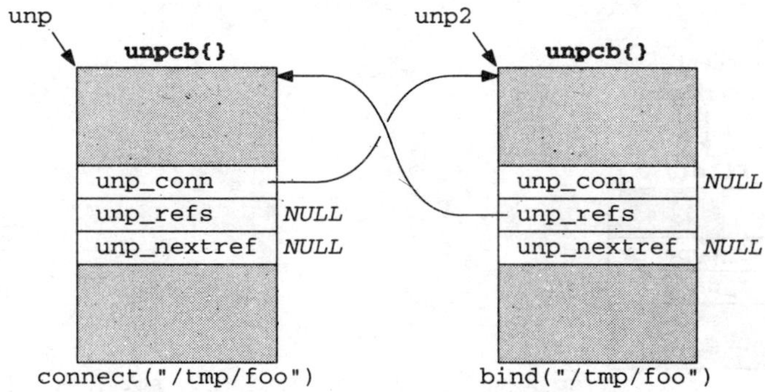

Figure 17.24 Connected datagram sockets.

For a datagram socket that has been connected to, the unp_refs member points to the first PCB on a linked list of all sockets that have connected to this socket. This linked list is traversed by following the unp_nextref pointers.

Figure 17.25 shows the state of the three PCBs after a third datagram socket (the one on the left) connects to the same server, /tmp/foo.

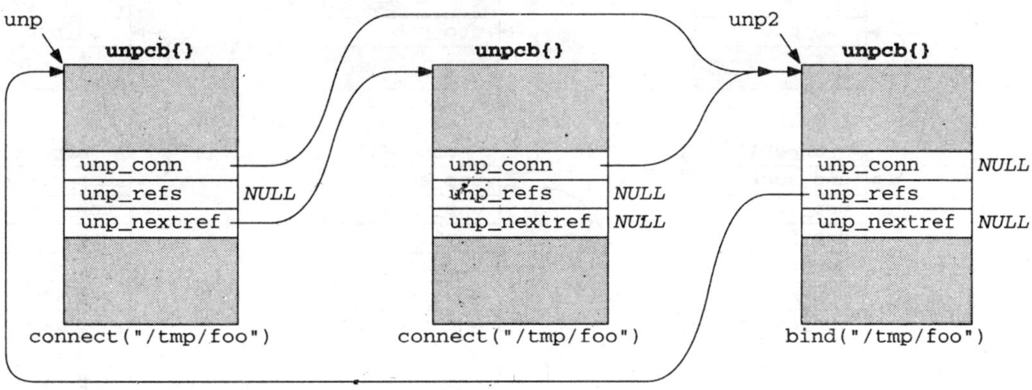

Figure 17.25 Another socket (on the left) connects to the socket on the right.

The two PCB fields unp_refs and unp_nextref must be separate because the socket on the right in Figure 17.25 can itself connect to some other datagram socket.

Connect stream sockets

443–447 The connection of a stream socket differs from the connection of a datagram socket because a stream socket (a server) can be connected to by only a single client socket. The unp_conn members of both PCBs point to the peer's PCB, as shown in Figure 17.26. This figure is a continuation of Figure 17.20.

Another change in this figure is that the call to soisconnected with an argument of so2 moves that socket from the incomplete connection queue of the listening socket (so_q0 in Figure 17.20) to the completed connection queue (so_q). This is the queue from which accept will take the newly created socket (p. 458 of Volume 2). Notice that soisconnected (p. 464 of Volume 2) also sets the SS_ISCONNECTED flag in the

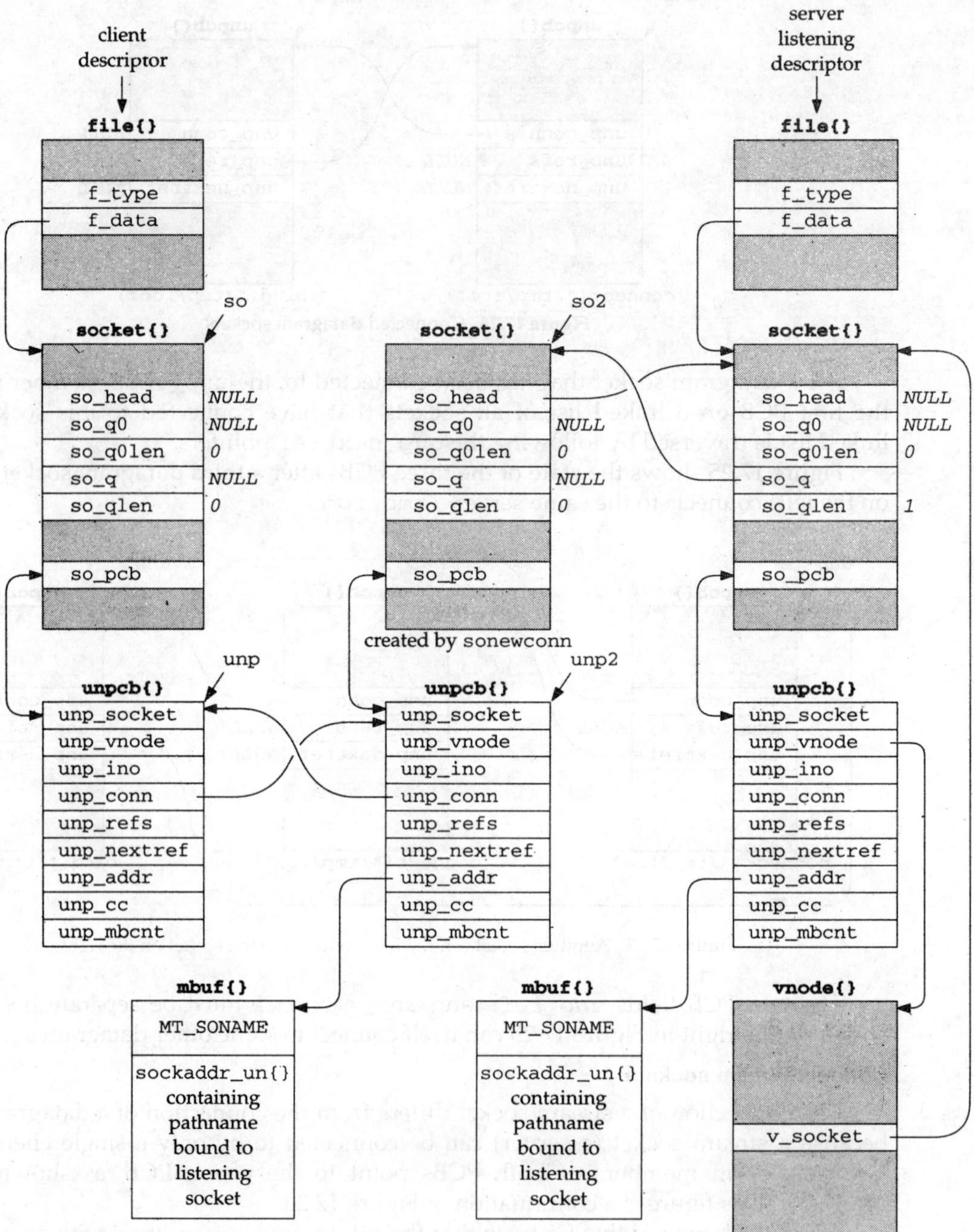

Figure 17.26 Connected stream sockets.

so_state but moves the socket from the incomplete queue to the completed queue only if the socket's so_head pointer is nonnull. (If the socket's so_head pointer is null, it is not on either queue.) Therefore the first call to soisconnected in Figure 17.23 with an argument of so changes only so_state.

17.12 socketpair System Call

The socketpair system call is supported only in the Unix domain. It creates two sockets and connects them, returning two descriptors, each one connected to the other. For example, a user process issues the call

```
int    fd[2];

socketpair(PF_UNIX, SOCK_STREAM, 0, fd);
```

to create a pair of full-duplex Unix domain stream sockets that are connected to each other. The first descriptor is returned in fd[0] and the second in fd[1]. If the second argument is SOCK_DGRAM a pair of connected Unix domain datagram sockets are created. The return value from socketpair is 0 on success, or –1 if an error occurs.

Figure 17.27 shows the implementation of the socketpair system call.

Arguments

229–239 The four integer arguments, domain through rsv, are the ones shown in the example user call to socketpair at the beginning of this section. The three arguments shown in the definition of the function socketpair (p, uap, and retval) are the arguments passed to the system call within the kernel.

Create two sockets and two descriptors

244–261 socreate is called twice, creating the two sockets. The first of the two descriptors is allocated by falloc. The descriptor value is returned in fd and the pointer to the corresponding file structure is returned in fp1. The FREAD and FWRITE flags are set (since the socket is full duplex), the file type is set to DTYPE_SOCKET, f_ops is set to point to the array of five function pointers for sockets (Figure 15.13 on p. 446 of Volume 2), and the f_data pointer is set to point to the socket structure. The second descriptor is allocated by falloc and the corresponding file structure is initialized.

Connect the two sockets

262–270 soconnect2 issues the PRU_CONNECT2 request, which is supported in the Unix domain only. If the system call is creating stream sockets, on return from soconnect2 we have the arrangement of structures shown in Figure 17.28.

If two datagram sockets are created, it requires two calls to soconnect2, with each call connecting in one direction. After the second call we have the arrangement shown in Figure 17.29.

uipc_syscalls.c

```
struct socketpair_args {
    int     domain;
    int     type;
    int     protocol;
    int    *rsv;
};

socketpair(p, uap, retval)
struct proc *p;
struct socketpair_args *uap;
int     retval[];
{
    struct filedesc *fdp = p->p_fd;
    struct file *fp1, *fp2;
    struct socket *so1, *so2;
    int     fd, error, sv[2];

    if (error = socreate(uap->domain, &so1, uap->type, uap->protocol))
        return (error);
    if (error = socreate(uap->domain, &so2, uap->type, uap->protocol))
        goto free1;

    if (error = falloc(p, &fp1, &fd))
        goto free2;
    sv[0] = fd;
    fp1->f_flag = FREAD | FWRITE;
    fp1->f_type = DTYPE_SOCKET;
    fp1->f_ops = &socketops;
    fp1->f_data = (caddr_t) so1;
    if (error = falloc(p, &fp2, &fd))
        goto free3;
    fp2->f_flag = FREAD | FWRITE;
    fp2->f_type = DTYPE_SOCKET;
    fp2->f_ops = &socketops;
    fp2->f_data = (caddr_t) so2;
    sv[1] = fd;

    if (error = soconnect2(so1, so2))
        goto free4;
    if (uap->type == SOCK_DGRAM) {
        /*
         * Datagram socket connection is asymmetric.
         */
        if (error = soconnect2(so2, so1))
            goto free4;
    }
    error = copyout((caddr_t) sv, (caddr_t) uap->rsv, 2 * sizeof(int));
    retval[0] = sv[0];          /* XXX ??? */
    retval[1] = sv[1];          /* XXX ??? */
    return (error);

  free4:
    ffree(fp2);
    fdp->fd_ofiles[sv[1]] = 0;
```

```
free3:
  ffree(fp1);
  fdp->fd_ofiles[sv[0]] = 0;
free2:
  (void) soclose(so2);
free1:
  (void) soclose(so1);
  return (error);
}
```
uipc_syscalls.c

Figure 17.27 socketpair system call.

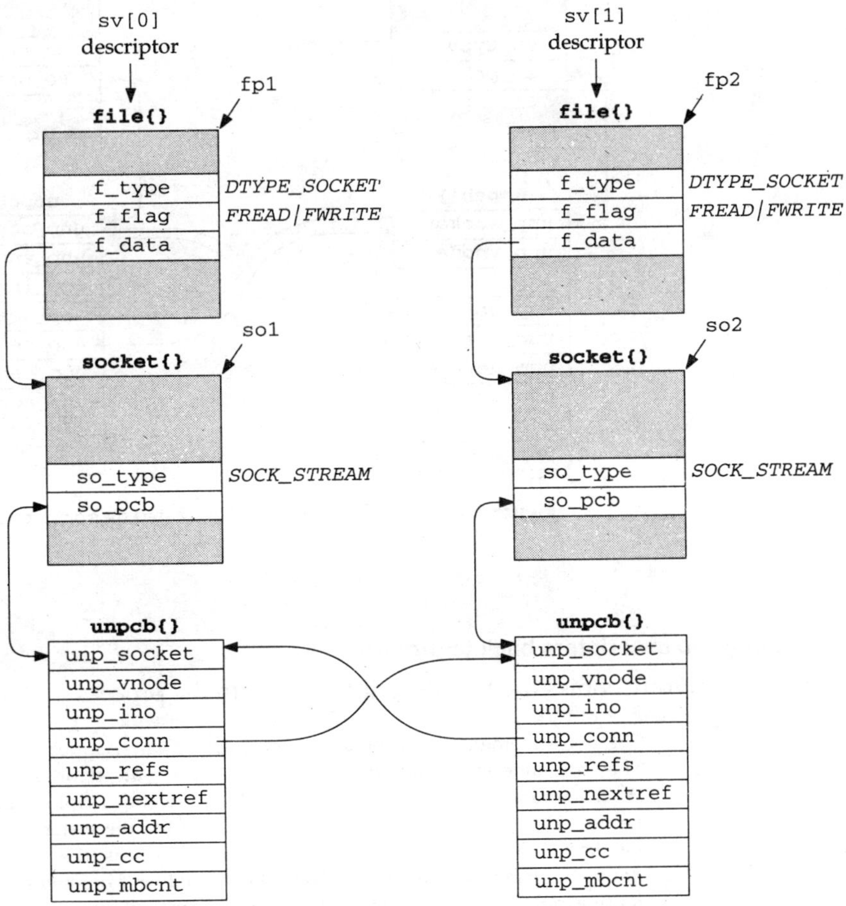

Figure 17.28 Two stream sockets created by socketpair.

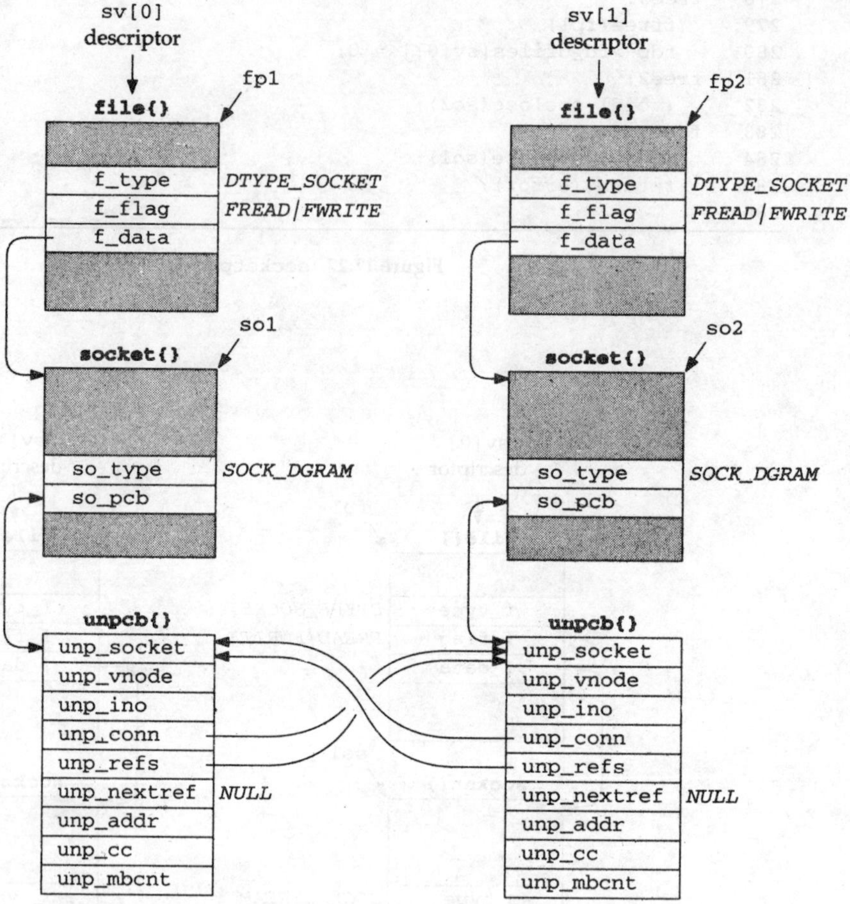

Figure 17.29 Two datagram sockets created by `socketpair`.

Copy two descriptors back to process

271–274 `copyout` copies the two descriptors back to the process.

The two statements with the comments `XXX ???` first appeared in the 4.3BSD Reno release. They are unnecessary because the two descriptors are returned to the process by `copyout`. We'll see that the `pipe` system call returns two descriptors by setting `retval[0]` and `retval[1]`, where `retval` is the third argument to the system call. The assembler routine in the kernel that handles system calls always returns the two integers `retval[0]` and `retval[1]` in machine registers as part of the return from any system call. But the assembler routine in the user process that invokes the system call must be coded to look at these registers and return the values as expected by the process. The `pipe` function in the C library does indeed do this, but the `socketpair` function does not.

soconnect2 Function

This function, shown in Figure 17.30, issues the PRU_CONNECT2 request. This function is called only by the socketpair system call.

uipc_socket.c

```
soconnect2(so1, so2)
struct socket *so1;
struct socket *so2;
{
    int     s = splnet();
    int     error;

    error = (*so1->so_proto->pr_usrreq) (so1, PRU_CONNECT2,
                 (struct mbuf *) 0, (struct mbuf *) so2, (struct mbuf *) 0);
    splx(s);
    return (error);
}
```

uipc_socket.c

Figure 17.30 soconnect2 function.

17.13 pipe System Call

The pipe system call, shown in Figure 17.31, is nearly identical to the socketpair system call.

654–686 The calls to socreate create two Unix domain stream sockets. The only differences in this system call from the socketpair system call are that pipe sets the first of the two descriptors to read-only and the second descriptor to write-only; the two descriptors are returned through the retval argument, not by copyout; and pipe calls unp_connect2 directly, instead of going through soconnect2.

Some versions of Unix, notably SVR4, create pipes with both ends read–write.

17.14 PRU_ACCEPT Request

Most of the work required to accept a new connection for a stream socket is handled by other kernel functions: sonewconn creates the new socket structure and issues the PRU_ATTACH request, and the accept system call processing removes the socket from the completed connection queue and calls soaccept. This function (p. 460 of Volume 2) just issues the PRU_ACCEPT request, which we show in Figure 17.33 for the Unix domain.

Return client's pathname

94–108 If the client called bind, and if the client is still connected, this request copies the sockaddr_un containing the client's pathname into the mbuf pointed to by the nam argument. Otherwise, the null pathname (sun_noname) is returned.

uipc_syscalls.c

```
pipe(p, uap, retval)
struct proc *p;
struct pipe_args *uap;
int     retval[];
{
    struct filedesc *fdp = p->p_fd;
    struct file *rf, *wf;
    struct socket *rso, *wso;
    int     fd, error;

    if (error = socreate(AF_UNIX, &rso, SOCK_STREAM, 0))
        return (error);
    if (error = socreate(AF_UNIX, &wso, SOCK_STREAM, 0))
        goto free1;
    if (error = falloc(p, &rf, &fd))
        goto free2;
    retval[0] = fd;
    rf->f_flag = FREAD;
    rf->f_type = DTYPE_SOCKET;
    rf->f_ops = &socketops;
    rf->f_data = (caddr_t) rso;
    if (error = falloc(p, &wf, &fd))
        goto free3;
    wf->f_flag = FWRITE;
    wf->f_type = DTYPE_SOCKET;
    wf->f_ops = &socketops;
    wf->f_data = (caddr_t) wso;
    retval[1] = fd;
    if (error = unp_connect2(wso, rso))
        goto free4;
    return (0);
  free4:
    ffree(wf);
    fdp->fd_ofiles[retval[1]] = 0;
  free3:
    ffree(rf);
    fdp->fd_ofiles[retval[0]] = 0;
  free2:
    (void) soclose(wso);
  free1:
    (void) soclose(rso);
    return (error);
}
```

uipc_syscalls.c

Figure 17.31 pipe system call.

uipc_usrreq.c

```
    case PRU_DISCONNECT:
        unp_disconnect(unp);
        break;
```

uipc_usrreq.c

Figure 17.32 PRU_DISCONNECT request.

uipc_usrreq.c

```
    case PRU_ACCEPT:
        /*
         * Pass back name of connected socket,
         * if it was bound and we are still connected
         * (our peer may have closed already!)
         */
        if (unp->unp_conn && unp->unp_conn->unp_addr) {
            nam->m_len = unp->unp_conn->unp_addr->m_len;
            bcopy(mtod(unp->unp_conn->unp_addr, caddr_t),
                  mtod(nam, caddr_t), (unsigned) nam->m_len);
        } else {
            nam->m_len = sizeof(sun_noname);
            *(mtod(nam, struct sockaddr *)) = sun_noname;
        }
        break;
```

uipc_usrreq.c

Figure 17.33 PRU_ACCEPT request.

17.15 PRU_DISCONNECT Request and unp_disconnect Function

If a socket is connected, the close system call issues the PRU_DISCONNECT request, which we show in Figure 17.32.

91–93 All the work is done by the unp_disconnect function, shown in Figure 17.34.

Check whether socket is connected

458–460 If this socket is not connected to another socket, the function returns immediately. Otherwise, the unp_conn member is set to 0, to indicate that this socket is not connected to another.

Remove closing datagram PCB from linked list

462–478 This code removes the PCB corresponding to the closing socket from the linked list of connected datagram PCBs. For example, if we start with Figure 17.25 and then close the leftmost socket, we end up with the data structures shown in Figure 17.35. Since unp2->unp_refs equals unp (the closing PCB is the head of the linked list), the unp_nextref pointer of the closing PCB becomes the new head of the linked list.

If we start again with Figure 17.25 and close the middle socket, we end up with the data structures shown in Figure 17.36. This time the PCB corresponding to the closing socket is not the head of the linked list. unp2 starts at the head of the list looking for the PCB that precedes the closing PCB. unp2 is left pointing to this PCB (the leftmost one in Figure 17.36). The unp_nextref pointer of the closing PCB is then copied into the unp_nextref field of the preceding PCB on the list (unp).

Complete disconnect of stream socket

479–483 Since a Unix domain stream socket can only be connected to by a single peer, the disconnect is simpler since a linked list is not involved. The peer's unp_conn pointer is set to 0 and soisdisconnected is called for both sockets.

uipc_usrreq.c

```
void
unp_disconnect(unp)
struct unpcb *unp;
{
    struct unpcb *unp2 = unp->unp_conn;

    if (unp2 == 0)
        return;
    unp->unp_conn = 0;
    switch (unp->unp_socket->so_type) {

    case SOCK_DGRAM:
        if (unp2->unp_refs == unp)
            unp2->unp_refs = unp->unp_nextref;
        else {
            unp2 = unp2->unp_refs;
            for (;;) {
                if (unp2 == 0)
                    panic("unp_disconnect");
                if (unp2->unp_nextref == unp)
                    break;
                unp2 = unp2->unp_nextref;
            }
            unp2->unp_nextref = unp->unp_nextref;
        }
        unp->unp_nextref = 0;
        unp->unp_socket->so_state &= ~SS_ISCONNECTED;
        break;

    case SOCK_STREAM:
        soisdisconnected(unp->unp_socket);
        unp2->unp_conn = 0;
        soisdisconnected(unp2->unp_socket);
        break;
    }
}
```

uipc_usrreq.c

Figure 17.34 unp_disconnect function.

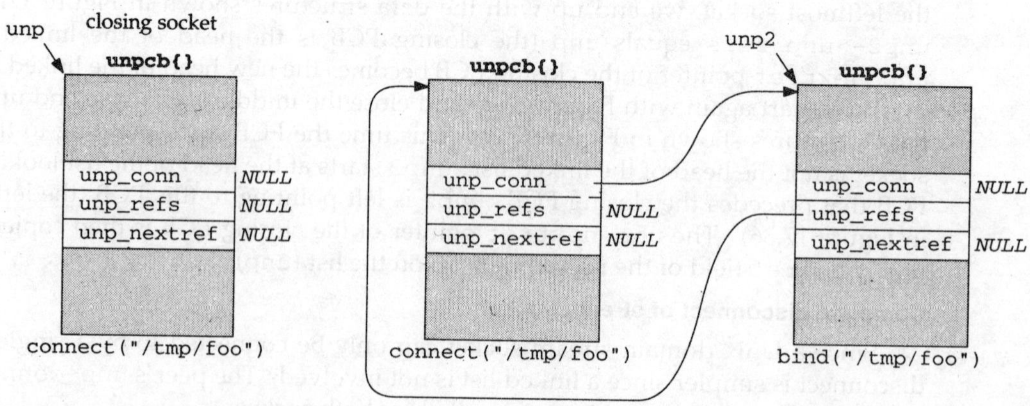

Figure 17.35 Transition from Figure 17.25 after leftmost socket is closed.

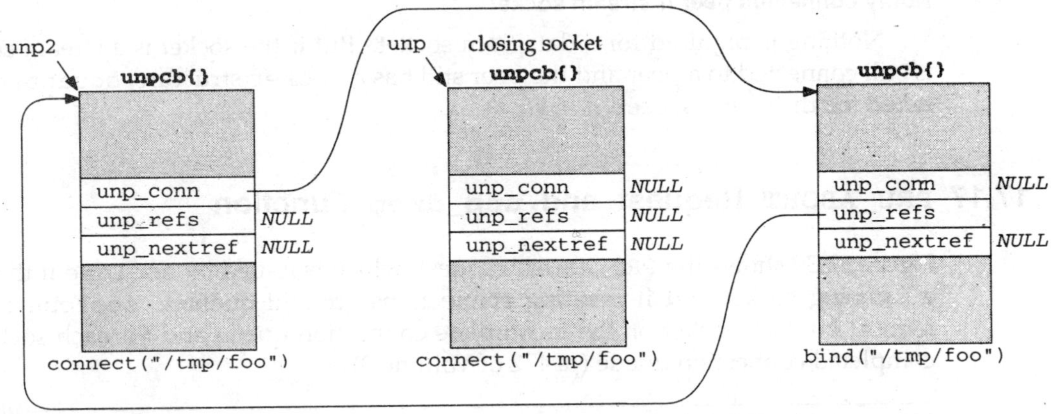

Figure 17.36 Transition from Figure 17.25 after middle socket is closed.

17.16 PRU_SHUTDOWN Request and unp_shutdown Function

The PRU_SHUTDOWN request, shown in Figure 17.37, is issued when the process calls shutdown to prevent any further output.

uipc_usrreq.c

```
109     case PRU_SHUTDOWN:
110         socantsendmore(so);
111         unp_shutdown(unp);
112         break;
```

uipc_usrreq.c

Figure 17.37 PRU_SHUTDOWN request.

109–112 socantsendmore sets the socket's flags to prevent any further output. unp_shutdown, shown in Figure 17.38, is then called.

uipc_usrreq.c

```
void
unp_shutdown(unp)
struct unpcb *unp;
{
    struct socket *so;

    if (unp->unp_socket->so_type == SOCK_STREAM && unp->unp_conn &&
        (so = unp->unp_conn->unp_socket))
        socantrcvmore(so);
}
```

uipc_usrreq.c

Figure 17.38 unp_shutdown function.

Notify connected peer if stream socket

499–502 Nothing is required for a datagram socket. But if the socket is a stream socket that is still connected to a peer and the peer still has a `socket` structure, `socantrcvmore` is called for the peer's socket.

17.17 PRU_ABORT Request and unp_drop Function

Figure 17.39 shows the PRU_ABORT request, which is issued by `soclose` if the socket is a listening socket and if pending connections are still queued. `soclose` issues this request for each socket on the incomplete connection queue and for each socket on the completed connection queue (p. 472 of Volume 2).

uipc_usrreq.c

```
209       case PRU_ABORT:
210           unp_drop(unp, ECONNABORTED);
211           break;
```

uipc_usrreq.c

Figure 17.39 PRU_ABORT request.

209–211 The `unp_drop` function (shown in Figure 17.40) generates an error of ECONNABORTED. We saw in Figure 17.14 that `unp_detach` also calls `unp_drop` with an argument of ECONNRESET.

uipc_usrreq.c

```
503 void
504 unp_drop(unp, errno)
505 struct unpcb *unp;
506 int     errno;
507 {
508     struct socket *so = unp->unp_socket;

509     so->so_error = errno;
510     unp_disconnect(unp);
511     if (so->so_head) {
512         so->so_pcb = (caddr_t) 0;
513         m_freem(unp->unp_addr);
514         (void) m_free(dtom(unp));
515         sofree(so);
516     }
517 }
```

uipc_usrreq.c

Figure 17.40 unp_drop function.

Save error and disconnect socket

509–510 The socket's `so_error` value is set and if the socket is connected, `unp_disconnect` is called.

Discard data structures if on listening server's queue

511–516 If the socket's `so_head` pointer is nonnull, the socket is currently on either the incomplete connection queue or the completed connection queue of a listening socket.

The pointer from the socket to the unpcb is set to 0. The call to m_freem releases the mbuf containing the name bound to the listening socket (recall Figure 17.20) and the next call to m_free releases the unpcb structure. sofree releases the socket structure. While on either of the listening server's queues, the socket cannot have an associated file structure, since that is allocated by accept when a socket is removed from the completed connection queue.

17.18 Miscellaneous Requests

Figure 17.41 shows six of the remaining requests.

uipc_usrreq.c

```
    case PRU_SENSE:
        ((struct stat *) m)->st_blksize = so->so_snd.sb_hiwat;
        if (so->so_type == SOCK_STREAM && unp->unp_conn != 0) {
            so2 = unp->unp_conn->unp_socket;
            ((struct stat *) m)->st_blksize += so2->so_rcv.sb_cc;
        }
        ((struct stat *) m)->st_dev = NODEV;
        if (unp->unp_ino == 0)
            unp->unp_ino = unp_ino++;
        ((struct stat *) m)->st_ino = unp->unp_ino;
        return (0);

    case PRU_RCVOOB:
        return (EOPNOTSUPP);

    case PRU_SENDOOB:
        error = EOPNOTSUPP;
        break;

    case PRU_SOCKADDR:
        if (unp->unp_addr) {
            nam->m_len = unp->unp_addr->m_len;
            bcopy(mtod(unp->unp_addr, caddr_t),
                  mtod(nam, caddr_t), (unsigned) nam->m_len);
        } else
            nam->m_len = 0;
        break;

    case PRU_PEERADDR:
        if (unp->unp_conn && unp->unp_conn->unp_addr) {
            nam->m_len = unp->unp_conn->unp_addr->m_len;
            bcopy(mtod(unp->unp_conn->unp_addr, caddr_t),
                  mtod(nam, caddr_t), (unsigned) nam->m_len);
        } else
            nam->m_len = 0;
        break;

    case PRU_SLOWTIMO:
        break;
```

uipc_usrreq.c

Figure 17.41 Miscellaneous PRU_*xxx* requests.

PRU_SENSE request

212–217 This request is issued by the fstat system call. The current value of the socket's send buffer high-water mark is returned as the st_blksize member of the stat structure. Additionally, if the socket is a connected stream socket, the number of bytes currently in the peer's socket receive buffer is added to this value. When we examine the PRU_SEND request in Section 18.2 we'll see that the sum of these two values is the true capacity of the "pipe" between the two connected stream sockets.

218 The st_dev member is set to NODEV (a constant value of all one bits, representing a nonexistent device).

219–221 I-node numbers identify files within a filesystem. The value returned as the i-node number of a Unix domain socket (the st_ino member of the stat structure) is just a unique value from the global unp_ino. If this unpcb has not yet been assigned one of these fake i-node numbers, the value of the global unp_ino is assigned and then incremented. These are called *fake* because they do not refer to actual files within the filesystem. They are just generated from a global counter when needed. If Unix domain sockets were required to be bound to a pathname in the filesystem (which is not the case), the PRU_SENSE request could use the st_dev and st_ino values corresponding to a bound pathname.

> The increment of the global unp_ino should be done before the assignment instead of after. The first time fstat is called for a Unix domain socket after the kernel reboots, the value stored in the socket's unpcb will be 0. But if fstat is called again for the same socket, since the saved value was 0, the current nonzero value of the global unp_ino is stored in the PCB.

PRU_RCVOOB and PRU_SENDOOB requests

223–227 Out-of-band data is not supported in the Unix domain.

PRU_SOCKADDR request

228–235 This request returns the protocol address (a pathname in the case of Unix domain sockets) that was bound to the socket. If a pathname was bound to the socket, unp_addr points to the mbuf containing the sockaddr_un with the name. The nam argument to uipc_usrreq points to an mbuf allocated by the caller to receive the result. m_copy makes a copy of the socket address structure. If a pathname was not bound to the socket, the length field of the resulting mbuf is set to 0.

PRU_PEERADDR request

236–243 This request is handled similarly to the previous request, but the pathname desired is the name bound to the socket that is connected to the calling socket. If the calling socket is connected to a peer, unp_conn will be nonnull.

> The handling by these two requests of a socket that has not bound a pathname differs from the PRU_ACCEPT request (Figure 17.33). The getsockname and getpeername system calls return a value of 0 through their third argument when no name exists. The accept function, however, returns a value of 16 through its third argument, and the pathname contained in the sockaddr_un returned through its second argument consists of a null byte. (sun_noname is a generic sockaddr structure, and its size is 16 bytes.)

PRU_SLOWTIMO request

244–245 This request should never be issued since the Unix domain protocols do not use any timers.

17.19 Summary

The implementation of the Unix domain protocols that we've seen in this chapter is simple and straightforward. Stream and datagram sockets are provided, with the stream protocol looking like TCP and the datagram protocol looking like UDP.

Pathnames can be bound to Unix domain sockets. The server `bind`s its well-known pathname and the client `connect`s to this pathname. Datagram sockets can also be connected and, similar to UDP, multiple clients can `connect` to a single server. Unnamed Unix domain sockets can also be created by the `socketpair` function. The Unix `pipe` system call just creates two Unix domain stream sockets that are connected to each other. Pipes on a Berkeley-derived system are really Unix domain stream sockets.

The protocol control block used with Unix domain sockets is the `unpcb` structure. Unlike other domains, however, these PCBs are not maintained in a linked list. Instead, when a Unix domain socket needs to rendezvous with another Unix domain socket (for a `connect` or `sendto`), the destination `unpcb` is located by the kernel's pathname lookup function (`namei`), which leads to a `vnode` structure, which leads to the desired `unpcb`.

18

Unix Domain Protocols: I/O and Descriptor Passing

18.1 Introduction

This chapter continues the implementation of the Unix domain protocols from the previous chapter. The first section of this chapter deals with I/O, the PRU_SEND and PRU_RCVD requests, and the remaining sections deal with descriptor passing.

18.2 PRU_SEND and PRU_RCVD Requests

The PRU_SEND request is issued whenever a process writes data or control information to a Unix domain socket. The first part of the request, which handles control information and then datagram sockets, is shown in Figure 18.1.

Internalize any control information

141–142 If the process passed control information using `sendmsg`, the function `unp_internalize` converts the embedded descriptors into `file` pointers. We describe this function in Section 18.4.

Temporarily connect an unconnected datagram socket

146–153 If the process passes a socket address structure with the destination address (that is, the `nam` argument is nonnull), the socket must be unconnected or an error of EISCONN is returned. The unconnected socket is connected by `unp_connect`. This temporary connecting of an unconnected datagram socket is similar to the UDP code shown on p. 762 of Volume 2.

154–159 If the process did not pass a destination address, an error of ENOTCONN is returned for an unconnected socket.

uipc_usrreq.c

```
140     case PRU_SEND:
141         if (control && (error = unp_internalize(control, p)))
142             break;
143         switch (so->so_type) {

144         case SOCK_DGRAM:{
145                 struct sockaddr *from;

146                 if (nam) {
147                     if (unp->unp_conn) {
148                         error = EISCONN;
149                         break;
150                     }
151                     error = unp_connect(so, nam, p);
152                     if (error)
153                         break;
154                 } else {
155                     if (unp->unp_conn == 0) {
156                         error = ENOTCONN;
157                         break;
158                     }
159                 }
160                 so2 = unp->unp_conn->unp_socket;
161                 if (unp->unp_addr)
162                     from = mtod(unp->unp_addr, struct sockaddr *);
163                 else
164                     from = &sun_noname;
165                 if (sbappendaddr(&so2->so_rcv, from, m, control)) {
166                     sorwakeup(so2);
167                     m = 0;
168                     control = 0;
169                 } else
170                     error = ENOBUFS;
171                 if (nam)
172                     unp_disconnect(unp);
173                 break;
174             }
```

uipc_usrreq.c

Figure 18.1 PRU_SEND request for datagram sockets.

Pass sender's address

160–164 so2 points to the socket structure of the destination socket. If the sending socket (unp) has bound a pathname, from points to the sockaddr_un structure containing the pathname. Otherwise from points to sun_noname, which is a sockaddr_un structure with a null byte as the first character of the pathname.

> If the sender of a Unix domain datagram does not bind a pathname to its socket, the recipient of the datagram cannot send a reply since it won't have a destination address (i.e., pathname) for its sendto. This differs from UDP, which automatically assigns an ephemeral port to an unbound datagram socket the first time a datagram is sent on the socket. One reason UDP can automatically choose port numbers on behalf of applications is that these port numbers are

used only by UDP. Pathnames in the filesystem, however, are not reserved to only Unix domain sockets. Automatically choosing a pathname for an unbound Unix domain socket could create a conflict at a later time.

Whether a reply is needed depends on the application. The `syslog` function, for example, does not bind a pathname to its Unix domain datagram socket. It just sends a message to the local `syslogd` daemon and does not expect a reply.

Append control, address, and data mbufs to socket receive queue

165–170 `sbappendaddr` appends the control information (if any), the sender's address, and the data to the receiving socket's receive queue. If this function is successful, `sorwakeup` wakes up any readers waiting for this data, and the mbuf pointers `m` and `control` are set to 0 to prevent their release at the end of the function (Figure 17.10). If an error occurs (probably because there is not enough room for the data, address, and control information on the receive queue), `ENOBUFS` is returned.

The handling of this error differs from UDP. With a Unix domain datagram socket the *sender* receives an error return from its output operation if there is not enough room on the receive queue. With UDP, the sender's output operation is successful if there is room on the interface output queue. If the receiving UDP finds no room on the receiving socket's receive queue it normally sends an ICMP port unreachable error to the sender, but the sender will not receive this error unless the sender has connected to the receiver (as described on pp. 748–749 of Volume 2).

Why doesn't the Unix domain sender block when the receiver's buffer is full, instead of receiving the `ENOBUFS` error? Datagram sockets are traditionally considered unreliable with no guarantee of delivery. [Rago 1993] notes that under SVR4 it is a vendor's choice, when the kernel is compiled, whether to provide flow control or not with a Unix domain datagram socket.

Disconnect temporarily connected socket

171–172 `unp_disconnect` disconnects the temporarily connected socket.

Figure 18.2 shows the processing of the `PRU_SEND` request for stream sockets.

Verify socket status

175–183 If the sending side of the socket has been closed, `EPIPE` is returned. The socket must also be connected or the kernel `panic`s, because `sosend` verifies that a socket that requires a connection is connected (p. 495 of Volume 2).

The first test appears to be a leftover from an earlier release. `sosend` already makes this test (p. 495 of Volume 2).

Append mbufs to receive buffer

184–194 `so2` points to the `socket` structure for the receiving socket. If control information was passed by the process using `sendmsg`, the control mbuf and any data mbufs are appended to the receiving socket receive buffer by `sbappendcontrol`. Otherwise `sbappend` appends the data mbufs to the receive buffer. If `sbappendcontrol` fails, the `control` pointer is set to 0 to prevent the call to `m_freem` at the end of the function (Figure 17.10), since `sbappendcontrol` has already released the mbuf.

uipc_usrreq.c

```
    case SOCK_STREAM:
#define rcv (&so2->so_rcv)
#define snd (&so->so_snd)
        if (so->so_state & SS_CANTSENDMORE) {
            error = EPIPE;
            break;
        }
        if (unp->unp_conn == 0)
            panic("uipc 3");
        so2 = unp->unp_conn->unp_socket;
        /*
         * Send to paired receive port, and then reduce
         * send buffer hiwater marks to maintain backpressure.
         * Wake up readers.
         */
        if (control) {
            if (sbappendcontrol(rcv, m, control))
                control = 0;
        } else
            sbappend(rcv, m);
        snd->sb_mbmax -=
            rcv->sb_mbcnt - unp->unp_conn->unp_mbcnt;
        unp->unp_conn->unp_mbcnt = rcv->sb_mbcnt;
        snd->sb_hiwat -= rcv->sb_cc - unp->unp_conn->unp_cc;
        unp->unp_conn->unp_cc = rcv->sb_cc;
        sorwakeup(so2);
        m = 0;
#undef snd
#undef rcv
        break;

    default:
        panic("uipc 4");
    }
    break;
```

uipc_usrreq.c

Figure 18.2 PRU_SEND request for stream sockets.

Update sender and receiver counters (end-to-end flow control)

95–199 The two variables sb_mbmax (the maximum number of bytes allowed for all the mbufs in the buffer) and sb_hiwat (the maximum number of bytes allowed for the actual data in the buffer) are updated for the sender. In Volume 2 (p. 495) we noted that the limit on the mbufs prevents lots of small messages from consuming too many mbufs.

With Unix domain stream sockets these two limits refer to the sum of these two counters in the receive buffer and in the send buffer. For example, the initial value of sb_hiwat is 4096 for both the send buffer and the receive buffer of a Unix domain stream socket (Figure 17.2). If the sender writes 1024 bytes to the socket, not only does the receiver's sb_cc (the current count of bytes in the socket buffer) go from 0 to 1024 (as we expect), but the sender's sb_hiwat goes from 4096 to 3072 (which we do not expect). With other protocols such as TCP, the value of a buffer's sb_hiwat never changes unless explicitly set with a socket option. The same thing happens with sb_mbmax: as the receiver's sb_mbcnt value goes up, the sender's sb_mbmax goes down.

This manipulation of the sender's limit and the receiver's current count is performed because data sent on a Unix domain stream socket is never placed on the sending socket's send buffer. The data is appended immediately onto the receiving socket's receive buffer. There is no need to waste time placing the data onto the sending socket's send queue, and then moving it onto the receive queue, either immediately or later. If there is not room in the receive buffer for the data, the sender must be blocked. But for sosend to block the sender, the amount of room in the send buffer must reflect the amount of room in the corresponding receive buffer. Instead of modifying the send buffer counts, when there is no data in the send buffer, it is easier to modify the send buffer limits to reflect the amount of room in the corresponding receive buffer.

198–199 If we examine just the manipulation of the sender's sb_hiwat and the receiver's unp_cc (the manipulation of sb_mbmax and unp_mbcnt is nearly identical), at this point rcv->sb_cc contains the number of bytes in the receive buffer, since the data was just appended to the receive buffer. unp->unp_conn->unp_cc is the previous value of rcv->sb_cc, so their difference is the number of bytes just appended to the receive buffer (i.e., the number of bytes written). snd->sb_hiwat is decremented by this amount. The current number of bytes in the receive buffer is saved in unp->unp_conn->unp_cc so the next time through this code, we can calculate how much data was written.

For example, when the sockets are created, the sender's sb_hiwat is 4096 and the receiver's sb_cc and unp_cc are both 0. If 1024 bytes are written, the sender's sb_hiwat becomes 3072 and the receiver's sb_cc and unp_cc are both 1024. We'll also see in Figure 18.3 that when the receiving process reads these 1024 bytes, the sender's sb_hiwat is incremented to 4096 and the receiver's sb_cc and unp_cc are both decremented to 0.

Wake up any processes waiting for the data

200–201 sorwakeup wakes up any processes waiting for the data. m is set to 0 to prevent the call to m_freem at the end of the function, since the mbuf is now on the receiver's queue.

The final piece of the I/O code is the PRU_RCVD request, shown in Figure 18.3. This request is issued by soreceive (p. 523 of Volume 2) when data is read from a socket and the protocol has set the PR_WANTRCVD flag, which was set for the Unix domain stream protocol in Figure 17.5. The purpose of this request is to let the protocol layer get control when the socket layer removes data from a socket's receive buffer. TCP uses this, for example, to check if a window advertisement should be sent to the peer, since the socket receive buffer now has more free space. The Unix domain stream protocol uses this to update the sender and receiver buffer counters.

uipc_usrreq.c

```
113     case PRU_RCVD:
114         switch (so->so_type) {

115         case SOCK_DGRAM:
116             panic("uipc 1");
117             /* NOTREACHED */

118         case SOCK_STREAM:
119 #define rcv (&so->so_rcv)
120 #define snd (&so2->so_snd)
121             if (unp->unp_conn == 0)
122                 break;
123             so2 = unp->unp_conn->unp_socket;
124             /*
125              * Adjust backpressure on sender
126              * and wake up any waiting to write.
127              */
128             snd->sb_mbmax += unp->unp_mbcnt - rcv->sb_mbcnt;
129             unp->unp_mbcnt = rcv->sb_mbcnt;
130             snd->sb_hiwat += unp->unp_cc - rcv->sb_cc;
131             unp->unp_cc = rcv->sb_cc;
132             sowwakeup(so2);
133 #undef snd
134 #undef rcv
135             break;

136         default:
137             panic("uipc 2");
138         }
139         break;
```

uipc_usrreq.c

Figure 18.3 PRU_RCVD request.

Check if peer is gone

121–122 If the peer that wrote the data has already terminated, there is nothing to do. Note that the receiver's data is not discarded; the sender's buffer counters cannot be updated, however, since the sending process has closed its socket. There is no need to update the buffer counters, since the sender will not write any more data to the socket.

Update buffer counters

123–131 `so2` points to the sender's `socket` structure. The sender's `sb_mbmax` and `sb_hiwat` are updated by what was read. For example, `unp->unp_cc` minus `rcv->sb_cc` is the number of bytes of data just read.

Wake up any writers

132 When the data is read from the receive queue, the sender's `sb_hiwat` is incremented. Therefore any processes waiting to write data to the socket are awakened since there might be room.

18.3 Descriptor Passing

Descriptor passing is a powerful technique for interprocess communication. Chapter 15 of [Stevens 1992] provides examples of this technique under both 4.4BSD and SVR4. Although the system calls differ between the two implementations, those examples provide library functions that can hide the implementation differences from the application.

Historically the passing of descriptors has been called the passing of *access rights*. One capability represented by a descriptor is the right to perform I/O on the underlying object. (If we didn't have that right, the kernel would not have opened the descriptor for us.) But this capability has meaning only in the context of the process in which the descriptor is open. For example, just passing the descriptor number, say, 4, from one process to another does not convey these rights because descriptor 4 may not be open in the receiving process and, even if it is open, it probably refers to a different file from the one in the sending process. A descriptor is simply an identifier that only has meaning within a given process. The passing of a descriptor from one process to another, along with the rights associated with that descriptor, requires additional support from the kernel. The only type of access rights that can be passed from one process to another are descriptors.

Figure 18.4 shows the data structures that are involved in passing a descriptor from one process to another. The following steps take place.

1. We assume the top process is a server with a Unix domain stream socket on which it accepts connections. The client is the bottom process and it creates a Unix domain stream socket and connects it to the server's socket. The client references its socket as *fdm* and the server references its socket as *fdi*. In this example we use stream sockets, but we'll see that descriptor passing also works with Unix domain datagram sockets. We also assume that *fdi* is the server's connected socket, returned by `accept` as shown in Section 17.10. For simplicity we do not show the structures for the server's listening socket.

2. The server opens some other file that it references as *fdj*. This can be *any* type of file that is referenced through a descriptor: file, device, socket, and so on. We show it as a file with a `vnode`. The file's reference count, the `f_count` member of its `file` structure, is 1 when it is opened for the first time.

3. The server calls `sendmsg` on *fdi* with control information containing a type of `SCM_RIGHTS` and a value of *fdj*. This "passes the descriptor" across the Unix domain stream socket to the recipient, *fdm* in the client process. The reference count in the `file` structure associated with *fdj* is incremented to 2.

4. The client calls `recvmsg` on *fdm* specifying a control buffer. The control information that is returned has a type of `SCM_RIGHTS` and a value of *fdn*, the lowest unused descriptor in the client.

5. After `sendmsg` returns in the server, the server typically closes the descriptor that it just passed (*fdj*). This causes the reference count to be decremented to 1.

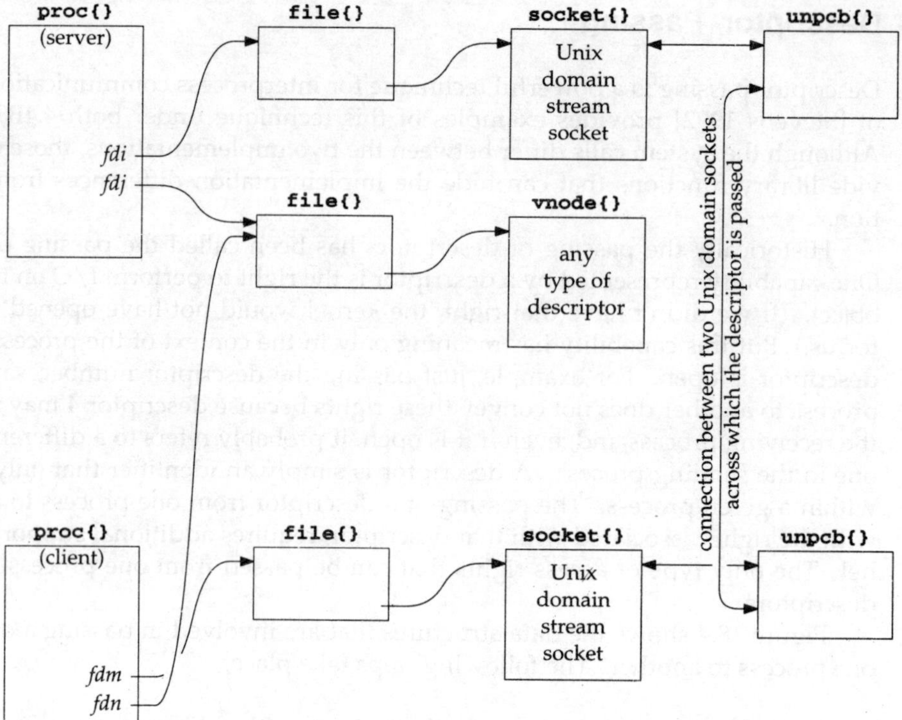

Figure 18.4 Data structures involved in descriptor passing.

We say the descriptor is *in flight* between the `sendmsg` and the `recvmsg`.

Three counters are maintained by the kernel that we will encounter with descriptor passing.

1. `f_count` is a member of the `file` structure and counts the number of current references to this structure. When multiple descriptors share the same `file` structure, this member counts the number of descriptors. For example, when a process opens a file, the file's `f_count` is set to 1. If the process then calls `fork`, the `f_count` member becomes 2 since the `file` structure is shared between the parent and child, and each has a descriptor that points to the same `file` structure. When a descriptor is closed the `f_count` value is decremented by one, and if it becomes 0, the corresponding file or socket is closed and the `file` structure can be reused.

2. `f_msgcount` is also a member of the `file` structure but is nonzero only while the descriptor is being passed. When the descriptor is passed by `sendmsg`, the `f_msgcount` member is incremented by one. When the descriptor is received by `recvmsg`, the `f_msgcount` value is decremented by one. The `f_msgcount`

value is a count of the references to this `file` structure held by descriptors in socket receive queues (i.e., currently in flight).

3. `unp_rights` is a kernel global that counts the number of descriptors currently being passed, that is, the total number of descriptors currently in socket receive queues.

For an open descriptor that is not being passed, `f_count` is greater than 0 and `f_msgcount` is 0. Figure 18.5 shows the values of the three variables when a descriptor is passed. We assume that no other descriptors are currently being passed by the kernel.

	f_count	f_msgcount	unp_rights
after open by sender	1	0	0
after sendmsg by sender	2	1	1
on receiver's queue	2	1	1
after recvmsg by receiver	2	0	0
after close by sender	1	0	0

Figure 18.5 Values of kernel variables during descriptor passing.

We assume in this figure that the sender closes the descriptor after the receiver's `recvmsg` returns. But the sender is allowed to close the descriptor while it is being passed, before the receiver calls `recvmsg`. Figure 18.6 shows the values of the three variables when this happens.

	f_count	f_msgcount	unp_rights
after open by sender	1	0	0
after sendmsg by sender	2	1	1
on receiver's queue	2	1	1
after close by sender	1	1	1
on receiver's queue	1	1	1
after recvmsg by receiver	1	0	0

Figure 18.6 Values of kernel variables during descriptor passing.

The end result is the same regardless of whether the sender closes the descriptor before or after the receiver calls `recvmsg`. We can also see from both figures that `sendmsg` increments all three counters, while `recvmsg` decrements just the final two counters in the table.

The kernel code for descriptor passing is conceptually simple. The descriptor being passed is converted into its corresponding `file` pointer and passed to the other end of the Unix domain socket. The receiver converts the `file` pointer into the lowest unused descriptor in the receiving process. Problems arise, however, when handling possible errors. For example, the receiving process can close its Unix domain socket while a descriptor is on its receive queue.

The conversion of a descriptor into its corresponding `file` pointer by the sending process is called *internalizing* and the subsequent conversion of this `file` pointer into the lowest unused descriptor in the receiving process is called *externalizing*. The function `unp_internalize` was called by the `PRU_SEND` request in Figure 18.1 if control information was passed by the process. The function `unp_externalize` is called by `soreceive` if an mbuf of type `MT_CONTROL` is being read by the process (p. 518 of Volume 2).

Figure 18.7 shows the definition of the control information passed by the process to `sendmsg` to pass a descriptor. A structure of the same type is filled in by `recvmsg` when a descriptor is received.

socket.h

```
struct cmsghdr {
    u_int   cmsg_len;                /* data byte count, including hdr */
    int     cmsg_level;              /* originating protocol */
    int     cmsg_type;               /* protocol-specific type */
/* followed by  u_char  cmsg_data[]; */
};
```

socket.h

Figure 18.7 cmsghdr structure.

For example, if the process is sending two descriptors, with values 3 and 7, Figure 18.8 shows the format of the control information. We also show the two fields in the `msghdr` structure that describe the control information.

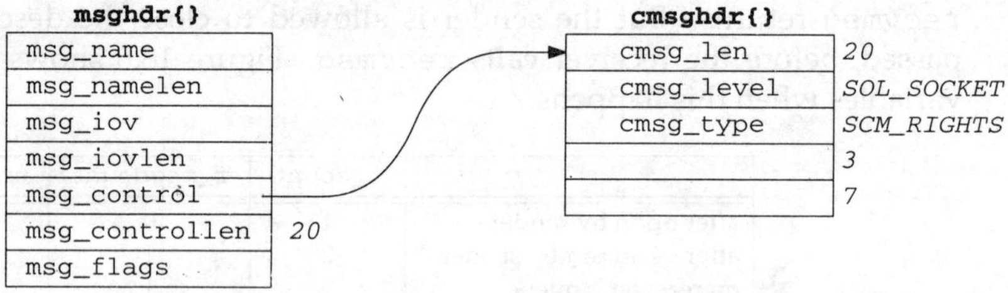

Figure 18.8 Example of control information to pass two descriptors.

In general a process can send any number of descriptors using a single `sendmsg`, but applications that pass descriptors typically pass just one descriptor. There is an inherent limit that the total size of the control information must fit into a single mbuf (imposed by the `sockargs` function, which is called by the `sendit` function, pp. 452 and 488, respectively, of Volume 2), limiting any process to passing a maximum of 24 descriptors.

> Prior to 4.3BSD Reno the `msg_control` and `msg_controllen` members of the `msghdr` structure were named `msg_accrights` and `msg_accrightslen`.

> The reason for the apparently redundant `cmsg_len` field, which always equals the `msg_controllen` field, is to allow multiple control messages to appear in a single control buffer. But we'll see that the code does not support this, requiring instead a single control message per control buffer.

> The only control information supported in the Internet domain is returning the destination IP address for a UDP datagram (p. 775 of Volume 2). The OSI protocols support four different types of control information for various OSI-specific purposes.

Figure 18.9 summarizes the functions that are called to send and receive descriptors. The shaded functions are covered in this text and the remaining functions are all covered in Volume 2.

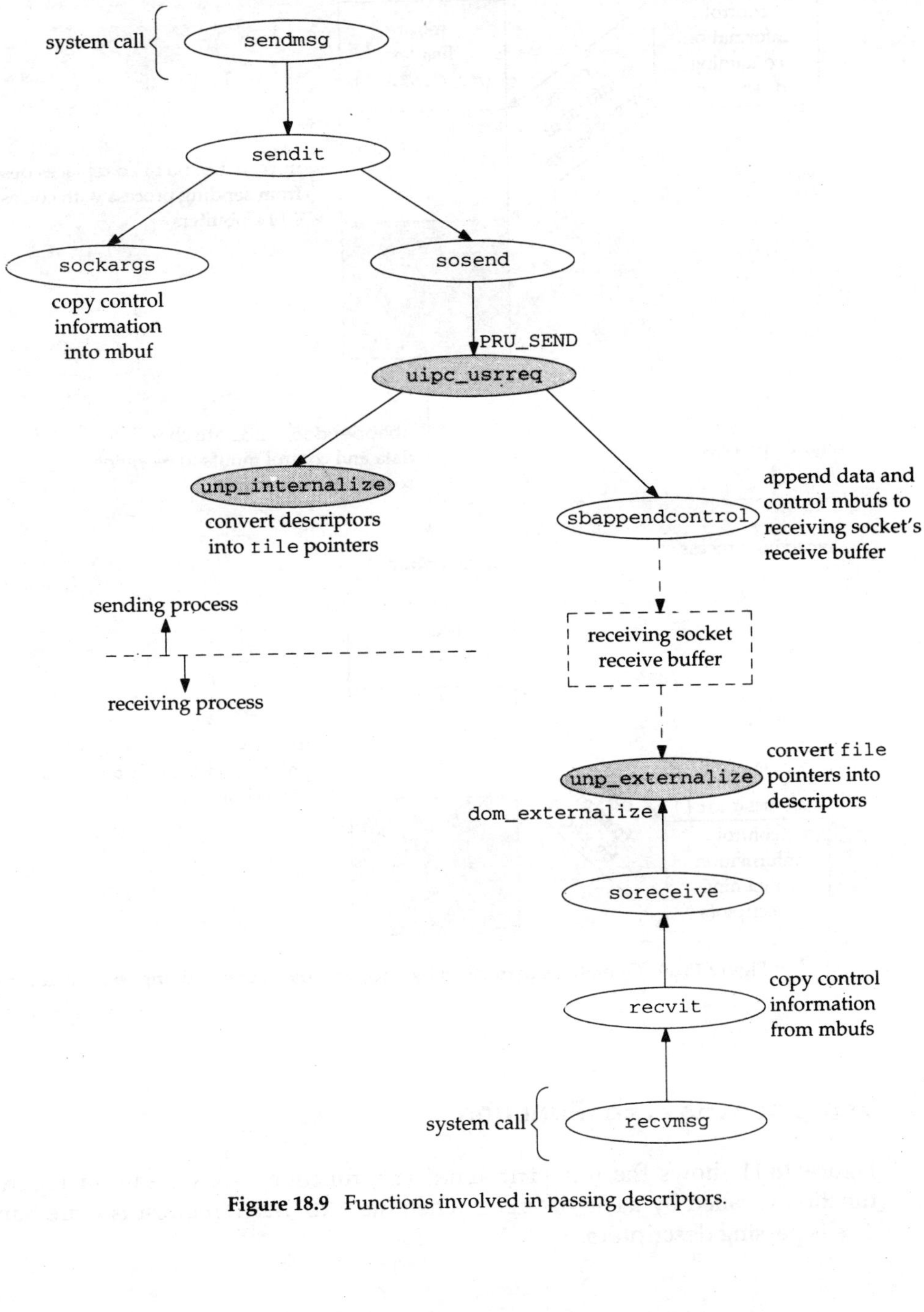

Figure 18.9 Functions involved in passing descriptors.

Figure 18.10 summarizes the actions of `unp_internalize` and `unp_externalize`, with regard to the descriptors and `file` pointers in the user's control buffer and in the kernel's mbuf.

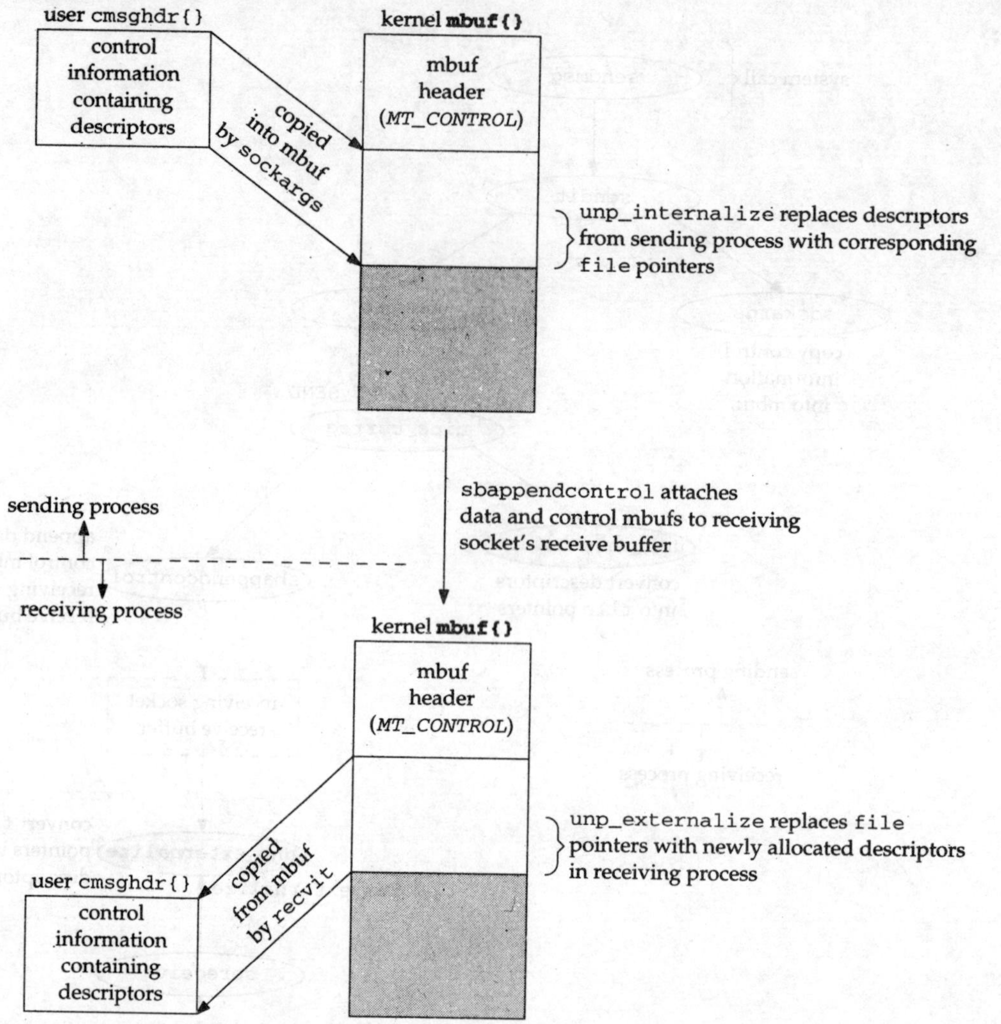

Figure 18.10 Operations performed by `unp_internalize` and `unp_externalize`.

18.4 `unp_internalize` Function

Figure 18.11 shows the `unp_internalize` function. As we saw in Figure 18.1, this function is called by `uipc_usrreq` when the `PRU_SEND` request is issued and the process is passing descriptors.

uipc_usrreq.c

```
553 int
554 unp_internalize(control, p)
555 struct mbuf *control;
556 struct proc *p;
557 {
558     struct filedesc *fdp = p->p_fd;
559     struct cmsghdr *cm = mtod(control, struct cmsghdr *);
560     struct file **rp;
561     struct file *fp;
562     int     i, fd;
563     int     oldfds;

564     if (cm->cmsg_type != SCM_RIGHTS || cm->cmsg_level != SOL_SOCKET ||
565         cm->cmsg_len != control->m_len)
566         return (EINVAL);
567     oldfds = (cm->cmsg_len - sizeof(*cm)) / sizeof(int);
568     rp = (struct file **) (cm + 1);
569     for (i = 0; i < oldfds; i++) {
570         fd = *(int *) rp++;
571         if ((unsigned) fd >= fdp->fd_nfiles ||
572             fdp->fd_ofiles[fd] == NULL)
573             return (EBADF);
574     }
575     rp = (struct file **) (cm + 1);
576     for (i = 0; i < oldfds; i++) {
577         fp = fdp->fd_ofiles[*(int *) rp];
578         *rp++ = fp;
579         fp->f_count++;
580         fp->f_msgcount++;
581         unp_rights++;
582     }
583     return (0);
584 }
```

uipc_usrreq.c

Figure 18.11 unp_internalize function.

Verify cmsghdr fields

564–566 The user's cmsghdr structure must specify a type of SCM_RIGHTS, a level of SOL_SOCKET, and its length field must equal the amount of data in the mbuf (which is a copy of the msg_controllen member of the msghdr structure that was passed by the process to sendmsg).

Verify validity of descriptors being passed

567–574 oldfds is set to the number of descriptors being passed and rp points to the first descriptor. For each descriptor being passed, the for loop verifies that the descriptor is not greater than the maximum descriptor currently used by the process and that the pointer is nonnull (that is, the descriptor is open).

Replace descriptors with file pointers

575–578 rp is reset to point to the first descriptor and this for loop replaces each descriptor with the referenced file pointer, fp.

Increment three counters

579–581 The f_count and f_msgcount members of the file structure are incremented. The former is decremented each time the descriptor is closed, while the latter is decremented by unp_externalize. Additionally, the global unp_rights is incremented for each descriptor passed by unp_internalize. We'll see that it is then decremented for each descriptor received by unp_externalize. Its value at any time is the number of descriptors currently in flight within the kernel. We saw in Figure 17.14 that when any Unix domain socket is closed and this counter is nonzero, the garbage collection function unp_gc is called, in case the socket being closed contains any descriptors in flight on its receive queue.

18.5 unp_externalize Function

Figure 18.12 shows the unp_externalize function. It is called as the dom_externalize function by soreceive (p. 518 of Volume 2) when an mbuf is encountered on the socket's receive queue with a type of MT_CONTROL and if the process is prepared to receive the control information.

Verify receiving process has enough available descriptors

532–541 newfds is a count of the number of file pointers in the mbuf being externalized. fdavail is a kernel function that checks whether the process has enough available descriptors. If there are not enough descriptors, unp_discard (shown in the next section) is called for each descriptor and EMSGSIZE is returned to the process.

Convert file pointers to descriptors

542–546 For each file pointer being passed, the lowest unused descriptor for the process is allocated by fdalloc. The second argument of 0 to fdalloc tells it not to allocate a file structure, since all that is needed at this point is a descriptor. The descriptor is returned by fdalloc in f. The descriptor in the process points to the file pointer.

Decrement two counters

547–548 The two counters f_msgcount and unp_rights are both decremented for each descriptor passed.

Replace file pointer with descriptor

549 The newly allocated descriptor replaces the file pointer in the mbuf. This is the value returned to the process as control information.

> What if the control buffer passed by the process to recvmsg is not large enough to receive the passed descriptors? unp_externalize still allocates the required number of descriptors in the process, and the descriptors all point to the correct file structure. But recvit (p. 504 of Volume 2) returns only the control information that fits into the buffer allocated by the process. If this causes truncation of the control information, the MSG_CTRUNC flag in the msg_flags field is set, which the process can test on return from recvmsg.

uipc_usrreq.c

```
int
unp_externalize(rights)
struct mbuf *rights;
{
    struct proc *p = curproc;     /* XXX */
    int     i;
    struct cmsghdr *cm = mtod(rights, struct cmsghdr *);
    struct file **rp = (struct file **) (cm + 1);
    struct file *fp;
    int     newfds = (cm->cmsg_len - sizeof(*cm)) / sizeof(int);
    int     f;

    if (!fdavail(p, newfds)) {
        for (i = 0; i < newfds; i++) {
            fp = *rp;
            unp_discard(fp);
            *rp++ = 0;
        }
        return (EMSGSIZE);
    }
    for (i = 0; i < newfds; i++) {
        if (fdalloc(p, 0, &f))
            panic("unp_externalize");
        fp = *rp;
        p->p_fd->fd_ofiles[f] = fp;
        fp->f_msgcount--;
        unp_rights--;
        *(int *) rp++ = f;
    }
    return (0);
}
```

uipc_usrreq.c

Figure 18.12 unp_externalize function.

18.6 unp_discard Function

unp_discard, shown in Figure 18.13, was called in Figure 18.12 for each descriptor being passed when it was determined that the receiving process did not have enough available descriptors.

uipc_usrreq.c

```
void
unp_discard(fp)
struct file *fp;
{

    fp->f_msgcount--;
    unp_rights--;
    (void) closef(fp, (struct proc *) NULL);
}
```

uipc_usrreq.c

Figure 18.13 unp_discard function.

Decrement two counters

730–731 The two counters `f_msgcount` and `unp_rights` are both decremented.

Call `closef`

732 The `file` is closed by `closef`, which decrements `f_count` and calls the descriptor's `fo_close` function (p. 471 of Volume 2) if `f_count` is now 0.

18.7 `unp_dispose` Function

Recall from Figure 17.14 that `unp_detach` calls `sorflush` when a Unix domain socket is closed if the global `unp_rights` is nonzero (i.e., there are descriptors in flight). One of the last actions performed by `sorflush` (p. 470 of Volume 2) is to call the domain's `dom_dispose` function, if defined and if the protocol has set the `PR_RIGHTS` flag (Figure 17.5). This call is made because the mbufs that are about to be flushed (released) might contain descriptors that are in flight. Since the two counters `f_count` and `f_msgcount` in the `file` structure and the global `unp_rights` were incremented by `unp_internalize`, these counters must all be adjusted for the descriptors that were passed but never received.

The `dom_dispose` function for the Unix domain is `unp_dispose` (Figure 17.4), which we show in Figure 18.14.

uipc_usrreq.c

```
682 void
683 unp_dispose(m)
684 struct mbuf *m;
685 {

686     if (m)
687         unp_scan(m, unp_discard);
688 }
```

uipc_usrreq.c

Figure 18.14 `unp_dispose` function.

Call `unp_scan`

686–687 All the work is done by `unp_scan`, which we show in the next section. The second argument in the call is a pointer to the function `unp_discard`, which, as we saw in the previous section, discards any descriptors that `unp_scan` finds in control buffers on the socket receive queue.

18.8 `unp_scan` Function

`unp_scan` is called from `unp_dispose`, with a second argument of `unp_discard`, and it is also called later from `unp_gc`, with a second argument of `unp_mark`. We show `unp_scan` in Figure 18.15.

uipc_usrreq.c

```
689 void
690 unp_scan(m0, op)
691 struct mbuf *m0;
692 void    (*op) (struct file *);
693 {
694     struct mbuf *m;
695     struct file **rp;
696     struct cmsghdr *cm;
697     int     i;
698     int     qfds;

699     while (m0) {
700         for (m = m0; m; m = m->m_next)
701             if (m->m_type == MT_CONTROL &&
702                 m->m_len >= sizeof(*cm)) {
703                 cm = mtod(m, struct cmsghdr *);
704                 if (cm->cmsg_level != SOL_SOCKET ||
705                     cm->cmsg_type != SCM_RIGHTS)
706                     continue;
707                 qfds = (cm->cmsg_len - sizeof *cm)
708                     / sizeof(struct file *);
709                 rp = (struct file **) (cm + 1);
710                 for (i = 0; i < qfds; i++)
711                     (*op) (*rp++);
712                 break;          /* XXX, but saves time */
713             }
714         m0 = m0->m_nextpkt;
715     }
716 }
```

uipc_usrreq.c

Figure 18.15 unp_scan function.

Look for control mbufs

699–706 This function goes through all the packets on the socket receive queue (the `m0` argument) and scans the mbuf chain of each packet, looking for an mbuf of type `MT_CONTROL`. When a control message is found, if the level is `SOL_SOCKET` and the type is `SCM_RIGHTS`, the mbuf contains descriptors in flight that were never received.

Release held `file` references

707–716 `qfds` is the number of `file` table pointers in the control message and the `op` function (`unp_discard` or `unp_mark`) is called for each `file` pointer. The argument to the `op` function is the `file` pointer contained in the control message. When this control mbuf has been processed, the `break` moves to the next packet on the receive buffer.

The `XXX` comment is because the `break` assumes there is only one control mbuf per mbuf chain, which is true.

18.9 unp_gc Function

We have already seen one form of garbage collection for descriptors in flight: in unp_detach, whenever a Unix domain socket is closed and descriptors are in flight, sorflush releases any descriptors in flight contained on the receive queue of the closing socket. Nevertheless, descriptors that are being passed across a Unix domain socket can still be "lost." There are three ways this can happen.

1. When the descriptor is passed, an mbuf of type MT_CONTROL is placed on the socket receive queue by sbappendcontrol (Figure 18.2). But if the receiving process calls recvmsg without specifying that it wants to receive control information, or calls one of the other input functions that cannot receive control information, soreceive calls MFREE to remove the mbuf of type MT_CONTROL from the socket receive buffer and release it (p. 518 of Volume 2). But when the file structure that was referenced by this mbuf is closed by the sender, its f_count and f_msgcount will both be 1 (recall Figure 18.6) and the global unp_rights still indicates that this descriptor is in flight. This is a file structure that is not referenced by any descriptor, will never be referenced by a descriptor, but is on the kernel's linked list of active file structures.

   Page 305 of [Leffler et al. 1989] notes that the problem is that the kernel does not permit a protocol to access a message after the message has been passed to the socket layer for delivery. They also comment that with hindsight this problem should have been handled with a per-domain disposal function that is invoked when an mbuf of type MT_CONTROL is released.

2. When a descriptor is passed but the receiving socket does not have room for the message, the descriptor in flight is discarded without being accounted for. This should never happen with a Unix domain stream socket, since we saw in Section 18.2 that the sender's high-water mark reflects the amount of space in the receiver's buffer, causing the sender to block until there is room in the receive buffer. But with a Unix domain datagram socket, failure is possible. If the receive buffer does not have enough room, sbappendaddr (called in Figure 18.1) returns 0, error is set to ENOBUFS, and the code at the label release (Figure 17.10) discards the mbuf containing the control information. This leads to the same scenario as in the previous case: a file structure that is not referenced by any descriptor and will never be referenced by a descriptor.
3. When a Unix domain socket *fdi* is passed on another Unix domain socket *fdj*, and *fdj* is also passed on *fdi*. If both Unix domain sockets are then closed, without receiving the descriptors that were passed, the descriptors can be lost. We'll see that 4.4BSD explicitly handles this problem (Figure 18.18).

The key fact in the first two cases is that the "lost" file structure is one whose f_count equals its f_msgcount (i.e., the only references to this descriptor are in control messages) *and* the file structure is not currently referenced from any control message found in the receive queues of all the Unix domain sockets in the kernel. If a file structure's f_count exceeds its f_msgcount, then the difference is the number of descriptors in processes that reference the structure, so the structure is not lost. (A file's f_count value must never be less than its f_msgcount value, or something is broken.) If f_count equals f_msgcount but the file structure is referenced by a control message on a Unix domain socket, it is OK since some process can still receive the descriptor from that socket.

The garbage collection function unp_gc locates these lost file structures and reclaims them. A file structure is reclaimed by calling closef, as is done in Figure 18.13, since closef returns an unused file structure to the kernel's free pool. Notice that this function is called only when there are descriptors in flight, that is, when unp_rights is nonzero (Figure 17.14), and when some Unix domain socket is closed. Therefore even though the function appears to involve much overhead, it should rarely be called.

unp_gc uses a mark-and-sweep algorithm to perform its garbage collection. The first half of the function, the mark phase, goes through every file structure in the kernel and marks those that are in use: either the file structure is referenced by a descriptor in a process or the file structure is referenced by a control message on a Unix domain socket's receive queue (that is, the structure corresponds to a descriptor that is currently in flight). The next half of the function, the sweep, reclaims all the unmarked file structures, since they are not in use.

Figure 18.16 shows the first half of unp_gc.

Prevent function from being called recursively

594–596 The global unp_gcing prevents the function from being called recursively, since unp_gc can call sorflush, which calls unp_dispose, which calls unp_discard, which calls closef, which can call unp_detach, which calls unp_gc again.

Clear FMARK and FDEFER flags

598–599 This first loop goes through all the file structures in the kernel and clears both the FMARK and FDEFER flags.

Loop until unp_defer equals 0

600–622 The do while loop is executed as long as the flag unp_defer is nonzero. We'll see that this flag is set when we discover that a file structure that we previously processed, which we thought was not in use, is actually in use. When this happens we may need to go back through all the file structures again, because there is a chance that the structure that we just marked as busy is itself a Unix domain socket containing file references on its receive queue.

Loop through all file structures

601–603 This loop examines all file structures in the kernel. If the structure is not in use (f_count is 0), we skip this entry.

Process deferred structures

604–606 If the FDEFER flag was set, the flag is turned off and the unp_defer counter is decremented. When the FDEFER flag is set by unp_mark, the FMARK flag is also set, so we know this entry is in use and will check if it is a Unix domain socket at the end of the if statement.

uipc_usrreq.c

```
587 void
588 unp_gc()
589 {
590     struct file *fp, *nextfp;
591     struct socket *so;
592     struct file **extra_ref, **fpp;
593     int     nunref, i;

594     if (unp_gcing)
595         return;
596     unp_gcing = 1;
597     unp_defer = 0;
598     for (fp = filehead.lh_first; fp != 0; fp = fp->f_list.le_next)
599         fp->f_flag &= ~(FMARK | FDEFER);
600     do {
601         for (fp = filehead.lh_first; fp != 0; fp = fp->f_list.le_next) {
602             if (fp->f_count == 0)
603                 continue;
604             if (fp->f_flag & FDEFER) {
605                 fp->f_flag &= ~FDEFER;
606                 unp_defer--;
607             } else {
608                 if (fp->f_flag & FMARK)
609                     continue;
610                 if (fp->f_count == fp->f_msgcount)
611                     continue;
612                 fp->f_flag |= FMARK;
613             }

614             if (fp->f_type != DTYPE_SOCKET ||
615                 (so = (struct socket *) fp->f_data) == 0)
616                 continue;
617             if (so->so_proto->pr_domain != &unixdomain ||
618                 (so->so_proto->pr_flags & PR_RIGHTS) == 0)
619                 continue;
620             unp_scan(so->so_rcv.sb_mb, unp_mark);
621         }
622     } while (unp_defer);
```

uipc_usrreq.c

Figure 18.16 unp_gc function: first part, the mark phase.

Skip over already-processed structures

607–609 If the FMARK flag is set, the entry is in use and has already been processed.

Do not mark lost structures

610–611 If f_count equals f_msgcount, this entry is potentially lost. It is not marked and is skipped over. Since it does not appear to be in use, we cannot check if it is a Unix domain socket with descriptors in flight on its receive queue.

Mark structures that are in use

612 At this point we know that the entry is in use so its FMARK flag is set.

Check if structure is associated with a Unix domain socket

614–619 Since this entry is in use, we check to see if it is a socket that has a socket structure. The next check determines whether the socket is a Unix domain socket with the PR_RIGHTS flag set. This flag is set for the Unix domain stream and datagram protocols. If any of these tests is false, the entry is skipped.

Scan Unix domain socket receive queue for descriptors in flight

620 At this point the file structure corresponds to a Unix domain socket. unp_scan traverses the socket's receive queue, looking for an mbuf of type MT_CONTROL containing descriptors in flight. If found, unp_mark is called.

> At this point the code should also process the completed connection queue (so_q) for the Unix domain socket [McKusick et al. 1996]. It is possible for a descriptor to be passed by a client to a newly created server socket that is still waiting to be accepted.

Figure 18.17 shows an example of the mark phase and the potential need for multiple passes through the list of file structures. This figure shows the state of the structures at the end of the first pass of the mark phase, at which time unp_defer is 1, necessitating another pass through all the file structures. The following processing takes place as each of the four structures is processed, from left to right.

1. This file structure has two descriptors in processes that refer to it (f_count equals 2) and no references from descriptors in flight (f_msgcount equals 0). The code in Figure 18.16 turns on the FMARK bit in the f_flag field. This structure points to a vnode. (We omit the DTYPE_ prefix in the value shown for the f_type field. Also, we show only the FMARK and FDEFER flags in the f_flag field; other flags may be turned on in this field.)
2. This structure appears unreferenced because f_count equals f_msgcount. When processed by the mark phase, the f_flag field is not changed.
3. The FMARK flag is set for this structure because it is referenced by one descriptor in a process. Furthermore, since this structure corresponds to a Unix domain socket, unp_scan processes any control messages on the socket receive queue.

   The first descriptor in the control message points to the second file structure, and since its FMARK flag was not set in step 2, unp_mark turns on both the FMARK and FDEFER flags. unp_defer is also incremented to 1 since this structure was already processed and found unreferenced.

   The second descriptor in the control message points to the fourth file structure and since its FMARK flag is not set (it hasn't even been processed yet), its FMARK and FDEFER flags are set. unp_defer is incremented to 2.
4. This structure has its FDEFER flag set, so the code in Figure 18.16 turns off this flag and decrements unp_defer to 1. Even though this structure is also referenced by a descriptor in a process, its f_count and f_msgcount values are not examined since it is already known that the structure is referenced by a descriptor in flight.

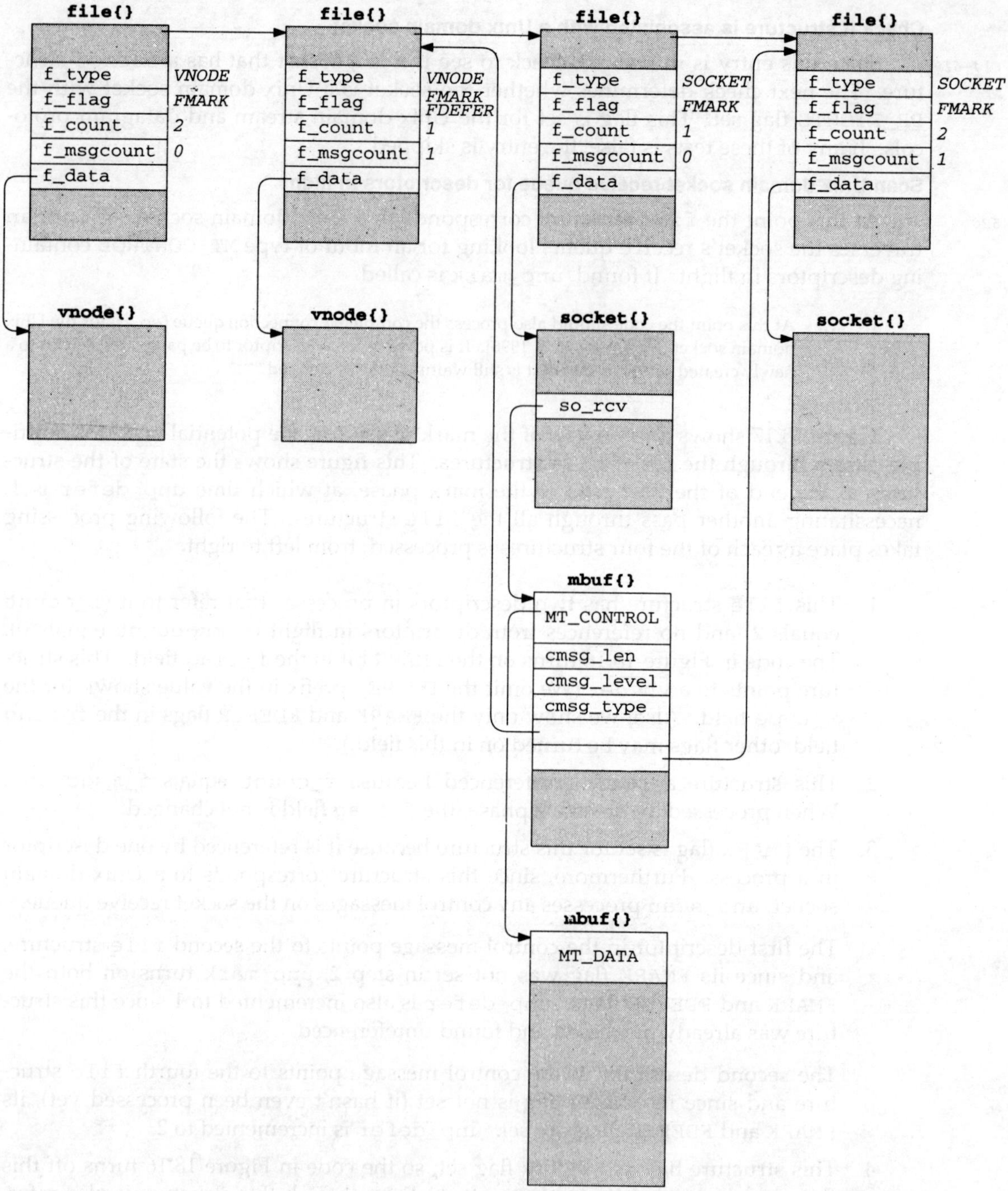

Figure 18.17 Data structures at end of first pass of mark phase.

At this point, all four `file` structures have been processed but the value of `unp_defer` is 1, so another loop is made through all the structures. This additional loop is made because the second structure, believed to be unreferenced the first time around, might be a Unix domain socket with a control message on its receive queue (which it is not in our example). That structure needs to be processed again, and when it is, it might turn on the `FMARK` and `FDEFER` flags in some other structure that was earlier in the list that was believed to be unreferenced.

At the end of the mark phase, which may involve multiple passes through the kernel's linked list of `file` structures, the unmarked structures are not in use. The second phase, the sweep, is shown in Figure 18.18.

uipc_usrreq.c

```
    /*
     * We grab an extra reference to each of the file table entries
     * that are not otherwise accessible and then free the rights
     * that are stored in messages on them.
     *
     * The bug in the orginal code is a little tricky, so I'll describe
     * what's wrong with it here.
     *
     * It is incorrect to simply unp_discard each entry for f_msgcount
     * times -- consider the case of sockets A and B that contain
     * references to each other.  On a last close of some other socket,
     * we trigger a gc since the number of outstanding rights (unp_rights)
     * is non-zero.  If during the sweep phase the gc code unp_discards,
     * we end up doing a (full) closef on the descriptor.  A closef on A
     * results in the following chain.  Closef calls soo_close, which
     * calls soclose.   Soclose calls first (through the switch
     * uipc_usrreq) unp_detach, which re-invokes unp_gc.  Unp_gc simply
     * returns because the previous instance had set unp_gcing, and
     * we return all the way back to soclose, which marks the socket
     * with SS_NOFDREF, and then calls sofree.  Sofree calls sorflush
     * to free up the rights that are queued in messages on the socket A,
     * i.e., the reference on B.  The sorflush calls via the dom_dispose
     * switch unp_dispose, which unp_scans with unp_discard.  This second
     * instance of unp_discard just calls closef on B.
     *
     * Well, a similar chain occurs on B, resulting in a sorflush on B,
     * which results in another closef on A.  Unfortunately, A is already
     * being closed, and the descriptor has already been marked with
     * SS_NOFDREF, and soclose panics at this point.
     *
     * Here, we first take an extra reference to each inaccessible
     * descriptor.  Then, we call sorflush ourself, since we know
     * it is a Unix domain socket anyhow.  After we destroy all the
     * rights carried in messages, we do a last closef to get rid
     * of our extra reference.  This is the last close, and the
     * unp_detach etc will shut down the socket.
     *
     * 91/09/19, bsy@cs.cmu.edu
     */
```

```
662     extra_ref = malloc(nfiles * sizeof(struct file *), M_FILE, M_WAITOK);
663     for (nunref = 0, fp = filehead.lh_first, fpp = extra_ref; fp != 0;
664          fp = nextfp) {
665         nextfp = fp->f_list.le_next;
666         if (fp->f_count == 0)
667             continue;
668         if (fp->f_count == fp->f_msgcount && !(fp->f_flag & FMARK)) {
669             *fpp++ = fp;
670             nunref++;
671             fp->f_count++;
672         }
673     }
674     for (i = nunref, fpp = extra_ref; --i >= 0; ++fpp)
675         if ((*fpp)->f_type == DTYPE_SOCKET)
676             sorflush((struct socket *) (*fpp)->f_data);
677     for (i = nunref, fpp = extra_ref; --i >= 0; ++fpp)
678         closef(*fpp, (struct proc *) NULL);
679     free((caddr_t) extra_ref, M_FILE);
680     unp_gcing = 0;
681 }
```

uipc_usrreq.c

Figure 18.18 unp_gc function: second part, the sweep phase.

Bug fix comments

623–661 The comments refer to a bug that was in the 4.3BSD Reno and Net/2 releases. The bug was fixed in 4.4BSD by Bennet S. Yee. We show the old code referred to by these comments in Figure 18.19.

Allocate temporary region

662 `malloc` allocates room for an array of pointers to all of the kernel's `file` structures. `nfiles` is the number of `file` structures currently in use. `M_FILE` identifies what the memory is to be used for. (The `vmstat -m` command outputs information on kernel memory usage.) `M_WAITOK` says it is OK to put the process to sleep if the memory is not immediately available.

Loop through all `file` structures

663–665 To find all the unreferenced (lost) structures, this loop examines all the `file` structures in the kernel again.

Skip unused structures

666–667 If the structure's `f_count` is 0, the structure is skipped.

Check for unreferenced structure

668 The entry is unreferenced if `f_count` equals `f_msgcount` (the only references are from descriptors in flight) and the `FMARK` flag was not set in the mark phase (the descriptors in flight did not appear on any Unix domain socket receive queue).

Save pointer to unreferenced `file` structure

669–671 A copy of `fp`, the pointer to the `file` structure, is saved in the array that was allocated, the counter `nunref` is incremented, and the structure's `f_count` is incremented.

Call sorflush for unreferenced sockets

674–676 For each unreferenced file that is a socket, sorflush is called. This function (p. 470 of Volume 2) calls the domain's dom_dispose function, unp_dispose, which calls unp_scan to discard any descriptors in flight currently on the socket's receive queue. It is unp_discard that decrements both f_msgcount and unp_rights and calls closef for all the file structures found in control messages on the socket receive queue. Since we have an extra reference to this file structure (the increment of f_count done earlier) and since that loop ignored structures with an f_count of 0, we are guaranteed that f_count is 2 or greater. Therefore the call to closef as a result of the sorflush will just decrement the structure's f_count to a nonzero value, avoiding a complete close of the structure. This is why the extra reference to the structure was taken earlier.

Perform last close

677–678 closef is called for all the unreferenced file structures. This is the last close, that is, f_count should be decremented from 1 to 0, causing the socket to be shut down and returning the file structure to the kernel's free pool.

Return temporary array

679–680 The array that was obtained earlier by malloc is returned and the flag unp_gcing is cleared.

Figure 18.19 shows the sweep phase of unp_gc as it appeared in the Net/2 release. This code was replaced by Figure 18.18.

```
    for (fp = filehead; fp; fp = fp->f_filef) {
        if (fp->f_count == 0)
            continue;
        if (fp->f_count == fp->f_msgcount && (fp->f_flag & FMARK) == 0)
            while (fp->f_msgcount)
                unp_discard(fp);
    }
    unp_gcing = 0;
}
```

Figure 18.19 Incorrect code for sweep phase of unp_gc from Net/2.

This is the code referred to in the comments at the beginning of Figure 18.18.

> Unfortunately, despite the improvements in the Net/3 code shown in this section over Figure 18.19, and the correction of the bug described at the beginning of Figure 18.18, the code is still not correct. It is still possible for file structures to become lost, with the first two scenarios mentioned at the beginning of this section.

18.10 unp_mark Function

This function is called by unp_scan, when called by unp_gc, to mark a file structure. The marking is done when descriptors in flight are discovered on the socket's receive queue. Figure 18.20 shows the function.

uipc_usrreq.c

```
717 void
718 unp_mark(fp)
719 struct file *fp;
720 {
721     if (fp->f_flag & FMARK)
722         return;
723     unp_defer++;
724     fp->f_flag |= (FMARK | FDEFER);
725 }
```

uipc_usrreq.c

Figure 18.20 unp_mark function.

717–720 The argument fp is the pointer to the file structure that was found in the control message on the Unix domain socket's receive queue.

Return if entry already marked

721–722 If the file structure has already been marked, there is nothing else to do. The file structure is already known to be in use.

Set FMARK and FDEFER flags

723–724 The unp_defer counter is incremented and both the FMARK and FDEFER flags are set. If this file structure occurs earlier in the kernel's list than the Unix domain socket's file structure (i.e., it was already processed by unp_gc and did not appear to be in use so it was not marked), incrementing unp_defer will cause another loop through all the file structures in the mark phase of unp_gc.

18.11 Performance (Revisited)

Having examined the implementation of the Unix domain protocols we now return to their performance to see why they are twice as fast as TCP (Figure 16.2).

All socket I/O goes through sosend and soreceive, regardless of protocol. This is both good and bad. Good because these two functions service the requirements of many different protocols, from byte streams (TCP), to datagram protocols (UDP), to record-based protocols (OSI TP4). But this is also bad because the generality hinders performance and complicates the code. Optimized versions of these two functions for the various forms of protocols would increase performance.

Comparing output performance, the path through sosend for TCP is nearly identical to the path for the Unix domain stream protocol. Assuming large application writes (Figure 16.2 used 32768-byte writes), sosend packages the user data into mbuf clusters and passes each 2048-byte cluster to the protocol using the PRU_SEND request.

Therefore both TCP and the Unix domain will process the same number of PRU_SEND requests. The difference in speed for output must be the simplicity of the Unix domain PRU_SEND (Figure 18.2) compared to TCP output (which calls IP output to append each segment to the loopback driver output queue).

On the receive side the only function involved with the Unix domain socket is soreceive, since the PRU_SEND request placed the data onto the receiving socket's receive buffer. With TCP, however, the loopback driver places each segment onto the IP input queue, followed by IP processing, followed by TCP input demultiplexing the segment to the correct socket and then placing the data onto the socket's receive buffer.

18.12 Summary

When data is written to a Unix domain socket, the data is appended immediately to the receiving socket's receive buffer. There is no need to buffer the data on the sending socket's send buffer. For this to work correctly for stream sockets, the PRU_SEND and PRU_RCVD requests manipulate the send buffer high-water mark so that it always reflects the amount of room in the peer's receive buffer.

Unix domain sockets provide the mechanism for passing descriptors from one process to another. This is a powerful technique for interprocess communication. When a descriptor is passed from one process to another, the descriptor is first internalized—converted into its corresponding file pointer—and this pointer is passed to the receiving socket. When the receiving process reads the control information, the file pointer is externalized—converted into the lowest unnumbered descriptor in the receiving process—and this descriptor is returned to the process.

One error condition that is easily handled is when a Unix domain socket is closed while its receive buffer contains control messages with descriptors in flight. Unfortunately two other error conditions can occur that are not as easily handled: when the receiving process doesn't ask for the control information that is in its receive buffer, and when the receive buffer does not have adequate room for the control buffer. In these two conditions the file structures are lost; that is, they are not in the kernel's free pool and are not in use. A garbage collection function is required to reclaim these lost structures.

The garbage collection function performs a mark phase, in which all the kernel's file structures are scanned and the ones in use are marked, followed by a sweep phase in which all unmarked structures are reclaimed. Although this function is required, it is rarely used.

Appendix A

Measuring Network Times

Throughout the text we measure the time required to exchange packets across a network. This appendix provides some details and examples of the various times that we can measure. We look at RTT measurements using the Ping program, measurements of how much time is taken going up and down the protocol stack, and the difference between latency and bandwidth.

A network programmer or system administrator normally has two ways to measure the time required for an application transaction:

1. Use an application timer. For example, in the UDP client in Figure 1.1 we fetch the system's clock time before the call to `sendto` and fetch the clock time again after `recvfrom` returns. The difference is the time measured by the application to send a request and receive a reply.

   If the kernel provides a high-resolution clock (on the order of microsecond resolution), the values that we measure (a few milliseconds or more) are fairly accurate. Appendix A of Volume 1 provides additional details about these types of measurements.

2. Use a software tool such as Tcpdump that taps into the data-link layer, watch for the desired packets, and calculate the corresponding time difference. Additional details on these tools are provided in Appendix A of Volume 1.

   In this text we assume the data-link tap is provided by Tcpdump using the BSD packet filter (BPF). Chapter 31 of Volume 2 provides additional details on the implementation of BPF. Pages 103 and 113 of Volume 2 show where the calls to BPF appear in a typical Ethernet driver, and p. 151 of Volume 2 shows the call to BPF in the loopback driver.

The most reliable method is to attach a network analyzer to the network cable, but this option is usually not available.

We note that the systems used for the examples in this text (Figure 1.13), BSD/OS 2.0 on an 80386 and Solaris 2.4 on a Sparcstation ELC, both provide a high-resolution timer for application timing and Tcpdump timestamps.

A.1 RTT Measurements Using Ping

The ubiquitous Ping program, described in detail in Chapter 7 of Volume 1, uses an application timer to calculate the RTT for an ICMP packet. The program sends an ICMP echo request packet to a server, which the server returns to the client as an ICMP echo reply packet. The client stores the clock time at which the packet is sent as optional user data in the echo request packet, and this data is returned by the server. When the echo reply is received by the client, the current clock time is fetched and the RTT is calculated and printed. Figure A.1 shows the format of a Ping packet.

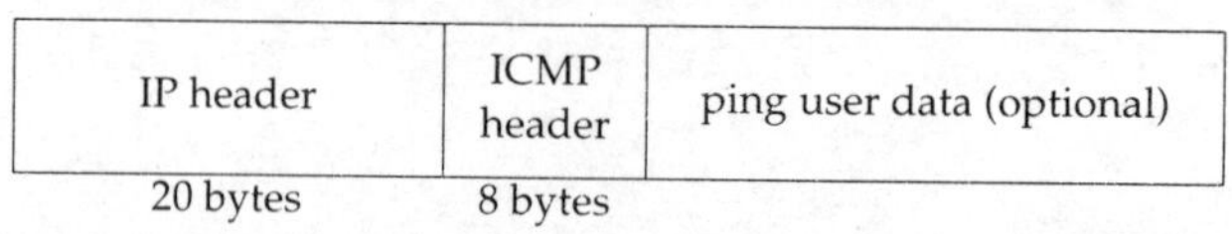

Figure A.1 Ping packet: ICMP echo request or ICMP echo reply.

The Ping program lets us specify the amount of optional user data in the packet, allowing us to measure the effect of the packet size on the RTT. The amount of optional data must be at least 8 bytes, however, for Ping to measure the RTT (because the timestamp that is sent by the client and echoed by the server occupies 8 bytes). If we specify less than 8 bytes as the amount of user data, Ping still works but it cannot calculate and print the RTT.

Figure A.2 shows some typical Ping RTTs between hosts on three different Ethernet LANs. The middle line in the figure is between the two hosts `bsdi` and `sun` in Figure 1.13.

Fifteen different packet sizes were measured: 8 bytes of user data and from 100 to 1400 bytes of user data (in 100-byte increments). With a 20-byte IP header and an 8-byte ICMP header, the IP datagrams ranged from 36 to 1428 bytes. Ten measurements were made for each packet size, and the minimum of the 10 values was plotted. As we expect, the RTT increases as the packet size increases. The differences between the three lines are caused by differences in processor speeds, interface cards, and operating systems.

Figure A.3 shows some typical Ping RTTs between various hosts across the Internet, a WAN. Note the difference in the scale of the y-axis from Figure A.2.

The same types of measurements were made for the WAN as for the LAN: 10 measurements for each of 15 different packet sizes, with the minimum of the 10 values plotted for each size. We also note the number of hops between each pair of hosts in parentheses.

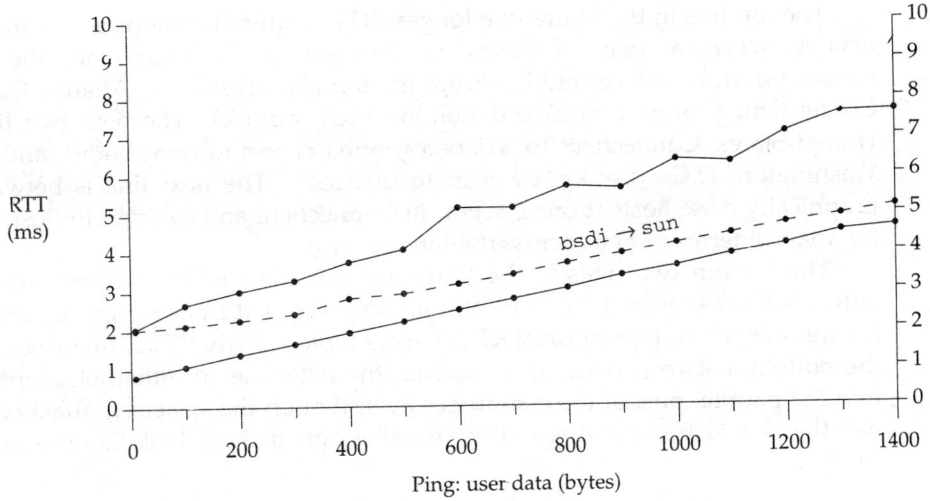

Figure A.2 Ping RTTs between hosts on three Ethernet LANs.

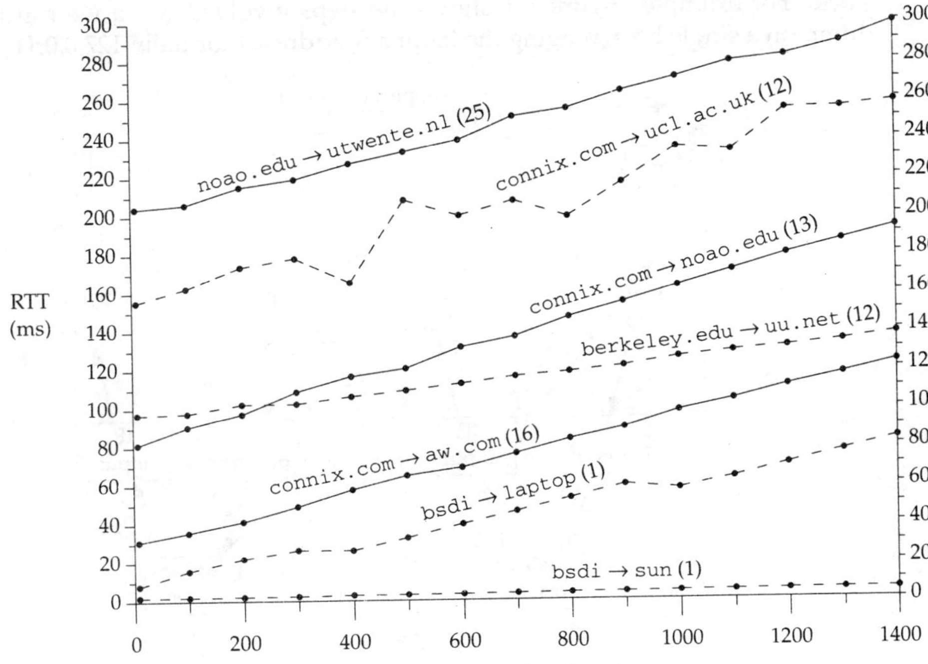

Figure A.3 Ping RTTs between hosts across the Internet (a WAN).

The top line in the figure (the longest RTT) required 25 hops across the Internet and was between a pair of hosts in Arizona (noao.edu) and the Netherlands (utwente.nl). The second line from the top also crosses the Atlantic Ocean, between Connecticut (connix.com) and London (ucl.ac.uk). The next two lines span the United States, Connecticut to Arizona (connix.com to noao.edu), and California to Washington, D.C. (berkeley.edu to uu.net). The next line is between two geographically close hosts (connix.com in Connecticut and aw.com in Boston), which are far apart in terms of hops across the Internet (16).

The bottom two lines in the figure (the smallest RTTs) are between hosts on the author's LAN (Figure 1.13). The bottom line is copied from Figure A.2 and is provided for comparison of typical LAN RTTs versus typical WAN RTTs. In the second line from the bottom, between bsdi and laptop, the latter has an Ethernet adapter that plugs into the parallel port of the computer. Even though the system is attached to an Ethernet, the slower transfer times of the parallel port make it look like it is connected to a WAN.

A.2 Protocol Stack Measurements

We can also use Ping, along with Tcpdump, to measure the time spent in the protocol stack. For example, Figure A.4 shows the steps involved when we run Ping and Tcpdump on a single host, pinging the loopback address (normally 127.0.0.1).

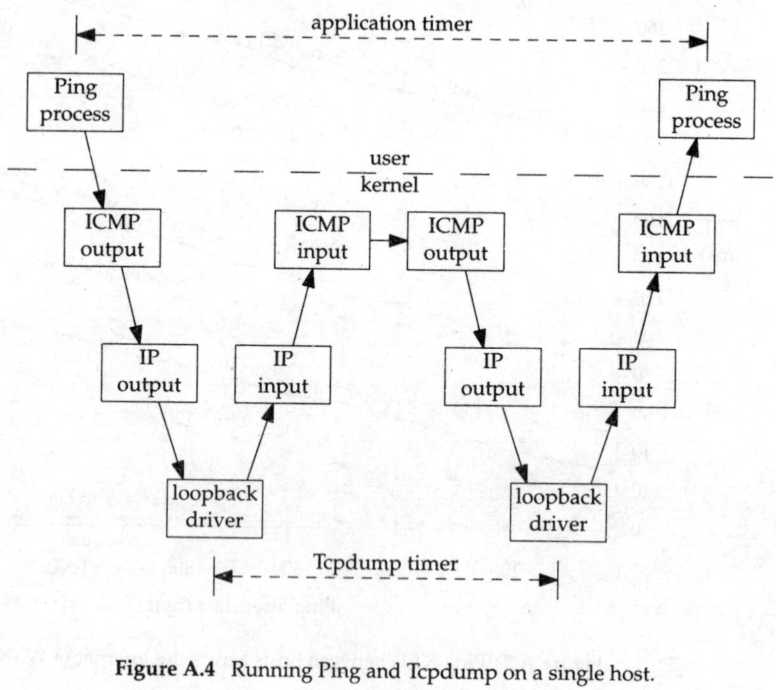

Figure A.4 Running Ping and Tcpdump on a single host.

Assuming the application starts its timer when it is about to send the echo request packet to the operating system, and stops the timer when the operating system returns the echo reply, the difference between the application measurement and the Tcpdump measurement is the amount of time required for ICMP output, IP output, IP input, and ICMP input.

We can measure similar values for any client–server application. Figure A.5 shows the processing steps for our UDP client–server from Section 1.2, when the client and server are on the same host.

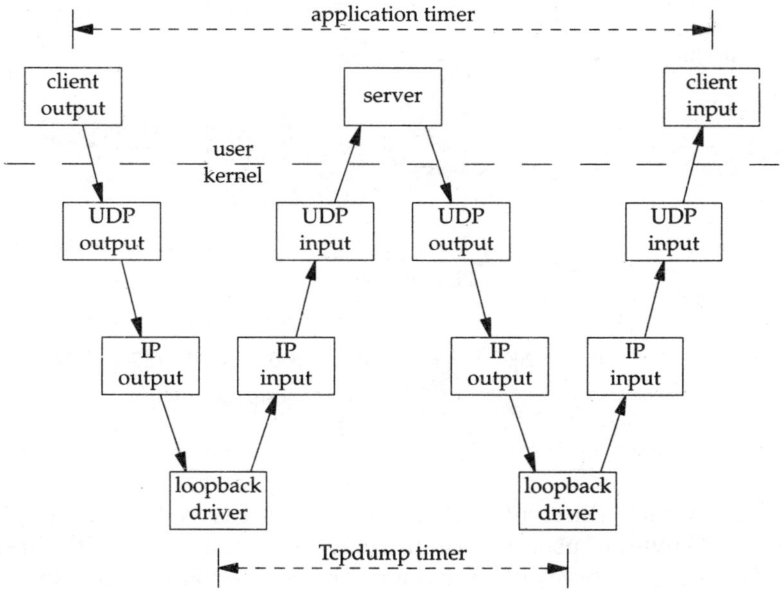

Figure A.5 Processing steps for UDP client–server transaction.

One difference between this UDP client–server and the Ping example from Figure A.4 is that the UDP server is a user process, whereas the Ping server is part of the kernel's ICMP implementation (p. 317 of Volume 2). Hence the UDP server requires two more copies of the client data between the kernel and the user process: server input and server output. Copying data between the kernel and a user process is normally an expensive operation.

Figure A.6 shows the results of various measurements made on the host `bsdi`. We compare the Ping client–server and the UDP client–server. We label the *y*-axis "measured transaction time" because the term RTT normally refers to the network round-trip time or to the time output by Ping (which we'll see in Figure A.8 is as close to the network RTT as we can come). With our UDP, TCP, and T/TCP client–servers we are measuring the application's transaction time. In the case of TCP and T/TCP, this can involve multiple packets and multiple network RTTs.

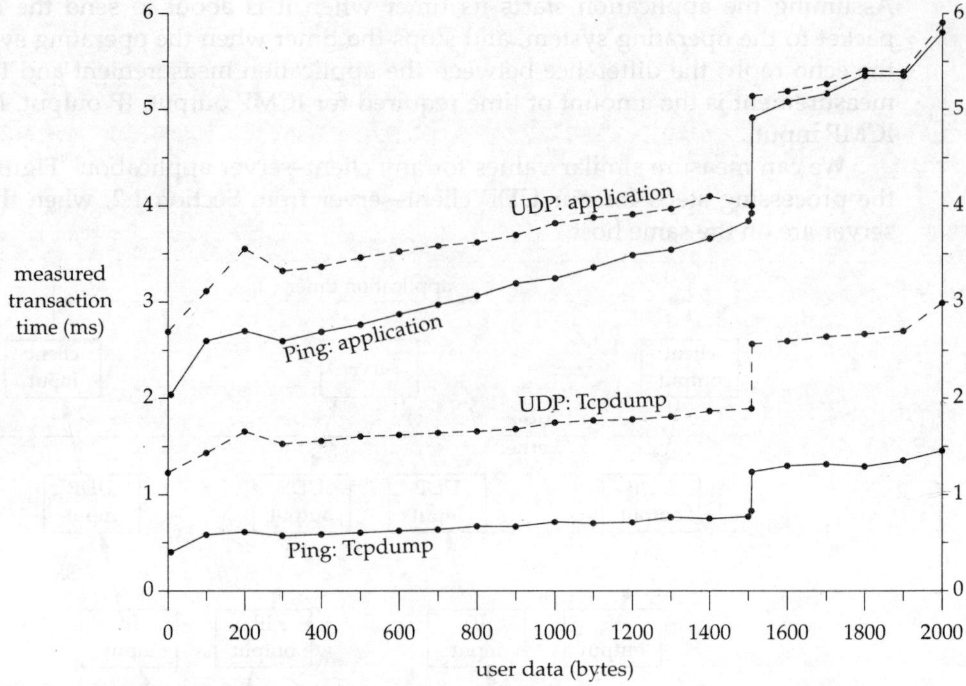

Figure A.6 Ping and Tcpdump measurements on a single host (loopback interface).

Twenty-three different packet sizes were measured using Ping for this figure: from 100 to 2000 bytes of user data (in increments of 100), along with three measurements for 8, 1508, and 1509 bytes of user data. The 8-byte value is the smallest amount of user data for which Ping can measure the RTT. The 1508-byte value is the largest value that avoids fragmentation of the IP datagram, since BSD/OS uses an MTU of 1536 for the loopback interface (1508 + 20 + 8). The 1509-byte value is the first one that causes fragmentation.

Twenty-three similar packet sizes were measured for UDP: from 100 to 2000 bytes of user data (in increments of 100), along with 0, 1508, and 1509. A 0-byte UDP datagram is allowable. Since the UDP header is the same size as the ICMP echo header (8 bytes), 1508 is again the largest value that avoids fragmentation on the loopback interface, and 1509 is the smallest value that causes fragmentation.

We first notice the jump in time at 1509 bytes of user data, when fragmentation occurs. This is expected. When fragmentation occurs, the calls to IP output on the left in Figures A.4 and A.5 result in two calls to the loopback driver, one per fragment. Even though the amount of user data increases by only 1 byte, from 1508 to 1509, the application sees approximately a 25% increase in the transaction time, because of the additional per-packet processing.

The increase in all four lines at the 200-byte point is caused by an artifact of the BSD mbuf implementation (Chapter 2 of Volume 2). For the smallest packets (0 bytes of user data for the UDP client and 8 bytes of user data for the Ping client), the data and protocol headers fit into a single mbuf. For the 100-byte point, a second mbuf is required, and for the 200-byte point, a third mbuf is required. Finally at the 300-byte point, the kernel chooses to use a 2048-byte mbuf cluster instead of the smaller mbufs. It appears that an mbuf cluster should be used sooner (e.g., for the 100-byte point) to reduce the processing time. This is an example of the classic time-versus-space trade-off. The decision to switch from smaller mbufs to the larger mbuf cluster only when the amount of data exceeds 208 bytes was made many years ago when memory was a scarce resource.

The timings in Figure 1.14 were done with a modified BSD/OS kernel in which the constant `MINCLSIZE` (pp. 37 and 497 of Volume 2) was changed from 208 to 101. This causes an mbuf cluster to be allocated as soon as the amount of user data exceeds 100 bytes. We note that the spike at the 200-byte point is gone from Figure 1.14.

We also described this problem in Section 14.11, where we noted that many Web client requests fall between 100 and 200 bytes.

The difference between the two UDP lines in Figure A.6 is between 1.5–2 ms until fragmentation occurs. Since this difference accounts for UDP output, IP output, IP input, and UDP input (Figure A.5), if we assume that the protocol output approximately equals the protocol input, then it takes just under 1 ms to send a packet down the protocol stack and just under 1 ms to receive a packet up the protocol stack. These times include the expensive copies of data from the process to the kernel when the data is sent, and from the kernel to the process when the data returns.

Since the same four steps are accounted for in the Tcpdump measurements in Figure A.5 (IP input, UDP input, UDP output, and IP output), we expect the UDP Tcpdump values to be between 1.5–2 ms also (considering only the values before fragmentation occurs). Other than the first data point, the remaining data are between 1.5–2 ms in Figure A.6.

If we consider the values after fragmentation occurs, the difference between the two UDP lines in Figure A.6 is between 2.5–3 ms. As expected, the UDP Tcpdump values are also between 2.5–3 ms.

Finally notice in Figure A.6 that the Tcpdump line for Ping is nearly flat while the application measurement for Ping has a definite positive slope. This is probably because the application time measures two copies of the data between the user process and the kernel, while none of these copies is measured by the Tcpdump line (since the Ping server is part of the kernel's implementation of ICMP). Also, the very slight positive slope of the Tcpdump line for Ping is probably caused by the two operations performed by the Ping server in the kernel that are performed on every byte: verification of the received ICMP checksum and calculation of the outgoing ICMP checksum.

We can also modify our TCP and T/TCP client–servers from Sections 1.3 and 1.4 to measure the time for each transaction (as described in Section 1.6) and perform measurements for different packet sizes. These are shown in Figure A.7. (In the remaining transaction measurements in this appendix we stop at 1400 bytes of user data, since TCP avoids fragmentation.)

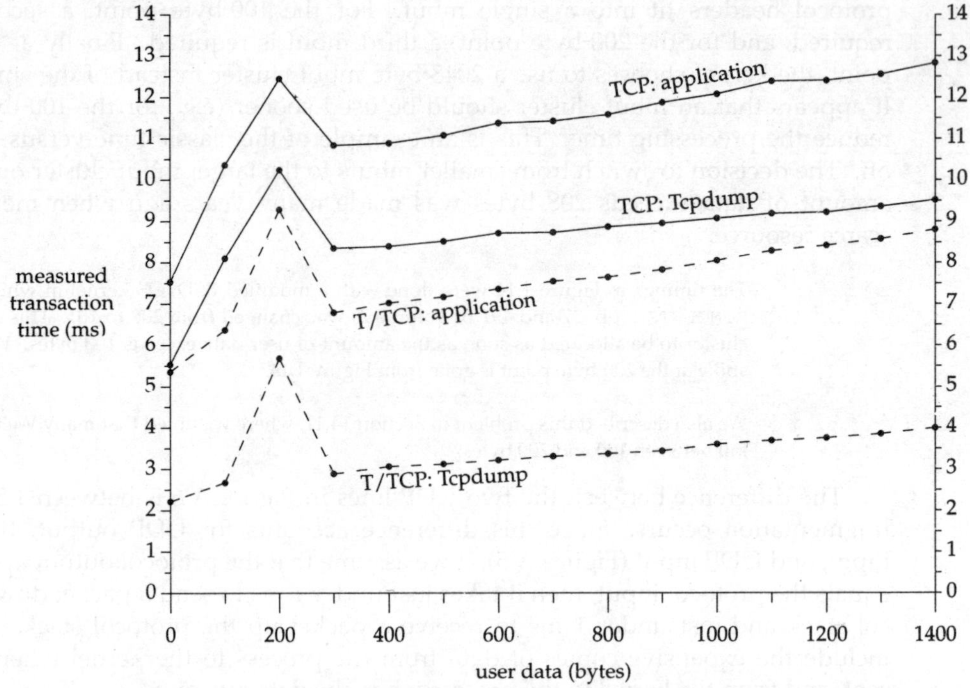

Figure A.7 TCP and T/TCP client–server transaction times on a single host (loopback interface).

The Tcpdump lines were measured from the first segment sent by the client (a SYN for the TCP client, and the combination of the SYN, data, and FIN for the T/TCP client) through the final segment received from the server (a FIN for the TCP client, and the combination of the data and a FIN for the T/TCP client). The difference between the TCP application line and the TCP Tcpdump line is then the amount of time required by the protocol stack to process the `connect` and the final FIN (Figure 1.8 shows the packet exchange). The difference between the application line and the Tcpdump line for the T/TCP client–server is the amount of time required by the protocol stack to process the client's `sendto`, which includes the client data, and the final FIN (Figure 1.12 shows the packet exchange). We notice that the difference between the two T/TCP lines (about 4 ms) is greater than the difference between the two TCP lines (about 2.5 ms), which makes sense since the protocol stack is doing more for T/TCP (sending the SYN, data, and FIN in the first segment), than for TCP (a stand-alone SYN as the first segment).

The increase in all four lines seen at the 200-byte point reiterates that the kernel should be using an mbuf cluster sooner. Notice that the increase at the 200-byte point for TCP and T/TCP is much larger than the increase we saw in Figure A.6 for Ping and UDP. With the datagram protocols (ICMP and UDP), even though three mbufs are used to hold the headers and user data, only one call is made by the socket layer in the kernel to the protocol's output routine. (This is done by the `sosend` function, Section 16.7 of Volume 2.) But for the stream protocol (TCP), two calls are made to the TCP output routine: one for the first 100 bytes of user data, and another for the next 100 bytes of user data. Indeed, Tcpdump verifies that two 100-byte segments are transmitted for this case. The additional call to the protocol's output routine is expensive.

The difference between the TCP and T/TCP application times, about 4 ms across all packet sizes, results because fewer segments are processed by T/TCP. Figures 1.8 and 1.12 showed nine segments for TCP and three segments for T/TCP. Reducing the number of segments obviously reduces the host processing on both ends.

Figure A.8 summarizes the application timing for the Ping, UDP, T/TCP, and TCP client–servers from Figures A.6 and A.7. We omit the Tcpdump timing.

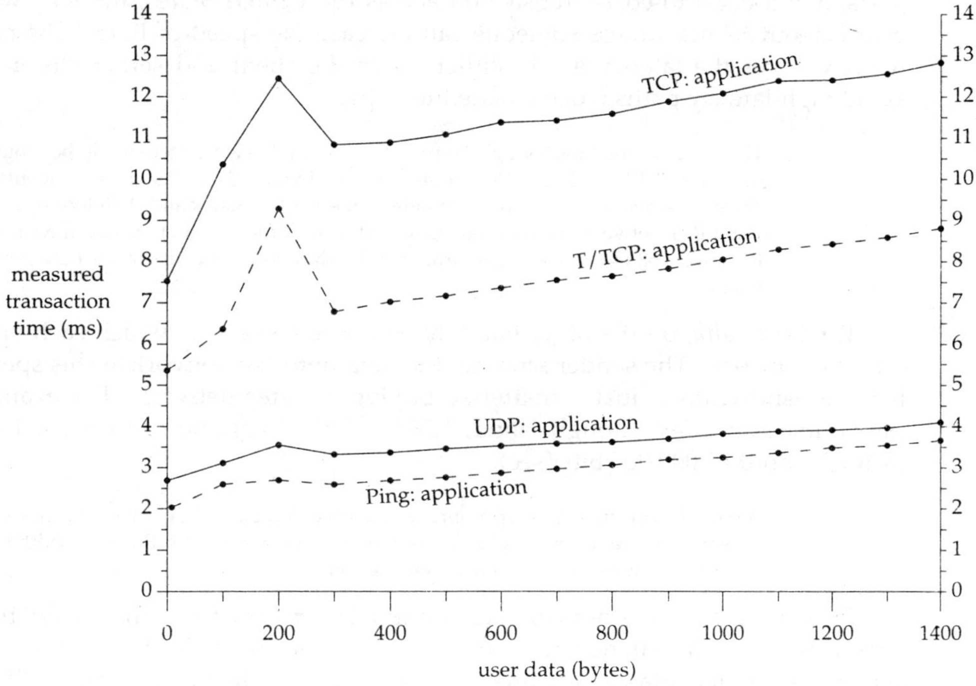

Figure A.8 Ping, UDP, T/TCP, and TCP client–server transaction times on a single host (loopback interface).

The results are what we expect. The Ping times are the lowest, and we cannot go faster than this, since the Ping server is within the kernel. The UDP transaction times are slightly larger than the ones for Ping, since the data is copied two more times between the kernel and the server, but not much larger, given the minimal amount of processing done by UDP. The T/TCP transaction times are about double those for UDP, which is caused by more protocol processing, even though the number of packets is the same as for UDP (our application timer does not include the final ACK shown in Figure 1.12). The transaction times for TCP are about 50% greater than the T/TCP values, caused by the larger number of packets that are processed by the protocol. The relative differences between the UDP, T/TCP, and TCP times in Figure A.8 are not the same as in Figure 1.14 because the measurements in Chapter 1 were made on an actual network while the measurements in this appendix were made using the loopback interface.

A.3 Latency and Bandwidth

In network communications two factors determine the amount of time required to exchange information: the latency and the bandwidth [Bellovin 1992]. This ignores the server processing time and the network load, additional factors that obviously affect the client's transaction time.

The *latency* (also called the propagation delay) is the fixed cost of moving one bit from the client to the server and back. It is limited by the speed of light and therefore depends on the distance that the electrical or optical signals travel between the two hosts. On a coast-to-coast transaction across the United States, the RTT will never go below about 60 ms, unless someone can increase the speed of light. The only controls we have over the latency are to either move the client and server closer together, or avoid high-latency paths (such as satellite hops).

Theoretically the time for light to travel across the United States should be around 16 ms, for a minimum RTT of 32 ms. But 60 ms is the real-world RTT. As an experiment the author ran Traceroute between hosts on each side of the United States and then looked at only the minimum RTT between the two routers at each end of the link that crossed the United States. The RTTs were 58 ms between California and Washington, D.C. and 80 ms between California and Boston.

The *bandwidth*, on the other hand, measures the speed at which each bit can be put into the network. The sender *serializes* the data onto the network at this speed. Increasing the bandwidth is just a matter of buying a faster network. For example, if a T1 phone line is not fast enough (about 1,544,000 bits/sec) you can lease a T3 phone line instead (about 45,000,000 bits/sec).

A garden hose analogy is appropriate (thanks to Ian Lance Taylor): the latency is the amount of time it takes the water to get from the faucet to the nozzle, and the bandwidth is the volume of water that comes out of the nozzle each second.

One problem is that networks are getting faster over time (that is, the bandwidth is increasing) but the latency remains constant. For example, to send 1 million bytes across the United States (assume a 30-ms one-way latency) using a T1 phone line requires 5.21 seconds: 5.18 because of the bandwidth and 0.03 because of the latency. Here the bandwidth is the overriding factor. But with a T3 phone line the total time is 208 ms: 178 ms because of the bandwidth and 30 ms because of the latency. The latency is now one-sixth the bandwidth. At 150,000,000 bits/sec the time is 82 ms: 52 because of the bandwidth and 30 because of the latency. The latency is getting closer to the bandwidth in this final example and with even faster networks the latency becomes the dominant factor, not the bandwidth.

In Figure A.3 the round-trip latency is approximately the *y*-axis intercept of each line. The top two lines (intercepting around 202 and 155 ms) are between the United States and Europe. The next two (intercepting around 98 and 80 ms) both cross the entire United States. The next one (intercepting around 30 ms) is between two hosts on the East coast of the United States.

The fact that latency is becoming more important as bandwidth increases makes T/TCP more desirable. T/TCP reduces the latency by at least one RTT.

Serialization Delay and Routers

If we lease a T1 phone line to an Internet service provider and send data to another host connected with a T1 phone line to the Internet, knowing that all intermediate links are T1 or faster, we'll be surprised at the result.

For example, in Figure A.3 if we examine the line starting at 80 ms and ending around 193 ms, which is between the hosts `connix.com` in Connecticut and `noao.edu` in Arizona, the y-axis intercept around 80 ms is reasonable for a coast-to-coast RTT. (Running the Traceroute program, described in detail in Chapter 8 of Volume 1, shows that the packets actually go from Arizona, back to California, then to Texas, Washington, DC, and then Connecticut.) But if we calculate the amount of time required to send 1400 bytes on a T1 phone line, it is about 7.5 ms, so we would estimate an RTT for a 1400-byte packet around 95 ms, which is way off from the measured value of 193 ms.

What's happening here is that the *serialization delay* is linear in the number of intermediate routers, since each router must receive the entire datagram before forwarding it to the outgoing interface. Consider the example in Figure A.9. We are sending a 1428-byte packet from the host on the left to the host on the right, through the router in the middle. We assume both links are T1 phone lines, which take about 7.5 ms to send 1428 bytes. Time is shown going down the page.

The first arrow, from time 0 to 1, is the host processing of the outgoing datagram, which we assume to be 1 ms from our earlier measurements in this appendix. The data is then serialized onto the network, which takes 7.5 ms from the first bit to the last bit. Additionally there is a 5-ms latency between the two ends of the line, so the first bit appears at the router at time 6, and the last bit at time 13.5.

Only after the final bit has arrived at time 13.5 does the router forward the packet, and we assume this forwarding takes another 1 ms. The first bit is then sent by the router at time 14.5 and appears at the destination host 1 ms later (the latency of the second link). The final bit arrives at the destination host at time 23. Finally, we assume the host processing takes another 1 ms at the destination.

The actual data rate is 1428 bytes in 24 ms, or 476,000 bits/sec, less than one-third the T1 rate. If we ignore the 3 ms needed by the hosts and router to process the packet, the data rate is then 544,000 bits/sec.

As we said earlier, the serialization delay is linear in the number of routers that the packet traverses. The effect of this delay depends on the line speed (bandwidth), the size of each packet, and the number of intermediate hops (routers). For example, the serialization delay for a 552-byte packet (a typical TCP segment containing 512 bytes of data) is almost 80 ms at 56,000 bits/sec, 2.86 ms at T1 speed, and only 0.10 ms at T3 speed. Therefore 10 T1 hops add 28.6 ms to the total time (which is almost the same as the one-way coast-to-coast latency), whereas 10 T3 hops add only 1 ms (which is probably negligible compared to the latency).

Finally, the serialization delay is a latency effect, not a bandwidth effect. For example, in Figure A.9 the sending host on the left can send the first bit of the next packet at time 8.5; it does not wait until time 24 to send the next packet. If the host on the left sends 10 back-to-back 1428-byte packets, assuming no dead time between packets, the last bit of the final packet arrives at time 91.5 $(24 + 9 \times 7.5)$. This is a data rate of

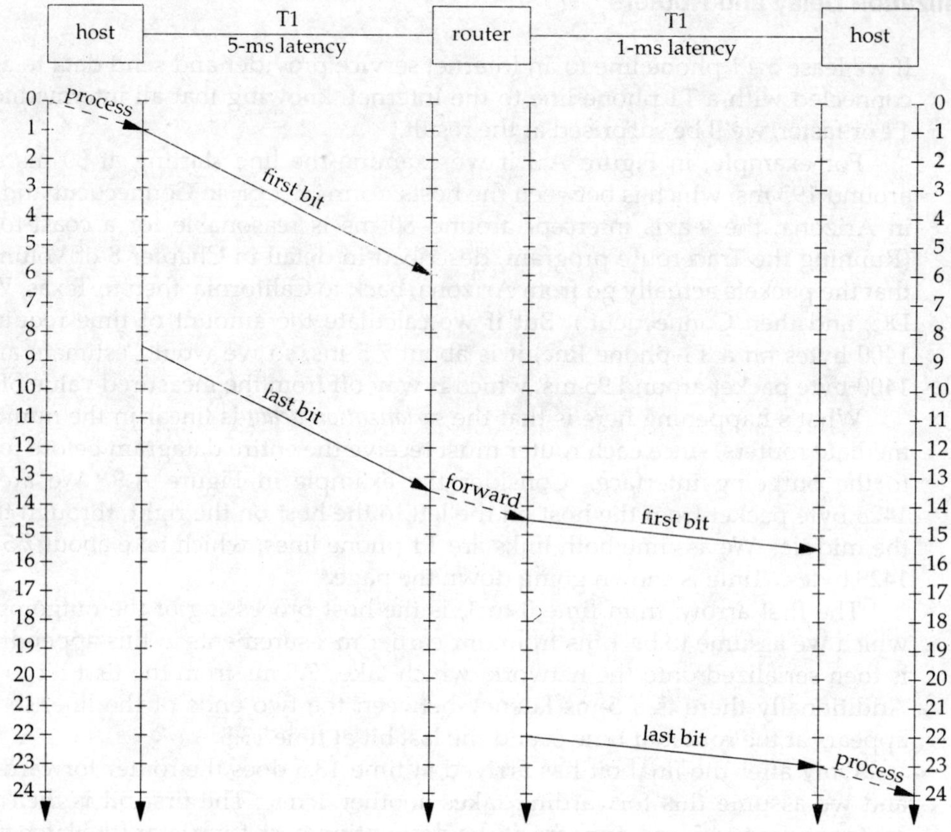

Figure A.9 Serialization of data.

1,248,525 bits/sec, which is much closer to the T1 rate. With regard to TCP, it just needs a larger window to compensate for the serialization delay.

Returning to our example from `connix.com` to `noao.edu`, if we determine the actual path using Traceroute, and know the speed of each link, we can take into account the serialization delay at each of the 12 routers between the two hosts. Doing this, and assuming an 80-ms latency, and assuming a 0.5-ms processing delay at each intermediate hop, our estimate becomes 187 ms. This is much closer to the measured value of 193 ms than our earlier estimate of 95 ms.

Appendix B

Coding Applications for T/TCP

In Part 1 we described two benefits from T/TCP:

1. Avoidance of the TCP three-way handshake.
2. Reducing the amount of time in the TIME_WAIT state when the connection duration is less than MSL.

If both hosts involved in a TCP connection support T/TCP, then the second benefit is available to *all* TCP applications, with no source code changes whatsoever.

To avoid the three-way handshake, however, the application must be coded to call sendto or sendmsg instead of calling connect and write. To combine the FIN flag with data, the application must specify the MSG_EOF flag in the final call to send, sendto, or sendmsg, instead of calling shutdown. Our TCP and T/TCP clients and servers in Chapter 1 showed these differences.

For maximum portability we need to code applications to take advantage of T/TCP if

1. the host on which the program is being compiled supports T/TCP, and
2. the application was compiled to support T/TCP.

With the second condition we also need to determine at run time if the host on which the program is running supports T/TCP, because it is sometimes possible to compile a program on one version of an operating system and run it on another version.

The host on which a program is being compiled supports T/TCP if the MSG_EOF flag is defined in the <sys/socket.h> header. This can be used with the C preprocessor #ifdef statement.

```
#ifdef  MSG_EOF
    /* host supports T/TCP */
#else
    /* host does not support T/TCP */
#endif
```

The second condition requires that the application issue the implied open (sendto or sendmsg specifying a destination address, without calling connect) but handle its failure if the host does not support T/TCP. All the output functions return ENOTCONN when applied to a connection-oriented socket that is not connected on a host that does not support T/TCP (p. 495 of Volume 2). This applies to both Berkeley-derived systems and SVR4 socket libraries. If the application receives this error from a call to sendto, for example, it must then call connect.

TCP or T/TCP Client and Server

We can implement these ideas in the following programs, which are simple modifications of the T/TCP and TCP clients and servers from Chapter 1. As with the C programs in Chapter 1, we don't explain these in detail, assuming some familiarity with the sockets API. The first, shown in Figure B.1 is the client main function.

8–13 An Internet socket address structure is filled in with the server's IP address and port number. Both are taken from the command line.

15–17 The function send_request sends the request to the server. This function returns either a socket descriptor if all is OK, or a negative value on an error. The third argument (1) tells the function to send an end-of-file after sending the request.

18–19 The function read_stream is unchanged from Figure 1.6.

The function send_request is shown in Figure B.2.

Try T/TCP sendto

13–29 If the compiling host supports T/TCP, this code is executed. We discussed the TCP_NOPUSH socket option in Section 3.6. If the run-time host doesn't understand T/TCP, the call to setsockopt returns ENOPROTOOPT, and we branch ahead to issue the normal TCP connect. We then call sendto, and if this fails with ENOTCONN, we branch ahead to issue the normal TCP connect. An end-of-file is sent following the request if the third argument to the function is nonzero.

Issue normal TCP calls

30–40 This is the normal TCP code: connect, write, and optionally shutdown.

The server main function, shown in Figure B.3, has minimal changes.

27–31 The only change is to always call send (in Figure 1.7 write was called) but with a fourth argument of 0 if the host does not support T/TCP. Even if the compile-time host supports T/TCP, but the run-time host does not (hence the compile-time value of MSG_EOF will not be understood by the run-time kernel), the sosend function in Berkeley-derived kernels does not complain about flags that it does not understand.

client.c

```
#include    "cliserv.h"

int
main(int argc, char *argv[])
{                               /* T/TCP or TCP client */
    struct sockaddr_in serv;
    char    request[REQUEST], reply[REPLY];
    int     sockfd, n;

    if (argc != 3)
        err_quit("usage: client <IP address of server> <port#>");

    memset(&serv, 0, sizeof(serv));
    serv.sin_family = AF_INET;
    serv.sin_addr.s_addr = inet_addr(argv[1]);
    serv.sin_port = htons(atoi(argv[2]));

    /* form request[] ... */

    if ((sockfd = send_request(request, REQUEST, 1,
                               (SA) &serv, sizeof(serv))) < 0)
        err_sys("send_request error %d", sockfd);

    if ((n = read_stream(sockfd, reply, REPLY)) < 0)
        err_sys("read error");

    /* process "n" bytes of reply[] ... */

    exit(0);
}
```

client.c

Figure B.1 Client `main` function for either T/TCP or TCP.

sendrequest.c

```
#include    "cliserv.h"
#include    <errno.h>
#include    <netinet/tcp.h>

/* Send a transaction request to a server, using T/TCP if possible,
 * else TCP.  Returns < 0 on error, else nonnegative socket descriptor. */

int
send_request(const void *request, size_t nbytes, int sendeof,
             const SA servptr, int servsize)
{
    int     sockfd, n;

    if ((sockfd = socket(PF_INET, SOCK_STREAM, 0)) < 0)
        return (-1);

#ifdef  MSG_EOF                     /* T/TCP is supported on compiling host */
    n = 1;
    if (setsockopt(sockfd, IPPROTO_TCP, TCP_NOPUSH,
                   (char *) &n, sizeof(n)) < 0) {
        if (errno == ENOPROTOOPT)
            goto doconnect;
        return (-2);
    }
    if (sendto(sockfd, request, nbytes, sendeof ? MSG_EOF : 0,
               servptr, servsize) != nbytes) {
        if (errno == ENOTCONN)
            goto doconnect;
        return (-3);
    }
    return (sockfd);                /* success */

  doconnect:                        /* run-time host does not support T/TCP */
#endif

    /*
     * Must include following code even if compiling host supports
     * T/TCP, in case run-time host does not support T/TCP.
     */

    if (connect(sockfd, servptr, servsize) < 0)
        return (-4);
    if (write(sockfd, request, nbytes) != nbytes)
        return (-5);
    if (sendeof && shutdown(sockfd, 1) < 0)
        return (-6);

    return (sockfd);                /* success */
}
```

sendrequest.c

Figure B.2 send_request function: send request using T/TCP or TCP.

server.c

```
#include    "cliserv.h"

int
main(int argc, char *argv[])
{                                   /* T/TCP or TCP server */
    struct sockaddr_in serv, cli;
    char    request[REQUEST], reply[REPLY];
    int     listenfd, sockfd, n, clilen;

    if (argc != 2)
        err_quit("usage: server <port#>");

    if ((listenfd = socket(PF_INET, SOCK_STREAM, 0)) < 0)
        err_sys("socket error");

    memset(&serv, 0, sizeof(serv));
    serv.sin_family = AF_INET;
    serv.sin_addr.s_addr = htonl(INADDR_ANY);
    serv.sin_port = htons(atoi(argv[1]));

    if (bind(listenfd, (SA) &serv, sizeof(serv)) < 0)
        err_sys("bind error");

    if (listen(listenfd, SOMAXCONN) < 0)
        err_sys("listen error");

    for (;;) {
        clilen = sizeof(cli);
        if ((sockfd = accept(listenfd, (SA) &cli, &clilen)) < 0)
            err_sys("accept error");

        if ((n = read_stream(sockfd, request, REQUEST)) < 0)
            err_sys("read error");

        /* process "n" bytes of request[] and create reply[] ... */

#ifndef MSG_EOF
#define MSG_EOF 0                   /* send() with flags=0 identical to write() */
#endif

        if (send(sockfd, reply, REPLY, MSG_EOF) != REPLY)
            err_sys("send error");

        close(sockfd);
    }
}
```

server.c

Figure B.3 Server `main` function.

Bibliography

All RFCs are available at no charge through electronic mail, anonymous FTP, or the World Wide Web. A starting point is `http://www.internic.net`. The directory `ftp://ds.internic.net/rfc` is one location for RFCs.

Items marked "Internet Draft" are works in progress of the Internet Engineering Task Force (IETF). They are available at no charge across the Internet, similar to the RFCs. These drafts expire 6 months after publication. The appropriate version of the draft may change after this book is published, or the draft may be published as an RFC.

Whenever the author was able to locate an electronic copy of papers and reports referenced in this bibliography, its URL (Uniform Resource Locator) is included. The filename portion of the URL for each Internet Draft is also included, since the filename contains the version number. A major repository for Internet Drafts is in the directory `ftp://ds.internic.net/internet-drafts`. URLs are not specified for the RFCs.

Anklesaria, F., McCahill, M., Lindner, P. Johnson, D., Torrey, D., and Alberti, B. 1993. "The Internet Gopher Protocol," RFC 1436, 16 pages (Mar.).

Baker, F., ed. 1995. "Requirements for IP Version 4 Routers," RFC 1812, 175 pages (June).

The router equivalent of RFC 1122 [Braden 1989]. This RFC makes RFC 1009 and RFC 1716 obsolete.

Barber, S. 1995. "Common NNTP Extensions," Internet Draft (June).

`draft-barber-nntp-imp-01.txt`

Bellovin, S. M. 1989. "Security Problems in the TCP/IP Protocol Suite," *Computer Communication Review*, vol. 19, no. 2, pp. 32–48 (Apr.).

`ftp://ftp.research.att.com/dist/internet_security/ipext.ps.Z`

Bellovin, S. M. 1992. *A Best-Case Network Performance Model.* Private Communication.

Berners-Lee, T. 1993. "Hypertext Transfer Protocol," Internet Draft, 31 pages (Nov.).

This is an Internet Draft that has now expired. Nevertheless, it is the original protocol specification for HTTP version 1.0.

`draft-ietf-iiir-http-00.txt`

Berners-Lee, T. 1994. "Universal Resource Identifiers in WWW: A Unifying Syntax for the Expression of Names and Addresses of Objects on the Network as Used in the World-Wide Web," RFC 1630, 28 pages (June).

`http://www.w3.org/hypertext/WWW/Addressing/URL/URI_Overview.html`

Berners-Lee, T., and Connolly, D. 1995. "Hypertext Markup Language—2.0," Internet Draft (Aug.).

`draft-ietf-html-spec-05.txt`

Berners-Lee, T., Fielding, R. T., and Nielsen, H. F. 1995. "Hypertext Transfer Protocol—HTTP/1.0," Internet Draft, 45 pages (Aug.).

`draft-ietf-http-v10-spec-02.ps`

Berners-Lee, T., Masinter, L., and McCahill, M., eds. 1994. "Uniform Resource Locators (URL)," RFC 1738, 25 pages (Dec.).

Braden, R. T. 1985. "Towards a Transport Service for Transaction Processing Applications," RFC 955, 10 pages (Sept.).

Braden, R. T., ed. 1989. "Requirements for Internet Hosts—Communication Layers," RFC 1122, 116 pages (Oct.).

The first half of the Host Requirements RFC. This half covers the link layer, IP, TCP, and UDP.

Braden, R. T. 1992a. "TIME-WAIT Assassination Hazards in TCP," RFC 1337, 11 pages (May).

Braden, R. T. 1992b. "Extending TCP for Transactions—Concepts," RFC 1379, 38 pages (Nov.).

Braden, R. T. 1993. "TCP Extensions for High Performance: An Update," Internet Draft, 10 pages (June).

This is an update to RFC 1323 [Jacobson, Braden, and Borman 1992].

`http://www.noao.edu/~rstevens/tcplw-extensions.txt`

Braden, R. T. 1994. "T/TCP—TCP Extensions for Transactions, Functional Specification," RFC 1644, 38 pages (July).

Brakmo, L. S., and Peterson, L. L., 1994. *Performance Problems in BSD4.4 TCP.*

`ftp://cs.arizona.edu/xkernel/Papers/tcp_problems.ps`

Braun, H-W., and Claffy, K. C. 1994. "Web Traffic Characterization: An Assessment of the Impact of Caching Documents from NCSA's Web Server," *Proceedings of the Second World Wide Web Conference '94: Mosaic and the Web*, pp. 1007–1027 (Oct.), Chicago, Ill.

`http://www.ncsa.uiuc.edu/SDG/IT94/Proceedings/DDay/claffy/main.html`

Cheriton, D. P. 1988. "VMTP: Versatile Message Transaction Protocol," RFC 1045, 123 pages (Feb.).

Cunha, C. R., Bestavros, A., and Crovella, M. E. 1995. "Characteristics of WWW Client-based Traces," BU-CS-95-010, Computer Science Department, Boston University (July).

ftp://cs-ftp.bu.edu/techreports/95-010-www-client-traces.ps.Z

Fielding, R. T. 1995. "Relative Uniform Resource Locators," RFC 1808, 16 pages (June).

Floyd, S., Jacobson, V., McCanne, S., Liu, C.-G., and Zhang, L. 1995. "A Reliable Multicast Framework for Lightweight Sessions and Application Level Framing," *Computer Communication Review*, vol. 25, no. 4, pp. 342–356 (Oct.).

ftp://ftp.ee.lbl.gov/papers/srm1.tech.ps.Z

Horton, M., and Adams, R. 1987. "Standard for Interchange of USENET Messages," RFC 1036, 19 pages (Dec.).

Jacobson, V. 1988. "Congestion Avoidance and Control," *Computer Communication Review*, vol. 18, no. 4, pp. 314–329 (Aug.).

A classic paper describing the slow start and congestion avoidance algorithms for TCP.

ftp://ftp.ee.lbl.gov/papers/congavoid.ps.Z

Jacobson, V. 1994. "Problems with Arizona's Vegas," March 14, 1994, end2end-tf mailing list (Mar.).

http://www.noao.edu/~rstevens/vanj.94mar14.txt

Jacobson, V., Braden, R. T., and Borman, D. A. 1992. "TCP Extensions for High Performance," RFC 1323, 37 pages (May).

Describes the window scale option, the timestamp option, and the PAWS algorithm, along with the reasons these modifications are needed. [Braden 1993] updates this RFC.

Jacobson, V., Braden, R. T., and Zhang, L. 1990. "TCP Extensions for High-Speed Paths," RFC 1185, 21 pages (Oct.).

Despite this RFC being made obsolete by RFC 1323, the appendix on protection against old duplicate segments in TCP is worth reading.

Kantor, B., and Lapsley, P. 1986. "Network News Transfer Protocol," RFC 977, 27 pages (Feb.).

Kleiman, S. R. 1986. "Vnodes: An Architecture for Multiple File System Types in Sun UNIX," *Proceedings of the 1986 Summer USENIX Conference*, pp. 238–247, Atlanta, Ga.

Kwan, T. T., McGrath, R. E., and Reed, D. A., 1995. *User Access Patterns to NCSA's World Wide Web Server*.

http://www-pablo.cs.uiuc.edu/Papers/WWW.ps.Z

Leffler, S. J., McKusick, M. K., Karels, M. J., and Quarterman, J. S. 1989. *The Design and Implementation of the 4.3BSD UNIX Operating System*. Addison-Wesley, Reading, Mass.

This book describes the 4.3BSD Tahoe release. It will be superseded in 1996 by [McKusick et al. 1996].

McKenney, P. E., and Dove, K. F. 1992. "Efficient Demultiplexing of Incoming TCP Packets," *Computer Communication Review*, vol. 22, no. 4, pp. 269–279 (Oct.).

McKusick, M. K., Bostic, K., Karels, M. J., and Quarterman, J. S. 1996. *The Design and Implementation of the 4.4BSD Operating System*. Addison-Wesley, Reading, Mass.

Miller, T. 1985. "Internet Reliable Transaction Protocol Functional and Interface Specification," *RFC 938*, 16 pages (Feb.).

Mogul, J. C. 1995a. "Operating Systems Support for Busy Internet Servers," TN-49, Digital Western Research Laboratory (May).

`http://www.research.digital.com/wrl/techreports/abstracts/TN-49.html`

Mogul, J. C. 1995b. "The Case for Persistent-Connection HTTP," *Computer Communication Review*, vol. 25, no. 4, pp. 299–313 (Oct.).

`http://www.research.digital.com/wrl/techreports/abstracts/95.4.html`

Mogul, J. C. 1995c. Private Communication.

Mogul, J. C. 1995d. "Network Behavior of a Busy Web Server and its Clients," WRL Research Report 95/5, Digital Western Research Laboratory (Oct.).

`http://www.research.digital.com/wrl/techreports/abstracts/95.5.html`

Mogul, J. C., and Deering, S. E. 1990. "Path MTU Discovery," RFC 1191, 19 pages (Apr.).

Olah, A. 1995. Private Communication.

Padmanabhan, V. N. 1995. "Improving World Wide Web Latency," UCB/CSD-95-875, Computer Science Division, University of California, Berkeley (May).

`http://www.cs.berkeley.edu/~padmanab/papers/masters-tr.ps`

Partridge, C. 1987. "Implementing the Reliable Data Protocol (RDP)," *Proceedings of the 1987 Summer USENIX Conference*, pp. 367–379, Phoenix, Ariz.

Partridge, C. 1990a. "Re: Reliable Datagram Protocol," Message-ID <60240@bbn.BBN.COM>, Usenet, comp.protocols.tcp-ip Newsgroup (Oct.).

Partridge, C. 1990b. "Re: Reliable Datagram ??? Protocols," Message-ID <60340@bbn.BBN.COM>, Usenet, comp.protocols.tcp-ip Newsgroup (Oct.).

Partridge, C., and Hinden, R. 1990. "Version 2 of the Reliable Data Protocol (RDP)," RFC 1151, 4 pages (Apr.).

Paxson, V. 1994a. "Growth Trends in Wide-Area TCP Connections," *IEEE Network*, vol. 8, no. 4, pp. 8–17 (July/Aug.).

`ftp://ftp.ee.lbl.gov/papers/WAN-TCP-growth-trends.ps.Z`

Paxson, V. 1994b. "Empirically-Derived Analytic Models of Wide-Area TCP Connections," *IEEE/ACM Transactions on Networking*, vol. 2, no. 4, pp. 316–336 (Aug.).

`ftp://ftp.ee.lbl.gov/papers/WAN-TCP-models.ps.Z`

Paxson, V. 1995a. Private Communication.

Paxson, V. 1995b. "Re: Traceroute and TTL," Message-ID <48407@dog.ee.lbl.gov>, Usenet, comp.protocols.tcp-ip Newsgroup (Sept.).

`http://www.noao.edu/~rstevens/paxson.95sep29.txt`

Postel, J. B., ed. 1981a. "Internet Protocol," RFC 791, 45 pages (Sept.).

Postel, J. B., ed. 1981b. "Transmission Control Protocol," RFC 793, 85 pages (Sept.).

Raggett, D., Lam, J., and Alexander, I. 1996. *The Definitive Guide to HTML 3.0: Electronic Publishing on the World Wide Web.* Addison-Wesley, Reading, Mass.

Rago, S. A. 1993. *UNIX System V Network Programming.* Addison-Wesley, Reading, Mass.

Reynolds, J. K., and Postel, J. B. 1994. "Assigned Numbers," RFC 1700, 230 pages (Oct.).

This RFC is updated regularly. Check the RFC index for the current number.

Rose, M. T. 1993. *The Internet Message: Closing the Book with Electronic Mail.* Prentice-Hall, Upper Saddle River, N.J.

Salus, P. H. 1995. *Casting the Net: From ARPANET to Internet and Beyond.* Addison-Wesley, Reading, Mass.

Shimomura, Tsutomu. 1995. "Technical details of the attack described by Markoff in NYT," Message-ID <3g5gkl$5j1@ariel.sdsc.edu>, Usenet, comp.protocols.tcp-ip Newsgroup (Jan.).

A detailed technical analysis of the Internet break-in of December 1994, along with the corresponding CERT advisory.

`http://www.noao.edu/~rstevens/shimomura.95jan25.txt`

Spero, S. E., 1994a. *Analysis of HTTP Performance Problems.*

`http://sunsite.unc.edu/mdma-release/http-prob.html`

Spero, S. E., 1994b. *Progress on HTTP-NG.*

`http://www.w3.org/hypertext/WWW/Protocols/HTTP-NG/http-ng-status.html`

Stein, L. D. 1995. *How to Set Up and Maintain a World Wide Web Site: The Guide for Information Providers.* Addison-Wesley, Reading, Mass.

Stevens, W. R. 1990. *UNIX Network Programming.* Prentice-Hall, Upper Saddle River, N.J.

Stevens, W. R. 1992. *Advanced Programming in the UNIX Environment.* Addison-Wesley, Reading, Mass.

Stevens, W. R. 1994. *TCP/IP Illustrated, Volume 1: The Protocols.* Addison-Wesley, Reading, Mass.

The first volume in this series, which provides a complete introduction to the Internet protocols.

Velten, D., Hinden, R., and Sax, J. 1984. "Reliable Data Protocol," RFC 908, 57 pages (July).

Wright, G. R., and Stevens, W. R. 1995. *TCP/IP Illustrated, Volume 2: The Implementation.* Addison-Wesley, Reading, Mass.

The second volume in this series, which examines the implementation of the Internet protocols in the 4.4BSD-Lite operating system.

Index

Rather than provide a separate glossary (with most of the entries being acronyms), this index also serves as a glossary for all the acronyms used in the book. The primary entry for the acronym appears under the acronym name. For example, all references to the Hypertext Transfer Protocol appear under HTTP. The entry under the compound term "Hypertext Transfer Protocol" refers back to the main entry under HTTP. Additionally, a list of all these acronyms with their compound terms is found on the inside front cover.

The two end papers at the back of the book contain a list of all the structures, functions, and macros presented or described in the text, along with the starting page number of the source code. Those structures, functions, and macros from Volume 2 that are referenced in this text also appear in these tables. These end papers should be the starting point to locate the definition of a structure, function, or macro.

Structure	Vol. 2	Vol. 3
cmsghdr		272
ifnet	67	
in_ifaddr	161	
inpcb	716	
mbuf	38	
radix_node	575	
radix_node_head	574	75
rmxp_tao		76
route	220	106
rtentry	579	75
rt_metrics	580	76
rtqk_arg		80
sockaddr	75	
sockaddr_in	160	
sockaddr_un		230
socket	438	
tcpcb	804	93
tcphdr	801	
tcpiphdr	803	
tcpopt		121
timeval	106	
unixdomain		229
unixsw		229
unpcb		231